THE NEW
OXFORD BOOK OF
VICTORIAN
VERSE

Edited by
CHRISTOPHER RICKS

Oxford   New York
OXFORD UNIVERSITY PRESS

821·
808
NEW

Oxford University Press, Walton Street, Oxford OX2 6DP

Oxford New York Toronto
Delhi Bombay Calcutta Madras Karachi
Petaling Jaya Singapore Hong Kong Tokyo
Nairobi Dar es Salaam Cape Town
Melbourne Auckland

and associated companies in
Berlin Ibadan

Oxford is a trade mark of Oxford University Press

Introduction, notes, and selection © Christopher Ricks 1987

First published 1987
First issued as an Oxford University Press paperback 1990
Reprinted 1991

British Library Cataloguing in Publication Data
The New Oxford book of Victorian verse.—(Oxford
paperbacks).
1. Poetry in English, 1837–1900—Anthologies
I. Ricks, Christopher, 1933–
821.808
ISBN 0-19-282778-2

Library of Congress Cataloging in Publication Data
The new Oxford book of Victorian verse/edited by Christopher Ricks.
p.   cm.
1. English poetry—19th century.   I. Ricks, Christopher, B.
PR1223.N48   1990
821'.808—dc20
90–32683
ISBN 0-19-282778-2

Printed in Great Britain by
Richard Clay Ltd., Bungay, Suffolk

21/09/92

CONTENTS

CONTENTS

CONTENTS

CONTENTS

CONTENTS

CONTENTS

CONTENTS

CONTENTS

CONTENTS

CONTENTS

CONTENTS

CONTENTS

CONTENTS

CONTENTS

CONTENTS

CONTENTS

INTRODUCTION

'WHEN a man writes a preface, he tries only to say an antithesis, and never thinks of the truth' (Charles James Fox). An anthologist's self-introduction is a tricky business. Taste, discretion, and decision have, one likes to think, been exercised so as to manifest the variety of an age's poems, the felicitous heterogeneity, the diverting diversity, and the buoyant resistance which a world of poems will always put up even to the best literary historian's summary justice. Whereupon the work of variety is to be pre-emptively undone, and the world of poems 'cramped into a planisphere'. The powers of unmisgiving generalization which make for a good strong introduction are likely to be the opposite of those needed to choose the anthology in the first place; which is why good anthologies have often been introduced by A. N. Other and why the most popular anthology ever, Palgrave's (and Tennyson's, and even in a way Queen Victoria's) *Golden Treasury*, had to all intents no introduction at all. Then there is the anthologist's temptation to write a review, or at least to see that the reviewers have their work cut out for them; perhaps by covert self-congratulation on the choices and the finds (Remark how unknown are A and B! How hitherto misprized were X and Y!); perhaps, with sheer statistics, by implicit deprecation of the beknighted predecessor. So: thirty-four of the poets in this *New Oxford Book of Victorian Verse* were not in Sir Arthur Quiller-Couch's *Oxford Book of Victorian Verse* (1912); and fifty-two of them were not in John Hayward's more extended, and therefore less roomy, *Oxford Book of Nineteenth-Century English Verse* (1964).

T. S. Eliot said that every good poem is to a degree a surprise to its creator. Some such thing might be said to those who are less important than creators but who do partake of others' creativity: critics, literary historians, anthologists. The anthologist ought at least not to preclude the chance of being truly surprised, and not just by an unexpected instance of something anticipated; and the trouble with narrowingly circular definitions is that they ensure that the unexpected becomes not only the unlooked-for (and therefore missed) but the uncalled-for (and therefore resisted and resented).

To his surprise, surprise of another sort, Quiller-Couch found that it was after all not difficult to decide where an anthology of Victorian verse ought to begin and end. 'Though Wordsworth happened to be the first

Laureate of Queen Victoria's reign, no one will argue that he belonged to it.' Quiller-Couch must mean that Wordsworth was the first Laureate appointed by Queen Victoria (for the first half-dozen years of her reign, Southey was her Laureate); moreover, Wordsworth did not 'happen' to be Laureate, but was appointed because not only his earlier work but his continuing art was deeply consonant with so much which was esteemed in that Victorian England which could remember Regency England. 'This laurel greener from the brows/Of him that uttered nothing base', Tennyson was to write in his dedicatory poem 'To the Queen' (1851), the year after he succeeded Wordsworth as Laureate. But the more important point is not whether Wordsworth may be thought of as a Victorian poet but whether the poems which he both wrote and published in the 1840s should be allowed to be Victorian poems. A stiff price is paid for denying that they are, the price of a stultifying self-fulfilling notion, by which from a narrow range of Victorian poems a restrictive practice is first extracted and then erected.

Abetted by the loose, thrilling word 'modern', W. B. Yeats in his *Oxford Book of Modern Verse* (1936) permitted himself a similar victory. By selecting for his auspices such poems from Victorian England as were creatively at odds with certain tendencies of Victorian literature, and then dubbing them modern and not effectively Victorian at all, he was able the more roundly (not squarely) to condemn Victorian poetry. The fact that so much of Hopkins was not published until 1918 facilitated this sleight, and so did the misrepresentation of Hopkins's poems as altogether unVictorian.

This is not to deny that there are historical terms, categorizings, which are to be understood more exclusively than their literal sense. A. E. Housman in 1928 was within his rights in sending his message of refusal to A. J. A. Symons:

He may be consoled, and also amused, if you tell him that to include me in an anthology of the Nineties would be just as technically correct, and just as essentially inappropriate, as to include Lot in a book on Sodomites.

Anyway, copyright is might. But A. J. A. Symons had been within his rights in seeking to include Housman; more, Symons was right to think that the anthology would have been all the better for including Housman's poems, very good in themselves and very good as challenging the coterie notion of the Nineties with the less narrow literalism of the nineties. It is another of the cases where, as Eliot said, the spirit killeth but the letter giveth life.

As for where to end, Quiller-Couch was equally unperturbed by questions of technical correctness, as if such correctness were not one of our few protections against wilful imposition. 'For the close', he wrote,

> I have thought it no insult to include any English poet, born in our time, under
> the great name 'Victorian'; a title the present misprision of which will no less
> surely go its way as a flippancy of fashion than it will be succeeded by fresh
> illustration of the habit, constant in fallen Man, of belittling his contemporaries
> in particular and the age before his own in the gross.

This left him free to include, for instance, Ezra Pound, whose poems are
as Victorian as they are English. Quiller-Couch could hardly have
foreseen the process by which 'misprision' would become both a term of
the critic's art and a warrant for the critic's arrested development (What
do you mean, I'm misunderstanding? I'm misprisioning); but by 1912
the reaction against the Victorians was clearly already potent. The
defiant-defensive tone of 'the great name "Victorian" ' is one which,
dangerous and even counterproductive though it is, is even now not
entirely avoidable, since to travesty or to calumniate the Victorians is still
such a cheap holiday.

For the *Oxford English Dictionary*, that last reward of consummated
Victorian scholarship, the definition of 'Victorian' was simple and in its
way neutral: 'Of or belonging to, designating, or typical of the reign of
Queen Victoria (1837–1901).' For the *Supplement* (vol. iv) to the *OED* in
1986, 'Victorian' is admitted as opprobrious, though 'supposedly' does
keep its distance:

> 2. *fig.* Resembling or typified by the attitudes supposedly characteristic of the
> Victorian era; prudish, strict; old-fashioned, out-dated.

The *Supplement*'s first citation is 1934, *Webster's Dictionary*; its second is
from that eminent Victorian, George Bernard Shaw (1950): 'He was
helping the movement against Victorian prudery in a very practical way
as a nudist.' This, from *Farfetched Fables*, is farfetched, fabulous, and
entirely Victorian in its critique of Victorian *moeurs* and *moues*.

The *OED* does not record the figurative pejorative use until 1934,
then, but the impulse was more than twenty years older than that. An
understanding of Victorian literature is certainly not helped by the
unseemly vying which has characterized party politicians in the 1980s,
with their packing and packaging of something called 'Victorian values'
to be conservatively owned or liberally disowned; but it is of course
unlikely that Victorian literature could be found valuable if Victorian
values were indeed to be found valueless.

The disparagement of Victorian poetry by the ensuing great inaugur-
ators—Yeats, Pound, Eliot—was so swift and deft as still to be potent.

These repudiators were also, naturally, the most cunning assimilators of their predecessors, and Arthur Carr's influential essay on 'Tennyson as a Modern Poet' (1950) has been complemented by many an essay on, say, Eliot as a Victorian poet. Overt repudiation (with covert predation) was assisted by the fact that the word 'Victorian' had from the start been so associated with writers; the *OED*'s first instance of the adjective is Stedman's *Victorian Poets* (1875), and the first sense of the noun is 'a person, especially an author, who lived in the reign of Queen Victoria', where especially an author means very especially a poet: Browning as 'the strongest, truest poet of the Victorians' (1876), and Tennyson as, 'alone of the Victorians', having 'definitely entered the immortal group of our English poets' (1886).

Yeats, Pound, and Eliot needed, as a new wave, to do this dissociating of themselves from the Victorians, though one thing that never can entirely dissociate itself is a new wave. For Yeats, 'Victorianism had been defeated':

The revolt against Victorianism meant to the young poet a revolt against irrelevant descriptions of nature, the scientific and moral discursiveness of *In Memoriam*—'When he should have been broken-hearted', said Verlaine, 'he had many reminiscences'—the political eloquence of Swinburne, the psychological curiosity of Browning, and the poetical diction of everybody.

Such a revolt against, essentially, complacency has since been seen to be open—like all accusations of complacency including this sentence—to the charge of complacency. For are Yeats's words truly cogent either as descriptions of Victorian poetry or as principles of indictment? Or, more widely, is it not the case that any 'revolt' against predecessors ought always to concede that pure gain is not of this world? The best thing ever said about literary revolution, by Bishop Hurd in his *Letters on Chivalry and Romance* (1762), finds its force in its magnanimity, in its knowing that an honest opponent would not have to deny the account but would simply ask to reverse the columns: 'What we have gotten by this revolution, you will say, is a great deal of good sense. What we have lost, is a world of fine fabling.'

Ezra Pound in 1918 made clear that the revolt against Victorianism was a revolt against Romanticism; indeed, one of the fiercest features of the literary reaction against the Victorian fathers is that it did not—as literary manifestos so often do—appeal over the head of the fathers to the grandfathers. Pound wrote:

As for the nineteenth century, with all respect to its achievements, I think we shall look back upon it as a rather blurry, messy sort of a period, or rather sentimentalistic, mannerish sort of a period. I say this without any self-righteousness, with no self-satisfaction.

But it is for us, not for him, to say whether he says this with self-righteousness and self-satisfaction; and there is something rather blurry and messy about Pound's couple of 'rather's and couple of 'sort of's.

As for Eliot's indictment, wisely it was less concerned with false matters of self-righteousness than with true righteousness:

Tennyson lived in a time which was already acutely time-conscious: a great many things seemed to be happening, railways were being built, discoveries were being made, the face of the world was changing. That was a time busy in keeping up to date. It had, for the most part, no hold on permanent truths about man and God and life and death.

Victorian poetry was ill-fated in two historical ways. The more important is the profound deprivation which it suffered by the extinction in early manhood of the three geniuses who constituted the second generation of the Romantics: Byron, Shelley, and Keats, dead in 1824, 1822, and 1821 respectively. There has been no other such extinction and deprivation in English literary history, for not even the Great War, when it took Owen and Rosenberg and many others, was really taking the greatest inaugurative poets of its day. The profound loss in the 1820s was not only to Romantic poetry but to Victorian poetry. This, not just in the sense that Byron, Shelley, and Keats could all have been expected to write poems which would now be legitimately gracing these pages, but in the sense that the Victorian poets were denied a unique critique of second-generation Romanticism. The most important, because most fecundating, critique of the art of any age is the art of the subsequent age; and one invaluable form of this continuing creative critique is a poet's criticism, in new art, of his or her own earlier work. The dialogue of the mind with itself enlists the dialogue of the mind with its past self. This is a more taxing business than any repudiation could ever be, and it has the internal vitality, the self-challenge, which constitutes heroism. But Victorian poetry was never to know what Byron, Shelley, and Keats would have made of and from their young selves and their young art. Add the young death of Emily Jane Brontë in 1848, and the early madness and incarceration of John Clare, and you have a grim curtailment. No amount of longevity in Wordsworth or in Landor, the earlier surviving masters, could atone for this; indeed, in some ways it made things worse, since it the more let the waters close over the heads of a lost generation which had feared its names might be writ in water.

Not that Victorian poetry then reneged on the obligation—which it would have had anyway—to furnish its own creative criticism of its immediate predecessors, Byron, Shelley, and Keats, but it did have to engage this on its own, and many of Victorian poetry's worst misjudgements were a consequence of its being so alone, so deprived of any chance to join a revisionary company.

The other misfortune, less tragic and more mischievous, is that of Victorian poetry's later reputation, where it happened that the usual or even inevitable repudiation by a succeeding movement coincided with something so unusual as to be entirely new: the establishing of English literary studies as an educational institution. In this establishing too there have been—as Arnold foresaw there would be—losses and gains, and our whole literary culture has for three-quarters of a century now been the victim-beneficiary of this new lease, sometimes one of life, sometimes—to apply Beckett's words—a new lease of apathy. Yet for Victorian poetry the coinciding of creative revolt with academic institutionalizing meant the seconding and consolidating, in an unprecedented way, of the reaction against Victorian poetry. Here the key-figure is clearly F. R. Leavis, whose early mission was the prosecution of this deep, wide revaluation; deploring 'the Victorian poetic tradition', Leavis was explicit about Eliot's agency and about his own: 'It was Mr Eliot who made us fully conscious of the weaknesses of that tradition.' But what of its strengths?

The weaknesses and vices of bad Victorian poems are what Leavis judged them to be. 'The inferiority, in rigour and force, of the intellectual content is compensated for'—by which he means that it isn't—'by nobility, sonority and finish of phrasing'. The 'spilt religion' which T. E. Hulme thought was Romanticism, and which is indeed Romanticism's vice, was often compounded by a forcible-feeble poetic diction that issued in religiosity's hollowness. Leavis stigmatized Dante Gabriel Rossetti's 'profundity' as 'an uninhibited proffer of large drafts on a merely nominal account ("Life", "love", "death", "terror", "mystery", "Beauty"—it is a bankrupt's lavishness)'. This is telling, but is too close to the narrowed eyes of a bank-teller to be entirely persuasive—can poems be so exactly accountable as wise national housekeeping? Still, the accusations were, and therefore are, true of the bad poems or the bad poets, where insensitivity of rhythm, over-emphasis (those *italicisings*), narrowness of countenanced feelings, and plangent poeticalities all conspired to create—in Arnold's words—the grand name without the grand thing.

It was a time, too, when minor talent was especially liable to make its greatest mistake, that of trying to write as the great had successfully done. Genius such as Tennyson's could do wonders with studied archaism, with unexpected scrannel Gothic notes, and with 'finest verbalism'; and Whitman sounded a self-warning note even in his handsome praise:

To me, Tennyson shows more than any poet I know (perhaps has been a warning to me) how much there is in finest verbalism. There is such a latent charm in mere words, cunning collocutions, and in the voice ringing them, which he has caught and brought out, beyond all others—as in the line, 'And hollow, hollow, hollow, all delight', in 'The Passing of Arthur'.

But Tennyson could do things that were entirely beyond the capabilities of Tennyson's apes. Inerrancy about one's own powers is not a mark of the Victorian poets, nor even is a simple prudence about not over-reaching or over-archaizing. The Victorian poetaster over 'weens'.

Yet the varied achievements of Victorian poetry are a wonder. There is no need to name names, of poets or of poems, since an anthology gives hostages which it believes to be worth a king's ransom. Yet it may be worth naming impulses and kinds. The sheer originality, for instance, of the dramatic monologue, and of nonsense-verse (the very opposite of that escapism which is often laid at Victorian poetry's door), outdoes in its speed of consummated enterprise even the precedent of the Augustan mock-heroic. The dramatic monologue and nonsense-verse are beautifully different but equally inaugurative, and they equally helped to heal the breach which had opened up for Joseph Warton in 1756, when his pre-Victorian predilections led him to prefer the less great poems of Pope to the more great: 'For WIT and SATIRE are transitory and perishable, but NATURE and PASSION are eternal'.

Again, Victorian light verse offers unique combinations of acumen and pathos; what W. H. Auden was to say of the Regency art of Praed ('Praed, whose serious poems are as trivial as his *vers de société* are profound') is often applicable to those who learnt from Praed. Swinburne was moved to appreciate an art very different from his own when he deprecated the mis-allocation of Browning's 'Youth and Art':

There is hardly a more tragic touch in all the most tragic passages of Mr. Browning's vast and various work than that which winds up, with neither a smile nor a sigh, the unspoken expression of hopeless and inexpressible regret:

> And nobody calls you a dunce,
> And people suppose me clever:
> This could but have happened once,
> And we missed it, lost it for ever.

That is not a sample of social verse: it is an echo from the place of conscious or unconscious torment which is paved with penitence and roofed with despair. Its quiet note of commonplace resignation is more bitter and more impressive in the self-scornful sadness of its retrospect than any shriek of rebellion or any imprecation of appeal.

Such a poem as 'Youth and Art' brings out the most valuable legacy of Romantic verse to Victorian verse, that which enabled the Victorians not only to understand 'the true voice of feeling' but also to understand how feeling has many more true voices than even Keats had sensed. Here the crucial figure is the poet who owed so much to Browning: Thomas Hardy.

The recovery of the conviction of Hardy's greatness as a poet, and as a Victorian poet (even though many of his greatest poems were still to come), is itself a reaction against the reaction against the Victorians. Eliot and Yeats colluded to put Hardy to one side, and they did it the easy way, with condescension. Eliot wrote in 1935: 'But it should be apparent at least that Mr. Yeats has been the great poet of his time. Thomas Hardy, who for a few years had all the cry, appears now, what he always was, a minor poet.' The next year, Yeats returned this in a calculatedly small compliment to Hardy: 'Thomas Hardy, though his work lacked technical accomplishment, made the necessary correction through his mastery of the impersonal objective scene.'

The recovery of Hardy (seconded by Philip Larkin's praises, principles, and practice) has brought with it a recovery of the central substantial claims of other poets notable for their true voices of feeling, poets all represented here on a scale greatly beyond that which Quiller-Couch and John Hayward accorded them: Emily Jane Brontë, John Clare, William Barnes, and Christina G. Rossetti.

Great Britain was Victorian for two-thirds of a century. Things changed and counterchanged; even the Queen often proved a surprise, though it may be thought that she was a surprise like a Browning character, by being even more herself than one would ever have anticipated. Victorian poetry is no more amenable to settled summary than are its sixty years. 'Are the Victorians Coming Back?', asked in 1948 the man who did so much to establish the grounds for newly-restored confidence in the Victorian novel and Victorian poetry. But Humphry House knew that revivals can be lethal. 'It will be disastrous if the Victorians' stupidities, vulgarities, failures and unhappinesses are minimised or explained away, or accepted as something else. For many Victorians were in many respects stupid, vulgar, unhappy and unsuccessful; and these aspects of the age remain visible in the objects, the buildings, the pictures and the literature that have been left to us.' For House, early in the re-esteeming of the Victorians, 'the alarming thing in current attitudes to Victorians ... is that they utterly ignore the central criticism which the great Victorians themselves applied to their own age'. Dissent from and assent to the age engrave that deep form of cultural and social criticism which is poetry. The place to end now is where a great novelist of the Victorian age, who was great in assent as well as dissent, famously chose to begin, when he offered, as any historical novelist must, a tale of two ages:

Chapter 1 · *The Period*

It was the best of times, it was the worst of times, it was the age of wisdom, it was the age of foolishness, it was the epoch of belief, it was the epoch of incredulity, it was the season of Light, it was the season of Darkness, it was the spring of hope, it was the winter of despair, we had everything before us, we had nothing before us, we were all going direct to Heaven, we were all going direct the other way— in short, the period was so far like the present period, that some of its noisiest authorities insisted on its being received, for good or for evil, in the superlative degree of comparison only.

EDITORIAL PRINCIPLES

Inclusion. Queen Victoria reigned from 1837 to 1901. Most of the poems included here meet the strictest criterion, of being both written and published within those years. Cheating with terminal dates should be resisted, because the effect of it is always to produce a self-fulfilling definition and restriction, in this case of what it is to be Victorian; so if any datings here are wrong, the editor would wish to know and be chastened. But some latitude is an editor's duty. For the insistence that a poem have been published within the period would preclude most of Hopkins, who yet lived and died a Victorian; and the insistence that a poem have been written within the period would preclude much of Tennyson, whose 'Morte d'Arthur' (rightly judged a Victorian poem not because of its values but because of its publication and impinging), was written four years before Victoria's accession but was not released by the poet, not published, till five years after it. 'Morte d'Arthur', then, and 'Ulysses' on the same terms; but not 'Mariana' which was both written and published too early. The only truly tricky case is that of the first poet in the book, Thomas Lovell Beddoes. *Death's Jest-Book* (1850) he did not himself publish, but he worked on revising it until his death in 1849, so there need be no qualms about including it. The poems which he drafted in the 1820s are a more difficult case. They are included because none of them was published until 1851, when they contributed powerfully to Victorian not to Georgian literature, and because Beddoes was for half his adult life a Victorian.

Texts. Poets have here been allowed their prerogative of revision, and the texts are those finally approved. But there are a few exceptions. 'The Song of the Low', by Ernest Jones, is given in its politically immediate version of 1852. Edward FitzGerald's *Rubáiyát of Omar Khayyám* is given from the first edition (1859); FitzGerald so expanded and changed it as to make it a different poem and his editors have long had to include the first and the last version. William Renton in 1905 (Victoria being dead . . .) revised his 1876 poems so much for the worse as to make it now imperative reluctantly to wrong the poet rather than the poems. And three of the poems of W. B. Yeats are given in their 1890s versions, one being the famous site of subsequent revision, 'The Sorrow of Love'; Yeats's later authorized text is after all everywhere available, and an anthology of Victorian verse does him no injury by representing a few of his poems in their Victorian form. Some people have even been known to prefer the modesty of the original versions.

Cases of notorious textual difficulty, such as that of the Brontës, are alerted in the notes, where the source of every poem's text is given. No titles have been newly supplied. Texts are from a modern edition where one of authority exists, and they are unmodernized. The only poet who thereby presents any difficulty is John Clare; but until very recently Clare's poems had for so long been maltreated by editors that it is imperative now to present them authentically, awkward though this may initially seem. Patience, hard thing.

Dates. At the end of each poem, or of the last poem from the one work, dates are supplied: that of composition (when known to the editor), followed by that of first publication. Thus: (Wr. 1860; pub. 1872). When there is only one date, it is that of first publication. Thus: (1875). The formula (Wr. and pub. 1864) is used too, because it is unsatisfactory to use the single date to cover the two very different cases, of the poem's being known to be written as well as published in that year, and of our knowing only when it was published. In the case of excerpts, the dates are those of the work, not of the excerpt, except when the appending makes clear the specific application.

For most of these poets, bibliographical and biographical research has never been prosecuted; the dates of composition are therefore not only incomplete, but are sure to be imperfect. It is inevitable too that periodical publication will often have been missed, and very likely that volume publication will sometimes have been. It is not practicable newly to edit a hundred poets, but the editor would again wish to learn of facts missed or mistaken.

The ordering. All principles of ordering within an anthology (or edition) have not only advantages and disadvantages, but anomalies. The practice of grouping all the poems by a particular author immediately entails profound dislocations of chronology, yet it remains best for such an anthology as this. The ordering of the poets is here effected on the same principle as that of the poems by any one poet: chronologically, by year of composition. A poet therefore enters the sequence at the year of composition of the earliest poem included, and the particular poet's poems are then in order of their years of composition when known and otherwise by year of publication. A posthumous date of publication, though, yields to a date of death.

Excerpting. All but a very few of the poems are printed in their entirety, including the entire four substantial masterpieces, Lewis Carroll's *The Hunting of the Snark*, Clough's *Amours de Voyage*, FitzGerald's *Rubáiyát of Omar Khayyám*, and Christina G. Rossetti's *Goblin Market*. The only excerpting has been of units to which the poet gave a distinct autonomy, by separate numbering or by stanzaic and formal separation; in practice this mostly means sections from a sequence, or intercalations within a longer poem. Thus there are sections from *In Memoriam*, a song from *Idylls of the King*, and sonnets from *Modern Love*, but not, say, the closing vignette of *Sohrab and Rustum*. This principle is practicable for Victorian poetry as it would not be for Romantic poetry; practicable, in that it need not do any serious injustice to the art of the great poets. The sole exception to this principle, of excerpting only that which possesses its own subordinate completeness, is the case of Elizabeth Barrett Browning, whose *Aurora Leigh* cannot be represented on such a principle; the decision has been to minimize any violation by giving the opening of the poem, the first five hundred lines of the First Book. It is regretted that constraints of space prevented the inclusion of the First Book entire.

The poets' names. As a matter of historical authenticity and of respect for authors' wishes, the poets' names are given, it is hoped, in the form which they preferred or in some cases came to prefer, the evidence usually being that of title-pages. Thus, William Bell Scott, E. Nesbit, Christina G. Rossetti, and J. K. Stephen. Two poets fail to furnish a helpful title-page. Emily Jane Brontë is the form with which she signed the manuscript volume in which she transcribed the Gondal poems. The other such manuscript is initialled E. J. B. Emily Jane Brontë, which was adopted by her good editor C. W. Hatfield, is slightly to be preferred to Emily J. Brontë (with which she signed her French devoirs). More unignorably difficult is Hopkins. He has become known (the roll, the rise . . .) as Gerard Manley Hopkins, but only a handful of his letters (three or four early ones?) were ever signed so. During the last two years of his life, he vacillated—even to the same recent correspondent—between Gerard Hopkins and Gerard M. Hopkins, with the latter predominating. Perhaps he would have preferred Gerard Hopkins, the form which he used for the only things which he ever published above his name, the notes in *Nature* near the end of his life, in 1882–4. But Gerard M. Hopkins has the advantage of being both a not ignoble compromise and a substantial likelihood. The alternative to seeming ostentatious here would have been to be craven, which Hopkins was not.

Pseudonyms need to be treated with discretion rather than consistency. When a writer is universally known by the pseudonym, the pseudonym is given first, and the family name in brackets; thus Lewis Carroll (Charles Lutwidge Dodgson). When the pseudonym has largely lapsed but may still be of help (there being, for instance, more than one poet called James Thomson), the pseudonym is given second, in brackets and in inverted commas; thus James Thomson ('B.V.'). When the pseudonym has entirely yielded, it is not given at all; no Currer Bell, simply Charlotte Brontë. But the notes at the back supply a pseudonym when a book might otherwise be hard to trace.

Proportions. Any anthologist frets, or more, about proportions. The worth or importance of the poets chosen is not to be measured by the number of pages allotted, and not just because certain kinds of poem ask, from their writers and readers, more amplitude or more leisure. And yet . . . It needs to be acknowledged that the claims (and consequential proportions to some degree) are not only of one poet against another, but are also of one kind of poem against another, of one vantage-point, and of one decade or phase or moment against another. It has here been taken to be more important that justice be done to the poems of the period than to the poets; indeed, there would be little point in having a period-based anthology if it were not pre-eminently the period to which justice should be done. The justling of these competing claims is sure to leave inequity and bruises; the anthologist is more aware of sins of omission than of commission.

ACKNOWLEDGEMENTS

Help has been generously given by Juliet R. V. Barker, Archie Burnett, R. W. Crump, Ian Fletcher, William E. Fredeman, Janet Gezari, Bernard Jones, William Logan, David Powell, and Joan Rutter.

THOMAS LOVELL BEDDOES
1803–1849

1

A Crocodile

HARD by the lilied Nile I saw
A duskish river-dragon stretched along,
The brown habergeon of his limbs enamelled
With sanguine almandines and rainy pearl:
And on his back there lay a young one sleeping,
No bigger than a mouse; with eyes like beads,
And a small fragment of its speckled egg
Remaining on its harmless, pulpy snout;
A thing to laugh at, as it gaped to catch
The baulking merry flies. In the iron jaws   10
Of the great devil-beast, like a pale soul
Fluttering in rocky hell, lightsomely flew
A snowy trochilus, with roseate beak
Tearing the hairy leeches from his throat.

(Wr. 1823–5; pub. 1851)

2

Death Sweet

IS it not sweet to die? for, what is death,
But sighing that we ne'er may sigh again,
Getting a length beyond our tedious selves;
But trampling the last tear from poisonous sorrow,
Spilling our woes, crushing our frozen hopes,
And passing like an incense out of man?
Then, if the body felt, what were its sense,
Turning to daisies gently in the grave,
If not the soul's most delicate delight
When it does filtrate, through the pores of thought,   10
In love and the enamelled flowers of song?

(Wr. 1823–5; pub. 1851)

3

Hymn

AND many voices marshalled in one hymn
Wound through the night, whose still, translucent moments
Lay on each side their breath; and the hymn passed

Its long, harmonious populace of words
Between the silvery silences, as when
The slaves of Egypt, like a wind between
The head and trunk of a dismembered king
On a strewn plank, with blood and footsteps sealed,
Vallied the unaccustomed sea.

(Wr. 1823–5; pub. 1851)

4 *Humble Beginnings*

WHY, Rome was naked once, a bastard smudge,
Tumbled on straw, the den-fellow of whelps,
Fattened on roots, and, when athirst for milk,
He crept beneath and drank the swagging udder
Of Tyber's brave she-wolf; and Heaven's Judea
Was folded in a pannier.

(Wr. 1823–5; pub. 1851)

5 *Sonnet: To Tartar, a Terrier Beauty*

SNOWDROP of dogs, with ear of brownest dye,
Like the last orphan leaf of naked tree
Which shudders in bleak autumn; though by thee,
Of hearing careless and untutored eye,
Not understood articulate speech of men,
Nor marked the artificial mind of books,
—The mortal's voice eternized by the pen,—
Yet hast thou thought and language all unknown
To Babel's scholars; oft intensest looks,
Long scrutiny o'er some dark-veined stone   10
Dost thou bestow, learning dead mysteries
Of the world's birth-day, oft in eager tone
With quick-tailed fellows bandiest prompt replies,
Solicitudes canine, four-footed amities.

(Wr. 1823–5; pub. 1851)

6 *A Lake*

A lake
Is a river curled and asleep like a snake.

(Wr. 1823–5; pub. 1935)

from *Death's Jest-Book* (7–9)

7   *Song by Isbrand*

SQUATS on a toad-stool under a tree
  A bodiless childfull of life in the gloom,
Crying with frog voice, 'What shall I be?
Poor unborn ghost, for my mother killed me
  Scarcely alive in her wicked womb.
What shall I be? shall I creep to the egg
  That's cracking asunder yonder by Nile,
    And with eighteen toes,
    And a snuff-taking nose,
  Make an Egyptian crocodile?   10
Sing, "Catch a mummy by the leg
And crunch him with an upper jaw,
Wagging tail and clenching claw;
Take a bill-full from my craw,
Neighbour raven, caw, O caw,
Grunt, my crocky, pretty maw!"

'Swine, shall I be one? 'Tis a dear dog;
  But for a smile, and kiss, and pout,
  I much prefer *your* black-lipped snout,
    Little, gruntless, fairy hog,   20
    Godson of the hawthorn hedge.
  For, when Ringwood snuffs me out,
    And 'gins my tender paunch to grapple,
    Sing, " 'Twixt your ancles visage wedge,
      And roll up like an apple."

'Serpent Lucifer, how do you do?
Of your worms and your snakes I'd be one or two
  For in this dear planet of wool and of leather
'Tis pleasant to need no shirt, breeches or shoe,
  And have arm, leg, and belly together.   30
  Then aches your head, or are you lazy?
  Sing, "Round your neck your belly wrap,
  Tail-a-top, and make your cap
    Any bee and daisy."

'I'll not be a fool, like the nightingale
Who sits up all midnight without any ale,
  Making a noise with his nose;
Nor a camel, although 'tis a beautiful back;
Nor a duck, notwithstanding the music of quack
  And the webby, mud-patting toes.   40

3

I'll be a new bird with the head of an ass,
　　Two pigs' feet, two men's feet, and two of a hen;
Devil-winged; dragon-bellied; grave-jawed, because grass
　　Is a beard that's soon shaved, and grows seldom again
　　Before it is summer; so cow all the rest;
　　The new Dodo is finished. O! come to my nest.'

(Act III, scene iii)

8   *Song*

                      By female voices

　　WE have bathed, where none have seen us,
　　　　In the lake and in the fountain,
　　　　　Underneath the charmed statue
　　Of the timid, bending Venus,
　　　　When the water-nymphs were counting
　　In the waves the stars of night,
　　　　　And those maidens started at you,
　　Your limbs shone through so soft and bright.
　　　　　But no secrets dare we tell,
　　　　　　For thy slaves unlace thee,   10
　　　　　　And he, who shall embrace thee,
　　　　　Waits to try thy beauty's spell.

                       By male voices

　　We have crowned thee queen of women,
　　　　Since love's love, the rose, hath kept her
　　　　　Court within thy lips and blushes,
　　And thine eye, in beauty swimming,
　　　　Kissing, we rendered up the sceptre,
　　At whose touch the startled soul
　　　　　Like an ocean bounds and gushes,
　　And spirits bend at thy controul.   20
　　　　　But no secrets dare we tell,
　　　　　　For thy slaves unlace thee,
　　　　　　And he, who shall embrace thee,
　　　　　Is at hand, and so farewell.

(Act IV, scene iii)

9 *Dirge*

WE do lie beneath the grass
  In the moonlight, in the shade
Of the yew-tree. They that pass
  Hear us not. We are afraid
    They would envy our delight,
    In our graves by glow-worm night.
Come follow us, and smile as we;
  We sail to the rock in the ancient waves,
Where the snow falls by thousands into the sea,
  And the drowned and the shipwrecked have happy graves. 10

(Act V, scene iv; wr. 1825–49, pub. 1850)

ALFRED TENNYSON

1809–1892

10 *St Simeon Stylites*

ALTHO' I be the basest of mankind,
From scalp to sole one slough and crust of sin,
Unfit for earth, unfit for heaven, scarce meet
For troops of devils, mad with blasphemy,
I will not cease to grasp the hope I hold
Of saintdom, and to clamour, mourn and sob,
Battering the gates of heaven with storms of prayer,
Have mercy, Lord, and take away my sin.

Let this avail, just, dreadful, mighty God,
This not be all in vain, that thrice ten years, 10
Thrice multiplied by superhuman pangs,
In hungers and in thirsts, fevers and cold,
In coughs, aches, stitches, ulcerous throes and cramps,
A sign betwixt the meadow and the cloud,
Patient on this tall pillar I have borne
Rain, wind, frost, heat, hail, damp, and sleet, and snow;
And I had hoped that ere this period closed
Thou wouldst have caught me up into thy rest,
Denying not these weather-beaten limbs
The meed of saints, the white robe and the palm. 20

O take the meaning, Lord: I do not breathe,
Not whisper, any murmur of complaint.
Pain heap'd ten-hundred-fold to this, were still
Less burthen, by ten-hundred-fold, to bear,
Than were those lead-like tons of sin that crush'd
My spirit flat before thee.
                                    O Lord, Lord,
Thou knowest I bore this better at the first,
For I was strong and hale of body then;
And tho' my teeth, which now are dropt away,
Would chatter with the cold, and all my beard   30
Was tagg'd with icy fringes in the moon,
I drown'd the whoopings of the owl with sound
Of pious hymns and psalms, and sometimes saw
An angel stand and watch me, as I sang.
Now am I feeble grown; my end draws nigh;
I hope my end draws nigh: half deaf I am,
So that I scarce can hear the people hum
About the column's base, and almost blind,
And scarce can recognise the fields I know;
And both my thighs are rotted with the dew;   40
Yet cease I not to clamour and to cry,
While my stiff spine can hold my weary head,
Till all my limbs drop piecemeal from the stone,
Have mercy, mercy: take away my sin.

O Jesus, if thou wilt not save my soul,
Who may be saved? who is it may be saved?
Who may be made a saint, if I fail here?
Show me the man hath suffer'd more than I.
For did not all thy martyrs die one death?
For either they were stoned, or crucified,   50
Or burn'd in fire, or boil'd in oil, or sawn
In twain beneath the ribs; but I die here
To-day, and whole years long, a life of death.
Bear witness, if I could have found a way
(And heedfully I sifted all my thought)
More slowly-painful to subdue this home
Of sin, my flesh, which I despise and hate,
I had not stinted practice, O my God.

For not alone this pillar-punishment,
Not this alone I bore: but while I lived   60
In the white convent down the valley there,
For many weeks about my loins I wore
The rope that haled the buckets from the well,

Twisted as tight as I could knot the noose;
And spake not of it to a single soul,
Until the ulcer, eating thro' my skin,
Betray'd my secret penance, so that all
My brethren marvell'd greatly. More than this
I bore, whereof, O God, thou knowest all.

Three winters, that my soul might grow to thee,   70
I lived up there on yonder mountain side.
My right leg chain'd into the crag, I lay
Pent in a roofless close of ragged stones;
Inswathed sometimes in wandering mist, and twice
Black'd with thy branding thunder, and sometimes
Sucking the damps for drink, and eating not,
Except the spare chance-gift of those that came
To touch my body and be heal'd, and live:
And they say then that I work'd miracles,
Whereof my fame is loud amongst mankind,   80
Cured lameness, palsies, cancers. Thou, O God,
Knowest alone whether this was or no.
Have mercy, mercy! cover all my sin.

Then, that I might be more alone with thee,
Three years I lived upon a pillar, high
Six cubits, and three years on one of twelve;
And twice three years I crouch'd on one that rose
Twenty by measure; last of all, I grew
Twice ten long weary weary years to this,
That numbers forty cubits from the soil.   90

I think that I have borne as much as this—
Or else I dream—and for so long a time,
If I may measure time by yon slow light,
And this high dial, which my sorrow crowns—
So much—even so.
                         And yet I know not well,
For that the evil ones come here, and say,
'Fall down, O Simeon: thou hast suffer'd long
For ages and for ages!' then they prate
Of penances I cannot have gone thro',
Perplexing me with lies; and oft I fall,   100
Maybe for months, in such blind lethargies
That Heaven, and Earth, and Time are choked.
                                                      But yet
Bethink thee, Lord, while thou and all the saints
Enjoy themselves in heaven, and men on earth

House in the shade of comfortable roofs,
Sit with their wives by fires, eat wholesome food,
And wear warm clothes, and even beasts have stalls,
I, 'tween the spring and downfall of the light,
Bow down one thousand and two hundred times,
To Christ, the Virgin Mother, and the saints;   110
Or in the night, after a little sleep,
I wake: the chill stars sparkle; I am wet
With drenching dews, or stiff with crackling frost.
I wear an undress'd goatskin on my back;
A grazing iron collar grinds my neck;
And in my weak, lean arms I lift the cross,
And strive and wrestle with thee till I die:
O mercy, mercy! wash away my sin.

O Lord, thou knowest what a man I am;
A sinful man, conceived and born in sin: 120
'Tis their own doing; this is none of mine;
Lay it not to me. Am I to blame for this,
That here come those that worship me? Ha! ha!
They think that I am somewhat. What am I?
The silly people take me for a saint,
And bring me offerings of fruit and flowers:
And I, in truth (thou wilt bear witness here)
Have all in all endured as much, and more
Than many just and holy men, whose names
Are register'd and calendar'd for saints.   130

Good people, you do ill to kneel to me.
What is it I can have done to merit this?
I am a sinner viler than you all.
It may be I have wrought some miracles,
And cured some halt and maim'd; but what of that?
It may be, no one, even among the saints,
May match his pains with mine; but what of that?
Yet do not rise; for you may look on me,
And in your looking you may kneel to God.
Speak! is there any of you halt or maim'd?   140
I think you know I have some power with Heaven
From my long penance: let him speak his wish.

Yes, I can heal him. Power goes forth from me.
They say that they are heal'd. Ah, hark! they shout
'St Simeon Stylites.' Why, if so,
God reaps a harvest in me. O my soul,
God reaps a harvest in thee. If this be,

Can I work miracles and not be saved?
This is not told of any. They were saints.
It cannot be but that I shall be saved;   150
Yea, crown'd a saint. They shout, 'Behold a saint!'
And lower voices saint me from above.
Courage, St Simeon! This dull chrysalis
Cracks into shining wings, and hope ere death
Spreads more and more and more, that God hath now
Sponged and made blank of crimeful record all
My mortal archives.
        O my sons, my sons,
I, Simeon of the pillar, by surname
Stylites, among men; I, Simeon,
The watcher on the column till the end;   160
I, Simeon, whose brain the sunshine bakes;
I, whose bald brows in silent hours become
Unnaturally hoar with rime, do now
From my high nest of penance here proclaim
That Pontius and Iscariot by my side
Show'd like fair seraphs. On the coals I lay,
A vessel full of sin: all hell beneath
Made me boil over. Devils pluck'd my sleeve,
Abaddon and Asmodeus caught at me.
I smote them with the cross; they swarm'd again.   170
In bed like monstrous apes they crush'd my chest:
They flapp'd my light out as I read: I saw
Their faces grow between me and my book;
With colt-like whinny and with hoggish whine
They burst my prayer. Yet this way was left,
And by this way I 'scaped them. Mortify
Your flesh, like me, with scourges and with thorns;
Smite, shrink not, spare not. If it may be, fast
Whole Lents, and pray. I hardly, with slow steps,
With slow, faint steps, and much exceeding pain,   180
Have scrambled past those pits of fire, that still
Sing in mine ears. But yield not me the praise:
God only thro' his bounty hath thought fit,
Among the powers and princes of this world,
To make me an example to mankind,
Which few can reach to. Yet I do not say
But that a time may come—yea, even now,
Now, now, his footsteps smite the threshold stairs
Of life—I say, that time is at the doors
When you may worship me without reproach;   190
For I will leave my relics in your land,
And you may carve a shrine about my dust,

And burn a fragrant lamp before my bones,
When I am gather'd to the glorious saints.

While I spake then, a sting of shrewdest pain
Ran shrivelling thro' me, and a cloudlike change,
In passing, with a grosser film made thick
These heavy, horny eyes. The end! the end!
Surely the end! What's here? a shape, a shade,
A flash of light. Is that the angel there   200
That holds a crown? Come, blessed brother, come.
I know thy glittering face. I waited long;
My brows are ready. What! deny it now?
Nay, draw, draw, draw nigh. So I clutch it. Christ!
'Tis gone: 'tis here again; the crown! the crown!
So now 'tis fitted on and grows to me,
And from it melt the dews of Paradise,
Sweet! sweet! spikenard, and balm, and frankincense.
Ah! let me not be fool'd, sweet saints: I trust
That I am whole, and clean, and meet for Heaven.   210

Speak, if there be a priest, a man of God,
Among you there, and let him presently
Approach, and lean a ladder on the shaft,
And climbing up into my airy home,
Deliver me the blessed sacrament;
For by the warning of the Holy Ghost,
I prophesy that I shall die to-night,
A quarter before twelve.
                           But thou, O Lord,
Aid all this foolish people; let them take
Example, pattern: lead them to thy light.   220

(Wr. 1833; pub. 1842)

11   *Ulysses*

      IT little profits that an idle king,
      By this still hearth, among these barren crags,
      Match'd with an aged wife, I mete and dole
      Unequal laws unto a savage race,
      That hoard, and sleep, and feed, and know not me.

      I cannot rest from travel: I will drink
      Life to the lees: all times I have enjoy'd
      Greatly, have suffer'd greatly, both with those
      That loved me, and alone; on shore, and when

Thro' scudding drifts the rainy Hyades   10
Vext the dim sea: I am become a name;
For always roaming with a hungry heart
Much have I seen and known; cities of men
And manners, climates, councils, governments,
Myself not least, but honour'd of them all;
And drunk delight of battle with my peers,
Far on the ringing plains of windy Troy.
I am a part of all that I have met;
Yet all experience is an arch wherethro'
Gleams that untravell'd world, whose margin fades   20
For ever and for ever when I move.
How dull it is to pause, to make an end,
To rust unburnish'd, not to shine in use!
As tho' to breathe were life. Life piled on life
Were all too little, and of one to me
Little remains: but every hour is saved
From that eternal silence, something more,
A bringer of new things; and vile it were
For some three suns to store and hoard myself,
And this gray spirit yearning in desire   30
To follow knowledge like a sinking star,
Beyond the utmost bound of human thought.

    This is my son, mine own Telemachus,
To whom I leave the sceptre and the isle—
Well-loved of me, discerning to fulfil
This labour, by slow prudence to make mild
A rugged people, and thro' soft degrees
Subdue them to the useful and the good.
Most blameless is he, centred in the sphere
Of common duties, decent not to fail   40
In offices of tenderness, and pay
Meet adoration to my household gods,
When I am gone. He works his work, I mine.

    There lies the port; the vessel puffs her sail:
There gloom the dark broad seas. My mariners,
Souls that have toil'd, and wrought, and thought with me—
That ever with a frolic welcome took
The thunder and the sunshine, and opposed
Free hearts, free foreheads—you and I are old;
Old age hath yet his honour and his toil;   50
Death closes all: but something ere the end,
Some work of noble note, may yet be done,
Not unbecoming men that strove with Gods.

The lights begin to twinkle from the rocks:
The long day wanes: the slow moon climbs: the deep
Moans round with many voices. Come, my friends,
'Tis not too late to seek a newer world.
Push off, and sitting well in order smite
The sounding furrows; for my purpose holds
To sail beyond the sunset, and the baths   60
Of all the western stars, until I die.
It may be that the gulfs will wash us down:
It may be we shall touch the Happy Isles,
And see the great Achilles, whom we knew.
Tho' much is taken, much abides; and tho'
We are not now that strength which in old days
Moved earth and heaven; that which we are, we are;
One equal temper of heroic hearts,
Made weak by time and fate, but strong in will
To strive, to seek, to find, and not to yield.   70

(Wr. 1833; pub. 1842)

12   *Morte d'Arthur*

So all day long the noise of battle roll'd
Among the mountains by the winter sea;
Until King Arthur's table, man by man,
Had fallen in Lyonnesse about their Lord,
King Arthur: then, because his wound was deep,
The bold Sir Bedivere uplifted him,
Sir Bedivere, the last of all his knights,
And bore him to a chapel nigh the field,
A broken chancel with a broken cross,
That stood on a dark strait of barren land.   10
On one side lay the Ocean, and on one
Lay a great water, and the moon was full.

Then spake King Arthur to Sir Bedivere:
'The sequel of to-day unsolders all
The goodliest fellowship of famous knights
Whereof this world holds record. Such a sleep
They sleep—the men I loved. I think that we
Shall never more, at any future time,
Delight our souls with talk of knightly deeds,
Walking about the gardens and the halls   20
Of Camelot, as in the days that were.
I perish by this people which I made,—

Tho' Merlin sware that I should come again
To rule once more—but let what will be, be,
I am so deeply smitten thro' the helm
That without help I cannot last till morn.
Thou therefore take my brand Excalibur,
Which was my pride: for thou rememberest how
In those old days, one summer noon, an arm
Rose up from out the bosom of the lake,   30
Clothed in white samite, mystic, wonderful,
Holding the sword—and how I row'd across
And took it, and have worn it, like a king:
And, wheresoever I am sung or told
In aftertime, this also shall be known:
But now delay not: take Excalibur,
And fling him far into the middle mere:
Watch what thou seëst, and lightly bring me word.'

    To him replied the bold Sir Bedivere:
'It is not meet, Sir King, to leave thee thus,   40
Aidless, alone, and smitten thro' the helm.
A little thing may harm a wounded man.
Yet I thy hest will all perform at full,
Watch what I see, and lightly bring thee word.'

    So saying, from the ruin'd shrine he stept
And in the moon athwart the place of tombs,
Where lay the mighty bones of ancient men,
Old knights, and over them the sea-wind sang
Shrill, chill, with flakes of foam. He, stepping down
By zig-zag paths, and juts of pointed rock,   50
Came on the shining levels of the lake.

    There drew he forth the brand Excalibur,
And o'er him, drawing it, the winter moon,
Brightening the skirts of a long cloud, ran forth
And sparkled keen with frost against the hilt:
For all the haft twinkled with diamond sparks,
Myriads of topaz-lights, and jacinth-work
Of subtlest jewellery. He gazed so long
That both his eyes were dazzled, as he stood,
This way and that dividing the swift mind,   60
In act to throw: but at the last it seem'd
Better to leave Excalibur conceal'd
There in the many-knotted waterflags,
That whistled stiff and dry about the marge.
So strode he back slow to the wounded King.

Then spake King Arthur to Sir Bedivere:
'Hast thou perform'd my mission which I gave?
What is it thou hast seen? or what hast heard?'

And answer made the bold Sir Bedivere:
'I heard the ripple washing in the reeds,   70
And the wild water lapping on the crag.'

To whom replied King Arthur, faint and pale:
'Thou hast betray'd thy nature and thy name,
Not rendering true answer, as beseem'd
Thy fëalty, nor like a noble knight:
For surer sign had follow'd, either hand,
Or voice, or else a motion of the mere.
This is a shameful thing for men to lie.
Yet now, I charge thee, quickly go again
As thou art lief and dear, and do the thing   80
I bad thee, watch, and lightly bring me word.'

Then went Sir Bedivere the second time
Across the ridge, and paced beside the mere,
Counting the dewy pebbles, fix'd in thought;
But when he saw the wonder of the hilt,
How curiously and strangely chased, he smote
His palms together, and he cried aloud,

'And if indeed I cast the brand away,
Surely a precious thing, one worthy note,
Should thus be lost for ever from the earth,   90
Which might have pleased the eyes of many men.
What good should follow this, if this were done?
What harm, undone? deep harm to disobey,
Seeing obedience is the bond of rule.
Were it well to obey then, if a king demand
An act unprofitable, against himself?
The King is sick, and knows not what he does.
What record, or what relic of my lord
Should be to aftertime, but empty breath
And rumours of a doubt? but were this kept,   100
Stored in some treasure-house of mighty kings,
Some one might show it at a joust of arms,
Saying, "King Arthur's sword, Excalibur,
Wrought by the lonely maiden of the Lake.
Nine years she wrought it, sitting in the deeps
Upon the hidden bases of the hills."
So might some old man speak in the aftertime

To all the people, winning reverence.
But now much honour and much fame were lost.'

So spake he, clouded with his own conceit,   110
And hid Excalibur the second time,
And so strode back slow to the wounded King.

Then spoke King Arthur, breathing heavily:
'What is it thou hast seen? or what hast heard?'

And answer made the bold Sir Bedivere:
'I heard the water lapping on the crag,
And the long ripple washing in the reeds.'

To whom replied King Arthur, much in wrath:
'Ah, miserable and unkind, untrue,
Unknightly, traitor-hearted! Woe is me!   120
Authority forgets a dying king,
Laid widow'd of the power in his eye
That bow'd the will. I see thee what thou art,
For thou, the latest-left of all my knights,
In whom should meet the offices of all,
Thou wouldst betray me for the precious hilt;
Either from lust of gold, or like a girl
Valuing the giddy pleasure of the eyes.
Yet, for a man may fail in duty twice,
And the third time may prosper, get thee hence: 130
But, if thou spare to fling Excalibur,
I will arise and slay thee with my hands.'

Then quickly rose Sir Bedivere, and ran,
And, leaping down the ridges lightly, plunged
Among the bulrush-beds, and clutch'd the sword,
And strongly wheel'd and threw it. The great brand
Made lightnings in the splendour of the moon,
And flashing round and round, and whirl'd in an arch,
Shot like a streamer of the northern morn,
Seen where the moving isles of winter shock   140
By night, with noises of the northern sea.
So flash'd and fell the brand Excalibur:
But ere he dipt the surface, rose an arm
Clothed in white samite, mystic, wonderful,
And caught him by the hilt, and brandish'd him
Three times, and drew him under in the mere.
And lightly went the other to the King.

Then spoke King Arthur, drawing thicker breath:
'Now see I by thine eyes that this is done.
Speak out: what is it thou hast heard, or seen?'   150

And answer made the bold Sir Bedivere:
'Sir King, I closed mine eyelids, lest the gems
Should blind my purpose, for I never saw,
Nor shall see, here or elsewhere, till I die,
Not tho' I live three lives of mortal men,
So great a miracle as yonder hilt.
Then with both hands I flung him, wheeling him;
But when I look'd again, behold an arm,
Clothed in white samite, mystic, wonderful,
That caught him by the hilt, and brandish'd him   160
Three times, and drew him under in the mere.'

And answer made King Arthur, breathing hard:
'My end draws nigh; 'tis time that I were gone.
Make broad thy shoulders to receive my weight,
And bear me to the margin; yet I fear
My wound hath taken cold, and I shall die.'

So saying, from the pavement he half rose,
Slowly, with pain, reclining on his arm,
And looking wistfully with wide blue eyes
As in a picture. Him Sir Bedivere   170
Remorsefully regarded thro' his tears,
And would have spoken, but he found not words,
Then took with care, and kneeling on one knee,
O'er both his shoulders drew the languid hands,
And rising bore him thro' the place of tombs.

But, as he walk'd, King Arthur panted hard,
Like one that feels a nightmare on his bed
When all the house is mute. So sigh'd the King,
Muttering and murmuring at his ear, 'Quick, quick!
I fear it is too late, and I shall die.'   180
But the other swiftly strode from ridge to ridge,
Clothed with his breath, and looking, as he walk'd,
Larger than human on the frozen hills.
He heard the deep behind him, and a cry
Before. His own thought drove him, like a goad.
Dry clash'd his harness in the icy caves
And barren chasms, and all to left and right
The bare black cliff clang'd round him, as he based
His feet on juts of slippery crag that rang

Sharp-smitten with the dint of armed heels—   190
And on a sudden, lo! the level lake,
And the long glories of the winter moon.

   Then saw they how there hove a dusky barge,
Dark as a funeral scarf from stem to stern,
Beneath them; and descending they were ware
That all the decks were dense with stately forms
Black-stoled, black-hooded, like a dream—by these
Three Queens with crowns of gold—and from them rose
A cry that shiver'd to the tingling stars,
And, as it were one voice, an agony   200
Of lamentation, like a wind, that shrills
All night in a waste land, where no one comes,
Or hath come, since the making of the world.

   Then murmur'd Arthur, 'Place me in the barge,'
And to the barge they came. There those three Queens
Put forth their hands, and took the King, and wept.
But she, that rose the tallest of them all
And fairest, laid his head upon her lap,
And loosed the shatter'd casque, and chafed his hands,
And call'd him by his name, complaining loud,   210
And dropping bitter tears against his brow
Striped with dark blood: for all his face was white
And colourless, and like the wither'd moon
Smote by the fresh beam of the springing east;
And all his greaves and cuisses dash'd with drops
Of onset; and the light and lustrous curls—
That made his forehead like a rising sun
High from the daïs-throne—were parch'd with dust;
Or, clotted into points and hanging loose,
Mix'd with the knightly growth that fringed his lips.   220
So like a shatter'd column lay the King;
Not like that Arthur who, with lance in rest,
From spur to plume a star of tournament,
Shot thro' the lists at Camelot, and charged
Before the eyes of ladies and of kings.

   Then loudly cried the bold Sir Bedivere,
'Ah! my Lord Arthur, whither shall I go?
Where shall I hide my forehead and my eyes?
For now I see the true old times are dead,
When every morning brought a noble chance,   230
And every chance brought out a noble knight.
Such times have been not since the light that led

The holy Elders with the gift of myrrh.
But now the whole ROUND TABLE is dissolved
Which was an image of the mighty world;
And I, the last, go forth companionless,
And the days darken round me, and the years,
Among new men, strange faces, other minds.'

    And slowly answered Arthur from the barge:
'The old order changeth, yielding place to new,   240
And God fulfils Himself in many ways,
Lest one good custom should corrupt the world.
Comfort thyself: what comfort is in me?
I have lived my life, and that which I have done
May He within Himself make pure! but thou,
If thou shouldst never see my face again,
Pray for my soul. More things are wrought by prayer
Than this world dreams of. Wherefore, let thy voice
Rise like a fountain for me night and day.
For what are men better than sheep or goats   250
That nourish a blind life within the brain,
If, knowing God, they lift not hands of prayer
Both for themselves and those who call them friend?
For so the whole round earth is every way
Bound by gold chains about the feet of God.
But now farewell. I am going a long way
With these thou seëst—if indeed I go—
(For all my mind is clouded with a doubt)
To the island-valley of Avilion;
Where falls not hail, or rain, or any snow,   260
Nor ever wind blows loudly; but it lies
Deep-meadow'd, happy, fair with orchard-lawns
And bowery hollows crown'd with summer sea,
Where I will heal me of my grievous wound.'

    So said he, and the barge with oar and sail
Moved from the brink, like some full-breasted swan
That, fluting a wild carol ere her death,
Ruffles her pure cold plume, and takes the flood
With swarthy webs. Long stood Sir Bedivere
Revolving many memories, till the hull   270
Look'd one black dot against the verge of dawn,
And on the mere the wailing died away.

                (Wr. 1833–4; pub. 1842)

13

The Eagle

Fragment

HE clasps the crag with crooked hands;
Close to the sun in lonely lands,
Ring'd with the azure world, he stands.

The wrinkled sea beneath him crawls;
He watches from his mountain walls,
And like a thunderbolt he falls.

(Wr. 1833?; pub. 1851)

14

BREAK, break, break,
  On thy cold gray stones, O Sea!
And I would that my tongue could utter
  The thoughts that arise in me.

O well for the fisherman's boy,
  That he shouts with his sister at play!
O well for the sailor lad,
  That he sings in his boat on the bay!

And the stately ships go on
  To their haven under the hill;   10
But O for the touch of a vanish'd hand,
  And the sound of a voice that is still!

Break, break, break,
  At the foot of thy crags, O Sea!
But the tender grace of a day that is dead
  Will never come back to me.

(Wr. 1834?; pub. 1842)

15

Audley Court

'THE Bull, the Fleece are cramm'd, and not a room
For love or money. Let us picnic there
At Audley Court.'
                    I spoke, while Audley feast
Humm'd like a hive all round the narrow quay,
To Francis, with a basket on his arm,

To Francis just alighted from the boat,
And breathing of the sea. 'With all my heart,'
Said Francis. Then we shoulder'd thro' the swarm,
And rounded by the stillness of the beach
To where the bay runs up its latest horn.   10

We left the dying ebb that faintly lipp'd
The flat red granite; so by many a sweep
Of meadow smooth from aftermath we reach'd
The griffin-guarded gates, and pass'd thro' all
The pillar'd dusk of sounding sycamores,
And cross'd the garden to the gardener's lodge,
With all its casements bedded, and its walls
And chimneys muffled in the leafy vine.

There, on a slope of orchard, Francis laid
A damask napkin wrought with horse and hound,   20
Brought out a dusky loaf that smelt of home,
And, half-cut-down, a pasty costly-made,
Where quail and pigeon, lark and leveret lay,
Like fossils of the rock, with golden yolks
Imbedded and injellied; last, with these,
A flask of cider from his father's vats,
Prime, which I knew; and so we sat and eat
And talk'd old matters over; who was dead,
Who married, who was like to be, and how
The races went, and who would rent the hall: 30
Then touch'd upon the game, how scarce it was
This season; glancing thence, discuss'd the farm,
The four-field system, and the price of grain;
And struck upon the corn-laws, where we split,
And came again together on the king
With heated faces; till he laugh'd aloud;
And, while the blackbird on the pippin hung
To hear him, clapt his hand in mine and sang—

'Oh! who would fight and march and countermarch,
Be shot for sixpence in a battle-field,   40
And shovell'd up into some bloody trench
Where no one knows? but let me live my life.
    'Oh! who would cast and balance at a desk,
Perch'd like a crow upon a three-legg'd stool,
Till all his juice is dried, and all his joints
Are full of chalk? but let me live my life.
    'Who'd serve the state? for if I carved my name
Upon the cliffs that guard my native land,

I might as well have traced it in the sands;
The sea wastes all: but let me live my life.　　　　50
　　'Oh! who would love? I woo'd a woman once,
But she was sharper than an eastern wind,
And all my heart turn'd from her, as a thorn
Turns from the sea; but let me live my life.'

　　He sang his song, and I replied with mine:
I found it in a volume, all of songs,
Knock'd down to me, when old Sir Robert's pride,
His books—the more the pity, so I said—
Came to the hammer here in March—and this—
I set the words, and added names I knew.　　　　60

　　'Sleep, Ellen Aubrey, sleep, and dream of me:
Sleep, Ellen, folded in thy sister's arm,
And sleeping, haply dream her arm is mine.
　　'Sleep, Ellen, folded in Emilia's arm;
Emilia, fairer than all else but thou,
For thou art fairer than all else that is.
　　'Sleep, breathing health and peace upon her breast:
Sleep, breathing love and trust against her lip:
I go to-night: I come to-morrow morn.
　　'I go, but I return: I would I were　　　　70
The pilot of the darkness and the dream.
Sleep, Ellen Aubrey, love, and dream of me.'

　　So sang we each to either, Francis Hale,
The farmer's son, who lived across the bay,
My friend; and I, that having wherewithal,
And in the fallow leisure of my life
A rolling stone of here and everywhere,
Did what I would; but ere the night we rose
And saunter'd home beneath a moon, that, just
In crescent, dimly rain'd about the leaf　　　　80
Twilights of airy silver, till we reach'd
The limit of the hills; and as we sank
From rock to rock upon the glooming quay,
The town was hush'd beneath us: lower down
The bay was oily calm; the harbour-buoy,
Sole star of phosphorescence in the calm,
With one green sparkle ever and anon
Dipt by itself, and we were glad at heart.

　　　　　　　　(Wr. 1838; pub. 1842)

from *The Princess* (16–17)

16   NOW sleeps the crimson petal, now the white;
Nor waves the cypress in the palace walk;
Nor winks the gold fin in the porphyry font:
The fire-fly wakens: waken thou with me.

Now droops the milkwhite peacock like a ghost,
And like a ghost she glimmers on to me.

Now lies the Earth all Danaë to the stars,
And all thy heart lies open unto me.

Now slides the silent meteor on, and leaves
A shining furrow, as thy thoughts in me.   10

Now folds the lily all her sweetness up,
And slips into the bosom of the lake:
So fold thyself, my dearest, thou, and slip
Into my bosom and be lost in me.

17   COME down, O maid, from yonder mountain height:
What pleasure lives in height (the shepherd sang)
In height and cold, the splendour of the hills?
But cease to move so near the Heavens, and cease
To glide a sunbeam by the blasted Pine,
To sit a star upon the sparkling spire;
And come, for Love is of the valley, come,
For Love is of the valley, come thou down
And find him; by the happy threshold, he,
Or hand in hand with Plenty in the maize,   10
Or red with spirted purple of the vats,
Or foxlike in the vine; nor cares to walk
With Death and Morning on the silver horns,
Nor wilt thou snare him in the white ravine,
Nor find him dropt upon the firths of ice,
That huddling slant in furrow-cloven falls
To roll the torrent out of dusky doors:
But follow; let the torrent dance thee down
To find him in the valley; let the wild
Lean-headed Eagles yelp alone, and leave   20
The monstrous ledges there to slope, and spill
Their thousand wreaths of dangling water-smoke,

That like a broken purpose waste in air:
So waste not thou; but come; for all the vales
Await thee; azure pillars of the hearth
Arise to thee; the children call, and I
Thy shepherd pipe, and sweet is every sound,
Sweeter thy voice, but every sound is sweet;
Myriads of rivulets hurrying thro' the lawn,
The moan of doves in immemorial elms,   30
And murmuring of innumerable bees.

(*The Princess* wr. 1845–7, 'Come down' wr. 1846; pub. 1847)

from In Memoriam A. H. H. (18–29)

18   II

Old Yew, which graspest at the stones
          That name the under-lying dead,
          Thy fibres net the dreamless head,
Thy roots are wrapt about the bones.

The seasons bring the flower again,
          And bring the firstling to the flock;
          And in the dusk of thee, the clock
Beats out the little lives of men.

O not for thee the glow, the bloom,
          Who changest not in any gale,   10
          Nor branding summer suns avail
To touch thy thousand years of gloom:

And gazing on thee, sullen tree,
          Sick for thy stubborn hardihood,
          I seem to fail from out my blood
And grow incorporate into thee.

19   VII

Dark house, by which once more I stand
          Here in the long unlovely street,
          Doors, where my heart was used to beat
So quickly, waiting for a hand,

A hand that can be clasp'd no more—
 Behold me, for I cannot sleep,
 And like a guilty thing I creep
At earliest morning to the door.

He is not here; but far away
 The noise of life begins again, 10
 And ghastly thro' the drizzling rain
On the bald street breaks the blank day.

20 XI

CALM is the morn without a sound,
 Calm as to suit a calmer grief,
 And only thro' the faded leaf
The chestnut pattering to the ground:

Calm and deep peace on this high wold,
 And on these dews that drench the furze,
 And all the silvery gossamers
That twinkle into green and gold:

Calm and still light on yon great plain
 That sweeps with all its autumn bowers, 10
 And crowded farms and lessening towers,
To mingle with the bounding main:

Calm and deep peace in this wide air,
 These leaves that redden to the fall;
 And in my heart, if calm at all,
If any calm, a calm despair:

Calm on the seas, and silver sleep,
 And waves that sway themselves in rest,
 And dead calm in that noble breast
Which heaves but with the heaving deep. 20

21 L

BE near me when my light is low,
 When the blood creeps, and the nerves prick
 And tingle; and the heart is sick,
And all the wheels of Being slow.

Be near me when the sensuous frame
    Is rack'd with pangs that conquer trust;
    And Time, a maniac scattering dust,
And Life, a Fury slinging flame.

Be near me when my faith is dry,
    And men the flies of latter spring,   10
    That lay their eggs, and sting and sing
And weave their petty cells and die.

Be near me when I fade away,
    To point the term of human strife,
    And on the low dark verge of life
The twilight of eternal day.

22   LIV

OH yet we trust that somehow good
    Will be the final goal of ill,
    To pangs of nature, sins of will,
Defects of doubt, and taints of blood;

That nothing walks with aimless feet;
    That not one life shall be destroy'd,
    Or cast as rubbish to the void,
When God hath made the pile complete;

That not a worm is cloven in vain;
    That not a moth with vain desire   10
    Is shrivell'd in a fruitless fire,
Or but subserves another's gain.

Behold, we know not anything;
    I can but trust that good shall fall
    At last—far off—at last, to all,
And every winter change to spring.

So runs my dream: but what am I?
    An infant crying in the night:
    An infant crying for the light:
And with no language but a cry.   20

23   LV

THE wish, that of the living whole
        No life may fail beyond the grave,
        Derives it not from what we have
The likest God within the soul?

Are God and Nature then at strife,
        That Nature lends such evil dreams?
        So careful of the type she seems,
So careless of the single life;

That I, considering everywhere
        Her secret meaning in her deeds,   10
        And finding that of fifty seeds
She often brings but one to bear,

I falter where I firmly trod,
        And falling with my weight of cares
        Upon the great world's altar-stairs
That slope thro' darkness up to God,

I stretch lame hands of faith, and grope,
        And gather dust and chaff, and call
        To what I feel is Lord of all,
And faintly trust the larger hope.   20

24   LVI

'So careful of the type?' but no.
        From scarped cliff and quarried stone
        She cries, 'A thousand types are gone:
I care for nothing, all shall go.

'Thou makest thine appeal to me:
        I bring to life, I bring to death:
        The spirit does but mean the breath:
I know no more.' And he, shall he,

Man, her last work, who seem'd so fair,
        Such splendid purpose in his eyes,   10
        Who roll'd the psalm to wintry skies,
Who built him fanes of fruitless prayer,

Who trusted God was love indeed
    And love Creation's final law—
    Tho' Nature, red in tooth and claw
With ravine, shriek'd against his creed—

Who loved, who suffer'd countless ills,
    Who battled for the True, the Just,
    Be blown about the desert dust,
Or seal'd within the iron hills?   20

No more? A monster then, a dream,
    A discord. Dragons of the prime,
    That tare each other in their slime,
Were mellow music match'd with him.

O life as futile, then, as frail!
    O for thy voice to soothe and bless!
    What hope of answer, or redress?
Behind the veil, behind the veil.

25

LXX

I CANNOT see the features right,
    When on the gloom I strive to paint
    The face I know; the hues are faint
And mix with hollow masks of night;

Cloud-towers by ghostly masons wrought,
    A gulf that ever shuts and gapes,
    A hand that points, and palled shapes
In shadowy thoroughfares of thought;

And crowds that stream from yawning doors,
    And shoals of pucker'd faces drive;   10
    Dark bulks that tumble half alive,
And lazy lengths on boundless shores;

Till all at once beyond the will
    I hear a wizard music roll,
    And thro' a lattice on the soul
Looks thy fair face and makes it still.

26   LXXXIII

DIP down upon the northern shore,
    O sweet new-year delaying long;
    Thou doest expectant nature wrong;
Delaying long, delay no more.

What stays thee from the clouded noons,
    Thy sweetness from its proper place?
    Can trouble live with April days,
Or sadness in the summer moons?

Bring orchis, bring the foxglove spire,
    The little speedwell's darling blue,   10
    Deep tulips dash'd with fiery dew,
Laburnums, dropping-wells of fire.

O thou, new-year, delaying long,
    Delayest the sorrow in my blood,
    That longs to burst a frozen bud
And flood a fresher throat with song.

27   XCV

BY night we linger'd on the lawn,
    For underfoot the herb was dry;
    And genial warmth; and o'er the sky
The silvery haze of summer drawn;

And calm that let the tapers burn
    Unwavering: not a cricket chirr'd:
    The brook alone far-off was heard,
And on the board the fluttering urn:

And bats went round in fragrant skies,
    And wheel'd or lit the filmy shapes   10
    That haunt the dusk, with ermine capes
And woolly breasts and beaded eyes;

While now we sang old songs that peal'd
    From knoll to knoll, where, couch'd at ease,
    The white kine glimmer'd, and the trees
Laid their dark arms about the field.

But when those others, one by one,
    Withdrew themselves from me and night,
    And in the house light after light
Went out, and I was all alone,   20

A hunger seized my heart; I read
    Of that glad year which once had been,
    In those fall'n leaves which kept their green,
The noble letters of the dead:

And strangely on the silence broke
    The silent-speaking words, and strange
    Was love's dumb cry defying change
To test his worth; and strangely spoke

The faith, the vigour, bold to dwell
    On doubts that drive the coward back,   30
    And keen thro' wordy snares to track
Suggestion to her inmost cell.

So word by word, and line by line,
    The dead man touch'd me from the past,
    And all at once it seem'd at last
The living soul was flash'd on mine,

And mine in this was wound, and whirl'd
    About empyreal heights of thought,
    And came on that which is, and caught
The deep pulsations of the world,   40

Æonian music measuring out
    The steps of Time—the shocks of Chance—
    The blows of Death. At length my trance
Was cancell'd, stricken thro' with doubt.

Vague words! but ah, how hard to frame
    In matter-moulded forms of speech,
    Or ev'n for intellect to reach
Thro' memory that which I became:

Till now the doubtful dusk reveal'd
    The knolls once more where, couch'd at ease,   50
    The white kine glimmer'd, and the trees
Laid their dark arms about the field:

And suck'd from out the distant gloom
　　A breeze began to tremble o'er
　　The large leaves of the sycamore,
And fluctuate all the still perfume,

And gathering freshlier overhead,
　　Rock'd the full-foliaged elms, and swung
　　The heavy-folded rose, and flung
The lilies to and fro, and said　　　　　　　　60

'The dawn, the dawn,' and died away;
　　And East and West, without a breath,
　　Mixt their dim lights, like life and death,
To broaden into boundless day.

28　　　　　　　　　　　CXV

Now fades the last long streak of snow,
　　Now burgeons every maze of quick
　　About the flowering squares, and thick
By ashen roots the violets blow.

Now rings the woodland loud and long,
　　The distance takes a lovelier hue,
　　And drown'd in yonder living blue
The lark becomes a sightless song.

Now dance the lights on lawn and lea,
　　The flocks are whiter down the vale,　　　　10
　　And milkier every milky sail
On winding stream or distant sea;

Where now the seamew pipes, or dives
　　In yonder greening gleam, and fly
　　The happy birds, that change their sky
To build and brood; that live their lives

From land to land; and in my breast
　　Spring wakens too; and my regret
　　Becomes an April violet,
And buds and blossoms like the rest.　　　　　20

29   CXXIII

THERE rolls the deep where grew the tree.
          O earth, what changes hast thou seen!
          There where the long street roars, hath been
The stillness of the central sea.

The hills are shadows, and they flow
          From form to form, and nothing stands;
          They melt like mist, the solid lands,
Like clouds they shape themselves and go.

But in my spirit will I dwell,
          And dream my dream, and hold it true;   10
          For tho' my lips may breathe adieu,
I cannot think the thing farewell.

                              (Wr. 1833–50; pub. 1850)

30   *The Daisy*

                              Written at Edinburgh

O LOVE, what hours were thine and mine,
In lands of palm and southern pine;
          In lands of palm, of orange-blossom,
Of olive, aloe, and maize and vine.

What Roman strength Turbìa show'd
In ruin, by the mountain road;
          How like a gem, beneath, the city
Of little Monaco, basking, glow'd.

How richly down the rocky dell
The torrent vineyard streaming fell   10
          To meet the sun and sunny waters,
That only heaved with a summer swell.

What slender campanili grew
By bays, the peacock's neck in hue;
          Where, here and there, on sandy beaches
A milky-bell'd amaryllis blew.

                                     31

How young Columbus seem'd to rove,
Yet present in his natal grove,
   Now watching high on mountain cornice,
And steering, now, from a purple cove,   20

Now pacing mute by ocean's rim;
Till, in a narrow street and dim,
   I stay'd the wheels at Cogoletto,
And drank, and loyally drank to him.

Nor knew we well what pleased us most,
Not the clipt palm of which they boast;
   But distant colour, happy hamlet,
A moulder'd citadel on the coast,

Or tower, or high hill-convent, seen
A light amid its olives green;   30
   Or olive-hoary cape in ocean;
Or rosy blossom in hot ravine,

Where oleanders flush'd the bed
Of silent torrents, gravel-spread;
   And, crossing, oft we saw the glisten
Of ice, far up on a mountain head.

We loved that hall, tho' white and cold,
Those niched shapes of noble mould,
   A princely people's awful princes,
The grave, severe Genovese of old.   40

At Florence too what golden hours,
In those long galleries, were ours;
   What drives about the fresh Cascinè,
Or walks in Boboli's ducal bowers.

In bright vignettes, and each complete,
Of tower or duomo, sunny-sweet,
   Or palace, how the city glitter'd,
Thro' cypress avenues, at our feet.

But when we crost the Lombard plain
Remember what a plague of rain;   50
   Of rain at Reggio, rain at Parma;
At Lodi, rain, Piacenza, rain.

And stern and sad (so rare the smiles
Of sunlight) look'd the Lombard piles;
   Porch-pillars on the lion resting,
And sombre, old, colonnaded aisles.

O Milan, O the chanting quires,
The giant windows' blazon'd fires,
   The height, the space, the gloom, the glory!
A mount of marble, a hundred spires!   60

I climb'd the roofs at break of day;
Sun-smitten Alps before me lay.
   I stood among the silent statues,
And statued pinnacles, mute as they.

How faintly-flush'd, how phantom-fair,
Was Monte Rosa, hanging there
   A thousand shadowy-pencill'd valleys
And snowy dells in a golden air.

Remember how we came at last
To Como; shower and storm and blast   70
   Had blown the lake beyond his limit,
And all was flooded; and how we past

From Como, when the light was gray,
And in my head, for half the day,
   The rich Virgilian rustic measure
Of Lari Maxume, all the way,

Like ballad-burthen music, kept,
As on The Lariano crept
   To that fair port below the castle
Of Queen Theodolind, where we slept;   80

Or hardly slept, but watch'd awake
A cypress in the moonlight shake,
   The moonlight touching o'er a terrace
One tall Agavè above the lake.

What more? we took our last adieu,
And up the snowy Splugen drew,
   But ere we reach'd the highest summit
I pluck'd a daisy, I gave it you.

It told of England then to me,
And now it tells of Italy.   90
    O love, we two shall go no longer
To lands of summer across the sea;

So dear a life your arms enfold
Whose crying is a cry for gold:
    Yet here to-night in this dark city,
When ill and weary, alone and cold,

I found, tho' crush'd to hard and dry,
This nurseling of another sky
    Still in the little book you lent me,
And where you tenderly laid it by: 100

And I forgot the clouded Forth,
The gloom that saddens Heaven and Earth,
    The bitter east, the misty summer
And gray metropolis of the North.

Perchance, to lull the throbs of pain,
Perchance, to charm a vacant brain,
    Perchance, to dream you still beside me,
My fancy fled to the South again.

                                    (Wr. 1853; pub. 1855)

31   *To the Rev. F. D. Maurice*

COME, when no graver cares employ,
Godfather, come and see your boy:
    Your presence will be sun in winter,
Making the little one leap for joy.

For, being of that honest few,
Who give the Fiend himself his due,
    Should eighty-thousand college-councils
Thunder 'Anathema,' friend, at you;

Should all our churchmen foam in spite
At you, so careful of the right,   10
    Yet one lay-hearth would give you welcome
(Take it and come) to the Isle of Wight;

Where, far from noise and smoke of town,
I watch the twilight falling brown
 All round a careless-order'd garden
Close to the ridge of a noble down.

You'll have no scandal while you dine,
But honest talk and wholesome wine,
 And only hear the magpie gossip
Garrulous under a roof of pine: 20

For groves of pine on either hand,
To break the blast of winter, stand;
 And further on, the hoary Channel
Tumbles a billow on chalk and sand;

Where, if below the milky steep
Some ship of battle slowly creep,
 And on thro' zones of light and shadow
Glimmer away to the lonely deep,

We might discuss the Northern sin
Which made a selfish war begin;   30
 Dispute the claims, arrange the chances;
Emperor, Ottoman, which shall win:

Or whether war's avenging rod
Shall lash all Europe into blood;
 Till you should turn to dearer matters,
Dear to the man that is dear to God;

How best to help the slender store,
How mend the dwellings, of the poor;
 How gain in life, as life advances,
Valour and charity more and more.   40

Come, Maurice, come: the lawn as yet
Is hoar with rime, or spongy-wet;
 But when the wreath of March has blossom'd,
Crocus, anemone, violet,

Or later, pay one visit here,
For those are few we hold as dear;
 Nor pay but one, but come for many,
Many and many a happy year.

(Wr. 1854; pub. 1855)

32

The Charge of the Light Brigade

I

HALF a league, half a league,
  Half a league onward,
All in the valley of Death
  Rode the six hundred.
'Forward, the Light Brigade!
Charge for the guns!' he said:
Into the valley of Death
  Rode the six hundred.

II

'Forward, the Light Brigade!'
Was there a man dismay'd?   10
Not tho' the soldier knew
  Some one had blunder'd:
Their's not to make reply,
Their's not to reason why,
Their's but to do and die:
Into the valley of Death
  Rode the six hundred.

III

Cannon to right of them,
Cannon to left of them,
Cannon in front of them   20
  Volley'd and thunder'd;
Storm'd at with shot and shell,
Boldly they rode and well,
Into the jaws of Death,
Into the mouth of Hell
  Rode the six hundred.

IV

Flash'd all their sabres bare,
Flash'd as they turn'd in air
Sabring the gunners there,
Charging an army, while   30
  All the world wonder'd:
Plunged in the battery-smoke
Right thro' the line they broke;

Cossack and Russian
Reel'd from the sabre-stroke
  Shatter'd and sunder'd.
Then they rode back, but not
  Not the six hundred.

V

Cannon to right of them,
Cannon to left of them,   40
Cannon behind them
  Volley'd and thunder'd;
Storm'd at with shot and shell,
While horse and hero fell,
They that had fought so well
Came thro' the jaws of Death,
Back from the mouth of Hell,
All that was left of them,
  Left of six hundred.

VI

When can their glory fade?
O the wild charge they made!   50
  All the world wonder'd.
Honour the charge they made!
Honour the Light Brigade,
  Noble six hundred!

             (Wr. and pub. 1854)

from *Maud* (33–36)

I. xi

33

I

O LET the solid ground
  Not fail beneath my feet
Before my life has found
  What some have found so sweet;
Then let come what come may,
What matter if I go mad,
I shall have had my day.

II

Let the sweet heavens endure,
   Not close and darken above me
Before I am quite quite sure   10
   That there is one to love me;
Then let come what come may
To a life that has been so sad,
I shall have had my day.

34   I. xviii

I

I HAVE led her home, my love, my only friend.
There is none like her, none.
And never yet so warmly ran my blood
And sweetly, on and on
Calming itself to the long-wish'd-for end,
Full to the banks, close on the promised good.

II

None like her, none.
Just now the dry-tongued laurels' pattering talk
Seem'd her light foot along the garden walk,
And shook my heart to think she comes once more;   10
But even then I heard her close the door,
The gates of Heaven are closed, and she is gone.

III

There is none like her, none.
Nor will be when our summers have deceased.
O, art thou sighing for Lebanon
In the long breeze that streams to thy delicious East,
Sighing for Lebanon,
Dark cedar, tho' thy limbs have here increased,
Upon a pastoral slope as fair,
And looking to the South, and fed   20
With honey'd rain and delicate air,
And haunted by the starry head
Of her whose gentle will has changed my fate,
And made my life a perfumed altar-flame;
And over whom thy darkness must have spread
With such delight as theirs of old, thy great

Forefathers of the thornless garden, there
Shadowing the snow-limb'd Eve from whom she came.

IV

Here will I lie, while these long branches sway,
And you fair stars that crown a happy day   30
Go in and out as if at merry play,
Who am no more so all forlorn,
As when it seem'd far better to be born
To labour and the mattock-harden'd hand,
Than nursed at ease and brought to understand
A sad astrology, the boundless plan
That makes you tyrants in your iron skies,
Innumerable, pitiless, passionless eyes,
Cold fires, yet with power to burn and brand
His nothingness into man.   40

V

But now shine on, and what care I,
Who in this stormy gulf have found a pearl
The countercharm of space and hollow sky,
And do accept my madness, and would die
To save from some slight shame one simple girl.

VI

Would die; for sullen-seeming Death may give
More life to Love than is or ever was
In our low world, where yet 'tis sweet to live.
Let no one ask me how it came to pass;
It seems that I am happy, that to me   50
A livelier emerald twinkles in the grass,
A purer sapphire melts into the sea.

VII

Not die; but live a life of truest breath,
And teach true life to fight with mortal wrongs.
O, why should Love, like men in drinking-songs,
Spice his fair banquet with the dust of death?
Make answer, Maud my bliss,
Maud made my Maud by that long loving kiss,
Life of my life, wilt thou not answer this?
'The dusky strand of Death inwoven here   60
With dear Love's tie, makes Love himself more dear.'

VIII

Is that enchanted moan only the swell
Of the long waves that roll in yonder bay?
And hark the clock within, the silver knell
Of twelve sweet hours that past in bridal white,
And died to live, long as my pulses play;
But now by this my love has closed her sight
And given false death her hand, and stol'n away
To dreamful wastes where footless fancies dwell
Among the fragments of the golden day.   70
May nothing there her maiden grace affright!
Dear heart, I feel with thee the drowsy spell.
My bride to be, my evermore delight,
My own heart's heart, my ownest own, farewell;
It is but for a little space I go:
And ye meanwhile far over moor and fell
Beat to the noiseless music of the night!
Has our whole earth gone nearer to the glow
Of your soft splendours that you look so bright?
I have climb'd nearer out of lonely Hell.   80
Beat, happy stars, timing with things below,
Beat with my heart more blest than heart can tell,
Blest, but for some dark undercurrent woe
That seems to draw—but it shall not be so:
Let all be well, be well.

35
I. xxii

I

COME into the garden, Maud,
    For the black bat, night, has flown,
Come into the garden, Maud,
    I am here at the gate alone;
And the woodbine spices are wafted abroad,
    And the musk of the rose is blown.

II

For a breeze of morning moves,
    And the planet of Love is on high,
Beginning to faint in the light that she loves
    On a bed of daffodil sky,   10
To faint in the light of the sun she loves,
    To faint in his light, and to die.

III

All night have the roses heard
  The flute, violin, bassoon;
All night has the casement jessamine stirr'd
  To the dancers dancing in tune;
Till a silence fell with the waking bird,
  And a hush with the setting moon.

IV

I said to the lily, 'There is but one
  With whom she has heart to be gay.   20
When will the dancers leave her alone?
  She is weary of dance and play.'
Now half to the setting moon are gone,
  And half to the rising day;
Low on the sand and loud on the stone
  The last wheel echoes away.

V

I said to the rose, 'The brief night goes
  In babble and revel and wine.
O young lord-lover, what sighs are those,
  For one that will never be thine?   30
But mine, but mine,' so I sware to the rose,
  'For ever and ever, mine.'

VI

And the soul of the rose went into my blood,
  As the music clash'd in the hall;
And long by the garden lake I stood,
  For I heard your rivulet fall
From the lake to the meadow and on to the wood,
  Our wood, that is dearer than all;

VII

From the meadow your walks have left so sweet
  That whenever a March-wind sighs   40
He sets the jewel-print of your feet
  In violets blue as your eyes,
To the woody hollows in which we meet
  And the valleys of Paradise.

VIII

The slender acacia would not shake
  One long milk-bloom on the tree;
The white lake-blossom fell into the lake
  As the pimpernel dozed on the lea;
But the rose was awake all night for your sake,
  Knowing your promise to me;   50
The lilies and roses were all awake,
  They sigh'd for the dawn and thee.

IX

Queen rose of the rosebud garden of girls,
  Come hither, the dances are done,
In gloss of satin and glimmer of pearls,
  Queen lily and rose in one;
Shine out, little head, sunning over with curls,
  To the flowers, and be their sun.

X

There has fallen a splendid tear
  From the passion-flower at the gate.   60
She is coming, my dove, my dear;
  She is coming, my life, my fate;
The red rose cries, 'She is near, she is near;'
  And the white rose weeps, 'She is late;'
The larkspur listens, 'I hear, I hear;'
  And the lily whispers, 'I wait.'

XI

She is coming, my own, my sweet;
  Were it ever so airy a tread,
My heart would hear her and beat,
  Were it earth in an earthy bed;   70
My dust would hear her and beat,
  Had I lain for a century dead;
Would start and tremble under her feet,
  And blossom in purple and red.

42

36

II. iv

I

O THAT 'twere possible
After long grief and pain
To find the arms of my true love
Round me once again!

II

When I was wont to meet her
In the silent woody places
By the home that gave me birth,
We stood tranced in long embraces
Mixt with kisses sweeter sweeter
Than anything on earth.   10

III

A shadow flits before me,
Not thou, but like to thee:
Ah Christ, that it were possible
For one short hour to see
The souls we loved, that they might tell us
What and where they be.

IV

It leads me forth at evening,
It lightly winds and steals
In a cold white robe before me,
When all my spirit reels   20
At the shouts, the leagues of lights,
And the roaring of the wheels.

V

Half the night I waste in sighs,
Half in dreams I sorrow after
The delight of early skies;
In a wakeful doze I sorrow
For the hand, the lips, the eyes,
For the meeting of the morrow,
The delight of happy laughter,
The delight of low replies.   30

VI

'Tis a morning pure and sweet,
And a dewy splendour falls
On the little flower that clings
To the turrets and the walls;
'Tis a morning pure and sweet,
And the light and shadow fleet;
She is walking in the meadow,
And the woodland echo rings;
In a moment we shall meet;
She is singing in the meadow   40
And the rivulet at her feet
Ripples on in light and shadow
To the ballad that she sings.

VII

Do I hear her sing as of old,
My bird with the shining head,
My own dove with the tender eye?
But there rings on a sudden a passionate cry,
There is some one dying or dead,
And a sullen thunder is roll'd;
For a tumult shakes the city,   50
And I wake, my dream is fled;
In the shuddering dawn, behold,
Without knowledge, without pity,
By the curtains of my bed
That abiding phantom cold.

VIII

Get thee hence, nor come again,
Mix not memory with doubt,
Pass, thou deathlike type of pain,
Pass and cease to move about!
'Tis the blot upon the brain   60
That *will* show itself without.

IX

Then I rise, the eavedrops falls,
And the yellow vapours choke
The great city sounding wide;
The day comes, a dull red ball
Wrapt in drifts of lurid smoke
On the misty river-tide.

X

Thro' the hubbub of the market
I steal, a wasted frame,
It crosses here, it crosses there,   70
Thro' all that crowd confused and loud,
The shadow still the same;
And on my heavy eyelids
My anguish hangs like shame.

XI

Alas for her that met me,
That heard me softly call,
Came glimmering thro' the laurels
At the quiet evenfall,
In the garden by the turrets
Of the old manorial hall.   80

XII

Would the happy spirit descend,
From the realms of light and song,
In the chamber or the street,
As she looks among the blest,
Should I fear to greet my friend
Or to say 'Forgive the wrong,'
Or to ask her, 'Take me, sweet,
To the regions of thy rest'?

XIII

But the broad light glares and beats,
And the shadow flits and fleets   90
And will not let me be;
And I loathe the squares and streets,
And the faces that one meets,
Hearts with no love for me:
Always I long to creep
Into some still cavern deep,
There to weep, and weep, and weep
My whole soul out to thee.

(Wr. 1854–5; pub. 1855; 'O that 'twere possible' wr. 1833–4, revised for pub.
1837, and for 1855)

37   from *Idylls of the King: Merlin and Vivien*

IN Love, if Love be Love, if Love be ours,
Faith and unfaith can ne'er be equal powers:
Unfaith in aught is want of faith in all.

It is the little rift within the lute,
That by and by will make the music mute,
And ever widening slowly silence all.

The little rift within the lover's lute
Or little pitted speck in garner'd fruit,
That rotting inward slowly moulders all.

It is not worth the keeping: let it go: 10
But shall it? answer, darling, answer, no.
And trust me not at all or all in all.

                              (Wr. 1856; pub. 1859)

38   *Tithonus*

THE woods decay, the woods decay and fall,
The vapours weep their burthen to the ground,
Man comes and tills the field and lies beneath,
And after many a summer dies the swan.
Me only cruel immortality
Consumes: I wither slowly in thine arms,
Here at the quiet limit of the world,
A white-hair'd shadow roaming like a dream
The ever-silent spaces of the East,
Far-folded mists, and gleaming halls of morn.   10

Alas! for this gray shadow, once a man—
So glorious in his beauty and thy choice,
Who madest him thy chosen, that he seem'd
To his great heart none other than a God!
I ask'd thee, 'Give me immortality.'
Then didst thou grant mine asking with a smile,
Like wealthy men, who care not how they give.
But thy strong Hours indignant work'd their wills,
And beat me down and marr'd and wasted me,
And tho' they could not end me, left me maim'd   20
To dwell in presence of immortal youth,

Immortal age beside immortal youth,
And all I was, in ashes. Can thy love,
Thy beauty, make amends, tho' even now,
Close over us, the silver star, thy guide,
Shines in those tremulous eyes that fill with tears
To hear me? Let me go: take back thy gift:
Why should a man desire in any way
To vary from the kindly race of men
Or pass beyond the goal of ordinance   30
Where all should pause, as is most meet for all?

A soft air fans the cloud apart; there comes
A glimpse of that dark world where I was born.
Once more the old mysterious glimmer steals
From thy pure brows, and from thy shoulders pure,
And bosom beating with a heart renew'd.
Thy cheek begins to redden thro' the gloom,
Thy sweet eyes brighten slowly close to mine,
Ere yet they blind the stars, and the wild team
Which love thee, yearning for thy yoke, arise,   40
And shake the darkness from their loosen'd manes,
And beat the twilight into flakes of fire.

Lo! ever thus thou growest beautiful
In silence, then before thine answer given
Departest, and thy tears are on my cheek.

Why wilt thou ever scare me with thy tears,
And make me tremble lest a saying learnt,
In days far-off, on that dark earth, be true?
'The Gods themselves cannot recall their gifts.'

Ay me! ay me! with what another heart   50
In days far-off, and with what other eyes
I used to watch—if I be he that watch'd—
The lucid outline forming round thee; saw
The dim curls kindle into sunny rings;
Changed with thy mystic change, and felt my blood
Glow with the glow that slowly crimson'd all
Thy presence and thy portals, while I lay,
Mouth, forehead, eyelids, growing dewy-warm
With kisses balmier than half-opening buds
Of April, and could hear the lips that kiss'd   60
Whispering I knew not what of wild and sweet,
Like that strange song I heard Apollo sing,
While Ilion like a mist rose into towers.

Yet hold me not for ever in thine East:
How can my nature longer mix with thine?
Coldly thy rosy shadows bathe me, cold
Are all thy lights, and cold my wrinkled feet
Upon thy glimmering thresholds, when the steam
Floats up from those dim fields about the homes
Of happy men that have the power to die,   70
And grassy barrows of the happier dead.
Release me, and restore me to the ground;
Thou seëst all things, thou wilt see my grave:
Thou wilt renew thy beauty morn by morn;
I earth in earth forget these empty courts,
And thee returning on thy silver wheels.

                  (Wr. 1833; revised for pub. 1860)

39   *Northern Farmer. New Style*

I

Dosn't thou 'ear my 'erse's legs, as they canters awaäy?
Proputty, proputty, proputty—that's what I 'ears 'em saäy.
Proputty, proputty, proputty—Sam, thou's an ass for thy paaïns:
Theer's moor sense i' one o' 'is legs nor in all thy braaïns.

II

Woä—theer's a craw to pluck wi' tha, Sam: yon's parson's 'ouse—
Dosn't thou knaw that a man mun be eäther a man or a mouse?
Time to think on it then; for thou'll be twenty to weeäk.
Proputty, proputty—woä then woä—let ma 'ear mysén speäk.

III

Me an' thy muther, Sammy, 'as beän a-talkin' o' thee;
Thou's beän talkin' to muther, an' she beän a tellin' it me.   10
Thou'll not marry for munny—thou's sweet upo' parson's lass—
Noä—thou'll marry for luvv—an' we boäth on us thinks tha an ass.

IV

Seeä'd her todaäy goä by—Saäint's daäy—they was ringing the bells.
She's a beauty thou thinks—an' soä is scoors o' gells,
Them as 'as munny an' all—wot's a beauty?—the flower as blaws.
But proputty, proputty sticks, an' proputty, proputty graws.

         39   to weeäk] this week

48

V

Do'ant be stunt: taäke time: I knaws what maäkes tha sa mad.
Warn't I craäzed fur the lasses mysén when I wur a lad?
But I knaw'd a Quaäker feller as often 'as towd ma this:
'Doänt thou marry for munny, but goä wheer munny is!'   20

VI

An' I went wheer munny war: an' thy muther coom to 'and,
Wi' lots o' munny laaïd by, an' a nicetish bit o' land.
Maäybe she warn't a beauty:—I niver giv it a thowt—
But warn't she as good to cuddle an' kiss as a lass as 'ant nowt?

VII

Parson's lass 'ant nowt, an' she weänt 'a nowt when 'e's deäd,
Mun be a guvness, lad, or summut, and addle her breäd:
Why? fur 'e's nobbut a curate, an' weänt niver git hissen clear,
An' 'e maäde the bed as 'e ligs on afoor 'e coom'd to the shere.

VIII

An thin 'e coom'd to the parish wi' lots o' Varsity debt,
Stook to his taaïl they did, an' 'e 'ant got shut on 'em yet.   30
An' 'e ligs on 'is back i' the grip, wi' noän to lend 'im a shuvv,
Woorse nor a far-welter'd yowe: fur, Sammy, 'e married fur luvv.

IX

Luvv? what's luvv? thou can luvv thy lass an' 'er munny too,
Maakin' 'em goä togither as they've good right to do.
Could'n I luvv thy muther by cause o' 'er munny laaïd by?
Naäy—fur I luvv'd 'er a vast sight moor fur it: reäson why.

X

Ay an' thy muther says thou wants to marry the lass,
Cooms of a gentleman burn: an' we boäth on us thinks tha an ass.
Woä then, proputty, wiltha?—an ass as near as mays nowt—
Woä then, wiltha? dangtha!—the bees is as fell as owt.   40

XI

Breäk me a bit o' the esh for his 'eäd lad, out o' the fence!
Gentleman burn! what's gentleman burn? is it shillins an' pence?
Proputty, proputty's ivrything 'ere, an', Sammy, I'm blest
If it isn't the saäme oop yonder, fur them as 'as it's the best.

stunt] obstinate   addle] earn   far-welter'd] or fow-weltered—said of a sheep lying
on its back   mays nowt] makes nothing   the bees is as fell as owt] the flies are as
fierce as anything

49

XII

Tis'n them as 'as munny as breäks into 'ouses an' steäls,
Them as 'as coats to their backs an' taäkes their regular meäls.
Noä, but it's them as niver knaws wheer a meäl's to be 'ad.
Taäke my word for it, Sammy, the poor in a loomp is bad.

XIII

Them or thir feythers, tha sees, mun 'a beän a laäzy lot,
Fur work mun 'a gone to the gittin' whiniver munny was got.   50
Feyther 'ad ammost nowt; leästways 'is munny was 'id.
But 'e tued an' moil'd 'issén deäd, an 'e died a good un, 'e did.

XIV

Look thou theer wheer Wrigglesby beck cooms out by the 'ill!
Feyther run oop to the farm, an' I runs oop to the mill;
An' I'll run oop to the brig, an' that thou'll live to see;
And if thou marries a good un I'll leäve the land to thee.

XV

Thim's my noätions, Sammy, wheerby I means to stick;
But if thou marries a bad un, I'll leäve the land to Dick.—
Coom oop, proputty, proputty—that's what I 'ears 'im saäy—
Proputty, proputty, proputty—canter an' canter awaäy.   60

(Wr. 1865; pub. 1869)

40   *To E. FitzGerald*

OLD FITZ, who from your suburb grange,
    Where once I tarried for a while,
Glance at the wheeling Orb of change,
    And greet it with a kindly smile;
Whom yet I see as there you sit
    Beneath your sheltering garden-tree,
And while your doves about you flit,
    And plant on shoulder, hand and knee,
Or on your head their rosy feet,
    As if they knew your diet spares   10
Whatever moved in that full sheet
    Let down to Peter at his prayers;

Who live on milk and meal and grass;
   And once for ten long weeks I tried
Your table of Pythagoras,
   And seem'd at first 'a thing enskied'
(As Shakespeare has it) airy-light
   To float above the ways of men,
Then fell from that half-spiritual height
   Chill'd, till I tasted flesh again   20
One night when earth was winter-black,
   And all the heavens flash'd in frost;
And on me, half-asleep, came back
   That wholesome heat the blood had lost,
And set me climbing icy capes
   And glaciers, over which there roll'd
To meet me long-arm'd vines with grapes
   Of Eshcol hugeness; for the cold
Without, and warmth within me, wrought
   To mould the dream; but none can say   30
That Lenten fare makes Lenten thought,
   Who reads your golden Eastern lay,
Than which I know no version done
   In English more divinely well;
A planet equal to the sun
   Which cast it, that large infidel
Your Omar; and your Omar drew
   Full-handed plaudits from our best
In modern letters, and from two,
   Old friends outvaluing all the rest,   40
Two voices heard on earth no more;
   But we old friends are still alive,
And I am nearing seventy-four,
   While you have touch'd at seventy-five,
And so I send a birthday line
   Of greeting; and my son, who dipt
In some forgotten book of mine
   With sallow scraps of manuscript,
And dating many a year ago,
   Has hit on this, which you will take   50
My Fitz, and welcome, as I know
   Less for its own than for the sake
Of one recalling gracious times,
   When, in our younger London days,
You found some merit in my rhymes,
   And I more pleasure in your praise.

(Wr. 1883; pub. 1885)

41   *Crossing the Bar*

SUNSET and evening star,
    And one clear call for me!
And may there be no moaning of the bar,
    When I put out to sea,

But such a tide as moving seems asleep,
    Too full for sound and foam,
When that which drew from out the boundless deep
    Turns again home.

Twilight and evening bell,
    And after that the dark!   10
And may there be no sadness of farewell,
    When I embark;

For tho' from out our bourne of Time and Place
    The flood may bear me far,
I hope to see my Pilot face to face
    When I have crost the bar.

                                    (Wr. and pub. 1889)

EMILY JANE BRONTË
1818–1848

42   LONG neglect has worn away
            Half the sweet enchanting smile;
            Time has turned the bloom to grey;
            Mould and damp the face defile.

            But that lock of silky hair,
            Still beneath the picture twined,
            Tells what once those features were,
            Paints their image on the mind.

            Fair the hand that traced that line,
            'Dearest, ever deem me true';   10
            Swiftly flew the fingers fine
            When the pen that motto drew.

                            (Wr. 1837; pub. 1902)

43   THE night is darkening round me,
The wild winds coldly blow;
But a tyrant spell has bound me
And I cannot, cannot go.

The giant trees are bending
Their bare boughs weighed with snow,
And the storm is fast descending
And yet I cannot go.

Clouds beyond clouds above me,
Wastes beyond wastes below;   10
But nothing drear can move me;
I will not, cannot go.

(Wr. 1837; pub. 1902)

44   ALL hushed and still within the house;
Without—all wind and driving rain;
But something whispers to my mind,
Through rain and through the wailing wind,
    Never again.
Never again? Why not again?
Memory has power as real as thine.

(Wr. 1838; pub. 1910)

45   IT'S over now; I've known it all;
I'll hide it in my heart no more,
But back again that night recall,
And think the fearful vision o'er.

The evening sun, in cloudless shine,
Had pass'd from summer's heaven divine;
And dark the shades of twilight grew,
And stars were in the depth of blue;

And in the heath on mountains far
From human eye and human care,   10
With thoughtful heart and tearful eye
I sadly watched that solemn sky.

(Wr. 1838; pub. 1902)

46
IT will not shine again;
Its sad course is done;
I have seen the last ray wane
Of the cold, bright sun.

(Wr. 1838; pub. 1902)

47
O COME with me, thus ran the song,
The moon is bright in Autumn's sky,
And thou hast toiled and laboured long
With aching head and weary eye.

(Wr. 1838; pub. 1902)

48
O DREAM, where art thou now?
Long years have past away
Since last, from off thine angel brow
I saw the light decay.

Alas, alas for me
Thou wert so bright and fair,
I could not think thy memory
Would yield me nought but care!

The sun-beam and the storm,
The summer-eve divine,   10
The silent night of solemn calm,
The full moon's cloudless shine,

Were once entwined with thee,
But now with weary pain,
Lost vision! 'tis enough for me—
Thou canst not shine again.

(Wr. 1838; pub. 1902)

49
HOW still, how happy! Those are words
That once would scarce agree together;
I loved the plashing of the surge,
The changing heaven, the breezy weather,

More than smooth seas and cloudless skies
And solemn, soothing, softened airs
That in the forest woke no sighs
And from the green spray shook no tears.

How still, how happy! Now I feel
Where silence dwells is sweeter far   10
Than laughing mirth's most joyous swell
However pure its raptures are.

Come, sit down on this sunny stone:
'Tis wintry light o'er flowerless moors—
But sit—for we are all alone
And clear expand heaven's breathless shores.

I could think in the withered grass
Spring's budding wreaths we might discern;
The violet's eye might shyly flash
And young leaves shoot among the fern.   20

It is but thought—full many a night
The snow shall clothe those hills afar
And storms shall add a drearier blight
And winds shall wage a wilder war,

Before the lark may herald in
Fresh foliage twined with blossoms fair
And summer days again begin
Their glory-haloed crown to wear.

Yet my heart loves December's smile
As much as July's golden beam;   30
Then let us sit and watch the while
The blue ice curdling on the stream.

                              (Wr. 1838; pub. 1902)

50   WHAT winter floods, what showers of spring
          Have drenched the grass by night and day;
          And yet, beneath, that spectre ring,
          Unmoved and undiscovered lay

          A mute remembrancer of crime,
          Long lost, concealed, forgot for years,
          It comes at last to cancel time,
          And waken unavailing tears.

                              (Wr. 1839; pub. 1910)

51   I KNOW not how it falls on me,
This summer evening, hushed and lone;
Yet the faint wind comes soothingly
With something of an olden tone.

Forgive me if I've shunned so long
Your gentle greeting, earth and air!
But sorrow withers even the strong,
And who can fight against despair?

(Wr. 1839; pub. 1910)

52   SHE dried her tears, and they did smile
To see her cheeks' returning glow;
Nor did discern how all the while
That full heart throbbed to overflow.

With that sweet look and lively tone,
And bright eye shining all the day,
They could not guess, at midnight lone
How she would weep the time away.

(Wr. 1839?; pub. 1910)

53   MILD the mist upon the hill,
Telling not of storms to-morrow;
No; the day has wept its fill,
Spent its store of silent sorrow.

Oh, I'm gone back to the days of youth,
I am a child once more;
And 'neath my father's sheltering roof,
And near the old hall door,

I watch this cloudy evening fall,
After a day of rain: 10
Blue mists, sweet mists of summer pall
The horizon's mountain-chain.

The damp stands in the long, green grass
As thick as morning's tears;
And dreamy scents of fragrance pass
That breathe of other years.

(Wr. 1839; pub. 1910)

54 IT is too late to call thee now:
I will not nurse that dream again;
For every joy that lit my brow
Would bring its after-storm of pain.

Besides, the mist is half withdrawn;
The barren mountain-side lies bare;
And sunshine and awaking morn
Paint no more golden visions there.

Yet, ever in my grateful breast,
Thy darling shade shall cherished be;   10
For God alone doth know how blest
My early years have been in thee!

     (Wr. 1840; pub. 1902)

55 HAD there been falsehood in my breast
No thorns had marred my road,
This spirit had not lost its rest,
These tears had never flowed.

     (Wr. 1843?; pub. 1902)

56 COME, walk with me;
There's only thee
To bless my spirit now;
We used to love on winter nights
To wander through the snow.
Can we not woo back old delights?
The clouds rush dark and wild;
They fleck with shade our mountain heights
The same as long ago,
And on the horizon rest at last   10
In looming masses piled;
While moonbeams flash and fly so fast
We scarce can say they smiled.

Come, walk with me—come, walk with me;
We were not once so few;
But Death has stolen our company
As sunshine steals the dew:

He took them one by one, and we
Are left, the only two;
So closer would my feelings twine,   20
Because they have no stay but thine.

'Nay, call me not; it may not be;
Is human love so true?
Can Friendship's flower droop on for years
And then revive anew?
No; though the soil be wet with tears,
How fair soe'er it grew;
The vital sap once perishèd
Will never flow again;
And surer than that dwelling dread,   30
The narrow dungeon of the dead,
Time parts the hearts of men.'

(Wr. 1844; pub. 1902)

57   *Remembrance*

COLD in the earth—and the deep snow piled above thee,
Far, far, removed, cold in the dreary grave!
Have I forgot, my only Love, to love thee,
Severed at last by Time's all-severing wave?

Now, when alone, do my thoughts no longer hover
Over the mountains, on that northern shore,
Resting their wings where heath and fern-leaves cover
Thy noble heart for ever, ever more?

Cold in the earth—and fifteen wild Decembers,
From those brown hills, have melted into spring: 10
Faithful, indeed, is the spirit that remembers
After such years of change and suffering!

Sweet Love of youth, forgive, if I forget thee,
While the world's tide is bearing me along;
Other desires and other hopes beset me,
Hopes which obscure, but cannot do thee wrong!

No later light has lightened up my heaven,
No second morn has ever shone for me;
All my life's bliss from thy dear life was given,
All my life's bliss is in the grave with thee.   20

But, when the days of golden dreams had perished,
And even Despair was powerless to destroy;
Then did I learn how existence could be cherished,
Strengthened, and fed without the aid of joy.

Then did I check the tears of useless passion—
Weaned my young soul from yearning after thine;
Sternly denied its burning wish to hasten
Down to that tomb already more than mine.

And, even yet, I dare not let it languish,
Dare not indulge in memory's rapturous pain;   30
Once drinking deep of that divinest anguish,
How could I seek the empty world again?

(Wr. 1845; pub. 1846)

58   *The Prisoner*

                      A Fragment

IN the dungeon-crypts, idly did I stray,
Reckless of the lives wasting there away;
'Draw the ponderous bars! open, Warder stern!'
He dared not say me nay—the hinges harshly turn.

'Our guests are darkly lodged,' I whisper'd, gazing through
The vault, whose grated eye showed heaven more grey than blue;
(This was when glad spring laughed in awaking pride;)
'Aye, darkly lodged enough!' returned my sullen guide.

Then, God forgive my youth; forgive my careless tongue;
I scoffed, as the chill chains on the damp flag-stones rung: 10
'Confined in triple walls, art thou so much to fear,
That we must bind thee down and clench thy fetters here?'

The captive raised her face, it was as soft and mild
As sculptured marble saint, or slumbering unwean'd child;
It was so soft and mild, it was so sweet and fair,
Pain could not trace a line, nor grief a shadow there!

The captive raised her hand and pressed it to her brow;
'I have been struck,' she said, 'and I am suffering now;
Yet these are little worth, your bolts and irons strong,
And, were they forged in steel, they could not hold me long.'   20

Hoarse laughed the jailor grim: 'Shall I be won to hear;
Dost think, fond, dreaming wretch, that *I* shall grant thy prayer?
Or, better still, wilt melt my master's heart with groans?
Ah! sooner might the sun thaw down these granite stones.

'My master's voice is low, his aspect bland and kind,
But hard as hardest flint, the soul that lurks behind;
And I am rough and rude, yet not more rough to see
Than is the hidden ghost that has its home in me.'

About her lips there played a smile of almost scorn,
'My friend,' she gently said, 'you have not heard me mourn;   30
When you my kindred's lives, *my* lost life, can restore,
Then may I weep and sue,—but never, friend, before!

Still, let my tyrants know, I am not doomed to wear
Year after year in gloom, and desolate despair;
A messenger of Hope, comes every night to me,
And offers for short life, eternal liberty.

He comes with western winds, with evening's wandering airs,
With that clear dusk of heaven that brings the thickest stars.
Winds take a pensive tone, and stars a tender fire,
And visions rise, and change, that kill me with desire.   40

Desire for nothing known in my maturer years,
When Joy grew mad with awe, at counting future tears.
When, if my spirit's sky was full of flashes warm,
I knew not whence they came, from sun, or thunder storm.

But, first, a hush of peace—a soundless calm descends;
The struggle of distress, and fierce impatience ends.
Mute music soothes my breast, unuttered harmony,
That I could never dream, till Earth was lost to me.

Then dawns the Invisible; the Unseen its truth reveals;
My outward sense is gone, my inward essence feels: 50
Its wings are almost free—its home, its harbour found,
Measuring the gulph, it stoops, and dares the final bound.

Oh, dreadful is the check—intense the agony—
When the ear begins to hear, and the eye begins to see;
When the pulse begins to throb, the brain to think again,
The soul to feel the flesh, and the flesh to feel the chain.

Yet I would lose no sting, would wish no torture less,
The more that anguish racks, the earlier it will bless;
And robed in fires of hell, or bright with heavenly shine,
If it but herald death, the vision is divine!'   60

She ceased to speak, and we, unanswering, turned to go—
We had no further power to work the captive woe:
Her cheek, her gleaming eye, declared that man had given
A sentence, unapproved, and overruled by Heaven.

(Wr. 1845; pub. 1846)

EMILY JANE BRONTË and CHARLOTTE BRONTË

59   *The Visionary*

SILENT is the house: all are laid asleep:
One alone looks out o'er the snow-wreaths deep;
Watching every cloud, dreading every breeze
That whirls the wildering drift, and bends the groaning trees.

Cheerful is the hearth, soft the matted floor;
Not one shivering gust creeps through pane or door;
The little lamp burns straight, its rays shoot strong and far:
I trim it well, to be the wanderer's guiding-star.

Frown, my haughty sire! chide, my angry dame;
Set your slaves to spy; threaten me with shame: 10
But neither sire nor dame, nor prying serf shall know,
What angel nightly tracks that waste of frozen snow.

What I love shall come like visitant of air,
Safe in secret power from lurking human snare;
What loves me, no word of mine shall e'er betray,
Though for faith unstained my life must forfeit pay.

Burn, then, little lamp; glimmer straight and clear—
Hush! a rustling wing stirs, methinks, the air:
He for whom I wait, thus ever comes to me;
Strange Power! I trust thy might; trust thou my constancy.   20

(Wr. 1845; pub. 1850)

LEIGH HUNT

1784–1859

60   *Rondeau*

JENNY kissed me when we met,
    Jumping from the chair she sat in;
Time, you thief, who love to get
    Sweets into your list, put that in:
Say I'm weary, say I'm sad,
    Say that health and wealth have missed me,
Say I'm growing old, but add,
    Jenny kissed me.

                                                    (1838)

61   *On the Death of His Son Vincent*

WAKING at morn, with the accustomed sigh
For what no morn could ever bring me more,
And again sighing, while collecting strength
To meet the pangs that waited me, like one
Whose sleep the rack hath watched: I tried to feel
How good for me had been strange griefs of old,
That for long days, months, years, inured my wits
To bear the dreadful burden of one thought.
One thought with woful need turned many ways,
Which, shunned at first, and scaring me, as wounds   10
Thrusting in wound, became, oh! almost clasped
And blest, as saviours from the one dire pang
That mocked the will to move it.

                                        (Wr. 1852?; pub. 1862)

WALTER SAVAGE LANDOR
1775–1864

62   *How to Read Me*

To turn my volume o'er nor find
    To chide or discommend
Some vestige of a wandering mind,
    Sweet unsuspicious friend!

Believe that all were loved like you,
    With love from blame exempt,
Believe that all my griefs were true
    And all my joys were dreamt.

(Wr. 1839; pub. 1855)

63   TWENTY years hence my eyes may grow
If not quite dim, yet rather so,
Still yours from others they shall know
                    Twenty years hence.
Twenty years hence tho' it may hap
That I be call'd to take a nap
In a cool cell where thunder-clap
                    Was never heard.
There breathe but o'er my arch of grass
A not too sadly sigh'd *Alas*,   10
And I shall catch, ere you can pass,
                    That winged word.

(1846)

64   *Dying Speech of an Old Philosopher*

I STROVE with none, for none was worth my strife:
    Nature I loved, and, next to Nature, Art:
I warm'd both hands before the fire of Life;
    It sinks; and I am ready to depart.

(Wr. and pub. 1849)

65 *Age*

> DEATH, tho I see him not, is near
> And grudges me my eightieth year.
> Now, I would give him all these last
> For one that fifty have run past.
> Ah! he strikes all things, all alike,
> But bargains: those he will not strike.

(1853)

66 *Pigmies and Cranes*

> I LIVE among the Pigmies and the Cranes,
> Nor care a straw who loses or who gains.
> Peel doffs the harness, Russell puts it on,
> The late Sir Robert is the live Lord John,
> Close in the corner sits the abler man,
> But show me the more tricky if you can.

(1858)

67 *La Promessa Sposa*

> SLEEP, my sweet girl! and all the sleep
> You take away from others, keep:
> A night, no distant one, will come
> When those you took their slumbers from,
> Generous, ungenerous, will confess
> Their joy that you have slumber'd less,
> And envy more than they condemn
> The rival who avenges them.

(1858)

68 *Memory*

> THE mother of the Muses, we are taught,
> Is Memory: she has left me; they remain,
> And shake my shoulder, urging me to sing
> About the summer days, my loves of old.
> *Alas! alas!* is all I can reply.
> Memory has left with me that name alone,

Harmonious name, which other bards may sing,
But her bright image in my darkest hour
Comes back, in vain comes back, call'd or uncall'd.
Forgotten are the names of visitors   10
Ready to press my hand but yesterday;
Forgotten are the names of earlier friends
Whose genial converse and glad countenance
Are fresh as ever to mine ear and eye;
To these, when I have written, and besought
Remembrance of me, the word *Dear* alone
Hangs on the upper verge, and waits in vain.
A blessing wert thou, O oblivion,
If thy stream carried only weeds away,
But vernal and autumnal flowers alike   20
It hurries down to wither on the strand.

(1863)

WINTHROP MACKWORTH PRAED

1802–1839

69   *To Helen*

DEAREST, I did not think four years ago,
   When through your veil I saw your tears shine,
Caught your clear whisper, exquisitely low,
   And felt your soft hand tremble into mine,

That in so brief, so very brief a space,
   The all-seeing Ruler of our lot in life,
Would lay on you, so full of light, hope, grace,
   The darker, sadder duties of the wife.

Fears, hopes and frequent toil, and constant care
   For this poor frame, by sickness sore bested;   10
The daily tendance on the fractious chair,
   The nightly vigil by the restless bed.

Yet not unwelcomed must this morn arise,
   Though in less sullied beams it might have shone.
Strength of these weak hands, light of these dim eyes,
   In sickness as in health, bless you, my Own!

(Wr. 1839; pub. 1864)

THOMAS HOOD
1799–1845

from Miss Kilmansegg and her Precious Leg
(70–72)

70   *Her Christening*

THOUGH Shakespeare asks us, 'What's in a name?'
(As if cognomens were much the same),
    There's really a very great scope in it.
A name?—why, wasn't there Doctor Dodd,
That servant at once of Mammon and God,
Who found four thousand pounds and odd,
    A prison—a cart—and a rope in it?

A name?—if the party had a voice,
What mortal would be a Bugg by choice,
As a Hogg, a Grubb, or a Chubb rejoice,   10
    Or any such nauseous blazon?
Not to mention many a vulgar name,
That would make a doorplate blush for shame,
    If doorplates were not so brazen!

A name?—it has more than nominal worth,
And belongs to good or bad luck at birth—
    As dames of a certain degree know,
In spite of his Page's hat and hose,
His Page's jacket, and buttons in rows,
Bob only sounds like a page of prose   20
    Till turn'd into Rupertino.

Now to christen the infant Kilmansegg,
For days and days it was quite a plague,
    To hunt the list in the Lexicon:
And scores were tried like coin by the ring,
Ere names were found just the proper thing
    For a minor rich as a Mexican.

Then cards were sent, the presence to beg
Of all the kin of Kilmansegg,
    White, yellow, and brown relations: 30
Brothers, Wardens of City Halls,
And Uncles—rich as three Golden Balls
    From taking pledges of nations.

66

Nephews, whom Fortune seem'd to bewitch,
  Rising in life like rockets—
Nieces whose dowries knew no hitch—
Aunts as certain of dying rich
  As candles in golden sockets—
Cousins German and cousins' sons,
All thriving and opulent—some had tons   40
  Of Kentish hops in their pockets!

For money had stuck to the race thro' life
(As it did to the bushel when cash so rife
Posed Ali Baba's brother's wife)—
  And down to the Cousins and Cozlings,
The fortunate brood of the Kilmanseggs,
As if they had come out of golden eggs
  Were all as wealthy as 'Goslings.'

It would fill a Court Gazette to name
What East and West End people came   50
  To the rite of Christianity:
The lofty Lord and the titled Dame,
  All di'monds, plumes, and urbanity:
His Lordship the May'r with his golden chain,
And two Gold Sticks, and the Sheriffs twain,
Nine foreign Counts, and other great men
With their orders and stars, to help M or N
  To renounce all pomp and vanity.

To paint the maternal Kilmansegg,
The pen of an Eastern Poet would beg,   60
  And need an elaborate sonnet;
How she sparkled with gems whenever she stirr'd,
And her head niddle-noddled at every word,
And seem'd so happy, a Paradise Bird
  Had nidificated upon it.

And Sir Jacob the Father strutted and bow'd,
And smiled to himself, and laugh'd aloud,
  To think of his heiress and daughter—
And then in his pockets he made a grope,
And then, in the fulness of joy and hope,   70
Seem'd washing his hands with invisible soap,
  In imperceptible water.

He had roll'd in money like pigs in mud,
Till it seem'd to have enter'd into his blood
   By some occult projection:
And his cheeks, instead of a healthy hue,
As yellow as any guinea grew,
Making the common phrase seem true
   About a rich complexion.

And now came the Nurse, and during a pause,   80
Her dead-leaf satin would fitly cause
   A very autumnal rustle—
So full of figure, so full of fuss,
As she carried about the babe to buss,
   She seem'd to be nothing but bustle.

A wealthy Nabob was Godpapa,
And an Indian Begum was Godmamma,
   Whose jewels a Queen might covet—
And the Priest was a vicar, and Dean withal
Of that Temple we see with a Golden Ball,   90
   And a Golden Cross above it.

The Font was a bowl of American gold,
Won by Raleigh in days of old,
   In spite of Spanish bravado;
And the Book of Pray'r was so over-run
With gilt devices, it shone in the sun,
Like a copy—a presentation one—
   Of Humboldt's 'El Dorado.'

Gold! and gold! and nothing but gold!
The same auriferous shine behold   100
   Wherever the eye could settle!
On the walls—the sideboard—the ceiling-sky—
On the gorgeous footmen standing by,
In coats to delight a miner's eye,
   With seams of the precious metal.

Gold! and gold! and besides the gold,
The very robe of the infant told
A tale of wealth in every fold;
   It lapp'd her like a vapour!
So fine! so thin! the mind at a loss   110
Could compare it to nothing, except a cross
   Of cobwebs with bank-note paper.

Then her pearls—'twas a perfect sight, forsooth,
To see them, like 'the dew of her youth,'
    In such a plentiful sprinkle.
Meanwhile, the Vicar read through the form,
And gave her another, not overwarm,
    That made her little eyes twinkle.

Then the babe was cross'd, and bless'd amain,
But instead of the Kate, or Ann, or Jane,   120
    Which the humbler female endorses,
Instead of one name, as some people prefix,
Kilmansegg went at the tails of six,
    Like a carriage of state with its horses.

Oh, then the kisses she got and hugs!
The golden mugs and the golden jugs,
    That lent fresh rays to the midges!
The golden knives, and the golden spoons,
The gems that sparkled like fairy boons,
It was one of the Kilmanseggs' own saloons,   130
    But looked like Rundell and Bridge's!

Gold! and gold! the new and old!
The company ate and drank from gold,
    They revell'd, they sang, and were merry;
And one of the Gold Sticks rose from his chair,
And toasted 'the Lass with the golden hair'
    In a bumper of golden Sherry.

Gold! still gold! it rain'd on the Nurse,
Who, unlike Danäe, was none the worse;
There was nothing but guineas glistening!   140
    Fifty were given to Doctor James
    For calling the little Baby names,
        And for saying, Amen!
        The Clerk had ten,
And that was the end of the Christening.

71 *Her Precious Leg*

'As the twig is bent, the tree's inclined,'
Is an adage often recall'd to mind,
  Referring to juvenile bias:
And never so well is the verity seen,
As when to the weak, warp'd side we lean,
  While Life's tempests and hurricanes try us.

Even thus with Miss K. and her broken limb,
By a very, very remarkable whim,
  She show'd her early tuition:
While the buds of character came into blow   10
With a certain tinge that served to show
The nursery culture long ago,
  As the graft is known by fruition!

For the King's Physician, who nursed the case,
His verdict gave with an awful face,
  And three others concurr'd to egg it:
That the Patient to give old Death the slip,
Like the Pope, instead of a personal trip,
  Must send her Leg as a Legate.

The limb was doom'd—it couldn't be saved!   20
And like other people the patient behaved,
Nay, bravely that cruel parting braved,
  Which makes some persons so falter;
They rather would part without a groan,
With the flesh of their flesh, and bone of their bone,
  They obtained at St George's altar.

But when it came to fitting the stump
With a proxy limb—then flatly and plump
  She spoke, in the spirit olden;
She couldn't—she shouldn't—she wouldn't have wood!   30
Nor a leg of cork, if she never stood,
And she swore an oath, or something as good,
  The proxy limb should be golden!

A wooden leg! what, a sort of peg,
  For your common Jockeys and Jennies!
No, no, her mother might worry and plague—
Weep, go down on her knees, and beg,
But nothing would move Miss Kilmansegg!
She could—she would have a Golden Leg,
  If it cost ten thousand guineas!   40

Wood indeed, in Forest or Park,
With its sylvan honours and feudal bark,
  Is an aristocratical article;
But split and sawn, and hack'd about town,
Serving all needs of pauper or clown,
Trod on! staggered on! Wood cut down
  Is vulgar—fibre and particle!

And Cork!—when the noble Cork Tree shades
A lovely group of Castilian maids,
  'Tis a thing for a song or sonnet!—   50
But cork, as it stops the bottle of gin,
Or bungs the beer—the *small* beer!—in—
It pierced her heart like a corking-pin,
  To think of standing upon it!

A Leg of Gold—solid gold throughout,
Nothing else, whether slim or stout,
  Should ever support her, God willing!
She must—she could—she would have her whim,
Her father, she turned a deaf ear to him—
  He might kill her—she didn't mind killing!   60
He was welcome to cut off her other limb—
  He might cut her all off with a shilling!

All other promised gifts were in vain,
Golden Girdle, or Golden Chain,
She writhed with impatience more than pain,
  And uttered 'pshaws!' and 'pishes!'
But a Leg of Gold! as she lay in bed,
It danced before her—it ran in her head!
  It jump'd with her dearest wishes!

'Gold—gold—gold! Oh, let it be gold!'   70
Asleep or awake that tale she told,
  And when she grew delirious:
Till her parents resolved to grant her wish,
If they melted down plate, and goblet, and dish,
  The case was getting so serious.

So a Leg was made in a comely mould,
Of Gold, fine virgin glittering gold,
  As solid as man could make it—
Solid in foot, and calf, and shank,
A prodigious sum of money it sank;   80
In fact 'twas a Branch of the family Bank,
  And no easy matter to break it.

All sterling metal—not half-and-half,
The Goldsmith's mark was stamped on the calf—
   'Twas pure as from Mexican barter!
And to make it more costly, just over the knee—
Where another ligature used to be,
Was a circle of Jewels, worth shillings to see,
   A new-fangled Badge of the Garter!

'Twas a splendid, brilliant, beautiful Leg,   90
Fit for the Court of Scander-Beg,
That Precious Leg of Miss Kilmansegg!
   For, thanks to parental bounty,
Secure from Mortification's touch,
She stood on a Member that cost as much
   As a Member for all the County!

72   *Her Death*

'T IS a stern and startling thing to think
How often mortality stands on the brink
   Of its grave without any misgiving:
And yet in this slippery world of strife,
In the stir of human bustle so rife,
There are daily sounds to tell us that Life
   Is dying, and Death is living!

Ay, Beauty the Girl, and Love the Boy,
Bright as they are with hope and joy,
   How their souls would sadden instanter,   10
To remember that one of those wedding-bells,
That ring so merrily through the dells,
     Is the same that knells
     Our last farewells,
   Only broken into a canter!

But breath and blood set doom at nought—
How little the wretched Countess thought,
   When at night she unloos'd her sandal,
That the Fates had woven her burial-cloth,
And that Death, in the shape of a Death's Head Moth, 20
   Was fluttering round her candle!

As she look'd at her clock of or-molu,
For the hours she had gone so wearily through
　　At the end of a day of trial—
How little she saw in her pride of prime
The Dart of Death in the Hand of Time—
　　That hand which mov'd on the dial!

As she went with her taper up the stair,
How little her swollen eye was aware
　　That the shadow which follow'd was double!　　30
Or when she clos'd her chamber door,
It was shutting out, and for evermore,
　　The world—and its worldly trouble.

Little she dreamt, as she laid aside
Her jewels—after one glance of pride—
　　They were solemn bequests to Vanity—
Or when her robe she began to doff,
That she stood so near to the putting off
　　Of the flesh that clothes humanity.

And when she quench'd the taper's light,　　40
How little she thought as the smoke took flight,
That her day was done—and merg'd in a night
　　Of dreams and duration uncertain—
　　　　Or, along with her own,
　　　　That a hand of bone
Was closing mortality's curtain!

But life is sweet, and mortality blind,
And youth is hopeful, and Fate is kind
　　In concealing the day of sorrow;
And enough is the present tense of toil—　　50
For this world is, to all, a stiffish soil—
And the mind flies back with a glad recoil
　　From the debts not due till tomorrow.

Wherefore else does the Spirit fly
And bid its daily cares good-bye,
　　Along with its daily clothing?
Just as the Felon condemn'd to die—
　　With a very natural loathing—
Leaving the Sheriff to dream of ropes,
From his gloomy cell in a vision elopes,　　60
To caper on sunny greens and slopes,
　　Instead of the dance upon nothing.

Thus, even thus, the Countess slept,
While Death still nearer and nearer crept,
   Like the Thane who smote the sleeping—
But her mind was busy with early joys,
Her golden treasures and golden toys,
     That flash'd a bright
     And golden light
Under lids still red with weeping.   70

The golden doll that she used to hug!
Her coral of gold, and the golden mug!
   Her godfather's golden presents!
The golden service she had at her meals,
The golden watch, and chain, and seals,
Her golden scissors, and thread, and reels,
   And her golden fishes and pheasants!

The golden guineas in silken purse—
And the Golden Legends she heard from her nurse,
   Of the Mayor in his gilded carriage—   80
And London streets that were pav'd with gold—
And the Golden Eggs that were laid of old—
     With each golden thing
     To the golden ring
At her own auriferous Marriage!

And still the golden light of the sun
Through her golden dream appear'd to run,
Though the night that roar'd without was one
   To terrify seamen or gipsies—
While the moon, as if in malicious mirth,   90
Kept peeping down at the ruffled earth,
As though she enjoyed the tempest's birth,
   In revenge of her old eclipses.

But vainly, vainly, the thunder fell,
For the soul of the sleeper was under a spell
   That Time had lately embitter'd—
The Count, as once at her feet he knelt—
That Foot which now he wanted to melt!
But—hush!—'twas a stir at her pillow she felt—
   And some object before her glitter'd.   100

'Twas the Golden Leg!—she knew its gleam!
And up she started, and tried to scream,—

But ev'n in the moment she started—
Down came the limb with a frightful smash,
And, lost in the universal flash
That her eyeballs made at so mortal a crash,
  The Spark, called Vital, departed!

Gold, still gold! hard, yellow, and cold,
For gold she had lived, and she died for gold—
  By a golden weapon—not oaken;
In the morning they found her all alone—
Stiff, and bloody, and cold as stone—
But her Leg, the Golden Leg, was gone,
  And the 'Golden Bowl was broken!'

Gold, still gold! it haunted her yet—
At the Golden Lion the Inquest met—
  Its foreman, a carver and gilder—
And the jury debated from twelve till three
What the Verdict ought to be,
And they brought it in as Felo de Se,
  'Because her own Leg had killed her!'

(Wr. and pub. 1840)

WILLIAM BARNES
1801–1886

Uncle an' Aunt

73

How happy uncle us'd to be
O' zummer time, when aunt an' he
O' Zunday evenens, eärm in eärm,
Did walk about their tiny farm,
While birds did zing an' gnats did zwarm,
Drough grass a'most above their knees,
An' roun' by hedges an' by trees
  Wi' leafy boughs a-swaÿen.

His hat wer broad, his cwoat wer brown,
Wi' two long flaps a-hangen down;
An' vrom his knee went down a blue
Knit stocken to his buckled shoe;

An' aunt did pull her gown-taïl drough
Her pocket-hole, to keep en neat,
As she mid walk, or teäke a seat
    By leafy boughs a-swaÿen.

An' vu'st they'd goo to zee their lots
O' pot-eärbs in the geärden plots;
An' he, i'-may-be, by the hatch,   20
Would zee aunt's vowls upon a patch
O' zeeds, an' vow if he could catch
Em wi' his gun, they shoudden vlee
Noo mwore into their roosten tree,
    Wi' leafy boughs a-swaÿen.

An' then vrom geärden they did pass
Drough orcha'd out to zee the grass,
An' if the apple-blooth, so white,
Mid be at all a-touch'd wi' blight;
An' uncle, happy at the zight,
Did guess what cider there mid be   30
In all the orcha'd, tree wi' tree,
    Wi' tutties all a-swaÿen.

An' then they stump'd along vrom there
A-vield, to zee the cows an' meäre;
An' she, when uncle come in zight,
Look'd up, an' prick'd her ears upright,
An' whicker'd out wi' all her might;
An' he, a-chucklen, went to zee
The cows below the sheädy tree,
    Wi' leafy boughs a-swaÿen.   40

An' last ov all, they went to know   ·
How vast the grass in meäd did grow;
An' then aunt zaid 'twer time to goo
In hwome,—a-holden up her shoe,
To show how wet he wer wi' dew.
An' zoo they toddled hwome to rest,
Lik' doves a-vlee-en to their nest,
    In leafy boughs a-swaÿen.

                                        (1840)

tutties] nosegays   whicker'd] neighed

74 *Polly Be-En Upzides Wi' Tom*

AH! yesterday, d'ye know, I voun'
Tom Dumpy's cwoat an' smock-frock, down
Below the pollard out in groun';
    An' zoo I slyly stole
An' took the smock-frock up, an' tack'd
The sleeves an' collar up, an' pack'd
Zome nice sharp stwones, all fresh a-crack'd,
    'Ithin each pocket-hole.

An' in the evenen, when he shut
Off work, an' come an' donn'd his cwoat,   10
Their edges gi'ed en sich a cut,
    How we did stan' an' laugh!
An' when the smock-frock I'd a-zow'd
Kept back his head an' hands, he drow'd
Hizzelf about, an' teäv'd, an' blow'd,
    Lik' any up-tied calf.

Then in a veag away he flung
His frock, an' after me he sprung,
An' mutter'd out sich dreats, an' wrung
    His vist up sich a size!   20
But I, a-runnen, turn'd an' drow'd
Some doust, a-pick'd up vrom the road,
Back at en wi' the wind, that blow'd
    It right into his eyes.

An' he did blink, an' vow he'd catch
Me zomehow yet, an' be my match.
But I wer nearly down to hatch
    Avore he got vur on;
An' up in chammer, nearly dead
Wi' runnen, lik' a cat I vled,   30
An' out o' window put my head
    To zee if he wer gon.

An' there he wer, a-prowlen roun'
Upon the green; an' I look'd down
An' told en that I hoped he voun'

teäv'd] reached about strongly as in work or a struggle   veag] strong fit of anger

He mussen think to peck
Upon a body zoo, nor whip
The meäre to drow me off, nor tip
Me out o' cart ageän, nor slip
    Cut hoss-heäir down my neck.   40

        (1841)

75   *The Vaïces that Be Gone*

WHEN evenen sheädes o' trees do hide
A body by the hedge's zide,
An' twitt'ren birds, wi' plaÿsome flight,
Do vlee to roost at comen night,
Then I do saunter out o' zight
    In orcha'd, where the pleäce woonce rung
    Wi' laughs a-laugh'd an' zongs a-zung
        By vaïces that be gone.

There's still the tree that bore our swing,
An' others where the birds did zing;   10
But long-leav'd docks do overgrow
The groun' we trampled beäre below,
Wi' merry skippens to an' fro
    Bezide the banks, where Jim did zit
    A-plaÿen o' the clarinit
        To vaïces that be gone.

How mother, when we us'd to stun
Her head wi' all our naïsy fun,
Did wish us all a-gone vrom home:
An' now that zome be dead, an' zome   20
A-gone, an' all the pleäce is dum',
    How she do wish, wi' useless tears,
    To have ageän about her ears
        The vaïces that be gone.

Vor all the maïdens an' the bwoys
But I, be marri'd off all woys,
Or dead an' gone; but I do bide
At hwome, alwone, at mother's zide,
An' often, at the evenen-tide,
    I still do saunter out, wi' tears,
    Down drough the orcha'd, where my ears   30
        Do miss the vaïces gone.

        (1841)

76   *My Orcha'd in Linden Lea*

'ITHIN the woodlands, flow'ry gleäded,
    By the woak tree's mossy moot,
The sheenen grass-bleädes, timber-sheäded,
    Now do quiver under voot;
An' birds do whissle over head,
An' water's bubblen in its bed,
An' there vor me the apple tree
Do leän down low in Linden Lea.

When leaves that leätely wer a-springen
    Now do feäde 'ithin the copse,
An' päinted birds do hush their zingen   10
    Up upon the timber's tops;
An' brown-leav'd fruit's a-turnen red,
In cloudless zunsheen, over head,
Wi' fruit vor me, the apple tree
Do leän down low in Linden Lea.

Let other vo'k meäke money vaster
    In the aïr o' dark-room'd towns,
I don't dread a peevish meäster;
    Though noo man do heed my frowns,   20
I be free to goo abrode,
Or teäke ageän my homeward road
To where, vor me, the apple tree
Do leän down low in Linden Lea.

                                        (1856)

77   *False Friends-Like*

WHEN I wer still a bwoy, an' mother's pride,
A bigger bwoy spoke up to me so kind-like,
'If you do like, I'll treat ye wi' a ride
In theäse wheel-barrow here.' Zoo I wer blind-like
To what he had a-worken in his mind-like,
An' mounted vor a passenger inside;
An' comen to a puddle, perty wide,
He tipp'd me in, a-grinnen back behind-like.

        76 moot] the bottom and roots of a felled tree

                            79

Zoo when a man do come to me so thick-like,
An' sheäke my hand, where woonce he pass'd me by,   10
An' tell me he would do me this or that,
I can't help thinken o' the big bwoy's trick-like.
An' then, vor all I can but wag my hat
An' thank en, I do veel a little shy.

(1857)

78   *Childhood*

AYE, at that time our days wer but vew,
An' our lim's wer but small, an' a-growen;
An' then the feäir worold wer new,
An' life wer all hopevul an' gaÿ;
An' the times o' the sprouten o' leaves,
An' the cheäk-burnen seasons o' mowen,
An' binden o' red-headed sheaves,
Wer all welcome seasons o' jaÿ.

Then the housen seem'd high, that be low,
An' the brook did seem wide that is narrow,   10
An' time, that do vlee, did goo slow,
An' veelens now feeble wer strong,
An' our worold did end wi' the neämes
Ov the Sha'sbury Hill or Bulbarrow;
An' life did seem only the geämes
That we plaÿ'd as the days rolled along.

Then the rivers, an' high-timber'd lands,
An' the zilvery hills, 'ithout buyen,
Did seem to come into our hands
Vrom others that own'd em avore;   20
An' all zickness, an' sorrow, an' need,
Seem'd to die wi' the wold vo'k a-dyen,
An' leäve us vor ever a-freed
Vrom evils our vorefathers bore.

But happy be childern the while
They have elders a-liven to love em,
An' teäke all the wearisome tweil

78 tweil] toil

80

That zome hands or others mus' do;
Like the low-headed shrubs that be warm,
In the lewth o' the trees up above em,   30
A-screen'd vrom the cwold blowen storm
That the timber avore em must rue.

(1858)

79   *Light or Sheäde*

A MAŸTIDE'S evenen wer a-dyen,
Under moonsheen, into night,
Wi' a streamen wind a-sighen
By the thorns a-bloomen white,
Where in sheäde, a-zinken deeply,
Wer a nook, all dark but lew,
By a bank, a-risèn steeply,
Not to let the win' come drough.

Should my love goo out, a-showen
All her smiles, in open light;   10
Or, in lewth, wi' wind a-blowen,
Staÿ in darkness, dim to zight?
Staÿ in sheäde o' bank or wallen,
In the warmth, if not in light;
Words alwone vrom her a-vallèn,
Would be jaÿ vor all the night.

(Under 1859 in 1879)

80   *Slow to Come, Quick A-Gone*

AH! there's a house that I do know
Besouth o' yonder trees,
Where northern winds can hardly blow
But in a softest breeze.
An' there woonce sounded zongs an' teäles
Vrom vaïce o' maïd or youth,
An' sweeter than the nightengeäle's
Above the copses lewth.

78 lewth] lewness (lew, sheltered from cold wind) [as in next poem]

81

How swiftly there did run the brooks,
How swift wer winds in flight,   10
How swiftly to their roost the rooks
Did vlee o'er head at night;
Though slow did seem to us the peäce
O' comen days a-head,
That now do seem as in a reäce
Wi' aïr-birds to ha' vled.

(Under 1859 in 1879)

81   *The Turnstile*

AH! sad wer we as we did peäce
The wold church road, wi' downcast feäce,
The while the bells, that mwoan'd so deep
Above our child a-left asleep,
Wer now a-zingen all alive
Wi' tother bells to meäke the vive.
But up at woone pleäce we come by,
'Twer hard to keep woone's two eyes dry:
On Steän-cliff road, 'ithin the drong,
Up where, as vo'k do pass along,   10
The turnen stile, a-païnted white,
Do sheen by day an' show by night.
Vor always there, as we did goo
To church, thik stile did let us drough,
Wi' spreaden eärms that wheel'd to guide
Us each in turn to tother zide.
An' vu'st ov all the traïn he took
My wife, wi' winsome gaït an' look;
An' then zent on my little maïd,
A-skippen onward, overjaÿ'd   20
To reach ageän the pleäce o' pride,
Her comely mother's left han' zide.
An' then, a-wheelen roun', he took
On me, 'ithin his third white nook.
An' in the fourth, a-sheäkèn wild,
He zent us on our giddy child.
But eesterday he guided slow
My downcast Jenny, vull o' woe,
An' then my little maïd in black,
A-walken softly on her track;   30

81 drong] narrow way

An' after he'd a-turn'd ageän,
To let me goo along the leäne,
He had noo little bwoy to vill
His last white eärms, an' they stood still.

(1859)

82   *The Rwose in the Dark*

IN zummer, leäte at evenen tide,
    I zot to spend a moonless hour
'Ithin the window, wi' the zide
    A-bound wi' rwoses out in flow'r,
Bezide the bow'r, vorsook o' birds,
An' listen'd to my true-love's words.

A-risèn to her comely height,
    She push'd the swingen ceäsement round;
And I could hear, beyond my zight,
    The win'-blow'd beech-tree softly sound,   10
On higher ground, a-swaÿen slow,
On drough my happy hour below.

An' tho' the darkness then did hide
    The dewy rwose's blushen bloom,
He still did cast sweet aïr inside
    To Jeäne, a-chatten in the room;
An' though the gloom did hide her feäce,
Her words did bind me to the pleäce.

An' there, while she, wi' runnen tongue,
    Did talk unzeen 'ithin the hall,   20
I thought her like the rwose that flung
    His sweetness vrom his darken'd ball,
'Ithout the wall, an' sweet's the zight
Ov her bright feäce by mornen light.

(1861)

83   *The Zilver-Weed*

THE zilver-weed upon the green,
    Out where my sons an' daughters plaÿ'd,
Had never time to bloom between
    The litty steps o' bwoy an' maïd.

But rwose-trees down along the wall,
    That then wer all the maïdens' ceäre,
An' all a-trimm'd an' traïn'd, did bear
    Their bloomen buds vrom Spring to Fall.

But now the zilver leaves do show
    To zummer day their goolden crown,   10
Wi' noo swift shoe-zoles' litty blow,
    In merry plaÿ to beät em down.
An' where vor years zome busy hand
    Did traïn the rwoses wide an' high;
Now woone by woone the trees do die,
    An' vew of all the row do stand.

(1861)

84 *Lwonesomeness*

As I do zew, wi' nimble hand,
    In here avore the window's light,
How still do all the housegear stand
    Around my lwonesome zight.
How still do all the housegear stand
Since Willie now 've a-left the land.

The rwose-tree's window-sheäden bow
    Do hang in leaf, an' win'-blow'd flow'rs
Avore my lwonesome eyes do show
    Theäse bright November hours.   10
Avore my lwonesome eyes do show
Wi' nwone but I to zee em blow.

The sheädes o' leafy buds, avore
    The peänes, do sheäke upon the glass,
An' stir in light upon the vloor,
    Where now vew veet do pass.
An' stir in light upon the vloor
Where there's a-stirren nothen mwore.

This win' mid dreve upon the maïn,
    My brother's ship, a-plowen foam,   20
But not bring mother, cwold, nor raïn,
    At her now happy hwome.
But not bring mother, cwold, nor raïn,
Where she is out o' païn.

Zoo now that I'm a-mwopen dumb,
    A-keepen father's house, do you
Come of'en wi' your work vrom hwome,
    Vor company. Now do.
Come of'en wi' your work vrom hwome,
Up here a while. Do come.   30

                                    (1861)

85   *Leaves A-Vallen*

THERE the ash-tree leaves do vall
    In the wind a-blowen cwolder,
An' my childern, tall or small,
    Since last Fall be woone year wolder;
Woone year wolder, woone year dearer,
    Till when they do leäve my he'th,
I shall be noo mwore a hearer
    O' their vaïces or their me'th.

There dead ash leaves be a-toss'd
    In the wind, a-blowen stronger,   10
An' our life-time, since we lost
    Souls we lov'd, is woone year longer;
Woone year longer, woone year wider,
    Vrom the friends that death ha' took,
As the hours do teäke the rider
    Vrom the hand that last he shook.

No. If he do ride at night
    Vrom the zide the zun went under,
Woone hour vrom his western light
    Needen meäke woone hour asunder;   20
Woone hour onward, woone hour nigher
    To the hopevul eastern skies,
Where his mornen rim o' vier
    Soon ageän shall meet his eyes.

Leaves be now a-scatter'd round
    In the wind, a-blowen bleaker,
An' if we do walk the ground,
    Wi' our life-strangth woone year weaker;

    85   he'th] hearth   me'th] mirth

                    85

Woone year weaker, woone year nigher
    To the pleäce where we shall vind   30
Woone that's deathless vor the dier,
    Voremost they that dropp'd behind.

(1862)

86   *Jaÿ A-Pass'd*

WHEN leaves, in evenen winds, do vlee,
Where mornen aïr did strip the tree,
The mind can waït vor boughs in spring
To cool the elem-sheäded ring.
Where orcha'd blooth's white sceäles do vall
Mid come the apple's blushen ball.
Our hopes be new, as time do goo,
A-measur'd by the zun on high,
Avore our jaÿs do pass us by.

When ice did melt below the zun,   10
An' weäves along the stream did run,
I hoped in Maÿ's bright froth to roll,
Lik' jess'my in a lily's bowl.
Or, if I lost my loose-bow'd swing,
My wrigglen kite mid pull my string,
An' when noo ball did rise an' vall,
Zome other geäme wud still be nigh,
Avore my jaÿs all pass'd me by.

I look'd, as childhood pass'd along,
To walk, in leäter years, man-strong,   20
An' look'd ageän, in manhood's pride,
To manhood's sweetest chaïce, a bride:
An' then to childern, that mid come
To meäke my house a dearer hwome.
But now my mind do look behind
Vor jaÿs; an' wonder, wi' a sigh,
When 'twer my jaÿs all pass'd me by.

Wer it when, woonce, I miss'd a call
To rise, an' seem'd to have a vall?

86   blooth] blossom

86

Or when my Jeäne to my hands left   30
Her vew bright keys, a dolevul heft?
Or when avore the door I stood,
To watch a child a-gone vor good?
Or where zome crowd did laugh aloud;
Or when the leaves did spring, or die?
When did my jaÿ all pass me by?

(1864)

87   *The Vierzide Chairs*

THOUGH days do gaïn upon the night,
An' birds do teäke a leäter flight,
'Tis cwold enough to spread our hands
Oonce now an' then to glowen brands.
Zoo now we two, a-left alwone,
Can meäke a quiet hour our own,
Let's teäke, a-zitten feäce to feäce,
Our pleäces by the vier pleäce,
Where you shall have the window view
Outside, an' I can look on you.   10

When oonce I brought ye hwome my bride,
In yollow glow o' zummer tide,
I wanted you to teäke a chair
At that zide o' the vier, there,
And have the ground an' sky in zight
Wi' feäce toward the window light;
While I back here should have my brow
In sheäde, an' zit where I do now,
That you mid zee the land outside,
If I could look on you, my bride.   20

An' there the water-pool do spread,
Wi' swaÿen elems over head,
An' there's the knap where we did rove
At dusk, along the high-tree'd grove,
The while the wind did whisper down
Our whisper'd words; an' there's the crown
Ov Duncliffe hill, wi' wid'nen sheädes
Ov wood a-cast on slopen gleädes:
Zoo you injoy the green an' blue
Without, an' I will look on you.   30

86 heft] weight

An' there's the copse, where we did all
Goo out a-nutten in the fall,
That now would meäke, a-quiv'ren black,
But little lewth behind your back;
An' there's the tower, near the door,
That we at dusk did meet avore
As we did gather on the green,
An' you did zee, an' wer a-zeen:
All wold zights welcomer than new,
A-look'd on as I look'd on you.   40

(Wr. 1865; pub. 1962)

88   *All Still*

WHY call it dead, wi' life a-vled,
On land wi' lively birds on wing,
An' rooks on high, an' blackbirds nigh
The wheelen zwallows in a ring,
An' vish to zwim, where streams do roam
By bridge an' rock a-beät to foam?

Bezides the rock an' boughless stock
There's little dead as I can zee.
I don't bemwoan a stock or stwone,
But life that seem'd all life to me;   10
Where oone sweet vaïce noo mwore can come
Ageän, the pleäce is ever dumb.

(Wr. 1866; pub. 1962)

89   *The Vield Path*

HERE once did sound sweet words, a-spoke
        In wind that swum
        Where ivy clomb,
About the ribby woak;
An' still the words, though now a-gone,
Be dear to me, that linger on.

An' here, as comely vo'k did pass,
        Their sheädes did slide
        Below their zide,
Along the flow'ry grass,   10
An' though the sheädes be all a-gone,
Still dear's the ground they vell upon.

88

But could they come where then they stroll'd,
 However young
 Mid sound their tongue,
Their sheädes would show em wold;
But dear, though they be all a-gone,
Be sheädes o' trees that linger on.

O ashen poles, a-sheenen tall!
 You be too young   20
 To have a-sprung
In days when I wer small;
But you, broad woak, wi' ribby rind,
 Wer here so long as I can mind.

(Wr. 1867; pub. 1962)

90   *Seasons and Times*

AWHILE in the dead of the winter,
The wind hurries keen through the sunshine,
But finds no more leaves that may linger
On tree-boughs to strew on the ground.

Long streaks of bright snow-drift, bank-shaded,
Yet lie on the slopes, under hedges;
But still all the road out to Thorndon
Would not wet a shoe on the ground.

The days, though the cold seems to strengthen,
Outlengthen their span, and the evening   10
Seeks later and later its westing,
To cast its dim hue on the ground,

Till tree-heads shall thicken their shadow
With leaves of a glittering greenness,
And daisies shall fold up their blossoms
At evening, in dew on the ground;

And then, in the plum-warding garden,
Or shadowy orchard, the house-man
Shall smile at his fruit, really blushing,
Where sunheat shoots through on the ground. 20

89

What season do you feel the fairest—
The season of sowing or growing,
Or season of mowing and ripeness,
When hay may lie new on the ground?

And like you the glittering morning,
Or short-shaded noon, or the coming
Of slant-lighted evening, or moonlight,
When footsteps are few on the ground?

(1873)

91 *When We That Now Ha' Childern Wer Childern*

AH! where the hedge athirt the hill
Wi' high-grown boughs did grow,
An' ashes' limbs wer wide a-spread,
Wi' up-grown tips, up over head,
And out an' in, wi' broken brink,
The brook did run below.

Out there in wind a-driven dry
Down drove we then did goo,
Where vrost wer still a-ling'ren white,
In sheädes a-screen'd vrom noontide light,   10
A-heästenen hwome avore the night
Should hide our path vrom view.

As you did skim, wi' litty tips
O' tooes, the ground so fleet,
A-gath'ren in the wind so strong,
Behind your frock a-gone along,
The ruddy leaves, a-lifted up,
Did leäp behind your veet.

But now, ageän, a-treaden trim
Our track, the seäme wold waÿ,   20
We bwoth do walk wi' slower gaït
On veet a-bearen vull-grown waïght,
An' leäve our litty childern's tooes
To leäp an' run in plaÿ.

(1962)

92   *Walken Hwome at Night*

YOU then vor me meäde up your mind
To leäve your rights o' hwome behind,
Your width o' teäble-rim an' bit
O' virezide vloor, where you did zit,
An' all your walks by stiles an geätes
O' summer vields wi' maïden meätes,
To guide vor me my house, though small,
A-reckon'd, all my house mid be.
Come, hood your head; the wind is keen.
Come this zide, here. I'll be your screen.   10

The clothes your mother put ye on
Be now a-worn all out an' gone,
An' you do wear vrom top to tooe
What my true love ha' bought ye new,
That now in comely sheäpe's a-shown,
My own a-decken ov my own;
An' oh! ov all that I've a-got,
Vor your sweet lot a half is small.
Come, hood your head; wrap up, now do.
Walk clwose to me. I'll keep ye lew.   20

An' now when we be out to spend
A vrosty night wi' zome wold friend,
An' ringen clocks to tell at last
The evenen hour's a-gone too vast,
Noo vorked roads, to left an' right,
Do sunder us vor night or light;
But all my woe's vor you to veel,
An' all my weal's vor you to know.
Come, hood your head. You can't zee out?
I'll leäd ye right, you needen doubt.   30

                                        (1962)

lew] sheltered from cold wind

93 *Which Road?*

STILL green on the limbs o' the woak wer the leaves,
Where the black slooe did grow, a-meal'd over wi' grey,
Though leäzes, a-burnt, wer wi' bennets a-brown'd,
An' the stubble o' wheat wer a-witheren white,
While sooner the zunlight did zink vrom the zight,
An' longer did linger the dim-roaded night.

But bright wer the day-light a-dryen the dew,
As foam wer a-villen the pool in its vall,
An' a-sheenen did climb, by the chalk o' the cliff,
The white road a-voun' steep to the waweary step,   10
Where along by the knap, wi' a high-beäten breast,
Went the maïd an' the chap to the feäst in their best.

There hosses went by wi' their neck in a bow,
An' did toss up their nose over outspringen knees;
An' the ox, heäiryhided, wi' low-swingen head;
An' the sheep, little knee'd, wi' a quick-dippen nod;
An' a maïd, wi' her head a-borne on in a proud
Gaït o' walken, so smooth as an aïr-zwimmin cloud.

(1962)

94 *Shop o' Meat-Weäre*

Wi' Childern an' Other Vo'ks in House

A-ZELLEN meat-weäre I shall get noo meat,
I mussen keep a shop o' weäres to eat.
I have zome goods, but I do hardly think
They be a-zwold so vast as they do shrink.
I have zome goods, but zomehow all my stocks
Do weäste away lik' camphor in a box.
Hand after han' do come, and slily clips
A bit an' bit to veed zome peäir o' lips.
You vo'k in house don't waït vor gaïn o' treäde,
But teäke the store avore the gaïn's a-meäde.   10
I had zome aggs, an' I do miss zome aggs,
An' I don't think they went 'ithout zome lags.

93 bennets] flower-stalks of grass

I had zome aggs, an' zome ha' left my store,
But I don't think they travell'd out o' door.
I ha'n't a-got zome aggs that oonce wer mine,
But I don't think they brought me any cwein.
I bought zome aggs, as I do know vull well;
I bought zome aggs, but now ha' nwone to zell.

(1962)

95   *The Stwonen Steps*

THEÄSE stwonen steps a-zet so true
Wi' top on top, a voot each wide,
Did always clim' the slopen zide
O' theäse steep ledge, vor me an' you.
Had men a-built the steps avore
The mossy arch ov our wold door?
Wer theäse wold steäirs a-laid by man
Avore the bridge's archèd span?
Had vo'k a-put the stwones down here
Avore they piled the churches speer?   10
Ah! who do know how long agoo
The steps vu'st bore a shoe?

An' here bezide the slopen hump,
Vrom stwone to stwone, a-lyen flat,
The childern's little veet do pat,
An' men-vo'k's heavy zoles do clump.
Ah! which the last shall beät a shoe
On theäse grey stwones: shall I or you?
Which little boy o' mine shall clim'
The steps the last, my John or Jim?   20
Which maïd, child-quick or woman-slow,
Shall walk the last theäse stwones in row?
Who can ever tell us who
The last shall come or goo?

The road do leäd below the blocks
To yonder springhead's stwonen cove,
An' Squier's house, an elem grove,
An' mill bezide the foamy rocks.
An' aye, theäse well-wore blocks o' stwone
Wer here when I vu'st run alwone;   30
The stwonen steäirs wer here avore
My father put a voot to vloor.

'Twer up the steps that gramfer come
To court poor grammer at her hwome.
But who can ever tell what peäirs
O' veet trod vu'st the steäirs?

(1962)

JAMES CLARENCE MANGAN

1803–1849

96   *Twenty Golden Years Ago*

O, THE rain, the weary, dreary rain,
    How it plashes on the window-sill!
Night, I guess too, must be on the wane,
    Strass and Gass around are grown so still.
Here I sit, with coffee in my cup—
    Ah! 'twas rarely I beheld it flow
In the taverns where I loved to sup
        Twenty golden years ago!

Twenty years ago, alas!—but stay,
    On my life, 'tis half-past twelve o'clock!   10
After all, the hours *do* slip away—
    Come, here goes to burn another block!
For the night, or morn, is wet and cold,
    And my fire is dwindling rather low:—
I had fire enough, when young and bold,
        Twenty golden years ago!

Dear! I don't feel well at all, somehow:
    Few in Weimar dream how bad I am;
Floods of tears grow common with me now,
    High-Dutch floods, that Reason cannot dam.   20
Doctors think I'll neither live nor thrive
    If I mope at home so—I don't know—
Am I living *now*? I *was* alive
        Twenty golden years ago.

Wifeless, friendless, flagonless, alone,
    Not quite bookless, though, unless I chuse,
Left with nought to do, except to groan,
    Not a soul to woo, except the Muse—

96 Strass and Gass] street and lane

O! this, this is hard for *me* to bear,
　　Me, who whilome lived so much *en haut*,
Me, who broke all hearts like chinaware
　　　　Twenty golden years ago!

P'rhaps 'tis better:—Time's defacing waves
　　Long have quenched the radiance of my brow—
They who curse me nightly from their graves
　　Scarce could love me were they living now;
But my loneliness hath darker ills—
　　Such dun-duns as Conscience, Thought and Co.,
Awful Gorgons! worse than tailors' bills
　　　　Twenty golden years ago!

Did I paint a fifth of what I feel,
　　O, how plaintive you would ween I was!
But I won't, albeit I have a deal
　　More to wail about than Kerner has!
Kerner's tears are wept for withered flowers,
　　Mine for withered hopes; my Scroll of Woe
Dates, alas! from Youth's deserted bowers,
　　　　Twenty golden years ago!

Yet may Deutschland's bardlings flourish long!
　　Me, I tweak no beak among them;—hawks
Must not pounce on hawks; besides, in song
　　I could once beat all of them by chalks.
Though you find me, as I near my goal,
　　Sentimentalising like Rousseau,
Oh! I had a grand Byronian soul
　　　　Twenty golden years ago!

Tick-tick, tick-tick!—Not a sound save Time's,
　　And the windgust, as it drives the rain—
Tortured torturer of reluctant rhymes,
　　Go to bed, and rest thine aching brain!
Sleep!—no more the dupe of hopes or schemes;
　　Soon thou sleepest where the thistles blow—
Curious anticlimax to thy dreams
　　　　Twenty golden years ago!

(1840)

97   *Siberia*

IN Siberia's wastes
    The Ice-wind's breath
Woundeth like the toothèd steel;
Lost Siberia doth reveal
    Only blight and death.

Blight and death alone.
    No Summer shines.
Night is interblent with Day.
In Siberia's wastes alway
    The blood blackens, the heart pines.   10

In Siberia's wastes
    No tears are shed,
For they freeze within the brain.
Nought is felt but dullest pain,
    Pain acute, yet dead;

Pain as in a dream,
    When years go by
Funeral-paced, yet fugitive,
When man lives, and doth not live,
    Doth not live—nor die.   20

In Siberia's wastes
    Are sands and rocks.
Nothing blooms of green or soft,
But the snow-peaks rise aloft
    And the gaunt ice-blocks.

And the exile there
    Is one with those;
They are part, and he is part,
For the sands are in his heart,
    And the killing snows.   30

Therefore, in those wastes
    None curse the Czar.
Each man's tongue is cloven by
The North Blast, that heweth nigh
    With sharp scymitar.

And such doom each drees,
   Till, hunger-gnawn,
And cold-slain, he at length sinks there,
Yet scarce more a corpse than ere
   His last breath was drawn.   40

(1846)

ANONYMOUS

98   *A New Song on the Birth of the Prince of Wales*

Who was born on Tuesday, November 9, 1841

THERE'S a pretty fuss and bother both in country and in town,
Since we have got a present, and an heir unto the Crown,
A little Prince of Wales so charming and so sly,
And the ladies shout with wonder, What a pretty little boy!

He must have a little musket, a trumpet and a kite,
A little penny rattle, and silver sword so bright,
A little cap and feather with scarlet coat so smart,
And a pretty little hobby horse to ride about the park.

Prince Albert he will often take the young Prince on his lap,
And fondle him so lovingly, while he stirs about the pap,   10
He will pin on his flannel before he takes his nap,
Then dress him out so stylish with his little clouts and cap.

He must have a dandy suit to strut about the town,
John Bull must rake together six or seven thousand pound,
You'd laugh to see his daddy, at night he homeward runs,
With some peppermint or lollipops, sweet cakes and sugar plums.

He will want a little fiddle, and a little German flute,
A little pair of stockings and a pretty pair of boots,
With a handsome pair of spurs, and a golden headed cane,
And a stick of barley sugar, as long as Drury Lane.   20

An old maid ran through the palace, which did the nobs surprize,
Bawling out, he's got his daddy's mouth, his mammy's nose and eyes,
He will be as like his daddy as a frigate to a ship,
If he'd only got mustachios upon his upper lip.

Now to get these little niceties the taxes must be rose,
For the little Prince of Wales wants so many suits of clothes,
So they must tax the frying pan, the windows and the doors,
The bedsteads and the tables, kitchen pokers, and the floors.

(Wr. 1841; pub. 1841?, 1871)

WILLIAM MILLER
1810–1872

99   WEE Willie Winkie rins through the town,
Up stairs and doon stairs in his nicht-gown,
Tirling at the window, crying at the lock,
Are the weans in their bed, for it's now ten o'clock?

Hey, Willie Winkie, are ye coming ben?
The cat's singing grey thrums to the sleeping hen,
The dog's spelder'd on the floor, and disna gi'e a cheep,
But here's a waukrife laddie! that winna fa' asleep.

Onything but sleep, you rogue! glow'ring like the moon,
Rattling in an airn jug wi' an airn spoon,   10
Rumbling, tumbling round about, crawing like a cock,
Skirling like a kenna-what, wauk'ning sleeping fock.

Hey, Willie Winkie—the wean's in a creel!
Wambling aff a bodie's knee like a very eel,
Rugging at the cat's lug, and raveling a' her thrums—
Hey, Willie Winkie—see, there he comes!

Wearied is the mither that has a stoorie wean,
A wee stumpie stoussie, that canna rin his lane,
That has a battle aye wi' sleep before he'll close an ee—
But a kiss frae aff his rosy lips gi'es strength anew to me.   20

(1841)

CHARLES DICKENS

1812–1870

100   *The Fine Old English Gentleman*

New Version

(To be said or sung at all Conservative Dinners)

I'll sing you a new ballad, and I'll warrant it first-rate,
Of the days of that old gentleman who had that old estate;
When they spent the public money at a bountiful old rate
On ev'ry mistress, pimp, and scamp, at ev'ry noble gate,
     In the fine old English Tory times;
     Soon may they come again!

The good old laws were garnished well with gibbets, whips, and chains,
With fine old English penalties, and fine old English pains,
With rebel heads, and seas of blood once hot in rebel veins;
For all these things were requisite to guard the rich old gains   10
     Of the fine old English Tory times;
     Soon may they come again!

This brave old code, like Argus, had a hundred watchful eyes,
And ev'ry English peasant had his good old English spies,
To tempt his starving discontent with fine old English lies,
Then call the good old Yeomanry to stop his peevish cries,
     In the fine old English Tory times;
     Soon may they come again!

The good old times for cutting throats that cried out in their need,
The good old times for hunting men who held their fathers' creed,   20
The good old times when William Pitt, as all good men agreed,
Came down direct from Paradise at more than railroad speed. . . .
     Oh the fine old English Tory times;
     When will they come again!

In those rare days, the press was seldom known to snarl or bark,
But sweetly sang of men in pow'r, like any tuneful lark;
Grave judges, too, to all their evil deeds were in the dark;
And not a man in twenty score knew how to make his mark.
     Oh the fine old English Tory times;
     Soon may they come again!   30

Those were the days for taxes, and for war's infernal din;
For scarcity of bread, that fine old dowagers might win;
For shutting men of letters up, through iron bars to grin,
Because they didn't think the Prince was altogether thin,
  In the fine old English Tory times;
  Soon may they come again!

But Tolerance, though slow in flight, is strong-wing'd in the main;
That night must come on these fine days, in course of time was plain;
The pure old spirit struggled, but its struggles were in vain;
A nation's grip was on it, and it died in choking pain,   40
  With the fine old English Tory days,
  All of the olden time.

The bright old day now dawns again; the cry runs through the land,
In England there shall be dear bread—in Ireland, sword and brand;
And poverty, and ignorance, shall swell the rich and grand,
So, rally round the rulers with the gentle iron hand,
  Of the fine old English Tory days;
  Hail to the coming time!

            (Wr. and pub. 1841)

WILLIAM WORDSWORTH

1770–1850

101   THE most alluring clouds that mount the sky
    Owe to a troubled element their forms,
    Their hues to sunset. If with raptured eye
    We watch their splendor, shall we covet storms,
    And wish the Lord of day his slow decline
    Would hasten, that such pomp may float on high?
    Behold, already they forget to shine,
    Dissolve—and leave to him who gazed a sigh.
    Not loth to thank each moment for its boon
    Of pure delight, come whensoe'er it may,   10
    Peace let us seek—to stedfast things attune
    Calm expectations, leaving to the gay
    And volatile their love of transient bowers,
    The house that cannot pass away be ours.

          (Wr. ? and pub. 1842)

102   THE unremitting voice of nightly streams
That wastes so oft, we think, its tuneful powers,
If neither soothing to the worm that gleams
Through dewy grass, nor small birds hushed in bowers,
Nor unto silent leaves and drowsy flowers,—
That voice of unpretending harmony
(For who what is shall measure by what seems
To be, or not to be,
Or tax high Heaven with prodigality?)
Wants not a healing influence that can creep   10
Into the human breast, and mix with sleep
To regulate the motion of our dreams
For kindly issues—as though every clime
Was felt near murmuring brooks in earliest time;
As, at this day, the rudest swains who dwell
Where torrents roar, or hear the tinkling knell
Of water-breaks, with grateful heart could tell.

(Wr. 1846; pub. 1850)

ELIZABETH BARRETT BROWNING
1806–1861

103   *Grief*

I TELL you, hopeless grief is passionless;
That only men incredulous of despair,
Half-taught in anguish, through the midnight air
Beat upward to God's throne in loud access
Of shrieking and reproach. Full desertness,
In souls as countries, lieth silent-bare
Under the blanching, vertical eye-glare
Of the absolute Heavens. Deep-hearted man, express
Grief for thy Dead in silence like to death—
Most like a monumental statue set   10
In everlasting watch and moveless woe
Till itself crumble to the dust beneath.
Touch it; the marble eyelids are not wet:
If it could weep, it could arise and go.

(1842)

104　　　　from *Sonnets from the Portuguese*

XXIV

LET the world's sharpness, like a clasping knife,
Shut in upon itself and do no harm
In this close hand of Love, now soft and warm,
And let us hear no sound of human strife
After the click of the shutting. Life to life—
I lean upon thee, Dear, without alarm,
And feel as safe as guarded by a charm
Against the stab of worldlings, who if rife
Are weak to injure. Very whitely still
The lilies of our lives may reassure　　　　　　　10
Their blossoms from their roots, accessible
Alone to heavenly dews that drop not fewer,
Growing straight, out of man's reach, on the hill.
God only, who made us rich, can make us poor.

(Wr. 1846; pub. 1850)

105　　　　from *Aurora Leigh*

from *First Book*

OF writing many books there is no end;
And I who have written much in prose and verse
For others' uses, will write now for mine,—
Will write my story for my better self,
As when you paint your portrait for a friend,
Who keeps it in a drawer and looks at it
Long after he has ceased to love you, just
To hold together what he was and is.
I, writing thus, am still what men call young;
I have not so far left the coasts of life　　　　　10
To travel inward, that I cannot hear
That murmur of the outer Infinite
Which unweaned babies smile at in their sleep
When wondered at for smiling; not so far,
But still I catch my mother at her post
Beside the nursery door, with finger up,
'Hush, hush—here's too much noise!' while her sweet eyes
Leap forward, taking part against her word
In the child's riot. Still I sit and feel
My father's slow hand, when she had left us both,　　　20
Stroke out my childish curls across his knee,

And hear Assunta's daily jest (she knew
He liked it better than a better jest)
Inquire how many golden scudi went
To make such ringlets. O my father's hand,
Stroke heavily, heavily the poor hair down,
Draw, press the child's head closer to thy knee!
I'm still too young, too young, to sit alone.

I write. My mother was a Florentine,
Whose rare blue eyes were shut from seeing me   30
When scarcely I was four years old, my life
A poor spark snatched up from a failing lamp
Which went out therefore. She was weak and frail;
She could not bear the joy of giving life,
The mother's rapture slew her. If her kiss
Had left a longer weight upon my lips
It might have steadied the uneasy breath,
And reconciled and fraternised my soul
With the new order. As it was, indeed,
I felt a mother-want about the world,   40
And still went seeking, like a bleating lamb
Left out at night in shutting up the fold,—
As restless as a nest-deserted bird
Grown chill through something being away, though what
It knows not. I, Aurora Leigh, was born
To make my father sadder, and myself
Not overjoyous, truly. Women know
The way to rear up children (to be just),
They know a simple, merry, tender knack
Of tying sashes, fitting baby-shoes,   50
And stringing pretty words that make no sense,
And kissing full sense into empty words,
Which things are corals to cut life upon,
Although such trifles: children learn by such,
Love's holy earnest in a pretty play
And get not over-early solemnised,
But seeing, as in a rose-bush, Love's Divine
Which burns and hurts not,—not a single bloom,—
Become aware and unafraid of Love.
Such good do mothers. Fathers love as well   60
—Mine did, I know,—but still with heavier brains,
And wills more consciously responsible,
And not as wisely, since less foolishly;
So mothers have God's license to be missed.

My father was an austere Englishman,
Who, after a dry lifetime spent at home

103

In college-learning, law, and parish talk,
Was flooded with a passion unaware,
His whole provisioned and complacent past
Drowned out from him that moment. As he stood   70
In Florence, where he had come to spend a month
And note the secret of Da Vinci's drains,
He musing somewhat absently perhaps
Some English question . . . whether men should pay
The unpopular but necessary tax
With left or right hand—in the alien sun
In that great square of the Santissima
There drifted past him (scarcely marked enough
To move his comfortable island scorn)
A train of priestly banners, cross and psalm,   80
The white-veiled rose-crowned maidens holding up
Tall tapers, weighty for such wrists, aslant
To the blue luminous tremor of the air,
And letting drop the white wax as they went
To eat the bishop's wafer at the church;
From which long trail of chanting priests and girls,
A face flashed like a cymbal on his face
And shook with silent clangour brain and heart,
Transfiguring him to music. Thus, even thus,
He too received his sacramental gift   90
With eucharistic meanings; for he loved.

And thus beloved, she died. I've heard it said
That but to see him in the first surprise
Of widower and father, nursing me,
Unmothered little child of four years old,
His large man's hands afraid to touch my curls,
As if the gold would tarnish,—his grave lips
Contriving such a miserable smile
As if he knew needs must, or I should die,
And yet 'twas hard,—would almost make the stones   100
Cry out for pity. There's a verse he set
In Santa Croce to her memory,—
'Weep for an infant too young to weep much
When death removed this mother'—stops the mirth
To-day on women's faces when they walk
With rosy children hanging on their gowns,
Under the cloister to escape the sun
That scorches in the piazza. After which
He left our Florence and made haste to hide
Himself, his prattling child, and silent grief,   110

Among the mountains above Pelago;
Because unmothered babes, he thought, had need
Of mother nature more than others use,
And Pan's white goats, with udders warm and full
Of mystic contemplations, come to feed
Poor milkless lips of orphans like his own—
Such scholar-scraps he talked, I've heard from friends,
For even prosaic men who wear grief long
Will get to wear it as a hat aside
With a flower stuck in't. Father, then, and child,   120
We lived among the mountains many years,
God's silence on the outside of the house,
And we who did not speak too loud within,
And old Assunta to make up the fire,
Crossing herself whene'er a sudden flame
Which lightened from the firewood, made alive
That picture of my mother on the wall.
The painter drew it after she was dead,
And when the face was finished, throat and hands,
Her cameriera carried him, in hate   130
Of the English-fashioned shroud, the last brocade
She dressed in at the Pitti; 'he should paint
No sadder thing than that,' she swore, 'to wrong
Her poor signora.' Therefore very strange
The effect was. I, a little child, would crouch
For hours upon the floor with knees drawn up,
And gaze across them, half in terror, half
In adoration, at the picture there,—
That swan-like supernatural white life
Just sailing upward from the red stiff silk   140
Which seemed to have no part in it nor power
To keep it from quite breaking out of bounds.
For hours I sat and stared. Assunta's awe
And my poor father's melancholy eyes
Still pointed that way. That way went my thoughts
When wandering beyond sight. And as I grew
In years, I mixed, confused, unconsciously,
Whatever I last read or heard or dreamed,
Abhorrent, admirable, beautiful,
Pathetical, or ghastly, or grotesque,   150
With still that face ... which did not therefore change,
But kept the mystic level of all forms,
Hates, fears, and admirations, was by turns
Ghost, fiend, and angel, fairy, witch, and sprite,
A dauntless Muse who eyes a dreadful Fate,
A loving Psyche who loses sight of Love,

A still Medusa with mild milky brows
All curdled and all clothed upon with snakes
Whose slime falls fast as sweat will; or anon
Our Lady of the Passion, stabbed with swords   160
Where the Babe sucked; or Lamia in her first
Moonlighted pallor, ere she shrunk and blinked
And shuddering wriggled down to the unclean;
Or my own mother, leaving her last smile
In her last kiss upon the baby-mouth
My father pushed down on the bed for that,—
Or my dead mother, without smile or kiss,
Buried at Florence. All which images,
Concentred on the picture, glassed themselves
Before my meditative childhood, as   170
The incoherencies of change and death
Are represented fully, mixed and merged,
In the smooth fair mystery of perpetual Life.
And while I stared away my childish wits
Upon my mother's picture (ah, poor child!),
My father, who through love had suddenly
Thrown off the old conventions, broken loose
From chin-bands of the soul, like Lazarus,
Yet had no time to learn to talk and walk
Or grow anew familiar with the sun,—   180
Who had reached to freedom, not to action, lived,
But lived as one entranced, with thoughts, not aims,—
Whom love had unmade from a common man
But not completed to an uncommon man,—
My father taught me what he had learnt the best
Before he died and left me,—grief and love.
And, seeing we had books among the hills,
Strong words of counselling souls confederate
With vocal pines and waters,—out of books
He taught me all the ignorance of men,   190
And how God laughs in heaven when any man
Says 'Here I'm learned; this, I understand;
In that, I am never caught at fault or doubt.'
He sent the schools to school, demonstrating
A fool will pass for such through one mistake,
While a philosopher will pass for such,
Through said mistakes being ventured in the gross
And heaped up to a system.
                              I am like,
They tell me, my dear father. Broader brows
Howbeit, upon a slenderer undergrowth   200
Of delicate features,—paler, near as grave;

But then my mother's smile breaks up the whole,
And makes it better sometimes than itself.
So, nine full years, our days were hid with God
Among his mountains: I was just thirteen,
Still growing like the plants from unseen roots
In tongue-tied Springs,—and suddenly awoke
To full life and life's needs and agonies
With an intense, strong, struggling heart beside
A stone-dead father. Life, struck sharp on death,   210
Makes awful lightning. His last word was 'Love—'
'Love, my child, love, love!'—(then he had done with grief)
'Love, my child.' Ere I answered he was gone,
And none was left to love in all the world.

There, ended childhood. What succeeded next
I recollect as, after fevers, men
Thread back the passage of delirium,
Missing the turn still, baffled by the door;
Smooth endless days, notched here and there with knives,
A weary, wormy darkness, spurred i' the flank   220
With flame, that it should eat and end itself
Like some tormented scorpion. Then at last
I do remember clearly how there came
A stranger with authority, not right
(I thought not), who commanded, caught me up
From old Assunta's neck; how, with a shriek,
She let me go,—while I, with ears too full
Of my father's silence to shriek back a word,
In all a child's astonishment at grief
Stared at the wharf-edge where she stood and moaned,   230
My poor Assunta, where she stood and moaned!
The white walls, the blue hills, my Italy,
Drawn backward from the shuddering steamer-deck,
Like one in anger drawing back her skirts
Which suppliants catch at. Then the bitter sea
Inexorably pushed between us both
And, sweeping up the ship with my despair,
Threw us out as a pasture to the stars.

Ten nights and days we voyaged on the deep;
Ten nights and days without the common face   240
Of any day or night; the moon and sun
Cut off from the green reconciling earth,
To starve into a blind ferocity
And glare unnatural; the very sky
(Dropping its bell-net down upon the sea,

As if no human heart should 'scape alive)
Bedraggled with the desolating salt,
Until it seemed no more that holy heaven
To which my father went. All new and strange;
The universe turned stranger, for a child.   250

Then, land!—then, England! oh, the frosty cliffs
Looked cold upon me. Could I find a home
Among those mean red houses through the fog?
And when I heard my father's language first
From alien lips which had no kiss for mine
I wept aloud, then laughed, then wept, then wept,
And some one near me said the child was mad
Through much sea-sickness. The train swept us on:
Was this my father's England? the great isle?
The ground seemed cut up from the fellowship   260
Of verdure, field from field, as man from man;
The skies themselves looked low and positive,
As almost you could touch them with a hand,
And dared to do it they were so far off
From God's celestial crystals; all things blurred
And dull and vague. Did Shakespeare and his mates
Absorb the light here?—not a hill or stone
With heart to strike a radiant colour up
Or active outline on the indifferent air.

I think I see my father's sister stand   270
Upon the hall-step of her country-house
To give me welcome. She stood straight and calm,
Her somewhat narrow forehead braided tight
As if for taming accidental thoughts
From possible pulses; brown hair pricked with gray
By frigid use of life (she was not old,
Although my father's elder by a year),
A nose drawn sharply, yet in delicate lines;
A close mild mouth, a little soured about
The ends, through speaking unrequited loves   280
Or peradventure niggardly half-truths;
Eyes of no colour,—once they might have smiled,
But never, never have forgot themselves
In smiling; cheeks, in which was yet a rose
Of perished summers, like a rose in a book,
Kept more for ruth than pleasure,—if past bloom,
Past fading also.
                    She had lived, we'll say,
A harmless life, she called a virtuous life,

A quiet life, which was not life at all
(But that, she had not lived enough to know), 290
Between the vicar and the county squires,
The lord-lieutenant looking down sometimes
From the empyrean to assure their souls
Against chance vulgarisms, and, in the abyss,
The apothecary, looked on once a year
To prove their soundness of humility.
The poor-club exercised her Christian gifts
Of knitting stockings, stitching petticoats,
Because we are of one flesh, after all,
And need one flannel (with a proper sense 300
Of difference in the quality)—and still
The book-club, guarded from your modern trick
Of shaking dangerous questions from the crease,
Preserved her intellectual. She had lived
A sort of cage-bird life, born in a cage,
Accounting that to leap from perch to perch
Was act and joy enough for any bird.
Dear heaven, how silly are the things that live
In thickets, and eat berries!
              I, alas,
A wild bird scarcely fledged, was brought to her cage, 310
And she was there to meet me. Very kind.
Bring the clean water, give out the fresh seed.

She stood upon the steps to welcome me,
Calm, in black garb. I clung about her neck,—
Young babes, who catch at every shred of wool
To draw the new light closer, catch and cling
Less blindly. In my ears my father's word
Hummed ignorantly, as the sea in shells,
'Love, love, my child.' She, black there with my grief,
Might feel my love—she was his sister once— 320
I clung to her. A moment she seemed moved,
Kissed me with cold lips, suffered me to cling,
And drew me feebly through the hall into
The room she sat in.
             There, with some strange spasm
Of pain and passion, she wrung loose my hands
Imperiously, and held me at arm's length,
And with two grey-steel naked-bladed eyes
Searched through my face,—ay, stabbed it through and through,
Through brows and cheeks and chin, as if to find
A wicked murderer in my innocent face, 330
If not here, there perhaps. Then, drawing breath,

She struggled for her ordinary calm—
And missed it rather,—told me not to shrink,
As if she had told me not to lie or swear,—
'She loved my father and would love me too
As long as I deserved it.' Very kind.

I understood her meaning afterward;
She thought to find my mother in my face,
And questioned it for that. For she, my aunt,
Had loved my father truly, as she could,   340
And hated, with the gall of gentle souls,
My Tuscan mother who had fooled away
A wise man from wise courses, a good man
From obvious duties, and, depriving her,
His sister, of the household precedence,
Had wronged his tenants, robbed his native land,
And made him mad, alike by life and death,
In love and sorrow. She had pored for years
What sort of woman could be suitable
To her sort of hate, to entertain it with,   350
And so, her very curiosity
Became hate too, and all the idealism
She ever used in life was used for hate,
Till hate, so nourished, did exceed at last
The love from which it grew, in strength and heat,
And wrinkled her smooth conscience with a sense
Of disputable virtue (say not, sin)
When Christian doctrine was enforced at church.

And thus my father's sister was to me
My mother's hater. From that day she did   360
Her duty to me (I appreciate it
In her own word as spoken to herself),
Her duty, in large measure, well pressed out
But measured always. She was generous, bland,
More courteous than was tender, gave me still
The first place,—as if fearful that God's saints
Would look down suddenly and say 'Herein
You missed a point, I think, through lack of love.'
Alas, a mother never is afraid
Of speaking angerly to any child,   370
Since love, she knows, is justified of love.

And I, I was a good child on the whole,
A meek and manageable child. Why not?
I did not live, to have the faults of life:

There seemed more true life in my father's grave
Than in all England. Since *that* threw me off
Who fain would cleave (his latest will, they say,
Consigned me to his land), I only thought
Of lying quiet there where I was thrown
Like sea-weed on the rocks, and suffering her   380
To prick me to a pattern with her pin,
Fibre from fibre, delicate leaf from leaf,
And dry out from my drowned anatomy
The last sea-salt left in me.
               So it was.
I broke the copious curls upon my head
In braids, because she liked smooth-ordered hair.
I left off saying my sweet Tuscan words
Which still at any stirring of the heart
Came up to float across the English phrase
As lilies (*Bene* or *Che che*), because   390
She liked my father's child to speak his tongue.
I learnt the collects and the catechism,
The creeds, from Athanasius back to Nice,
The Articles, the Tracts *against* the times
(By no means Buonaventure's 'Prick of Love'),
And various popular synopses of
Inhuman doctrines never taught by John,
Because she liked instructed piety.
I learnt my complement of classic French
(Kept pure of Balzac and neologism)   400
And German also, since she liked a range
Of liberal education,—tongues, not books.
I learnt a little algebra, a little
Of the mathematics,—brushed with extreme flounce
The circle of the sciences, because
She misliked women who are frivolous.
I learnt the royal genealogies
Of Oviedo, the internal laws
Of the Burmese empire,—by how many feet
Mount Chimborazo outsoars Teneriffe.   410
What navigable river joins itself
To Lara, and what census of the year five
Was taken at Klagenfurt,—because she liked
A general insight into useful facts.
I learnt much music,—such as would have been
As quite impossible in Johnson's day
As still it might be wished—fine sleights of hand
And unimagined fingering, shuffling off
The hearer's soul through hurricanes of notes

To a noisy Tophet; and I drew . . . costumes 420
From French engravings, nereids neatly draped
(With smirks of simmering godship): I washed in
Landscapes from nature (rather say, washed out).
I danced the polka and Cellarius,
Spun glass, stuffed birds, and modelled flowers in wax,
Because she liked accomplishments in girls.
I read a score of books on womanhood
To prove, if women do not think at all,
They may teach thinking (to a maiden aunt
Or else the author),—books that boldly assert 430
Their right of comprehending husband's talk
When not too deep, and even of answering
With pretty 'may it please you,' or 'so it is,'—
Their rapid insight and fine aptitude,
Particular worth and general missionariness,
As long as they keep quiet by the fire
And never say 'no' when the world says 'ay',
For that is fatal,—their angelic reach
Of virtue, chiefly used to sit and darn,
And fatten household sinners,—their, in brief, 440
Potential faculty in everything
Of abdicating power in it: she owned
She liked a woman to be womanly,
And English women, she thanked God and sighed
(Some people always sigh in thanking God)
Were models to the universe. And last
I learnt cross-stitch, because she did not like
To see me wear the night with empty hands
A-doing nothing. So, my shepherdess
Was something after all (the pastoral saints 450
Be praised for't), leaning lovelorn with pink eyes
To match her shoes, when I mistook the silks;
Her head uncrushed by that round weight of hat
So strangely similar to the tortoise-shell
Which slew the tragic poet.
                              By the way,
The works of women are symbolical.
We sew, sew, prick our fingers, dull our sight,
Producing what? A pair of slippers, sir,
To put on when you're weary—or a stool
To stumble over and vex you . . . 'curse that stool!' 460
Or else at best, a cushion, where you lean
And sleep, and dream of something we are not
But would be for your sake. Alas, alas!
This hurts most, this—that, after all, we are paid

The worth of our work, perhaps.
                                    In looking down
Those years of education (to return)
I wonder if Brinvilliers suffered more
In the water-torture . . . flood succeeding flood
To drench the incapable throat and split the veins . . .
Than I did. Certain of your feebler souls   470
Go out in such a process; many pine
To a sick, inodorous light; my own endured:
I had relations in the Unseen, and drew
The elemental nutriment and heat
From nature, as earth feels the sun at nights,
Or as a babe sucks surely in the dark.
I kept the life thrust on me, on the outside
Of the inner life with all its ample room
For heart and lungs, for will and intellect,
Inviolable by conventions. God,   480
I thank thee for that grace of thine!
                                    At first
I felt no life which was not patience,—did
The thing she bade me, without heed to a thing
Beyond it, sat in just the chair she placed,
With back against the window, to exclude
The sight of the great lime-tree on the lawn,
Which seemed to have come on purpose from the woods
To bring the house a message,—ay, and walked
Demurely in her carpeted low rooms,
As if I should not, hearkening my own steps,   490
Misdoubt I was alive. I read her books,
Was civil to her cousin, Romney Leigh,
Gave ear to her vicar, tea to her visitors,
And heard them whisper, when I changed a cup
(I blushed for joy at that),—'The Italian child,
For all her blue eyes and her quiet ways,
Thrives ill in England: she is paler yet
Than when we came the last time; she will die.'

'Will die.' My cousin, Romney Leigh, blushed too,
With sudden anger, and approaching me   500
Said low between his teeth, 'You're wicked now?
You wish to die and leave the world a-dusk
For others, with your naughty light blown out?'
I looked into his face defyingly;
He might have known that, being what I was,
'Twas natural to like to get away
As far as dead folk can: and then indeed

Some people make no trouble when they die.
He turned and went abruptly, slammed the door,
And shut his dog out.
     Romney, Romney Leigh.   510
I have not named my cousin hitherto,
And yet I used him as a sort of friend;
My elder by few years, but cold and shy
And absent . . . tender, when he thought of it,
Which scarcely was imperative, grave betimes,
As well as early master of Leigh Hall,
Whereof the nightmare sat upon his youth,
Repressing all its seasonable delights,
And agonising with a ghastly sense
Of universal hideous want and wrong   520
To incriminate possession. When he came
From college to the country, very oft
He crossed the hill on visits to my aunt,
With gifts of blue grapes from the hothouses,
A book in one hand,—mere statistics (if
I chanced to lift the cover), count of all
The goats whose beards grow sprouting down toward hell
Against God's separative judgment-hour.
And she, she almost loved him,—even allowed
That sometimes he should seem to sigh my way;   530
It made him easier to be pitiful,
And sighing was his gift. So, undisturbed,
At whiles she let him shut my music up
And push my needles down, and lead me out
To see in that south angle of the house
The figs grow black as if by a Tuscan rock,
On some light pretext. She would turn her head
At other moments, go to fetch a thing,
And leave me breath enough to speak with him,
For his sake; it was simple.
      Sometimes too   540
He would have saved me utterly, it seemed,
He stood and looked so.
      Once, he stood so near,
He dropped a sudden hand upon my head
Bent down on woman's work, as soft as rain—
But then I rose and shook it off as fire,
The stranger's touch that took my father's place
Yet dared seem soft.
      I used him for a friend
Before I ever knew him for a friend.
'Twas better, 'twas worse also, afterward:

We came so close, we saw our differences 550
Too intimately. Always Romney Leigh
Was looking for the worms, I for the gods.
A godlike nature his; the gods look down,
Incurious of themselves; and certainly
'Tis well I should remember, how, those days,
I was a worm too, and he looked on me.

A little by his act perhaps, yet more
By something in me, surely not my will,
I did not die. But slowly, as one in swoon,
To whom life creeps back in the form of death, 560
With a sense of separation, a blind pain
Of blank obstruction, and a roar i' the ears
Of visionary chariots which retreat
As earth grows clearer . . . slowly, by degrees;
I woke, rose up . . . where was I? in the world;
For uses therefore I must count worth while.

(Wr. from 1853; pub. 1857)

106 *The Best Thing in the World*

WHAT'S the best thing in the world?
June-rose, by May-dew impearled;
Sweet south-wind, that means no rain;
Truth, not cruel to a friend;
Pleasure, not in haste to end;
Beauty, not self-decked and curled
Till its pride is over-plain;
Light, that never makes you wink;
Memory, that gives no pain;
Love, when, *so*, you're loved again. 10
What's the best thing in the world?
—Something out of it, I think.

(1862)

107 ## 'Died . . .'

(*The 'Times' Obituary*)

I

WHAT shall we add now? He is dead.
  And I who praise and you who blame,
  With wash of words across his name,
Find suddenly declared instead—
'*On Sunday, third of August, dead.*'

II

Which stops the whole we talked to-day.
  I quickened to a plausive glance
  At his large general tolerance
By common people's narrow way,
Stopped short in praising. Dead, they say.   10

III

And you, who had just put in a sort
  Of cold deduction—'rather, large
  Through weakness of the continent marge,
Than greatness of the thing contained'—
Broke off. Dead!—there, you stood restrained.

IV

As if we had talked in following one
  Up some long gallery. 'Would you choose
  An air like that? The gait is loose—
Or noble.' Sudden in the sun
An oubliette winks. Where *is* he? Gone.   20

V

Dead. Man's 'I was' by God's 'I am'—
  All hero-worship comes to that.
  High heart, high thought, high fame, as flat
As a gravestone. Bring your *Jacet jam*—
The epitaph's an epigram.

VI

Dead. There's an answer to arrest
  All carping. Dust's his natural place?
  He'll let the flies buzz round his face
And, though you slander, not protest?
—From such an one, exact the Best?   30

VII

Opinions gold or brass are null.
  We chuck our flattery or abuse,
  Called Cæsar's due, as Charon's dues,
I' the teeth of some dead sage or fool,
To mend the grinning of a skull.

VIII

Be abstinent in praise and blame.
  The man's still mortal, who stands first,
  And mortal only, if last and worst.
Then slowly lift so frail a fame,
Or softly drop so poor a shame.   40

(1862)

ROBERT BROWNING
1812–1889

108   *My Last Duchess*

Ferrara

THAT'S my last Duchess painted on the wall,
Looking as if she were alive. I call
That piece a wonder, now: Frà Pandolf's hands
Worked busily a day, and there she stands.
Will't please you sit and look at her? I said
'Frà Pandolf' by design, for never read
Strangers like you that pictured countenance,
The depth and passion of its earnest glance,
But to myself they turned (since none puts by
The curtain I have drawn for you, but I)   10
And seemed as they would ask me, if they durst,
How such a glance came there; so, not the first
Are you to turn and ask thus. Sir, 't was not
Her husband's presence only, called that spot
Of joy into the Duchess' cheek: perhaps
Frà Pandolf chanced to say 'Her mantle laps
'Over my lady's wrist too much,' or 'Paint
'Must never hope to reproduce the faint

'Half-flush that dies along her throat:' such stuff
Was courtesy, she thought, and cause enough   20
For calling up that spot of joy. She had
A heart—how shall I say?—too soon made glad,
Too easily impressed; she liked whate'er
She looked on, and her looks went everywhere.
Sir, 't was all one! My favour at her breast,
The dropping of the daylight in the West,
The bough of cherries some officious fool
Broke in the orchard for her, the white mule
She rode with round the terrace—all and each
Would draw from her alike the approving speech,   30
Or blush, at least. She thanked men,—good! but thanked
Somehow—I know not how—as if she ranked
My gift of a nine-hundred-years-old name
With anybody's gift. Who'd stoop to blame
This sort of trifling? Even had you skill
In speech—(which I have not)—to make your will
Quite clear to such an one, and say, 'Just this
'Or that in you disgusts me; here you miss,
'Or there exceed the mark'—and if she let
Herself be lessoned so, nor plainly set   40
Her wits to yours, forsooth, and made excuse,
—E'en then would be some stooping; and I choose
Never to stoop. Oh sir, she smiled, no doubt,
Whene'er I passed her; but who passed without
Much the same smile? This grew; I gave commands;
Then all smiles stopped together. There she stands
As if alive. Will 't please you rise? We'll meet
The company below, then. I repeat,
The Count your master's known munificence
Is ample warrant that no just pretence   50
Of mine for dowry will be disallowed;
Though his fair daughter's self, as I avowed
At starting, is my object. Nay, we'll go
Together down, sir. Notice Neptune, though,
Taming a sea-horse, thought a rarity,
Which Claus of Innsbruck cast in bronze for me!

(Wr. and pub. 1842)

Soliloquy of the Spanish Cloister

I

GR-R-R—there go, my heart's abhorrence!
  Water your damned flower-pots, do!
If hate killed men, Brother Lawrence,
  God's blood, would not mine kill you!
What? your myrtle-bush wants trimming?
  Oh, that rose has prior claims—
Needs its leaden vase filled brimming?
  Hell dry you up with its flames!

II

At the meal we sit together:
  Salve tibi! I must hear   10
Wise talk of the kind of weather,
  Sort of season, time of year:
Not a plenteous cork-crop: scarcely
  Dare we hope oak-galls, I doubt:
What's the Latin name for 'parsley'?
  What's the Greek name for Swine's Snout?

III

Whew! We'll have our platter burnished,
  Laid with care on our own shelf!
With a fire-new spoon we're furnished,
  And a goblet for ourself,   20
Rinsed like something sacrificial
  Ere 't is fit to touch our chaps—
Marked with L. for our initial!
  (He-he! There his lily snaps!)

IV

Saint, forsooth! While brown Dolores
  Squats outside the Convent bank
With Sanchicha, telling stories,
  Steeping tresses in the tank,
Blue-black, lustrous, thick like horsehairs,
  —Can't I see his dead eye glow,   30
Bright as 't were a Barbary corsair's?
  (That is, if he'd let it show!)

V

When he finishes refection,
   Knife and fork he never lays
Cross-wise, to my recollection,
   As do I, in Jesu's praise.
I the Trinity illustrate,
   Drinking watered orange-pulp—
In three sips the Arian frustrate;
   While he drains his at one gulp.   40

VI

Oh, those melons? If he's able
   We're to have a feast! so nice!
One goes to the Abbot's table,
   All of us get each a slice.
How go on your flowers? None double?
   Not one fruit-sort can you spy?
Strange!—And I, too, at such trouble,
   Keep them close-nipped on the sly!

VII

There's a great text in Galatians,
   Once you trip on it, entails   50
Twenty-nine distinct damnations,
   One sure, if another fails:
If I trip him just a-dying,
   Sure of heaven as sure can be,
Spin him round and send him flying
   Off to hell, a Manichee?

VIII

Or, my scrofulous French novel
   On grey paper with blunt type!
Simply glance at it, you grovel
   Hand and foot in Belial's gripe: 60
If I double down its pages
   At the woeful sixteenth print,
When he gathers his greengages,
   Ope a sieve and slip it in 't?

IX

Or, there's Satan!—one might venture
  Pledge one's soul to him, yet leave
Such a flaw in the indenture
  As he'd miss till, past retrieve,
Blasted lay that rose-acacia
  We're so proud of! *Hy, Zy, Hine* ...   70
'St, there's Vespers! *Plena gratiâ*
  Ave, Virgo! Gr-r-r—you swine!

(1842)

110   *The Bishop Orders His Tomb at Saint Praxed's*
                      Church

Rome 15—

VANITY, saith the preacher, vanity!
Draw round my bed: is Anselm keeping back?
Nephews—sons mine ... ah God, I know not! Well—
She, men would have to be your mother once,
Old Gandolf envied me, so fair she was!
What's done is done, and she is dead beside,
Dead long ago, and I am Bishop since,
And as she died so must we die ourselves,
And thence ye may perceive the world's a dream.
Life, how and what is it? As here I lie   10
In this state-chamber, dying by degrees,
Hours and long hours in the dead night, I ask
'Do I live, am I dead?' Peace, peace seems all.
Saint Praxed's ever was the church for peace;
And so, about this tomb of mine. I fought
With tooth and nail to save my niche, ye know:
—Old Gandolf cozened me, despite my care;
Shrewd was that snatch from out the corner South
He graced his carrion with, God curse the same!
Yet still my niche is not so cramped but thence   20
One sees the pulpit o' the epistle-side,
And somewhat of the choir, those silent seats,
And up into the aery dome where live
The angels, and a sunbeam's sure to lurk:
And I shall fill my slab of basalt there,
And 'neath my tabernacle take my rest,
With those nine columns round me, two and two,

The odd one at my feet where Anselm stands:
Peach-blossom marble all, the rare, the ripe
As fresh-poured red wine of a mighty pulse.   30
—Old Gandolf with his paltry onion-stone,
Put me where I may look at him! True peach,
Rosy and flawless: how I earned the prize!
Draw close: that conflagration of my church
—What then? So much was saved if aught were missed!
My sons, ye would not be my death? Go dig
The white-grape vineyard where the oil-press stood,
Drop water gently till the surface sink,
And if ye find . . . Ah God, I know not, I! . . .
Bedded in store of rotten fig-leaves soft,   40
And corded up in a tight olive-frail,
Some lump, ah God, of *lapis lazuli*,
Big as a Jew's head cut off at the nape,
Blue as a vein o'er the Madonna's breast . . .
Sons, all have I bequeathed you, villas, all,
That brave Frascati villa with its bath,
So, let the blue lump poise between my knees,
Like God the Father's globe on both his hands
Ye worship in the Jesu Church so gay,
For Gandolf shall not choose but see and burst!   50
Swift as a weaver's shuttle fleet our years:
Man goeth to the grave, and where is he?
Did I say basalt for my slab, sons? Black—
'T was ever antique-black I meant! How else
Shall ye contrast my frieze to come beneath?
The bas-relief in bronze ye promised me,
Those Pans and Nymphs ye wot of, and perchance
Some tripod, thyrsus, with a vase or so,
The Saviour at his sermon on the mount,
Saint Praxed in a glory, and one Pan   60
Ready to twitch the Nymph's last garment off,
And Moses with the tables . . . but I know
Ye mark me not! What do they whisper thee,
Child of my bowels, Anselm? Ah, ye hope
To revel down my villas while I gasp
Bricked o'er with beggar's mouldy travertine
Which Gandolf from his tomb-top chuckles at!
Nay, boys, ye love me—all of jasper, then!
'T is jasper ye stand pledged to, lest I grieve.
My bath must needs be left behind, alas!   70
One block, pure green as a pistachio-nut,
There's plenty jasper somewhere in the world—
And have I not Saint Praxed's ear to pray

Horses for ye, and brown Greek manuscripts,
And mistresses with great smooth marbly limbs?
—That's if ye carve my epitaph aright,
Choice Latin, picked phrase, Tully's every word,
No gaudy ware like Gandolf's second line—
Tully, my masters? Ulpian serves his need!
And then how I shall lie through centuries,   80
And hear the blessed mutter of the mass,
And see God made and eaten all day long,
And feel the steady candle-flame, and taste
Good strong thick stupefying incense-smoke!
For as I lie here, hours of the dead night,
Dying in state and by such slow degrees,
I fold my arms as if they clasped a crook,
And stretch my feet forth straight as stone can point,
And let the bedclothes, for a mortcloth, drop
Into great laps and folds of sculptor's-work: 90
And as yon tapers dwindle, and strange thoughts
Grow, with a certain humming in my ears,
About the life before I lived this life,
And this life too, popes, cardinals and priests,
Saint Praxed at his sermon on the mount,
Your tall pale mother with her talking eyes,
And new-found agate urns as fresh as day,
And marble's language, Latin pure, discreet,
—Aha, ELUCESCEBAT quoth our friend?
No Tully, said I, Ulpian at the best!   100
Evil and brief hath been my pilgrimage.
All *lapis*, all, sons! Else I give the Pope
My villas! Will ye ever eat my heart?
Ever your eyes were as a lizard's quick,
They glitter like your mother's for my soul,
Or ye would heighten my impoverished frieze,
Piece out its starved design, and fill my vase
With grapes, and add a vizor and a Term,
And to the tripod ye would tie a lynx
That in his struggle throws the thyrsus down,   110
To comfort me on my entablature
Whereon I am to lie till I must ask
'Do I live, am I dead?' There, leave me, there!
For ye have stabbed me with ingratitude
To death—ye wish it--God, ye wish it! Stone—
Gritstone, a-crumble! Clammy squares which sweat
As if the corpse they keep were oozing through—
And no more *lapis* to delight the world!
Well go! I bless ye. Fewer tapers there,

But in a row: and, going, turn your backs   120
—Ay, like departing altar-ministrants,
And leave me in my church, the church for peace,
That I may watch at leisure if he leers—
Old Gandolf, at me, from his onion-stone,
As still he envied me, so fair she was!

(Wr. 1844–5?; pub. 1845)

III   *Home-Thoughts, from Abroad*

I

O H, to be in England,
Now that April's there,
And whoever wakes in England
Sees, some morning, unaware,
That the lowest boughs and the brushwood sheaf
Round the elm-tree bole are in tiny leaf,
While the chaffinch sings on the orchard bough
In England—now!

II

And after April, when May follows,
And the whitethroat builds, and all the swallows!   10
Hark, where my blossomed pear-tree in the hedge
Leans to the field and scatters on the clover
Blossoms and dewdrops—at the bent spray's edge—
That's the wise thrush; he sings each song twice over,
Lest you should think he never could recapture
The first fine careless rapture!
And though the fields look rough with hoary dew
All will be gay when noontide wakes anew
The buttercups, the little children's dower
—Far brighter than this gaudy melon-flower!   20

(1845)

112 *Meeting at Night*

I

THE grey sea and the long black land;
And the yellow half-moon large and low;
And the startled little waves that leap
In fiery ringlets from their sleep,
As I gain the cove with pushing prow,
And quench its speed i' the slushy sand.

II

Then a mile of warm sea-scented beach;
Three fields to cross till a farm appears;
A tap at the pane, the quick sharp scratch
And blue spurt of a lighted match,   10
And a voice less loud, thro' its joys and fears,
Than the two hearts beating each to each!

(1845)

113 *Memorabilia*

I

AH, did you once see Shelley plain,
    And did he stop and speak to you
And did you speak to him again?
    How strange it seems and new!

II

But you were living before that,
    And also you are living after;
And the memory I started at—
    My starting moves your laughter.

III

I crossed a moor, with a name of its own
    And a certain use in the world no doubt,   10
Yet a hand's-breadth of it shines alone
    'Mid the blank miles round about:

IV

For there I picked up on the heather
And there I put inside my breast
A moulted feather, an eagle-feather!
Well, I forget the rest.

(Wr. after 1851?; pub. 1855)

114   *Andrea del Sarto*

(*Called 'The Faultless Painter'*)

BUT do not let us quarrel any more,
No, my Lucrezia; bear with me for once:
Sit down and all shall happen as you wish.
You turn your face, but does it bring your heart?
I'll work then for your friend's friend, never fear,
Treat his own subject after his own way,
Fix his own time, accept too his own price,
And shut the money into this small hand
When next it takes mine. Will it? tenderly?
Oh, I'll content him,—but to-morrow, Love!   10
I often am much wearier than you think,
This evening more than usual, and it seems
As if—forgive now—should you let me sit
Here by the window with your hand in mine
And look a half-hour forth on Fiesole,
Both of one mind, as married people use,
Quietly, quietly the evening through,
I might get up to-morrow to my work
Cheerful and fresh as ever. Let us try.
To-morrow, how you shall be glad for this!   20
Your soft hand is a woman of itself,
And mine the man's bared breast she curls inside.
Don't count the time lost, neither; you must serve
For each of the five pictures we require:
It saves a model. So! keep looking so—
My serpentining beauty, rounds on rounds!
—How could you ever prick those perfect ears,
Even to put the pearl there! oh, so sweet—
My face, my moon, my everybody's moon,
Which everybody looks on and calls his,   30
And, I suppose, is looked on by in turn,
While she looks—no one's: very dear, no less.
You smile? why, there's my picture ready made,

There's what we painters call our harmony!
A common greyness silvers everything,—
All in a twilight, you and I alike
—You, at the point of your first pride in me
(That's gone you know),—but I, at every point;
My youth, my hope, my art, being all toned down
To yonder sober pleasant Fiesole.   40
There's the bell clinking from the chapel-top;
That length of convent-wall across the way
Holds the trees safer, huddled more inside;
The last monk leaves the garden; days decrease,
And autumn grows, autumn in everything.
Eh? the whole seems to fall into a shape
As if I saw alike my work and self
And all that I was born to be and do,
A twilight-piece. Love, we are in God's hand.
How strange now, looks the life he makes us lead;   50
So free we seem, so fettered fast we are!
I feel he laid the fetter: let it lie!
This chamber for example—turn your head—
All that's behind us! You don't understand
Nor care to understand about my art,
But you can hear at least when people speak:
And that cartoon, the second from the door
—It is the thing, Love! so such things should be—
Behold Madonna!—I am bold to say.
I can do with my pencil what I know,   60
What I see, what at bottom of my heart
I wish for, if I ever wish so deep—
Do easily, too—what I say, perfectly,
I do not boast, perhaps: yourself are judge,
Who listened to the Legate's talk last week,
And just as much they used to say in France.
At any rate 't is easy, all of it!
No sketches first, no studies, that's long past:
I do what many dream of, all their lives,
—Dream? strive to do, and agonize to do,   70
And fail in doing. I could count twenty such
On twice your fingers, and not leave this town,
Who strive—you don't know how the others strive
To paint a little thing like that you smeared
Carelessly passing with your robes afloat,—
Yet do much less, so much less, Someone says,
(I know his name, no matter)—so much less!
Well, less is more, Lucrezia: I am judged.
There burns a truer light of God in them,

In their vexed beating stuffed and stopped-up brain,   80
Heart, or whate'er else, than goes on to prompt
This low-pulsed forthright craftsman's hand of mine.
Their works drop groundward, but themselves, I know,
Reach many a time a heaven that's shut to me,
Enter and take their place there sure enough,
Though they come back and cannot tell the world.
My works are nearer heaven, but I sit here.
The sudden blood of these men! at a word—
Praise them, it boils, or blame them, it boils too.
I, painting from myself and to myself,   90
Know what I do, am unmoved by men's blame
Or their praise either. Somebody remarks
Morello's outline there is wrongly traced,
His hue mistaken; what of that? or else,
Rightly traced and well ordered; what of that?
Speak as they please, what does the mountain care?
Ah, but a man's reach should exceed his grasp,
Or what's a heaven for? All is silver-grey
Placid and perfect with my art: the worse!
I know both what I want and what might gain,   100
And yet how profitless to know, to sigh
'Had I been two, another and myself,
'Our head would have o'erlooked the world!' No doubt.
Yonder's a work now, of that famous youth
The Urbinate who died five years ago.
('T is copied, George Vasari sent it me.)
Well, I can fancy how he did it all,
Pouring his soul, with kings and popes to see,
Reaching, that heaven might so replenish him,
Above and through his art—for it gives way;   110
That arm is wrongly put—and there again—
A fault to pardon in the drawing's lines,
Its body, so to speak: its soul is right,
He means right—that, a child may understand.
Still, what an arm! and I could alter it:
But all the play, the insight and the stretch—
Out of me, out of me! And wherefore out?
Had you enjoined them on me, given me soul,
We might have risen to Rafael, I and you!
Nay, Love, you did give all I asked, I think—   120
More than I merit, yes, by many times.
But had you—oh, with the same perfect brow,
And perfect eyes, and more than perfect mouth,
And the low voice my soul hears, as a bird
The fowler's pipe, and follows to the snare—

Had you, with these the same, but brought a mind!
Some women do so. Had the mouth there urged
'God and the glory! never care for gain.
'The present by the future, what is that?
'Live for fame, side by side with Agnolo!   130
'Rafael is waiting: up to God, all three!'
I might have done it for you. So it seems:
Perhaps not. All is as God over-rules.
Beside, incentives come from the soul's self;
The rest avail not. Why do I need you?
What wife had Rafael, or has Agnolo?
In this world, who can do a thing, will not;
And who would do it, cannot, I perceive:
Yet the will's somewhat—somewhat, too, the power—
And thus we half-men struggle. At the end,   140
God, I conclude, compensates, punishes.
'T is safer for me, if the award be strict,
That I am something underrated here,
Poor this long while, despised, to speak the truth.
I dared not, do you know, leave home all day,
For fear of chancing on the Paris lords.
The best is when they pass and look aside;
But they speak sometimes; I must bear it all.
Well may they speak! That Francis, that first time,
And that long festal year at Fontainebleau!   150
I surely then could sometimes leave the ground,
Put on the glory, Rafael's daily wear,
In that humane great monarch's golden look,—
One finger in his beard or twisted curl
Over his mouth's good mark that made the smile,
One arm about my shoulder, round my neck,
The jingle of his gold chain in my ear,
I painting proudly with his breath on me,
All his court round him, seeing with his eyes,
Such frank French eyes, and such a fire of souls   160
Profuse, my hand kept plying by those hearts,—
And, best of all, this, this, this face beyond,
This in the background, waiting on my work,
To crown the issue with a last reward!
A good time, was it not, my kingly days?
And had you not grown restless . . . but I know—
'T is done and past; 't was right, my instinct said;
Too live the life grew, golden and not grey,
And I'm the weak-eyed bat no sun should tempt
Out of the grange whose four walls make his world.   170
How could it end in any other way?

You called me, and I came home to your heart.
The triumph was—to reach and stay there; since
I reached it ere the triumph, what is lost?
Let my hands frame your face in your hair's gold,
You beautiful Lucrezia that are mine!
'Rafael did this, Andrea painted that;
'The Roman's is the better when you pray,
'But still the other's Virgin was his wife—'
Men will excuse me. I am glad to judge   180
Both pictures in your presence; clearer grows
My better fortune, I resolve to think.
For do you know, Lucrezia, as God lives,
Said one day Agnolo, his very self,
To Rafael . . . I have known it all these years . . .
(When the young man was flaming out his thoughts
Upon a palace-wall for Rome to see,
Too lifted up in heart because of it)
'Friend, there's a certain sorry little scrub
'Goes up and down our Florence, none cares how,   190
'Who, were he set to plan and execute
'As you are, pricked on by your popes and kings,
'Would bring the sweat into that brow of yours!'
To Rafael's!—And indeed the arm is wrong.
I hardly dare . . . yet, only you to see,
Give the chalk here—quick, thus the line should go!
Ay, but the soul! he's Rafael! rub it out!
Still, all I care for, if he spoke the truth,
(What he? why, who but Michel Agnolo?
Do you forget already words like those?)   200
If really there was such a chance, so lost,—
Is, whether you're—not grateful—but more pleased.
Well, let me think so. And you smile indeed!
This hour has been an hour! Another smile?
If you would sit thus by me every night
I should work better, do you comprehend?
I mean that I should earn more, give you more.
See, it is settled dusk now; there's a star;
Morello's gone, the watch-lights show the wall,
The cue-owls speak the name we call them by.   210
Come from the window, love,—come in, at last,
Inside the melancholy little house
We built to be so gay with. God is just.
King Francis may forgive me: oft at nights
When I look up from painting, eyes tired out,
The walls become illumined, brick from brick
Distinct, instead of mortar, fierce bright gold,

That gold of his I did cement them with!
Let us but love each other. Must you go?
That Cousin here again? he waits outside?   220
Must see you—you, and not with me? Those loans?
More gaming debts to pay? you smiled for that?
Well, let smiles buy me! have you more to spend?
While hand and eye and something of a heart
Are left me, work's my ware, and what's it worth?
I'll pay my fancy. Only let me sit
The grey remainder of the evening out,
Idle, you call it, and muse perfectly
How I could paint, were I but back in France,
One picture, just one more—the Virgin's face,   230
Not yours this time! I want you at my side
To hear them—that is, Michel Agnolo—
Judge all I do and tell you of its worth.
Will you? To-morrow, satisfy your friend.
I take the subjects for his corridor,
Finish the portrait out of hand—there, there,
And throw him in another thing or two
If he demurs; the whole should prove enough
To pay for this same Cousin's freak. Beside,
What's better and what's all I care about,   240
Get you the thirteen scudi for the ruff!
Love, does that please you? Ah, but what does he,
The Cousin! what does he to please you more?

    I am grown peaceful as old age to-night.
I regret little, I would change still less.
Since there my past life lies, why alter it?
The very wrong to Francis!—it is true
I took his coin, was tempted and complied,
And built this house and sinned, and all is said.
My father and my mother died of want.   250
Well, had I riches of my own? you see
How one gets rich! Let each one bear his lot.
They were born poor, lived poor, and poor they died:
And I have laboured somewhat in my time
And not been paid profusely. Some good son
Paint my two hundred pictures—let him try!
No doubt, there's something strikes a balance. Yes,
You loved me quite enough, it seems to-night.
This must suffice me here. What would one have?
In heaven, perhaps, new chances, one more chance—   260
Four great walls in the New Jerusalem,
Meted on each side by the angel's reed,

For Leonard, Rafael, Agnolo and me
To cover—the three first without a wife,
While I have mine! So—still they overcome
Because there's still Lucrezia,—as I choose.

Again the Cousin's whistle! Go, my Love.

(Wr. 1853?; pub. 1855)

115   *Two in the Campagna*

I

I WONDER do you feel to-day
   As I have felt since, hand in hand,
We sat down on the grass, to stray
   In spirit better through the land,
This morn of Rome and May?

II

For me, I touched a thought, I know,
   Has tantalized me many times,
(Like turns of thread the spiders throw
   Mocking across our path) for rhymes
To catch at and let go.   10

III

Help me to hold it! First it left
   The yellowing fennel, run to seed
There, branching from the brickwork's cleft,
   Some old tomb's ruin: yonder weed
Took up the floating weft,

IV

Where one small orange cup amassed
   Five beetles,—blind and green they grope
Among the honey-meal: and last,
   Everywhere on the grassy slope
I traced it. Hold it fast!   20

V

The champaign with its endless fleece
   Of feathery grasses everywhere!
Silence and passion, joy and peace,
   An everlasting wash of air—
Rome's ghost since her decease.

VI

Such life here, through such lengths of hours,
   Such miracles performed in play,
Such primal naked forms of flowers,
   Such letting nature have her way
While heaven looks from its towers!   30

VII

How say you? Let us, O my dove,
   Let us be unashamed of soul,
As earth lies bare to heaven above!
   How is it under our control
To love or not to love?

VIII

I would that you were all to me,
   You that are just so much, no more.
Nor yours nor mine, nor slave nor free!
   Where does the fault lie? What the core
O' the wound, since wound must be?   40

IX

I would I could adopt your will,
   See with your eyes, and set my heart
Beating by yours, and drink my fill
   At your soul's springs,—your part my part
In life, for good and ill.

X

No. I yearn upward, touch you close,
   Then stand away. I kiss your cheek,
Catch your soul's warmth,—I pluck the rose
   And love it more than tongue can speak—
Then the good minute goes.   50

XI

Already how am I so far
   Out of that minute? Must I go
Still like the thistle-ball, no bar,
   Onward, whenever light winds blow
Fixed by no friendly star?

XII

Just when I seemed about to learn!
  Where is the thread now? Off again!
The old trick! Only I discern—
  Infinite passion, and the pain
Of finite hearts that yearn.   60

(Wr. 1854?; pub. 1855)

116   *Love in a Life*

I

ROOM after room,
I hunt the house through
We inhabit together.
Heart, fear nothing, for, heart, thou shalt find her—
Next time, herself!—not the trouble behind her
Left in the curtain, the couch's perfume!
As she brushed it, the cornice-wreath blossomed anew:
Yon looking-glass gleamed at the wave of her feather.

II

Yet the day wears,
And door succeeds door;   10
I try the fresh fortune—
Range the wide house from the wing to the centre.
Still the same chance! she goes out as I enter.
Spend my whole day in the quest,—who cares?
But 't is twilight, you see,—with such suites to explore,
Such closets to search, such alcoves to importune!

(1855)

117   *A Toccata of Galuppi's*

I

OH Galuppi, Baldassaro, this is very sad to find!
I can hardly misconceive you; it would prove me deaf and blind;
But although I take your meaning, 't is with such a heavy mind!

II

Here you come with your old music, and here's all the good it brings.
What, they lived once thus at Venice where the merchants were the
    kings,
Where Saint Mark's is, where the Doges used to wed the sea with
    rings?

III

Ay, because the sea's the street there; and 't is arched by . . . what you
    call
. . . Shylock's bridge with houses on it, where they kept the carnival:
I was never out of England—it's as if I saw it all.

IV

Did young people take their pleasure when the sea was warm in May?   10
Balls and masks begun at midnight, burning ever to midday,
When they made up fresh adventures for the morrow, do you say?

V

Was a lady such a lady, cheeks so round and lips so red,—
On her neck the small face buoyant, like a bell-flower on its bed,
O'er the breast's superb abundance where a man might base his head?

VI

Well, and it was graceful of them—they'd break talk off and afford
—She, to bite her mask's black velvet—he, to finger on his sword,
While you sat and played Toccatas, stately at the clavichord?

VII

What? Those lesser thirds so plaintive, sixths diminished, sigh on sigh,
Told them something? Those suspensions, those solutions—'Must we
    die?'   20
Those commiserating sevenths—'Life might last! we can but try!'

VIII

'Were you happy?'—'Yes'—'And are you still as happy?'—'Yes. And
    you?'
—'Then, more kisses!'—'Did *I* stop them, when a million seemed so
    few?'
Hark, the dominant's persistence till it must be answered to!

IX

So, an octave struck the answer. Oh, they praised you, I dare say!
'Brave Galuppi! that was music! good alike at grave and gay!
'I can always leave off talking when I hear a master play!'

X

Then they left you for their pleasure: till in due time, one by one,
Some with lives that came to nothing, some with deeds as well undone,
Death stepped tacitly and took them where they never see the sun.   30

XI

But when I sit down to reason, think to take my stand nor swerve,
While I triumph o'er a secret wrung from nature's close reserve,
In you come with your cold music till I creep thro' every nerve.

XII

Yes, you, like a ghostly cricket, creaking where a house was burned:
'Dust and ashes, dead and done with, Venice spent what Venice
    earned.
'The soul, doubtless, is immortal—where a soul can be discerned.

XIII

'Yours for instance: you know physics, something of geology,
'Mathematics are your pastime; souls shall rise in their degree;
'Butterflies may dread extinction,—you'll not die, it cannot be!

XIV

'As for Venice and her people, merely born to bloom and drop,   40
'Here on earth they bore their fruitage, mirth and folly were the crop:
'What of soul was left, I wonder, when the kissing had to stop?

XV

'Dust and ashes!' So you creak it, and I want the heart to scold.
Dear dead women, with such hair, too—what's become of all the gold
Used to hang and brush their bosoms? I feel chilly and grown old.

(1855)

118   *'Childe Roland to the Dark Tower Came'*
         (*See Edgar's song in* 'LEAR')

I

MY first thought was, he lied in every word,
   That hoary cripple, with malicious eye
   Askance to watch the working of his lie
On mine, and mouth scarce able to afford
Suppression of the glee, that pursed and scored
   Its edge, at one more victim gained thereby.

II

What else should he be set for, with his staff?
   What, save to waylay with his lies, ensnare
   All travellers who might find him posted there,
And ask the road? I guessed what skull-like laugh   10
Would break, what crutch 'gin write my epitaph
   For pastime in the dusty thoroughfare,

III

If at his counsel I should turn aside
   Into that ominous tract which, all agree,
   Hides the Dark Tower. Yet acquiescingly
I did turn as he pointed: neither pride
Nor hope rekindling at the end descried,
   So much as gladness that some end might be.

IV

For, what with my whole world-wide wandering,
   What with my search drawn out thro' years, my hope   20
   Dwindled into a ghost not fit to cope
With that obstreperous joy success would bring,—
I hardly tried now to rebuke the spring
   My heart made, finding failure in its scope.

V

As when a sick man very near to death
   Seems dead indeed, and feels begin and end
   The tears and takes the farewell of each friend,
And hears one bid the other go, draw breath
Freelier outside, ('since all is o'er,' he saith,
   'And the blow fallen no grieving can amend;')   30

VI

While some discuss if near the other graves
   Be room enough for this, and when a day
   Suits best for carrying the corpse away,
With care about the banners, scarves and staves:
And still the man hears all, and only craves
   He may not shame such tender love and stay.

VII

Thus, I had so long suffered in this quest,
   Heard failure prophesied so oft, been writ
   So many times among 'The Band'—to wit,
The knights who to the Dark Tower's search addressed   40
Their steps—that just to fail as they, seemed best,
   And all the doubt was now—should I be fit?

VIII

So, quiet as despair, I turned from him,
   That hateful cripple, out of his highway
   Into the path he pointed. All the day
Had been a dreary one at best, and dim
Was settling to its close, yet shot one grim
   Red leer to see the plain catch its estray.

IX

For mark! no sooner was I fairly found
   Pledged to the plain, after a pace or two,   50
   Than, pausing to throw backward a last view
O'er the safe road, 't was gone; grey plain all round:
Nothing but plain to the horizon's bound.
   I might go on; nought else remained to do.

X

So, on I went. I think I never saw
   Such starved ignoble nature; nothing throve:
   For flowers—as well expect a cedar grove!
But cockle, spurge, according to their law
Might propagate their kind, with none to awe,
   You'd think; a burr had been a treasure-trove.   60

XI

No! penury, inertness and grimace,
　In some strange sort, were the land's portion. 'See
　'Or shut your eyes,' said Nature peevishly,
'It nothing skills: I cannot help my case:
''T is the Last Judgment's fire must cure this place,
　'Calcine its clods and set my prisoners free.'

XII

If there pushed any ragged thistle-stalk
　Above its mates, the head was chopped; the bents
　Were jealous else. What made those holes and rents
In the dock's harsh swarth leaves, bruised as to baulk　　70
All hope of greenness? 't is a brute must walk
　Pashing their life out, with a brute's intents.

XIII

As for the grass, it grew as scant as hair
　In leprosy; thin dry blades pricked the mud
　Which underneath looked kneaded up with blood.
One stiff blind horse, his every bone a-stare,
Stood stupefied, however he came there:
　Thrust out past service from the devil's stud!

XIV

Alive? he might be dead for aught I know,
　With that red gaunt and colloped neck a-strain,　　80
　And shut eyes underneath the rusty mane;
Seldom went such grotesqueness with such woe;
I never saw a brute I hated so;
　He must be wicked to deserve such pain.

XV

I shut my eyes and turned them on my heart.
　As a man calls for wine before he fights,
　I asked one draught of earlier, happier sights,
Ere fitly I could hope to play my part.
Think first, fight afterwards—the soldier's art:
　One taste of the old time sets all to rights.　　90

XVI

Not it! I fancied Cuthbert's reddening face
  Beneath its garniture of curly gold,
  Dear fellow, till I almost felt him fold
An arm in mine to fix me to the place,
That way he used. Alas, one night's disgrace!
  Out went my heart's new fire and left it cold.

XVII

Giles then, the soul of honour—there he stands
  Frank as ten years ago when knighted first.
  What honest man should dare (he said) he durst.
Good—but the scene shifts—faugh! what hangman-hands 100
Pin to his breast a parchment? His own bands
  Read it. Poor traitor, spit upon and curst!

XVIII

Better this present than a past like that;
  Back therefore to my darkening path again!
  No sound, no sight as far as eye could strain.
Will the night send a howlet or a bat?
I asked: when something on the dismal flat
  Came to arrest my thoughts and change their train.

XIX

A sudden little river crossed my path
  As unexpected as a serpent comes.   110
  No sluggish tide congenial to the glooms;
This, as it frothed by, might have been a bath
For the fiend's glowing hoof—to see the wrath
  Of its black eddy bespate with flakes and spumes.

XX

So petty yet so spiteful! All along,
  Low scrubby alders kneeled down over it;
  Drenched willows flung them headlong in a fit
Of mute despair, a suicidal throng:
The river which had done them all the wrong,
  Whate'er that was, rolled by, deterred no whit.   120

XXI

Which, while I forded,—good saints, how I feared
  To set my foot upon a dead man's cheek,
  Each step, or feel the spear I thrust to seek
For hollows, tangled in his hair or beard!
—It may have been a water-rat I speared,
  But, ugh! it sounded like a baby's shriek.

XXII

Glad was I when I reached the other bank.
  Now for a better country. Vain presage!
  Who were the strugglers, what war did they wage,
Whose savage trample thus could pad the dank   130
Soil to a plash? Toads in a poisoned tank,
  Or wild cats in a red-hot iron cage—

XXIII

The fight must so have seemed in that fell cirque.
  What penned them there, with all the plain to choose?
  No foot-print leading to that horrid mews,
None out of it. Mad brewage set to work
Their brains, no doubt, like galley-slaves the Turk
  Pits for his pastime, Christians against Jews.

XXIV

And more than that—a furlong on—why, there!
  What bad use was that engine for, that wheel,   140
  Or brake, not wheel—that harrow fit to reel
Men's bodies out like silk? with all the air
Of Tophet's tool, on earth left unaware,
  Or brought to sharpen its rusty teeth of steel.

XXV

Then came a bit of stubbed ground, once a wood,
  Next a marsh, it would seem, and now mere earth
  Desperate and done with; (so a fool finds mirth,
Makes a thing and then mars it, till his mood
Changes and off he goes!) within a rood—
  Bog, clay and rubble, sand and stark black dearth.   150

XXVI

Now blotches rankling, coloured gay and grim,
  Now patches where some leanness of the soil's
  Broke into moss or substances like boils;
Then came some palsied oak, a cleft in him
Like a distorted mouth that splits its rim
  Gaping at death, and dies while it recoils.

XXVII

And just as far as ever from the end!
  Nought in the distance but the evening, nought
  To point my footstep further! At the thought,
A great black bird, Apollyon's bosom-friend,   160
Sailed past, nor beat his wide wing dragon-penned
  That brushed my cap—perchance the guide I sought.

XXVIII

For, looking up, aware I somehow grew,
  'Spite of the dusk, the plain had given place
  All round to mountains—with such name to grace
Mere ugly heights and heaps now stolen in view.
How thus they had surprised me,—solve it, you!
  How to get from them was no clearer case.

XXIX

Yet half I seemed to recognize some trick
  Of mischief happened to me, God knows when—   170
  In a bad dream perhaps. Here ended, then,
Progress this way. When, in the very nick
Of giving up, one time more, came a click
  As when a trap shuts—you're inside the den!

XXX

Burningly it came on me all at once,
  This was the place! those two hills on the right,
  Crouched like two bulls locked horn in horn in fight;
While to the left, a tall scalped mountain ... Dunce,
Dotard, a-dozing at the very nonce,
  After a life spent training for the sight!   180

XXXI

What in the midst lay but the Tower itself?
  The round squat turret, blind as the fool's heart,
  Built of brown stone, without a counterpart
In the whole world. The tempest's mocking elf
Points to the shipman thus the unseen shelf
  He strikes on, only when the timbers start.

XXXII

Not see? because of night perhaps?—why, day
  Came back again for that! before it left,
  The dying sunset kindled through a cleft:
The hills, like giants at a hunting, lay,   190
Chin upon hand, to see the game at bay,—
  'Now stab and end the creature—to the heft!'

XXXIII

Not hear? when noise was everywhere! it tolled
  Increasing like a bell. Names in my ears
  Of all the lost adventurers my peers,—
How such a one was strong, and such was bold,
And such was fortunate, yet each of old
  Lost, lost! one moment knelled the woe of years.

XXXIV

There they stood, ranged along the hill-sides, met
  To view the last of me, a living frame   200
  For one more picture! in a sheet of flame
I saw them and I knew them all. And yet
Dauntless the slug-horn to my lips I set,
  And blew. '*Childe Roland to the Dark Tower came.*'

(1855)

119   *A Grammarian's Funeral*

Shortly after the Revival of Learning in Europe

LET us begin and carry up this corpse,
      Singing together.
  Leave we the common crofts, the vulgar thorpes
      Each in its tether

Sleeping safe on the bosom of the plain,
    Cared-for till cock-crow:
Look out if yonder be not day again
    Rimming the rock-row!
That's the appropriate country: there, man's thought,
    Rarer, intenser,   10
Self-gathered for an outbreak, as it ought,
    Chafes in the censer.
Leave we the unlettered plain its herd and crop;
    Seek we sepulture
On a tall mountain, citied to the top,
    Crowded with culture!
All the peaks soar, but one the rest excels;
    Clouds overcome it;
No! yonder sparkle is the citadel's
    Circling its summit.   20
Thither our path lies; wind we up the heights:
    Wait ye the warning?
Our low life was the level's and the night's;
    He's for the morning.
Step to a tune, square chests, erect each head,
    'Ware the beholders!
This is our master, famous calm and dead,
    Borne on our shoulders.

Sleep, crop and herd! sleep, darkling thorpe and croft,
    Safe from the weather!   30
He, whom we convoy to his grave aloft,
    Singing together,
He was a man born with thy face and throat,
    Lyric Apollo!
Long he lived nameless: how should spring take note
    Winter would follow?
Till lo, the little touch, and youth was gone!
    Cramped and diminished,
Moaned he, 'New measures, other feet anon!
    'My dance is finished?'   40
No, that's the world's way: (keep the mountain-side,
    Make for the city!)
He knew the signal, and stepped on with pride
    Over men's pity;
Left play for work, and grappled with the world
    Bent on escaping:
'What's in the scroll,' quoth he, 'thou keepest furled?
    'Show me their shaping,

'Theirs who most studied man, the bard and sage,—
      'Give!'—So, he gowned him,   50
Straight got by heart that book to its last page:
      Learned, we found him.
Yea, but we found him bald too, eyes like lead,
      Accents uncertain:
'Time to taste life,' another would have said,
      'Up with the curtain!'
This man said rather, 'Actual life comes next?
      'Patience a moment!
'Grant I have mastered learning's crabbed text,
      'Still there's the comment.   60
'Let me know all! Prate not of most or least,
      'Painful or easy!
'Even to the crumbs I'd fain eat up the feast,
      'Ay, nor feel queasy.'
Oh, such a life as he resolved to live,
      When he had learned it,
When he had gathered all books had to give!
      Sooner, he spurned it.
Image the whole, then execute the parts—
      Fancy the fabric   70
Quite, ere you build, ere steel strike fire from quartz,
      Ere mortar dab brick!

(Here's the town-gate reached: there's the market-place
      Gaping before us.)
Yea, this in him was the peculiar grace
      (Hearten our chorus!)
That before living he'd learn how to live—
      No end to learning:
Earn the means first—God surely will contrive
      Use for our earning.   80
Others mistrust and say, 'But time escapes:
      'Live now or never!'
He said, 'What's time? Leave Now for dogs and apes!
      'Man has Forever.'
Back to his book then: deeper drooped his head:
      Calculus racked him:
Leaden before, his eyes grew dross of lead:
      Tussis attacked him.
'Now, master, take a little rest!'—not he!
      (Caution redoubled,   90
Step two abreast, the way winds narrowly!)
      Not a whit troubled

Back to his studies, fresher than at first,
    Fierce as a dragon
He (soul-hydroptic with a sacred thirst)
    Sucked at the flagon.
Oh, if we draw a circle premature,
    Heedless of far gain,
Greedy for quick returns of profit, sure
    Bad is our bargain!   100
Was it not great? did not he throw on God,
    (He loves the burthen)—
God's task to make the heavenly period
    Perfect the earthen?
Did not he magnify the mind, show clear
    Just what it all meant?
He would not discount life, as fools do here,
    Paid by instalment.
He ventured neck or nothing—heaven's success
    Found, or earth's failure: 110
'Wilt thou trust death or not?' He answered 'Yes:
    'Hence with life's pale lure!'
That low man seeks a little thing to do,
    Sees it and does it:
This high man, with a great thing to pursue,
    Dies ere he knows it.
That low man goes on adding one to one,
    His hundred's soon hit:
This high man, aiming at a million,
    Misses an unit.   120
That, has the world here—should he need the next,
    Let the world mind him!
This, throws himself on God, and unperplexed
    Seeking shall find him.
So, with the throttling hands of death at strife,
    Ground he at grammar;
Still, thro' the rattle, parts of speech were rife:
    While he could stammer
He settled *Hoti's* business—let it be!—
    Properly based *Oun*—   130
Gave us the doctrine of the enclitic *De*,
    Dead from the waist down.
Well, here's the platform, here's the proper place:
    Hail to your purlieus,
All ye highfliers of the feathered race,
    Swallows and curlews!
Here's the top-peak; the multitude below
    Live, for they can, there:

This man decided not to Live but Know—
 Bury this man there?   140
Here—here's his place, where meteors shoot, clouds form,
 Lightnings are loosened,
Stars come and go! Let joy break with the storm,
 Peace let the dew send!
Lofty designs must close in like effects:
 Loftily lying,
Leave him—still loftier than the world suspects,
 Living and dying.

          (1855)

120   *Confessions*

I

WHAT is he buzzing in my ears?
 'Now that I come to die,
'Do I view the world as a vale of tears?'
 Ah, reverend sir, not I!

II

What I viewed there once, what I view again
 Where the physic bottles stand
On the table's edge,—is a suburb lane,
 With a wall to my bedside hand.

III

That lane sloped, much as the bottles do,
 From a house you could descry   10
O'er the garden-wall: is the curtain blue
 Or green to a healthy eye?

IV

To mine, it serves for the old June weather
 Blue above lane and wall;
And that farthest bottle labelled 'Ether'
 Is the house o'ertopping all.

V

At a terrace, somewhere near the stopper,
 There watched for me, one June,
A girl: I know, sir, it's improper,
 My poor mind's out of tune.   20

VI

Only, there was a way . . . you crept
   Close by the side, to dodge
Eyes in the house, two eyes except:
   They styled their house 'The Lodge'.

VII

What right had a lounger up their lane?
   But, by creeping very close,
With the good wall's help,—their eyes might strain
   And stretch themselves to Oes,

VIII

Yet never catch her and me together,
   As she left the attic, there,   30
By the rim of the bottle labelled 'Ether',
   And stole from stair to stair,

IX

And stood by the rose-wreathed gate. Alas,
   We loved, sir—used to meet:
How sad and bad and mad it was—
   But then, how it was sweet!

                             (Wr. 1859–60?; pub. 1864)

121   *Youth and Art*

I

It once might have been, once only:
   We lodged in a street together,
You, a sparrow on the housetop lonely,
   I, a lone she-bird of his feather.

II

Your trade was with sticks and clay,
   You thumbed, thrust, patted and polished,
Then laughed 'They will see some day
   'Smith made, and Gibson demolished.'

III

My business was song, song, song;
   I chirped, cheeped, trilled and twittered,   10
'Kate Brown's on the boards ere long,
   'And Grisi's existence embittered!'

IV

I earned no more by a warble
   Than you by a sketch in plaster;
You wanted a piece of marble,
   I needed a music-master.

V

We studied hard in our styles,
   Chipped each at a crust like Hindoos,
For air looked out on the tiles,
   For fun watched each other's windows.   20

VI

You lounged, like a boy of the South,
   Cap and blouse—nay, a bit of beard too;
Or you got it, rubbing your mouth
   With fingers the clay adhered to.

VII

And I—soon managed to find
   Weak points in the flower-fence facing,
Was forced to put up a blind
   And be safe in my corset-lacing.

VIII

No harm! It was not my fault
   If you never turned your eye's tail up   30
As I shook upon E *in alt*,
   Or ran the chromatic scale up:

IX

For spring bade the sparrows pair,
   And the boys and girls gave guesses,
And stalls in our street looked rare
   With bulrush and watercresses.

X

Why did you not pinch a flower
    In a pellet of clay and fling it?
Why did not I put a power
    Of thanks in a look, or sing it?   40

XI

I did look, sharp as a lynx,
    (And yet the memory rankles)
When models arrived, some minx
    Tripped up-stairs, she and her ankles.

XII

But I think I gave you as good!
    'That foreign fellow,—who can know
'How she pays, in a playful mood,
    'For his tuning her that piano?'

XIII

Could you say so, and never say
    'Suppose we join hands and fortunes,   50
'And I fetch her from over the way,
    'Her, piano, and long tunes and short tunes?'

XIV

No, no: you would not be rash,
    Nor I rasher and something over:
You've to settle yet Gibson's hash,
    And Grisi yet lives in clover.

XV

But you meet the Prince at the Board,
    I'm queen myself at *bals-paré*,
I've married a rich old lord,
    And you're dubbed knight and an R.A.   60

XVI

Each life unfulfilled, you see;
    It hangs still, patchy and scrappy:
We have not sighed deep, laughed free,
    Starved, feasted, despaired,—been happy.

XVII

And nobody calls you a dunce,
  And people suppose me clever:
This could but have happened once,
  And we missed it, lost it for ever.

(Wr. 1860?; pub. 1864)

122 *Caliban upon Setebos; or, Natural Theology in the Island*

'Thou thoughtest that I was altogether such a one as thyself'

['WILL sprawl, now that the heat of day is best,
Flat on his belly in the pit's much mire,
With elbows wide, fists clenched to prop his chin.
And, while he kicks both feet in the cool slush,
And feels about his spine small eft-things course,
Run in and out each arm, and make him laugh:
And while above his head a pompion-plant,
Coating the cave-top as a brow its eye,
Creeps down to touch and tickle hair and beard,
And now a flower drops with a bee inside,   10
And now a fruit to snap at, catch and crunch,—
He looks out o'er yon sea which sunbeams cross
And recross till they weave a spider-web
(Meshes of fire, some great fish breaks at times)
And talks to his own self, howe'er he please,
Touching that other, whom his dam called God.
Because to talk about Him, vexes—ha,
Could He but know! and time to vex is now,
When talk is safer than in winter-time.
Moreover Prosper and Miranda sleep   20
In confidence he drudges at their task,
And it is good to cheat the pair, and gibe,
Letting the rank tongue blossom into speech.]

Setebos, Setebos, and Setebos!
'Thinketh, He dwelleth i' the cold o' the moon.

'Thinketh He made it, with the sun to match,
But not the stars; the stars came otherwise;
Only made clouds, winds, meteors, such as that:

Also this isle, what lives and grows thereon,
And snaky sea which rounds and ends the same.   30

'Thinketh, it came of being ill at ease:
He hated that He cannot change His cold,
Nor cure its ache. 'Hath spied an icy fish
That longed to 'scape the rock-stream where she lived,
And thaw herself within the lukewarm brine
O' the lazy sea her stream thrusts far amid,
A crystal spike 'twixt two warm walls of wave;
Only, she ever sickened, found repulse
At the other kind of water, not her life,
(Green-dense and dim-delicious, bred o' the sun)   40
Flounced back from bliss she was not born to breathe,
And in her old bounds buried her despair,
Hating and loving warmth alike: so He.

'Thinketh, He made thereat the sun, this isle,
Trees and the fowls here, beast and creeping thing.
Yon otter, sleek-wet, black, lithe as a leech;
Yon auk, one fire-eye in a ball of foam,
That floats and feeds; a certain badger brown
He hath watched hunt with that slant white-wedge eye
By moonlight; and the pie with the long tongue   50
That pricks deep into oakwarts for a worm,
And says a plain word when she finds her prize,
But will not eat the ants; the ants themselves
That build a wall of seeds and settled stalks
About their hole—He made all these and more,
Made all we see, and us, in spite: how else?
He could not, Himself, make a second self
To be His mate; as well have made Himself:
He would not make what he mislikes or slights,
An eyesore to Him, or not worth His pains: 60
But did, in envy, listlessness or sport,
Make what Himself would fain, in a manner, be—
Weaker in most points, stronger in a few,
Worthy, and yet mere playthings all the while,
Things He admires and mocks too,—that is it.
Because, so brave, so better though they be,
It nothing skills if He begin to plague.
Look now, I melt a gourd-fruit into mash,
Add honeycomb and pods, I have perceived,
Which bite like finches when they bill and kiss,—   70
Then, when froth rises bladdery, drink up all,
Quick, quick, till maggots scamper through my brain;

Last, throw me on my back i' the seeded thyme,
And wanton, wishing I were born a bird.
Put case, unable to be what I wish,
I yet could make a live bird out of clay:
Would not I take clay, pinch my Caliban
Able to fly?—for, there, see, he hath wings,
And great comb like the hoopoe's to admire,
And there, a sting to do his foes offence,   80
There, and I will that he begin to live,
Fly to yon rock-top, nip me off the horns
Of grigs high up that make the merry din,
Saucy through their veined wings, and mind me not.
In which feat, if his leg snapped, brittle clay,
And he lay stupid-like,—why, I should laugh;
And if he, spying me, should fall to weep,
Beseech me to be good, repair his wrong,
Bid his poor leg smart less or grow again,—
Well, as the chance were, this might take or else   90
Not take my fancy: I might hear his cry,
And give the mankin three sound legs for one,
Or pluck the other off, leave him like an egg,
And lessoned he was mine and merely clay.
Were this no pleasure, lying in the thyme,
Drinking the mash, with brain become alive,
Making and marring clay at will? So He.

'Thinketh, such shows nor right nor wrong in Him,
Nor kind, nor cruel: He is strong and Lord.
'Am strong myself compared to yonder crabs   100
That march now from the mountain to the sea,
'Let twenty pass, and stone the twenty-first,
Loving not, hating not, just choosing so.
'Say, the first straggler that boasts purple spots
Shall join the file, one pincer twisted off;
'Say, this bruised fellow shall receive a worm,
And two worms he whose nippers end in red;
As it likes me each time, I do: so He.

Well then, 'supposeth He is good i' the main,
Placable if His mind and ways were guessed,   110
But rougher than His handiwork, be sure!
Oh, He hath made things worthier than Himself,
And envieth that, so helped, such things do more
Than He who made them! What consoles but this?
That they, unless through Him, do nought at all,
And must submit: what other use in things?

'Hath cut a pipe of pithless elder joint
That, blown through, gives exact the scream o' the jay
When from her wing you twitch the feathers blue:
Sound this, and little birds that hate the jay   120
Flock within stone's throw, glad their foe is hurt:
Put case such pipe could prattle and boast forsooth
'I catch the birds, I am the crafty thing,
'I make the cry my maker cannot make
'With his great round mouth; he must blow through mine!'
Would not I smash it with my foot? So He.

But wherefore rough, why cold and ill at ease?
Aha, that is a question! Ask, for that,
What knows,—the something over Setebos
That made Him, or He, may be, found and fought,   130
Worsted, drove off and did to nothing, perchance.
There may be something quiet o'er His head,
Out of His reach, that feels nor joy nor grief,
Since both derive from weakness in some way.
I joy because the quails come; would not joy
Could I bring quails here when I have a mind:
This Quiet, all it hath a mind to, doth.
'Esteemeth stars the outposts of its couch,
But never spends much thought nor care that way.
It may look up, work up,—the worse for those   140
It works on! 'Careth but for Setebos
The many-handed as a cuttle-fish,
Who, making Himself feared through what He does,
Looks up, first, and perceives he cannot soar
To what is quiet and hath happy life;
Next looks down here, and out of very spite
Makes this a bauble-world to ape yon real,
These good things to match those as hips do grapes.
'T is solace making baubles, ay, and sport.
Himself peeped late, eyed Prosper at his books   150
Careless and lofty, lord now of the isle:
Vexed, 'stitched a book of broad leaves, arrow-shaped,
Wrote thereon, he knows what, prodigious words;
Has peeled a wand and called it by a name;
Weareth at whiles for an enchanter's robe
The eyed skin of a supple oncelot;
And hath an ounce sleeker than youngling mole,
A four-legged serpent he makes cower and couch,
Now snarl, now hold its breath and mind his eye,
And saith she is Miranda and my wife: 160
'Keeps for his Ariel a tall pouch-bill crane

He bids go wade for fish and straight disgorge;
Also a sea-beast, lumpish, which he snared,
Blinded the eyes of, and brought somewhat tame,
And split its toe-webs, and now pens the drudge
In a hole o' the rock and calls him Caliban;
A bitter heart that bides its time and bites.
'Plays thus at being Prosper in a way,
Taketh his mirth with make-believes: so He.

His dam held that the Quiet made all things   170
Which Setebos vexed only: 'holds not so.
Who made them weak, meant weakness He might vex.
Had He meant other, while His hand was in,
Why not make horny eyes no thorn could prick,
Or plate my scalp with bone against the snow,
Or overscale my flesh 'neath joint and joint,
Like an orc's armour? Ay,—so spoil His sport!
He is the One now: only He doth all.

'Saith, He may like, perchance, what profits Him.
Ay, himself loves what does him good; but why?   180
'Gets good no otherwise. This blinded beast
Loves whoso places flesh-meat on his nose,
But, had he eyes, would want no help, but hate
Or love, just as it liked him: He hath eyes.
Also it pleaseth Setebos to work,
Use all His hands, and exercise much craft,
By no means for the love of what is worked.
'Tasteth, himself, no finer good i' the world
When all goes right, in this safe summer-time,
And he wants little, hungers, aches not much,   190
Than trying what to do with wit and strength.
'Falls to make something: 'piled yon pile of turfs,
And squared and stuck there squares of soft white chalk,
And, with a fish-tooth, scratched a moon on each,
And set up endwise certain spikes of tree,
And crowned the whole with a sloth's skull a-top,
Found dead i' the woods, too hard for one to kill.
No use at all i' the work, for work's sole sake;
'Shall some day knock it down again: so He.

'Saith He is terrible: watch His feats in proof!   200
One hurricane will spoil six good months' hope.
He hath a spite against me, that I know,
Just as He favours Prosper, who knows why?
So it is, all the same, as well I find.

'Wove wattles half the winter, fenced them firm
With stone and stake to stop she-tortoises
Crawling to lay their eggs here: well, one wave,
Feeling the foot of Him upon its neck,
Gaped as a snake does, lolled out its large tongue,
And licked the whole labour flat: so much for spite. 210
'Saw a ball flame down late (yonder it lies)
Where, half an hour before, I slept i' the shade:
Often they scatter sparkles: there is force!
'Dug up a newt He may have envied once
And turned to stone, shut up inside a stone.
Please Him and hinder this?—What Prosper does?
Aha, if He would tell me how! Not He!
There is the sport: discover how or die!
All need not die, for of the things o' the isle
Some flee afar, some dive, some run up trees; 220
Those at His mercy,—why, they please Him most
When . . . when . . . well, never try the same way twice!
Repeat what act has pleased, He may grow wroth.
You must not know His ways, and play Him off,
Sure of the issue. 'Doth the like himself:
'Spareth a squirrel that it nothing fears
But steals the nut from underneath my thumb,
And when I threat, bites stoutly in defence:
'Spareth an urchin that contrariwise,
Curls up into a ball, pretending death 230
For fright at my approach: the two ways please.
But what would move my choler more than this,
That either creature counted on its life
To-morrow and next day and all days to come,
Saying, forsooth, in the inmost of its heart,
'Because he did so yesterday with me,
'And otherwise with such another brute,
'So must he do henceforth and always.'—Ay?
Would teach the reasoning couple what 'must' means!
'Doth as he likes, or wherefore Lord? So He. 240

'Conceiveth all things will continue thus,
And we shall have to live in fear of Him
So long as He lives, keeps His strength: no change,
If He have done His best, make no new world
To please Him more, so leave off watching this,—
If He surprise not even the Quiet's self
Some strange day,—or, suppose, grow into it
As grubs grow butterflies: else, here are we,
And there is He, and nowhere help at all.

'Believeth with the life, the pain shall stop.   250
His dam held different, that after death
He both plagued enemies and feasted friends:
Idly! He doth His worst in this our life,
Giving just respite lest we die through pain,
Saving last pain for worst,—with which, an end.
Meanwhile, the best way to escape His ire
Is, not to seem too happy. 'Sees, himself,
Yonder two flies, with purple films and pink,
Bask on the pompion-bell above: kills both.
'Sees two black painful beetles roll their ball   260
On head and tail as if to save their lives:
Moves them the stick away they strive to clear.

Even so, 'would have Him misconceive, suppose
This Caliban strives hard and ails no less,
And always, above all else, envies Him;
Wherefore he mainly dances on dark nights,
Moans in the sun, gets under holes to laugh,
And never speaks his mind save housed as now:
Outside, 'groans, curses. If He caught me here,
O'erheard this speech, and asked 'What chucklest at?'   270
'Would, to appease Him, cut a finger off,
Or of my three kid yearlings burn the best,
Or let the toothsome apples rot on tree,
Or push my tame beast for the orc to taste:
While myself lit a fire, and made a song
And sung it, '*What I hate, be consecrate*
'*To celebrate Thee and Thy state, no mate*
'*For Thee; what see for envy in poor me?*'
Hoping the while, since evils sometimes mend,
Warts rub away and sores are cured with slime,   280
That some strange day, will either the Quiet catch
And conquer Setebos, or likelier He
Decrepit may doze, doze, as good as die.

[What, what? A curtain o'er the world at once!
Crickets stop hissing; not a bird—or, yes,
There scuds His raven that has told Him all!
It was fool's play, this prattling! Ha! The wind
Shoulders the pillared dust, death's house o' the move,
And fast invading fires begin! White blaze—
A tree's head snaps—and there, there, there, there, there, 290
His thunder follows! Fool to gibe at Him!
Lo! 'Lieth flat and loveth Setebos!

'Maketh his teeth meet through his upper lip,
Will let those quails fly, will not eat this month
One little mess of whelks, so he may 'scape!]

(1864)

123   *[Rhyme for a Child Viewing a Naked Venus in a
        Painting of 'The Judgement of Paris']*

HE gazed and gazed and gazed and gazed,
Amazed, amazed, amazed, amazed.

(Wr. 1872?; pub. 1925)

124   *Never the Time and the Place*

NEVER the time and the place
    And the loved one all together!
This path—how soft to pace!
    This May—what magic weather!
Where is the loved one's face?
In a dream that loved one's face meets mine,
    But the house is narrow, the place is bleak
Where, outside, rain and wind combine
    With a furtive ear, if I strive to speak,
    With a hostile eye at my flushing cheek,   10
With a malice that marks each word, each sign!
O enemy sly and serpentine,
    Uncoil thee from the waking man!
        Do I hold the Past
        Thus firm and fast
Yet doubt if the Future hold I can?
This path so soft to pace shall lead
Thro' the magic of May to herself indeed!
Or narrow if needs the house must be,
Outside are the storms and strangers: we—   20
Oh, close, safe, warm sleep I and she,
—I and she!

(Wr. 1882?; pub. 1883)

125 *Development*

My Father was a scholar and knew Greek.
When I was five years old, I asked him once
'What do you read about?'
                                    'The siege of Troy.'
'What is a siege and what is Troy?'
                                    Whereat
He piled up chairs and tables for a town,
Set me a-top for Priam, called our cat
—Helen, enticed away from home (he said)
By wicked Paris, who couched somewhere close
Under the footstool, being cowardly,
But whom—since she was worth the pains, poor puss—   10
Towzer and Tray,—our dogs, the Atreidai,—sought
By taking Troy to get possession of
—Always when great Achilles ceased to sulk,
(My pony in the stable)—forth would prance
And put to flight Hector—our page-boy's self.
This taught me who was who and what was what:
So far I rightly understood the case
At five years old: a huge delight it proved
And still proves—thanks to that instructor sage
My Father, who knew better than turn straight   20
Learning's full flare on weak-eyed ignorance,
Or, worse yet, leave weak eyes to grow sand-blind,
Content with darkness and vacuity.

It happened, two or three years afterward,
That—I and playmates playing at Troy's Siege—
My Father came upon our make-believe.
'How would you like to read yourself the tale
Properly told, of which I gave you first
Merely such notion as a boy could bear?
Pope, now, would give you the precise account   30
Of what, some day, by dint of scholarship,
You'll hear—who knows?—from Homer's very mouth.
Learn Greek by all means, read the "Blind Old Man,
Sweetest of Singers"—*tuphlos* which means "blind,"
Hedistos which means "sweetest," Time enough!
Try, anyhow, to master him some day;
Until when, take what serves for substitute,
Read Pope, by all means!'
                                    So I ran through Pope,
Enjoyed the tale—what history so true?

Also attacked my Primer, duly drudged,   40
Grew fitter thus for what was promised next—
The very thing itself, the actual words,
When I could turn—say, Buttmann to account.

Time passed, I ripened somewhat: one fine day,
'Quite ready for the Iliad, nothing less?
There's Heine, where the big books block the shelf:
Don't skip a word, thumb well the Lexicon!'

I thumbed well and skipped nowise till I learned
Who was who, what was what, from Homer's tongue,
And there an end of learning. Had you asked   50
The all-accomplished scholar, twelve years old,
'Who was it wrote the Iliad?'—what a laugh!
'Why, Homer, all the world knows: of his life
Doubtless some facts exist: it's everywhere:
We have not settled, though, his place of birth:
He begged, for certain, and was blind beside:
Seven cities claimed him—Scio, with best right,
Thinks Byron. What he wrote? Those Hymns we have.
Then there's the "Battle of the Frogs and Mice,"
That's all—unless they dig "Margites" up   60
(I'd like that) nothing more remains to know.'

Thus did youth spend a comfortable time;
Until—'What's this the Germans say is fact
That Wolf found out first? It's unpleasant work
Their chop and change, unsettling one's belief:
All the same, while we live, we learn, that's sure.'
So, I bent brow o'er *Prolegomena*.
And, after Wolf, a dozen of his like
Proved there was never any Troy at all,
Neither Besiegers nor Besieged,—nay, worse,—   70
No actual Homer, no authentic text,
No warrant for the fiction I, as fact,
Had treasured in my heart and soul so long—
Ay, mark you! and as fact held still, still hold,
Spite of new knowledge, in my heart of hearts
And soul of souls, fact's essence freed and fixed
From accidental fancy's guardian sheath.
Assuredly thenceforward—thank my stars!—
However it got there, deprive who could—
Wring from the shrine my precious tenantry,   80
Helen, Ulysses, Hector and his Spouse,

Achilles and his Friend?—though Wolf—ah, Wolf!
Why must he needs come doubting, spoil a dream?

But then 'No dream's worth waking'—Browning says:
And here's the reason why I tell thus much.
I, now mature man, you anticipate,
May blame my Father justifiably
For letting me dream out my nonage thus,
And only by such slow and sure degrees
Permitting me to sift the grain from chaff,   90
Get truth and falsehood known and named as such.
Why did he ever let me dream at all,
Not bid me taste the story in its strength?
Suppose my childhood was scarce qualified
To rightly understand mythology,
Silence at least was in his power to keep:
I might have—somehow—correspondingly—
Well, who knows by what method, gained my gains,
Been taught, by forthrights not meanderings,
My aim should be to loathe, like Peleus' son,   100
A lie as Hell's Gate, love my wedded wife,
Like Hector, and so on with all the rest.
Could not I have excogitated this
Without believing such men really were?
That is—he might have put into my hand
The 'Ethics'? In translation, if you please,
Exact, no pretty lying that improves,
To suit the modern taste: no more, no less—
The 'Ethics': 't is a treatise I find hard
To read aright now that my hair is grey,   110
And I can manage the original.
At five years old—how ill had fared its leaves!
Now, growing double o'er the Stagirite,
At least I soil no page with bread and milk,
Nor crumple, dogsear and deface—boys' way.

(Wr. 1888–9?; pub. 1889)

126   *Inapprehensiveness*

WE two stood simply friend-like side by side,
Viewing a twilight country far and wide,
Till she at length broke silence. 'How it towers
Yonder, the ruin o'er this vale of ours!

The West's faint flare behind it so relieves
Its rugged outline—sight perhaps deceives,
Or I could almost fancy that I see
A branch wave plain—belike some wind-sown tree
Chance-rooted where a missing turret was.
What would I give for the perspective glass   10
At home, to make out if 't is really so!
Has Ruskin noticed here at Asolo
That certain weed-growths on the ravaged wall
Seem' . . . something that I could not say at all,
My thought being rather—as absorbed she sent
Look onward after look from eyes distent
With longing to reach Heaven's gate left ajar—
'Oh, fancies that might be, oh, facts that are!
What of a wilding? By you stands, and may
So stand unnoticed till the Judgment Day,   20
One who, if once aware that your regard
Claimed what his heart holds,—woke, as from its sward
The flower, the dormant passion, so to speak—
Then what a rush of life would startling wreak
Revenge on your inapprehensive stare
While, from the ruin and the West's faint flare,
You let your eyes meet mine, touch what you term
Quietude—that's an universe in germ—
The dormant passion needing but a look
To burst into immense life!'   30
                             'No, the book
Which noticed how the wall-growths wave' said she
'Was not by Ruskin.'
                I said 'Vernon Lee?'

(Wr. and pub. 1889)

EBENEZER JONES

1820–1860

127   *High Summer*

I NEVER wholly feel that summer is high,
However green the trees, or loud the birds,
However movelessly eye-winking herds
Stand in field ponds, or under large trees lie,

Till I do climb all cultured pastures by,
That hedged by hedgerows studiously fretted trim,
Smile like a lady's face with lace laced prim,
And on some moor or hill that seeks the sky
Lonely and nakedly,—utterly lie down,
And feel the sunshine throbbing on body and limb,   10
My drowsy brain in pleasant drunkenness swim,
Each rising thought sink back and dreamily drown,
Smiles creep o'er my face, and smother my lips, and cloy,
Each muscle sink to itself, and separately enjoy.

          (1843)

128   *Whimper of Awakening Passion*

YOUR hands made a tent o'er mine eyes,
  As low in your lap I was lain,
Perhaps half from yourself to disguise
  The prayer that they could not restrain.

You sang, and your voice through me waved
  Such rapture, I heard myself say,
'Oh here is the heaven I have craved,
  Never hence will I wander astray.'

As I lay in your lap your limbs gave
  Such beautiful smooth rest to me,   10
I told you that thus to be slave
  I would never consent to be free.

But now mine eyes under their tent
  Think such distance from yours, love, is wrong;
And my mouth wants your mouth to be sent
  Down to him, all undrest, love, of song.

Oh I fear if your beautiful limbs
  Still to have me their slave feel inclined,
You must either prevent all these whims,
  Or a way, love, to humour them find.   20

          (1843)

129 *Eyeing the Eyes of One's Mistress*

WHEN down the crowded aisle my wandering eyes
'Lighted on thine fix'd scanningly on my face,
They struck not passion fire, but in their place
Did settlingly fix themselves, contemplative-wise,
Thine eyes to fathom;—for as one that lies
On mountain side where thick-leaved branches vein
'Twixt him and the sun, and gazes o'er the plain
That wide beneath him variedly amplifies;
I think my being was elevatedly lain
On its own thought, and in thy being gazing   10
With tranquil speculation, that did gain
Singular delight: thus mine eyes thine appraising,
By dial reckoning, only a moment spent;
Whole ages by the heart's right measurement.

But when thine eyelids bent into thy gaze
Nearing regard and instigating light;
Their lashes narrowing o'er the dewy blaze
That suddenly thine eyes did appetite;
Narrowing as if thou fear'd'st to invite
Too utterly, but truly that their motion   20
Caressingly closing faintly, might excite
My tranquil gaze to passionate devotion;—
Then suddenly seemed I an infinite life;
Infinitely falling down before thy shrine;
Infinitely praying thy descent; the strife
Of the aisle's crowd seem'd gone; thine eyes and mine,
Devouring distance, into each other grew;
While thine unfeigning lids gloriously upward flew.

(1843)

JOHN CLARE
1793–1864

130 *Love's Pains*

I

THIS love, I canna' bear it,
It cheats me night and day;
This love, I canna' wear it,
It takes my peace away.

2

This love, wa' once a flower;
But now it is a thorn,—
The joy o' evening hour,
Turn'd to a pain e're morn.

3

This love, it wa' a bud,
And a secret known to me;   10
Like a flower within a wood;
Like a nest within a tree.

4

This love, wrong understood,
Oft' turned my joy to pain;
I tried to throw away the bud,
But the blossom would remain.

(Wr. 1844; pub. 1949)

131   *I've Had Many an Aching Pain*

1

I'VE had many an aching pain,
A for sake o' somebody:
I have talked, but o' in vain,
When I thought o' somebody.

2

Nought could please me any where,
I could heed nor smile, nor tear;
And yet I sighed, for half a year!
And that for sake o' somebody.

3

She was like the lily fair,
The rose it blushed, for somebody;   10
Her neck was white, her cheek was rare,
I wot it smiled on somebody;—

4

Here's good luck to somebody;
And best o' health for somebody;
The dearest thought I keep mysell,
I keep for sake o' somebody.

(Wr. 1844; pub. 1984)

132   *Stanzas*

1

BLACK absence hides upon the past
    I quite forget thy face
And memory like the angry blast
    Will love's last smile erace
I try to think of what has been
    But all is blank to me
And other faces pass between
    My early love and thee

2

I try to trace thy memory now
    And only find thy name   10
Those inky lashes on thy brow
    Black hair, and eyes the same
Thy round pale face of snowy dyes
    There's nothing paints thee there
A darkness comes before my eyes
    For nothing seems so fair

3

I knew thy name so sweet and young
    'Twas music to my ears
A silent word upon my tongue
    A hidden thought for years   20
Dark hair and lashes swarthy too
    Arched on thy forehead pale
All else is vanished from my view
    Like voices on the gale

(Wr. 1844?; pub. 1949)

133   *A Vision*

1

I LOST the love, of heaven above;
I spurn'd the lust, of earth below;
I felt the sweets of fancied love,—
And hell itself my only foe.

2

I lost earths joys, but felt the glow,
Of heaven's flame abound in me:
'Till loveliness, and I did grow,
The bard of immortality.

3

I loved, but woman fell away;
I hid me, from her faded fame: 10
I snatch'd the sun's eternal ray,—
And wrote 'till earth was but a name.

4

In every language upon earth,
On every shore, o'er every sea;
I gave my name immortal birth,
And kep't my spirit with the free.

                              (Wr. 1844; pub. 1924)

134   THE thunder mutters louder & more loud
           With quicker motion hay folks ply the rake
           Ready to burst slow sails the pitch black cloud
           & all the gang a bigger haycock make
           To sit beneath—the woodland winds awake
           The drops so large wet all thro' in an hour
           A tiney flood runs down the leaning rake
           In the sweet hay yet dry the hay folks cower
           & some beneath the waggon shun the shower

                              (Wr. 1845; pub. 1984)

135　*The Old Year*

1

THE Old Year's gone away
To nothingness and night
We cannot find him all the day
Nor hear him in the night
He left no footstep mark or place
In either shade or sun
Tho' last year he'd a neighbours face
In this he's known by none

2

All nothing every where
Mists we on mornings see　　　　　　　　　10
They have more substance when they're here
And more of form than he
He was a friend by every fire
In every cot and hall
A guest to every hearts desire
And now he's nought at all

3

Old papers thrown away
Or garments cast aside
E'en the talk of yesterday
Are things identified　　　　　　　　　　20
But time once torn away
No voices can recall
The eve of new years day
Left the old one lost to all

(Wr. 1845; pub. 1873)

136　　　　　*'I Am'*

1

I AM—yet what I am, none cares or knows;
　My friends forsake me like a memory lost:—
I am the self-consumer of my woes;—
　They rise and vanish in oblivion's host,
Like shadows in love's frenzied stifled throes:—
And yet I am, and live—like vapours tost

2

Into the nothingness of scorn and noise,—
  Into the living sea of waking dreams,
Where there is neither sense of life or joys,
  But the vast shipwreck of my lifes esteems;   10
Even the dearest, that I love the best
Are strange—nay, rather stranger than the rest.

3

I long for scenes, where man hath never trod
  A place where woman never smiled or wept
There to abide with my Creator, God;
  And sleep as I in childhood, sweetly slept,
Untroubling, and untroubled where I lie,
The grass below—above the vaulted sky.

                 (Wr. 1846; pub. 1848)

137

The Winters Spring

1

THE winter comes I walk alone
I want no birds to sing
To those who keep their hearts their own
The winter is the Spring
No flowers to please—no bees to hum
The coming Springs already come

2

I never want the christmas rose
To come before its time
The seasons each as God bestows
Are simple and sublime   10
I love to see the snow storm hing
'Tis but the winter garb of Spring

3

I never want the grass to bloom
The snow-storm's best in white
I love to see the tempest come
And love its piercing light
The dazzled eyes that love to cling
O'er snow white meadows sees the Spring

137 hing] hang

169

4

I love the snow the crimpling snow
That hangs on every thing   20
It covers every thing below
Like white doves brooding wing
A landscape to the aching sight
A vast expance of dazzling light

5

It is the foliage of the woods
That winter's bring—The dress
White easter of the year in bud
That makes the winter Spring
The frost and snow his poseys bring
Natures white spirits of the Spring   30

(Wr. 1847; pub. 1949)

138   *Hesperus*

1

HESPERUS the day is gone
Soft falls the silent dew
A tear is now on many a flower
And heaven lives in you

2

Hesperus the evening mild
Falls round us soft and sweet
'Tis like the breathings of a child
When day and evening meet

3

Hesperus the closing flower
Sleeps on the dewy ground   10
While dews fall in a silent shower
And heaven breathes around

4

Hesperus thy twinkling ray
Beams in the blue of heaven
And tells the traveller on his way
That earth shall be forgiven

(Wr. and pub. 1847)

139   *An Invite to Eternity*

1

WILT thou go with me sweet maid
Say maiden wilt thou go with me
Through the valley depths of shade
Of night and dark obscurity
Where the path hath lost its way
Where the sun forgets the day
Where there's nor life nor light to see
Sweet maiden wilt thou go with me

2

Where stones will turn to flooding streams
Where plains will rise like ocean waves   10
Where life will fade like visioned dreams
And mountains darken into caves
Say maiden wilt thou go with me
Through this sad non-identity
Where parents live and are forgot
And sisters live and know us not

3

Say maiden wilt thou go with me
In this strange death of life to be
To live in death and be the same
Without this life, or home, or name   20
At once to be, & not to be
That was, and is not—yet to see
Things pass like shadows—and the sky
Above, below, around us lie

4

The land of shadows wilt thou trace
And look—nor know each others face
The present mixed with reasons gone
And past, and present all as one
Say maiden can thy life be led
To join the living with the dead   30
Then trace thy footsteps on with me
We're wed to one eternity

(Wr. 1847–8; pub. 1848)

140 *The Shepherd Boy*

1

THE fly or beetle on their track
Are things that know no sin
And when they whemble on their back
What terror they seem in
The shepherd boy wi' bits o' bents
Will turn them up again
And start them where they nimbly went
Along the grassy plain
And such the shepherd boy is found
While lying on the sun crackt ground   10

2

The lady-bird that seldom stops
From climbing all the day
Climbs up the rushes tassle tops
Spreads wings and flies away
He sees them—lying on the grass
Musing the whole day long
And clears the way to let them pass
And sings a nameless song
He watches pismires on the hill
Always busy never still   20

3

He sees the traveller beetle run
Where thick the grass wood weaves
To hide the black-snail from the sun
He props up plantain leaves
The lady-cows have got a house
Within the cowslip pip
The spider weaving for his spouse
On threads will often slip
So looks and lyes the shepherd boy
The summer long his whole employ—   30

(Wr. 1848; pub. 1964)

whemble] turn upside down   pip] single blossom in a flower-head

141   *Evening*

                             1

'TIS evening, the black snail has got on his track,
And gone to its nest is the wren;—
And the packman snail too, with his home on his back;
Clings on the bowed bents like a wen.

                             2

The shepherd has made a rude mark with his foot,
Where his shaddow reached when he first came;
And it just touched the tree where his secret love cut,
Two letters that stand for love's name.

                             3

The evening comes in with the wishes of love;—
And the shepherd he looks on the flowers;—   10
And thinks who would praise the soft song of the dove,
And meet joy in these dewfalling hours.

                             4

For nature is love, and the wishers of love;
When nothing can hear or intrude;
It hides from the eagle, and joins with the dove:
In beautiful green solitude.

                              (Wr. 1842–64; pub. 1873)

142   *Sonnet: 'I am'*

    I FEEL I am;—I only know I am,
    And plod upon the earth, as dull and void:
    Earth's prison chilled my body with its dram
    Of dullness, and my soaring thoughts destroyed,
    I fled to solitudes from passions dream,
    But strife persued—I only know, I am,
    I was a being created in the race
    Of men disdaining bounds of place and time:—
    A spirit that could travel o'er the space
    Of earth and heaven,—like a thought sublime,   10
    Tracing creation, like my maker, free,—
    A soul unshackled—like eternity,
    Spurning earth's vain and soul debasing thrall
    But now I only know I am,—that's all.

                              (Wr. 1842–64; pub. 1935)

143   *Stanzas*

1

THE passing of a dream
　　Are the thoughts I have to day
Cloud shadows they all seem
　　And pass as soon away
Their meaning and their shade
　　I cannot well define
The little left unsaid
　　Seems others, and not mine

2

Here's a place so dainty dress't
　　That o'er my vision swim   10
Like a land in the far west
　　But alas my vision's dim
The trees are not the trees
　　Under which I used to play
And the flowers they cannot please
　　For I am sad to day

3

Here's the shumac all on fire
　　Like hot coals amid the green
It might please my heart's desire
　　If elsewhere the place had been   20
Here dreams their troubles make
　　To a body without pain
When shall my mind awake
　　In its own loved scenes again

(Wr. 1842–64; pub. 1935)

144 *Song*

1

SOFT falls the sweet evening
  Bright shines the one star
The night clouds they're leaning
  On mountains afar
The moon in dim brightness
  The fern in its lightness
Tinge the valley with whiteness
  Both near and afar

2

O soft falls the evening
  Around those sweet glens   10
The hill's shadows leaning
  Half over the glen
There meet me my deary
  I'm lonely and weary
And nothing can cheer me
  So meet me agen

3

The gate it clap'd slightly
  The noise it was small
The footstep fell lightly
  And she pass'd the stone wall   20
And is it my deary
  I'm no longer weary
But happy and cheery
  For in thee I meet all

(Wr. 1842–64; pub. 1984)

145 *To Miss B*

1

ODD rot it what a shame it is
  That love should puzzles grow
That we the one we seek should miss
  And change from top to toe
    The Gilafers a Gilafer
And nature owns the plan
And strange a thing it is to me
A man cant be a man

175

2

I traced the woods and mountains brow
And felt as feels a man   10
Love pleased me then that puzzles now
    E'en do the best I can
Nature her same green mantle spread
    And boundless is her span
The same bright sun is o'er my head
    But I can't be a man

3

The turf is green and fair the sky
And nature still divine
And summot lovely fills my eye
Just like this love of mine   20
And though I love—it may not be
For do the best I can
Mong such disordered company
I cannot be a man

4

Th[r]ough married ties—affections ties
And all the ties of love
I struggled to be just and wise
But just I cannot prove
The Bible says that God is love
I like so wise a plan   30
But was it ordered from above
That love was [not] wi' man

5

This contradiction puzzles me
And it may puzzle all
Was Adam thus fore doomed to be
Our misery by his fall
Eves fall has been a fall to me
And do the best I can
Woman—I neither love nor see
And cannot be a man   40

(Wr. 1842–64; pub. 1964)

146 *Hymn to the Creator*

1

ALMIGHTY creator and ruler as well
Of the earth and the heaven and darkness and hell
We adore thee—and worship as simple as when
Adam knelt in the garden the first of all men
The God of that sun that yet brings the broad day
When Eve the first flower in the first garden lay
That mercy that yet ever falls from the sky
Says that the meanest of beings never shall die

2

Almighty creator of all we behold
The mountains bare rock and the meadows all gold   10
The wilderness old and the desert of sand
Are his in his glory and wild barren land
To cheer and to cherish in wonder and love
The earth well as heaven, his dwellings above
Almighty creator to seek and to save
We need from the cradle thy help to the grave

3

We need thee and fear thee so ought we to fear
When thou hast no mercy none other will hear
And mercy thou shewest every day to our land
In keeping us all as the work of thy hand   20
In helping the feeble in seeking the lost
For man neither springs from a pillar or post
But breath[e]s from his father eternally yet
His hell or his heaven in mercy is met

4

Almighty creator of heaven and earth
Creations protector its life and its birth
In thee all began and in thee all have end
Our father at first and at last the one friend
We love and adore thee or ought so to do
From the sunrise of morning to evenings bright dew   30
Through morning and evening and blackest midnight
Thou'rt our faith in nights darkness and love in morns light

(Wr. 1842–64; pub. 1984)

147   THERE is a charm in Solitude that cheers
A feeling that the world knows nothing of
A green delight the wounded mind endears
After the hustling world is broken off
Whose whole delight was crime at good to scoff
Green solitude his prison pleasure yields
The bitch fox heeds him not—birds seem to laugh
He lives the Crusoe of his lonely fields
Which dark green oaks his noontide leisure shields

(Wr. 1842–64; pub. 1949)

148   *Song*

1

I WENT my Sunday mornings rounds
   One pleasant summer day
And stood i' the green meadow grounds
   'Mong cocks and swaths o' hay
Up the green rush the Lady bird
   Clomb to its very tops
And there the crickets songs were heard
   Like organs without stops

2

The sun was climbing up the sky
   A looking glass of gold   10
It melts and quivers on the eye
   And blinds us to behold
Melting and shining to its height
   It shines from pole to pole
And sliddering down at dewy night
   Goes out a dying coal

3

I stood among the swathes and cocks
   How sweet the light did seem
When a sweet lass with inky locks
   Came tripping by the stream   20
Sweet one I said I do prefer
   To ask you why you walk
'Tis merely for my pleasure sir
   As you stand there to talk

4

The wind came from the southern sky
   And tokened flying showers
The busy bee and butterfly
   Her ribbons took for flowers
The wasp it buzzed about her mouth
   Her lips seemed cherries red   30
The wind shook from the balmy south
   The curls about her head

5

Young man she said you'l marry me
   And waited for reply
Why yes my dear but do'nt you see
   Love is the stronger tie
And then I kissed her lips and cheeks
   And made her merry hearted
I wed the maid in just three weeks
   From the first day we parted   40

(Wr. 1842–64; pub. 1964)

149   *First Love*

I NE'ER was struck before that hour
   With love so sudden and so sweet
Her face it bloomed like a sweet flower
   And stole my heart away complete
My face turned pale a deadly pale
   My legs refused to walk away
And when she looked what could I ail
My life and all seemed turned to clay

2

And then my blood rushed to my face
   And took my eyesight quite away   10
The trees and bushes round the place
   Seemed midnight at noon day
I could not see a single thing
   Words from my eyes did start
They spoke as chords do from the string
   And blood burnt round my heart

3

Are flowers the winters choice
Is love's bed always snow
She seemed to hear my silent voice
Not loves appeals to know   20
I never saw so sweet a face
As that I stood before
My heart has left its dwelling place
And can return no more—

(Wr. 1842–64; pub. 1920)

150   *Song*

I HID my love when young while I
Coud'nt bear the buzzing of a flye
I hid my love to my despite
Till I could not bear to look at light
I dare not gaze upon her face
But left her memory in each place
Where ere I saw a wild flower lye
I kissed and bade my love good bye

I met her in the greenest dells
Where dew drops pearl the wood blue bells   10
The lost breeze kissed her bright blue eye
The Bee kissed and went singing bye
A sun beam found a passage there
A gold chain round her neck so fair
As secret as the wild bees song
She lay there all the summer long

I hid my love in field and town
Till e'en the breeze would knock me down
The Bees seemed singing ballads oe'r
The flyes buzz turned a Lions roar   20
And even silence found a tongue
To haunt me all the summer long
The Riddle nature could not prove
Was nothing else but secret love

(Wr. 1842–64; pub. 1920)

151 ## *Song*

I WISH I was where I would be
With love alone to dwell
Was I but her or she but me
Then love would all be well

I wish to send my thoughts to her
As quick as thoughts can fly
But as the winds the waters stir
The mirrors change & flye

(Wr. 1842–64; pub. 1920)

152 ## *Fragment*

LOVE'S memories haunt my footsteps still
    Like ceaseless flowings of the river
Its mystic depths say what can fill?
    Sad disappointment waits for ever

(Wr. 1842–64; pub. 1949)

153 ## *The Yellowhammer*

WHEN shall I see the white thorn leaves agen
And Yellowhammers gath'ring the dry bents
By the Dyke side on stilly moor or fen
Feathered wi love and natures good intents
Rude is the nest this Architect invents
Rural the place wi cart ruts by dyke side
Dead grass, horse hair and downy headed bents
Tied to dead thistles she doth well provide
Close to a hill o' ants where cowslips bloom
And shed o'er meadows far their sweet perfume   10
In early Spring when winds blow chilly cold
The yellow hammer trailing grass will come
To fix a place and choose an early home
With yellow breast and head of solid gold

(Wr. 1842–64; pub. 1920)

154   *Song*

THE mist rauk is hanging
Over turnip fields green
The wood gate is banging
Where hunters are seen
The brown leaves are dancing
About on the green
The horses are prancing
Where the hounds hurry in

Where Lucy stands knocking
Her clogs at the gate   10
Bright shoes & white stocking
Are killing of late
Wi cotton or silk on
What man could forbear
Where Lucy sits milking
To kiss if he dare

The Maples turn yellow
Hazels crimson & brown
Oaks still keep their colour
Popples fade & fall down   20
When a milking goes Lucy
Where woodbramble weaves
T[he] winds wont excuse ye
But pelts her wi leaves

On her new gown and bonnet
They patter and fall
Leaving no stain upon it
They pat and thats all
Crows quawk & swoop over
Like chimney sweep crows   30
Lucy milks under cover
Nor sullies her clothes

Home rambles young Lucy
With her milk buckets twain
Oer grass fields were dews be
And rut brimming lane

rauk] mist, fog   Popples] poplars

She sings songs till sunday
When she offers her vows
And in drab frock on monday
Goes milking the cows   40

(Wr. 1842–64; pub. 1984)

155   *An Anecdote of Love*

WHEN April & dew brings primroses here
I think love of you at the Spring o' the year
Did I harbour bad words when your garter fell off
I to stoop was deterred but I stood not to scoff
A bitt of brown list of small value must be
But as it lay there 'twas a diamond to me

Ere back you turned to pick it up
I noticed well the place
For children there for violets stoop
With many a rosey face   10
I fain would stoop myself you see
But dare not well presume
The Blackbird sung out let it be
The maid was in her bloom

How beautiful that ancle was
From which that garter fell
And lusty was the bonny lass
Whose name I dare not tell
I know the colour of her gown
Her bonnet Ribbon too   20
The fairest maiden in the town
Is she that wears the blue

Though years have gone but when I see
The green spot where it fell
The stitchwort flower delighteth me
There blooming in the dell
And years may come no winter seers
The green haunts of the Dove
Those wild flowers stand the bl[i]ght of years
Sweet anecdotes of love—   30

(Wr. 1842–64; pub. 1964)

JOHN RUSKIN
1819–1900

156   *La Madonna dell' Acqua*

In the centre of the lagoon between Venice and the mouths of the Brenta, supported on a few mouldering piles, stands a small shrine dedicated to the Madonna dell' Acqua, which the gondolier never passes without a prayer.

AROUND her shrine no earthly blossoms blow,
No footsteps fret the pathway to and fro;
No sign nor record of departed prayer,
Print of the stone, nor echo of the air;
Worn by the lip, nor wearied by the knee,—
Only a deeper silence of the sea:
For there, in passing, pause the breezes bleak,
And the foam fades, and all the waves are weak.
The pulse-like oars in softer fall succeed,
The black prow falters through the wild seaweed—   10
Where, twilight-borne, the minute thunders reach
Of deep-mouthed surf, that bays by Lido's beach,
With intermittent motion traversed far,
And shattered glancing of the western star,
Till the faint storm-bird on the heaving flow
Drops in white circles, silently like snow.
Not here the ponderous gem, nor pealing note,
Dim to adorn—insentient to adore—
But purple-dyed, the mists of evening float,
In ceaseless incense from the burning floor   20
Of ocean, and the gathered gold of heaven
Laces its sapphire vault, and, early given,
The white rays of the rushing firmament
Pierce the blue-quivering night through wreath or rent
Of cloud inscrutable and motionless,
Hectic and wan, and moon-companioned cloud!
Oh! lone Madonna—angel of the deep—
When the night falls, and deadly winds are loud,
Will not thy love be with us while we keep
Our watch upon the waters, and the gaze   30
Of thy soft eyes, that slumber not, nor sleep?
Deem not thou, stranger, that such trust is vain;
Faith walks not on these weary waves alone,
Though weakness dread, or apathy disdain
The spot which God has hallowed for His own.

They sin who pass it lightly—ill divining
The glory of this place of bitter prayer;
And hoping against hope, and self-resigning,
And reach of faith, and wrestling with despair,
And resurrection of the last distress,   40
Into the sense of heaven, when earth is bare,
And of God's voice, when man's is comfortless.

(Wr. 1844; pub. 1845)

157   *The Zodiac Song*

1. *Aries* (sings) . . .   Horn for weapon, and wool for shield,
Windy weather and lambs afield.

2. *Taurus* . . . . .   Head in the sunshine, hoof in the hay,
Toss the last of the clouds away.

3. *Gemini* . . . . .   Double in leaf and double in light,
Flowers by day, and stars by night.

4. *Cancer* . . . . .   Cancer, Cancer, crooked and black,
Answer us, answer us—Forward or back?

5. *Leo* . . . . . .   Fierce at eve, at morning tame,
Crest of cloud, and claws of flame.   10

6. *Virgo* . . . . .   Sickle in hand, and sandal on feet,
Crowned with poppy, and swathed with
wheat.

7. *Libra* . . . . .   Libra, Libra, truth is treasure,
Fair the weight and full the measure.

8. *Scorpio* . . . . .   Sharp the sting, but grand the grief,
Shivering bough, and burning leaf.

9. *Sagittarius* . . .   Numb the finger: narrow the mark,
Frost on the feather, and flight in the dark.

10. *Capricorn* . . . .   Capricorn, Capricorn,
Cowardly heart, and crumpled horn.   20

11. *Aquarius* . . . .   Snow to flicker, or rain to fall,
Down with thy pitcher, and out with it all.

12. *Pisces* . . . . .   Fish, little fish, lying head to tail,
Daisies round the dish and a pearl on every
scale.

(Wr. *c*.1865; pub. 1903)

THOMAS BABINGTON MACAULAY
1800–1859

158   *Epitaph on a Jacobite*

TO my true king I offered free from stain
Courage and faith; vain faith, and courage vain.
For him, I threw lands, honours, wealth, away,
And one dear hope, that was more prized than they.
For him I languished in a foreign clime,
Grey-haired with sorrow in my manhood's prime;
Heard on Lavernia Scargill's whispering trees,
And pined by Arno for my lovelier Tees;
Beheld each night my home in fevered sleep,
Each morning started from the dream to weep;   10
Till God, who saw me tried too sorely, gave
The resting place I asked, an early grave.
Oh thou, whom chance leads to this nameless stone,
From that proud country which was once mine own,
By those white cliffs I never more must see,
By that dear language which I spake like thee,
Forget all feuds, and shed one English tear
O'er English dust. A broken heart lies here.

(Wr. 1845; pub. 1860)

LEWIS CARROLL
(CHARLES LUTWIDGE DODGSON)
1832–1898

159   *Rules and Regulations*

A SHORT direction
To avoid dejection,
By variations
In occupations,
And prolongation
Of relaxation,

And combinations
Of recreations,
And disputation
On the state of the nation   10
In adaptation
To your station,
By invitations
To friends and relations,
By evitation
Of amputation,
By permutation
In conversation,
And deep reflection
You'll avoid dejection.   20

Learn well your grammar,
And never stammer,
Write well and neatly,
And sing most sweetly,
Be enterprising,
Love early rising,
Go walk of six miles,
Have ready quick smiles,
With lightsome laughter,
Soft flowing after.   30
Drink tea, not coffee;
Never eat toffy.
Eat bread with butter.
Once more, don't stutter.
Don't waste your money,
Abstain from honey.
Shut doors behind you,
(Don't slam them, mind you.)
Drink beer, not porter.
Don't enter the water   40
Till to swim you are able.
Sit close to the table.
Take care of a candle.
Shut a door by the handle,
Don't push with your shoulder
Until you are older.
Lose not a button.
Refuse cold mutton.
Starve your canaries.
Believe in fairies.   50

If you are able,
Don't have a stable
With any mangers.
Be rude to strangers.

Moral: Behave.

(Wr. 1845; pub. 1954)

160   THEY told me you had been to her,
           And mentioned me to him:
        She gave me a good character,
           But said I could not swim.

        He sent them word I had not gone
           (We know it to be true):
        If she should push the matter on,
           What would become of you?

        I gave her one, they gave him two,
           You gave us three or more;   10
        They all returned from him to you,
           Though they were mine before.

        If I or she should chance to be
           Involved in this affair,
         He trusts to you to set them free,
           Exactly as we were.

        My notion was that you had been
           (Before she had this fit)
        An obstacle that came between
           Him, and ourselves, and it.   20

        Don't let him know she liked them best,
           For this must ever be
        A secret, kept from all the rest,
           Between yourself and me.

(1855)

161   How doth the little crocodile
           Improve his shining tail,
         And pour the waters of the Nile
           On every golden scale!

How cheerfully he seems to grin,
    How neatly spreads his claws,
And welcomes little fishes in,
    With gently smiling jaws!

(1865)

162 'YOU are old, Father William,' the young man said
        'And your hair has become very white;
    And yet you incessantly stand on your head—
        Do you think, at your age, it is right?'

'In my youth', Father William replied to his son,
    'I feared it might injure the brain;
But, now that I'm perfectly sure I have none,
    Why, I do it again and again.'

'You are old,' said the youth, 'as I mentioned before,
    And have grown most uncommonly fat;   10
Yet you turned a back-somersault in at the door—
    Pray, what is the reason of that?'

'In my youth', said the sage, as he shook his grey locks,
    'I kept all my limbs very supple
By the use of this ointment—one shilling the box—
    Allow me to sell you a couple?'

'You are old,' said the youth, 'and your jaws are too weak
    For anything tougher than suet;
Yet you finished the goose, with the bones and the beak—
    Pray, how did you manage to do it?'   20

'In my youth', said his father, 'I took to the law,
    And argued each case with my wife;
And the muscular strength, which it gave to my jaw
    Has lasted the rest of my life.'

'You are old,' said the youth, 'one would hardly suppose
    That your eye was as steady as ever;
Yet you balanced an eel on the end of your nose—
    What made you so awfully clever?'

'I have answered three questions, and that is enough,'
   Said his father, 'Don't give yourself airs!   30
Do you think I can listen all day to such stuff?
   Be off, or I'll kick you down-stairs!'

(1865)

163   *Jabberwocky*

'TWAS brillig, and the slithy toves
   Did gyre and gimble in the wabe:
All mimsy were the borogoves,
   And the mome raths outgrabe.

'Beware the Jabberwock, my son!
   The jaws that bite, the claws that catch!
Beware the Jubjub bird, and shun
   The frumious Bandersnatch!'

He took his vorpal sword in hand:
   Long time the manxome foe he sought—   10
So rested he by the Tumtum tree,
   And stood awhile in thought.

And, as in uffish thought he stood,
   The Jabberwock, with eyes of flame,
Came whiffling through the tulgey wood,
   And burbled as it came!

One, two! One, two! And through and through
   The vorpal blade went snicker-snack!
He left it dead, and with its head
   He went galumphing back.   20

'And hast thou slain the Jabberwock?
   Come to my arms, my beamish boy!
O frabjous day! Callooh! Callay!'
   He chortled in his joy.

'Twas brillig, and the slithy toves
   Did gyre and gimble in the wabe:
All mimsy were the borogoves,
   And the mome raths outgrabe.

(Wr. 1855 and 1867; pub. 1872)

THE sun was shining on the sea,
   Shining with all his might:
He did his very best to make
   The billows smooth and bright—
And this was odd, because it was
   The middle of the night.

The moon was shining sulkily,
   Because she thought the sun
Had got no business to be there
   After the day was done—   10
'It's very rude of him', she said,
   'To come and spoil the fun!'

The sea was wet as wet could be,
   The sands were dry as dry.
You could not see a cloud, because
   No cloud was in the sky:
No birds were flying overhead—
   There were no birds to fly.

The Walrus and the Carpenter
   Were walking close at hand:
They wept like anything to see   20
   Such quantities of sand:
'If this were only cleared away,'
   They said, 'it *would* be grand!'

'If seven maids with seven mops
   Swept it for half a year,
Do you suppose', the Walrus said,
   'That they could get it clear?'
'I doubt it,' said the Carpenter,
   And shed a bitter tear.   30

'O Oysters, come and walk with us!'
   The Walrus did beseech.
'A pleasant walk, a pleasant talk,
   Along the briny beach:
We cannot do with more than four,
   To give a hand to each.'

The eldest Oyster looked at him,
   But never a word he said:
The eldest Oyster winked his eye,
   And shook his heavy head— 40
Meaning to say he did not choose
   To leave the oyster-bed.

But four young Oysters hurried up,
   All eager for the treat:
Their coats were brushed, their faces washed,
   Their shoes were clean and neat—
And this was odd, because, you know,
   They hadn't any feet.

Four other Oysters followed them,
   And yet another four; 50
And thick and fast they came at last,
   And more, and more, and more—
All hopping through the frothy waves,
   And scrambling to the shore.

The Walrus and the Carpenter
   Walked on a mile or so,
And then they rested on a rock
   Conveniently low:
And all the little Oysters stood
   And waited in a row. 60

'The time has come', the Walrus said,
   'To talk of many things:
Of shoes—and ships—and sealing wax—
   Of cabbages—and kings—
And why the sea is boiling hot—
   And whether pigs have wings.'

'But wait a bit,' the Oysters cried,
   'Before we have our chat;
For some of us are out of breath,
   And all of us are fat!' 70
'No hurry!' said the Carpenter.
   They thanked him much for that.

'A loaf of bread', the Walrus said,
  'Is what we chiefly need:
Pepper and vinegar besides
  Are very good indeed—
Now, if you're ready, Oysters dear,
  We can begin to feed.'

'But not on us!' the Oysters cried,
  Turning a little blue.   80
'After such kindness, that would be
  A dismal thing to do!'
'The night is fine,' the Walrus said.
  'Do you admire the view?

'It was so kind of you to come!
  And you are very nice!'
The Carpenter said nothing but
  'Cut us another slice.
I wish you were not quite so deaf—
  I've had to ask you twice!'   90

'It seems a shame', the Walrus said,
  'To play them such a trick.
After we've brought them out so far,
  And made them trot so quick!'
The Carpenter said nothing but
  'The butter's spread too thick!'

'I weep for you,' the Walrus said:
  'I deeply sympathize.'
With sobs and tears he sorted out
  Those of the largest size,   100
Holding his pocket-handkerchief
  Before his streaming eyes.

'O Oysters,' said the Carpenter,
  'You've had a pleasant run!
Shall we be trotting home again?'
  But answer came there none—
And this was scarcely odd, because
  They'd eaten every one.

(Wr. from 1869; pub. 1872)

165
IN winter, when the fields are white,
I sing this song for your delight—

In spring, when woods are getting green,
I'll try and tell you what I mean:

In summer, when the days are long,
Perhaps you'll understand the song:

In autumn, when the leaves are brown,
Take pen and ink, and write it down.

I sent a message to the fish:
I told them 'This is what I wish.'   10

The little fishes of the sea,
They sent an answer back to me.

The little fishes' answer was
'We cannot do it, Sir, because—'

I sent to them again to say
'It will be better to obey'.

The fishes answered, with a grin,
'Why, what a temper you are in!'

I told them once, I told them twice:
They would not listen to advice.   20

I took a kettle large and new,
Fit for the deed I had to do.

My heart went hop, my heart went thump:
I filled the kettle at the pump.

Then some one came to me and said
'The little fishes are in bed.'

I said to him, I said it plain,
'Then you must wake them up again.'

I said it very loud and clear:
I went and shouted in his ear.   30

But he was very stiff and proud:
He said, 'You needn't shout so loud!'

And he was very proud and stiff:
He said 'I'd go and wake them, if—'

I took a corkscrew from the shelf:
I went to wake them up myself.

And when I found the door was locked,
I pulled and pushed and kicked and knocked.

And when I found the door was shut,
I tried to turn the handle, but—   40

(Wr. from 1869; pub. 1872)

166   *The Hunting of the Snark*

FIT THE FIRST

The Landing

'JUST the place for a Snark!' the Bellman cried,
    As he landed his crew with care;
Supporting each man on the top of the tide
    By a finger entwined in his hair.

'Just the place for a Snark! I have said it twice:
    That alone should encourage the crew.
Just the place for a Snark! I have said it thrice:
    What I tell you three times is true.'

The crew was complete: it included a Boots—
    A maker of Bonnets and Hoods—   10
A Barrister, brought to arrange their disputes—
    And a Broker, to value their goods.

A Billiard-marker, whose skill was immense,
    Might perhaps have won more than his share—
But a Banker, engaged at enormous expense,
    Had the whole of their cash in his care.

195

There was also a Beaver, that paced on the deck,
　　Or would sit making lace in the bow:
And had often (the Bellman said) saved them from wreck
　　Though none of the sailors knew how.　　　　　　20

There was one who was famed for the number of things
　　He forgot when he entered the ship:
His umbrella, his watch, all his jewels and rings,
　　And the clothes he had bought for the trip.

He had forty-two boxes, all carefully packed,
　　With his name painted clearly on each:
But, since he omitted to mention the fact,
　　They were all left behind on the beach.

The loss of his clothes hardly mattered, because
　　He had seven coats on when he came,　　　　　　30
With three pair of boots—but the worst of it was,
　　He had wholly forgotten his name.

He would answer to 'Hi' or to any loud cry,
　　Such as 'Fry me!' or 'Fritter my wig!'
To 'What-you-may-call-um!' or 'What-was-his-name!'
　　But especially 'Thing-um-a-jig!'

While, for those who preferred a more forcible word,
　　He had different names from these:
His intimate friends called him 'Candle-ends',
　　And his enemies 'Toasted-cheese'.　　　　　　40

'His form is ungainly—his intellect small—'
　　(So the Bellman would often remark)—
'But his courage is perfect! And that, after all,
　　Is the thing that one needs with a Snark.'

He would joke with hyænas, returning their stare
　　With an impudent wag of the head:
And he once went a walk, paw-in-paw, with a bear,
　　'Just to keep up its spirits,' he said.

He came as a Baker: but owned, when too late—
　　And it drove the poor Bellman half-mad—　　　　　　50
He could only bake Bridecake—for which, I may state,
　　No materials were to be had.

The last of the crew needs especial remark,
   Though he looked an incredible dunce:
He had just one idea—but, that one being 'Snark',
   The good Bellman engaged him at once.

He came as a Butcher: but gravely declared,
   When the ship had been sailing a week,
He could only kill Beavers. The Bellman looked scared,
   And was almost too frightened to speak: 60

But at length he explained, in a tremulous tone,
   There was only one Beaver on board;
And that was a tame one he had of his own,
   Whose death would be deeply deplored.

The Beaver, who happened to hear the remark,
   Protested, with tears in its eyes,
That not even the rapture of hunting the Snark
   Could atone for that dismal surprise!

It strongly advised that the Butcher should be
   Conveyed in a separate ship: 70
But the Bellman declared that would never agree
   With the plans he had made for the trip:

Navigation was always a difficult art,
   Though with only one ship and one bell:
And he feared he must really decline, for his part,
   Undertaking another as well.

The Beaver's best course was, no doubt, to procure
   A second-hand dagger-proof coat—
So the Baker advised it—and next, to insure
   Its life in some Office of note: 80

This the Baker suggested, and offered for hire
   (On moderate terms), or for sale,
Two excellent Policies, one Against Fire
   And one Against Damage From Hail.

Yet still, ever after that sorrowful day,
   Whenever the Butcher was by,
The Beaver kept looking the opposite way,
   And appeared unaccountably shy.

Fit the Second

The Bellman's Speech

The Bellman himself they all praised to the skies—
 Such a carriage, such ease and such grace!
Such solemnity, too! One could see he was wise,
 The moment one looked in his face!

He had bought a large map representing the sea,
 Without the least vestige of land:
And the crew were much pleased when they found it to be
 A map they could all understand.

'What's the good of Mercator's North Poles and Equators,
 Tropics, Zones, and Meridian Lines?'   10
So the Bellman would cry: and the crew would reply
 'They are merely conventional signs!

'Other maps are such shapes, with their islands and capes!
 But we've got our brave Captain to thank'
(So the crew would protest) 'that he's bought *us* the best—
 A perfect and absolute blank!'

This was charming, no doubt: but they shortly found out
 That the Captain they trusted so well
Had only one notion for crossing the ocean,
 And that was to tingle his bell.   20

He was thoughtful and grave—but the orders he gave
 Were enough to bewilder a crew.
When he cried 'Steer to starboard, but keep her head larboard!'
 What on earth was the helmsman to do?

Then the bowsprit got mixed with the rudder sometimes:
 A thing, as the Bellman remarked,
That frequently happens in tropical climes,
 When a vessel is, so to speak, 'snarked'.

But the principal failing occurred in the sailing,
 And the Bellman, perplexed and distressed,   30
Said he *had* hoped, at least, when the wind blew due East,
 That the ship would *not* travel due West!

But the danger was past—they had landed at last,
　With their boxes, portmanteaus, and bags:
Yet at first sight the crew were not pleased with the view
　Which consisted of chasms and crags.

The Bellman perceived that their spirits were low,
　And repeated in musical tone
Some jokes he had kept for a season of woe—
　But the crew would do nothing but groan.　　40

He served out some grog with a liberal hand,
　And bade them sit down on the beach:
And they could not but own that their Captain looked grand,
　As he stood and delivered his speech.

'Friends, Romans, and countrymen, lend me your ears!'
　(They were all of them fond of quotations:
So they drank to his health, and they gave him three cheers,
　While he served out additional rations).

'We have sailed many months, we have sailed many weeks,
　(Four weeks to the month you may mark),　　50
But never as yet ('tis your Captain who speaks)
　Have we caught the least glimpse of a Snark!

'We have sailed many weeks, we have sailed many days,
　(Seven days to the week I allow),
But a Snark, on the which we might lovingly gaze,
　We have never beheld till now!

'Come, listen, my men, while I tell you again
　The five unmistakable marks
By which you may know, wheresoever you go,
　The warranted genuine Snarks.　　60

'Let us take them in order. The first is the taste,
　Which is meagre and hollow, but crisp:
Like a coat that is rather too tight in the waist,
　With a flavour of Will-o'-the-Wisp.

'Its habit of getting up late you'll agree
　That it carries too far, when I say
That it frequently breakfasts at five-o'clock tea,
　And dines on the following day.

'The third is its slowness in taking a jest.
    Should you happen to venture on one,   70
It will sigh like a thing that is deeply distressed:
    And it always looks grave at a pun.

'The fourth is its fondness for bathing-machines,
    Which it constantly carries about,
And believes that they add to the beauty of scenes—
    A sentiment open to doubt.

'The fifth is ambition. It next will be right
    To describe each particular batch:
Distinguishing those that have feathers, and bite,
    From those that have whiskers, and scratch.   80

'For, although common Snarks do no manner of harm,
    Yet I feel it my duty to say
Some are Boojums—' The Bellman broke off in alarm,
    For the Baker had fainted away.

Fit the Third

The Baker's Tale

THEY roused him with muffins—they roused him with ice—
    They roused him with mustard and cress—
They roused him with jam and judicious advice—
    They set him conundrums to guess.

When at length he sat up and was able to speak,
    His sad story he offered to tell;
And the Bellman cried 'Silence! Not even a shriek!'
    And excitedly tingled his bell.

There was silence supreme! Not a shriek, not a scream,
    Scarcely even a howl or a groan,   10
As the man they called 'Ho!' told his story of woe
    In an antediluvian tone.

'My father and mother were honest, though poor—'
    'Skip all that!' cried the Bellman in haste.
'If it once becomes dark, there's no chance of a Snark—
    We have hardly a minute to waste!'

'I skip forty years,' said the Baker in tears,
  'And proceed without further remark
To the day when you took me aboard of your ship
  To help you in hunting the Snark.   20

'A dear uncle of mine (after whom I was named)
  Remarked, when I bade him farewell—'
'Oh, skip your dear uncle!' the Bellman exclaimed,
  As he angrily tingled his bell.

'He remarked to me then,' said that mildest of men,
  ' "If your Snark be a Snark, that is right:
Fetch it home by all means—you may serve it with greens
  And it's handy for striking a light.

' "You may seek it with thimbles—and seek it with care—
  You may hunt it with forks and hope;   30
You may threaten its life with a railway-share;
  You may charm it with smiles and soap—" '

('That's exactly the method,' the Bellman bold
  In a hasty parenthesis cried,
'That's exactly the way I have always been told
  That the capture of Snarks should be tried!')

' "But oh, beamish nephew, beware of the day,
  If your Snark be a Boojum! For then
You will softly and suddenly vanish away,
  And never be met with again!"   40

'It is this, it is this that oppresses my soul,
  When I think of my uncle's last words:
And my heart is like nothing so much as a bowl
  Brimming over with quivering curds!

'It is this, it is this—' 'We have had that before!'
  The Bellman indignantly said.
And the Baker replied 'Let me say it once more.
  It is this, it is this that I dread!

'I engage with the Snark—every night after dark—
  In a dreamy delirious fight: 50
I serve it with greens in those shadowy scenes,
  And I use it for striking a light:

'But if ever I meet with a Boojum, that day,
  In a moment (of this I am sure),
I shall softly and suddenly vanish away—
  And the notion I cannot endure!'

FIT THE FOURTH

The Hunting

THE Bellman looked uffish, and wrinkled his brow.
  'If only you'd spoken before!
It's excessively awkward to mention it now,
  With the Snark, so to speak, at the door!

'We should all of us grieve, as you well may believe,
  If you never were met with again—
But surely, my man, when the voyage began,
  You might have suggested it then?

'It's excessively awkward to mention it now—
  As I think I've already remarked.'   10
And the man they called 'Hi!' replied, with a sigh,
  'I informed you the day we embarked.

'You may charge me with murder—or want of sense—
  (We are all of us weak at times):
But the slightest approach to a false pretence
  Was never among my crimes!

'I said it in Hebrew—I said it in Dutch—
  I said it in German and Greek:
But I wholly forgot (and it vexes me much)
  That English is what you speak!'   20

''Tis a pitiful tale,' said the Bellman, whose face
  Had grown longer at every word:
'But, now that you've stated the whole of your case,
  More debate would be simply absurd.

'The rest of my speech' (he exclaimed to his men)
  'You shall hear when I've leisure to speak it.
But the Snark is at hand, let me tell you again!
  'Tis your glorious duty to seek it!

'To seek it with thimbles, to seek it with care;
   To pursue it with forks and hope;   30
To threaten its life with a railway-share;
   To charm it with smiles and soap!

'For the Snark's a peculiar creature, that wo'n't
   Be caught in a commonplace way.
Do all that you know, and try all that you don't:
   Not a chance must be wasted to-day!

'For England expects—I forbear to proceed:
   'Tis a maxim tremendous, but trite:
And you'd best be unpacking the things that you need
   To rig yourselves out for the fight.'   40

Then the Banker endorsed a blank cheque (which he crossed),
   And changed his loose silver for notes:
The Baker with care combed his whiskers and hair,
   And shook the dust out of his coats:

The Boots and the Broker were sharpening a spade—
   Each working the grindstone in turn:
But the Beaver went on making lace, and displayed
   No interest in the concern:

Though the Barrister tried to appeal to its pride,
   And vainly proceeded to cite   50
A number of cases, in which making laces
   Had been proved an infringement of right.

The maker of Bonnets ferociously planned
   A novel arrangement of bows:
While the Billiard-marker with quivering hand
   Was chalking the tip of his nose.

But the Butcher turned nervous, and dressed himself fine,
   With yellow kid gloves and a ruff—
Said he felt it exactly like going to dine,
   Which the Bellman declared was all 'stuff'.   60

'Introduce me, now there's a good fellow,' he said,
   'If we happen to meet it together!'
And the Bellman, sagaciously nodding his head,
   Said 'That must depend on the weather.'

The Beaver went simply galumphing about,
  At seeing the Butcher so shy:
And even the Baker, though stupid and stout,
  Made an effort to wink with one eye.

'Be a man!' said the Bellman in wrath, as he heard
  The Butcher beginning to sob.   70
'Should we meet with a Jubjub, that desperate bird,
  We shall need all our strength for the job!'

Fit the Fifth

The Beaver's Lesson

They sought it with thimbles, they sought it with care;
  They pursued it with forks and hope;
They threatened its life with a railway-share;
  They charmed it with smiles and soap.

Then the Butcher contrived an ingenious plan
  For making a separate sally;
And had fixed on a spot unfrequented by man,
  A dismal and desolate valley.

But the very same plan to the Beaver occurred:
  It had chosen the very same place: 10
Yet neither betrayed, by a sign or a word,
  The disgust that appeared in his face.

Each thought he was thinking of nothing but 'Snark'
  And the glorious work of the day;
And each tried to pretend that he did not remark
  That the other was going that way.

But the valley grew narrower and narrower still,
  And the evening got darker and colder,
Till (merely from nervousness, not from good will)
  They marched along shoulder to shoulder.   20

Then a scream, shrill and high, rent the shuddering sky
  And they knew that some danger was near:
The Beaver turned pale to the tip of its tail,
  And even the Butcher felt queer.

He thought of his childhood, left far behind—
    That blissful and innocent state—
The sound so exactly recalled to his mind
    A pencil that squeaks on a slate!

''Tis the voice of the Jubjub!' he suddenly cried.
    (This man, that they used to call 'Dunce'.)   30
'As the Bellman would tell you,' he added with pride,
    'I have uttered that sentiment once.

''Tis the note of the Jubjub! Keep count, I entreat.
    You will find I have told it you twice.
'Tis the song of the Jubjub! The proof is complete.
    If only I've stated it thrice.'

The Beaver had counted with scrupulous care,
    Attending to every word:
But it fairly lost heart, and outgrabe in despair,
    When the third repetition occurred.   40

It felt that, in spite of all possible pains,
    It had somehow contrived to lose count,
And the only thing now was to rack its poor brains
    By reckoning up the amount.

'Two added to one—if that could but be done',
    It said, 'with one's fingers and thumbs!'
Recollecting with tears how, in earlier years,
    It had taken no pains with its sums.

'The thing can be done,' said the Butcher, 'I think.
    The thing must be done, I am sure.   50
The thing shall be done! Bring me paper and ink,
    The best there is time to procure.'

The Beaver brought paper, portfolio, pens,
    And ink in unfailing supplies:
While strange creepy creatures came out of their dens,
    And watched them with wondering eyes.

So engrossed was the Butcher, he heeded them not,
    As he wrote with a pen in each hand,
And explained all the while in a popular style
    Which the Beaver could well understand.   60

'Taking Three as the subject to reason about—
  A convenient number to state—
We add Seven, and Ten, and then multiply out
  By One Thousand diminished by Eight.

'The result we proceed to divide, as you see,
  By Nine Hundred and Ninety and Two:
Then subtract Seventeen, and the answer must be
  Exactly and perfectly true.

'The method employed I would gladly explain,
  While I have it so clear in my head,   70
If I had but the time and you had but the brain—
  But much yet remains to be said.

'In one moment I've seen what has hitherto been
  Enveloped in absolute mystery,
And without extra charge I will give you at large
  A Lesson in Natural History.'

In his genial way he proceeded to say
  (Forgetting all laws of propriety,
And that giving instruction, without introduction,
  Would have caused quite a thrill in Society),   80

'As to temper the Jubjub's a desperate bird.
  Since it lives in perpetual passion:
Its taste in costume is entirely absurd—
  It is ages ahead of the fashion:

'But it knows any friend it has met once before:
  It never will look at a bribe:
And in charity-meetings it stands at the door,
  And collects—though it does not subscribe.

'Its flavour when cooked is more exquisite far
  Than mutton, or oysters, or eggs: 90
(Some think it keeps best in an ivory jar,
  And some, in mahogany kegs:)

'You boil it in sawdust: you salt it in glue:
  You condense it with locusts and tape:
Still keeping one principal object in view—
  To preserve its symmetrical shape.'

The Butcher would gladly have talked till next day,
  But he felt that the Lesson must end,
And he wept with delight in attempting to say
  He considered the Beaver his friend: 100

While the Beaver confessed, with affectionate looks
  More eloquent even than tears,
It had learned in ten minutes far more than all books
  Would have taught it in seventy years.

They returned hand-in-hand, and the Bellman, unmanned
  (For a moment) with noble emotion,
Said 'This amply repays all the wearisome days
  We have spent on the billowy ocean!'

Such friends, as the Beaver and Butcher became,
  Have seldom if ever been known;   110
In winter or summer, 'twas always the same—
  You could never meet either alone.

And when quarrels arose—as one frequently finds
  Quarrels will, spite of every endeavour—
The song of the Jubjub recurred to their minds,
  And cemented their friendship for ever!

Fit the Sixth

The Barrister's Dream

THEY sought it with thimbles, they sought it with care;
  They pursued it with forks and hope;
They threatened its life with a railway-share;
  They charmed it with smiles and soap.

But the Barrister, weary of proving in vain
  That the Beaver's lace-making was wrong,
Fell asleep, and in dreams saw the creature quite plain
  That his fancy had dwelt on so long.

He dreamed that he stood in a shadowy Court,
  Where the Snark, with a glass in its eye,   10
Dressed in gown, bands, and wig, was defending a pig
  On the charge of deserting its sty.

The Witnesses proved, without error or flaw,
  That the sty was deserted when found:
And the Judge kept explaining the state of the law
  In a soft under-current of sound.

The indictment had never been clearly expressed,
  And it seemed that the Snark had begun,
And had spoken three hours, before any one guessed
  What the pig was supposed to have done.   20

The Jury had each formed a different view
  (Long before the indictment was read),
And they all spoke at once, so that none of them knew
  One word that the others had said.

'You must know—' said the Judge: but the Snark exclaimed 'Fudge!
  That statute is obsolete quite!
Let me tell you, my friends, the whole question depends
  On an ancient manorial right.

'In the matter of Treason the pig would appear   .
  To have aided, but scarcely abetted:
While the charge of Insolvency fails, it is clear,   30
  If you grant the plea "never indebted".

'The fact of Desertion I will not dispute:
  But its guilt, as I trust, is removed
(So far as relates to the costs of this suit)
  By the Alibi which has been proved.

'My poor client's fate now depends on your votes.'
  Here the speaker sat down in his place,
And directed the Judge to refer to his notes
  And briefly to sum up the case.   40

But the Judge said he never had summed up before;
  So the Snark undertook it instead,
And summed it so well that it came to far more
  Than the Witnesses ever had said!

When the verdict was called for, the Jury declined,
  As the word was so puzzling to spell;
But they ventured to hope that the Snark wouldn't mind
  Undertaking that duty as well.

So the Snark found the verdict, although, as it owned,
   It was spent with the toils of the day: 50
When it said the word 'GUILTY!' the Jury all groaned
   And some of them fainted away.

Then the Snark pronounced sentence, the Judge being quite
   Too nervous to utter a word:
When it rose to its feet, there was silence like night,
   And the fall of a pin might be heard.

'Transportation for life' was the sentence it gave,
   'And *then* to be fined forty pound.'
The Jury all cheered, though the Judge said he feared
   That the phrase was not legally sound.   60

But their wild exultation was suddenly checked
   When the jailer informed them, with tears,
Such a sentence would have not the slightest effect,
   As the pig had been dead for some years.

The Judge left the Court, looking deeply disgusted
   But the Snark, though a little aghast,
As the lawyer to whom the defence was intrusted,
   Went bellowing on to the last.

Thus the Barrister dreamed, while the bellowing seemed
   To grow every moment more clear: 70
Till he woke to the knell of a furious bell,
   Which the Bellman rang close at his ear.

FIT THE SEVENTH

The Banker's Fate

THEY sought it with thimbles, they sought it with care;
   They pursued it with forks and hope;
They threatened its life with a railway-share;
   They charmed it with smiles and soap.

And the Banker, inspired with a courage so new
   It was matter for general remark,
Rushed madly ahead and was lost to their view
   In his zeal to discover the Snark.

But while he was seeking with thimbles and care,
   A Bandersnatch swiftly drew nigh   10
And grabbed at the Banker, who shrieked in despair,
   For he knew it was useless to fly.

He offered large discount—he offered a cheque
   (Drawn 'to bearer') for seven-pounds-ten:
But the Bandersnatch merely extended its neck
   And grabbed at the Banker again.

Without rest or pause—while those frumious jaws
   Went savagely snapping around—
He skipped and he hopped, and he floundered and flopped,
   Till fainting he fell to the ground.   20

The Bandersnatch fled as the others appeared
   Led on by that fear-stricken yell:
And the Bellman remarked 'It is just as I feared!'
   And solemnly tolled on his bell.

He was black in the face, and they scarcely could trace
   The least likeness to what he had been:
While so great was his fright that his waistcoat turned white—
   A wonderful thing to be seen!

To the horror of all who were present that day,
   He uprose in full evening dress,   30
And with senseless grimaces endeavoured to say
   What his tongue could no longer express.

Down he sank in a chair—ran his hands through his hair—
   And chanted in mimsiest tones
Words whose utter inanity proved his insanity,
   While he rattled a couple of bones.

'Leave him here to his fate—it is getting so late!'
   The Bellman exclaimed in a fright.
'We have lost half the day. Any further delay,
   And we sha'n't catch a Snark before night!'   40

Fit the Eighth

The Vanishing

They sought it with thimbles, they sought it with care;
   They pursued it with forks and hope;
They threatened its life with a railway-share;
   They charmed it with smiles and soap.

They shuddered to think that the chase might fail,
   And the Beaver, excited at last,
Went bounding along on the tip of its tail,
   For the daylight was nearly past.

'There is Thingumbob shouting!' the Bellman said.
   'He is shouting like mad, only hark!   10
He is waving his hands, he is wagging his head,
   He has certainly found a Snark!'

They gazed in delight, while the Butcher exclaimed
   'He was always a desperate wag!'
They beheld him—their Baker—their hero unnamed—
   On the top of a neighbouring crag,

Erect and sublime, for one moment of time,
   In the next, that wild figure they saw
(As if stung by a spasm) plunge into a chasm,
   While they waited and listened in awe.   20

'It's a Snark!' was the sound that first came to their ears,
   And seemed almost too good to be true.
Then followed a torrent of laughter and cheers:
   Then the ominous words 'It's a Boo—'

Then, silence. Some fancied they heard in the air
   A weary and wandering sigh
That sounded like '—jum!' but the others declare
   It was only a breeze that went by.

They hunted till darkness came on, but they found
   Not a button, or feather, or mark,   30
By which they could tell that they stood on the ground
   Where the Baker had met with the Snark.

In the midst of the word he was trying to say,
   In the midst of his laughter and glee,
He had softly and suddenly vanished away—
   For the Snark *was* a Boojum, you see.

                (Wr. 1875–6; pub. 1876)

167

(i)

'He thought he saw an Elephant,
  That practised on a fife:
He looked again, and found it was
  A letter from his wife.
"At length I realise", he said,
  "The bitterness of Life!" '

(ii)

'He thought he saw a Buffalo
  Upon the chimney-piece:
He looked again, and found it was
  His Sister's Husband's Niece.
"Unless you leave this house", he said,
  "I'll send for the Police!" '

(iii)

'He thought he saw a Banker's Clerk
  Descending from the bus:
He looked again, and found it was
  A Hippopotamus:
"If this should stay to dine", he said,
  "There wo'n't be much for us!" '

(iv)

'He thought he saw a Kangaroo
  That worked a coffee-mill:
He looked again, and found it was
  A Vegetable-Pill.
"Were I to swallow this", he said,
  "I should be very ill!" '

(v)

'He thought he saw a Coach-and-Four
  That stood beside his bed:
He looked again, and found it was
  A Bear without a Head.
"Poor thing," he said, "poor silly thing!
  It's waiting to be fed!" '

(vi)

'He thought he saw an Albatross
    That fluttered round the lamp:
He looked again, and found it was
    A Penny-Postage-Stamp.
"You'd best be getting home," he said:
    "The nights are very damp!" '

(vii)

'He thought he saw a Garden-Door
    That opened with a key:
He looked again, and found it was
    A Double Rule of Three:
"And all its mystery", he said,
    "Is clear as day to me!" '

(viii)

'He thought he saw an Argument
    That proved he was the Pope:
He looked again, and found it was
    A Bar of Mottled Soap.
"A fact so dread", he faintly said,
    "Extinguishes all hope!" '

(i–vii wr. from 1867; pub. 1889; viii, 1893)

CHARLOTTE BRONTË
1816–1855

168

THE Autumn day its course has run—the Autumn evening falls
Already risen the Autumn moon gleams quiet on these walls
And Twilight to my lonely house a silent guest is come
In mask of gloom through every room she passes dusk and dumb
Her veil is spread, her shadow shed o'er stair and chamber void
And now I feel her presence steal even to my lone fireside
Sit silent Nun—sit there and be
Comrade and Confidant to me

(Wr. *c.* 1844–6; pub. 1924)

213

169   THE house was still—the room was still
'Twas eventide in June
A caged canary to the sun
Then setting—trilled a tune

A free bird on that lilac bush
Outside the lattice heard
He listened long—there came a hush
He dropped an answering word—

The prisoner to the free replied

(1915)

170   I NOW had only to retrace
The long and lonely road
So lately in the rainbow chase
With fearless ardour trod

Behind I left the sunshine now
The evening setting sun,
Before a storm rolled dark and low
Some gloomy hills upon

It came with rain—it came with wind
With swollen stream it howled   10
And night advancing black and blind
In ebon horror scowled

Lost in the hills—all painfully
I climbed a heathy peak
I sought I longed afar to see
My life's light's parting streak

The West was black as if no day
Had ever lingered there
As if no red expiring ray
Had tinged the enkindled air   20

And morning's portals could not lie
Where yon dark Orient spread
The funeral North—the black dark sky
Alike mourned [   ] dead

(1934)

171   THE Nurse believed the sick man slept
          For motionless he lay
       She rose and from the bed-side crept
          With cautious step away.

                              (Wr. 1845?; pub. 1984)

CHARLOTTE BRONTË
(perhaps EMILY JANE BRONTË)

172   *Stanzas*

OFTEN rebuked, yet always back returning
   To those first feelings that were born with me,
And leaving busy chase of wealth and learning
   For idle dreams of things which cannot be:

To-day, I will seek not the shadowy region;
   Its unsustaining vastness waxes drear;
And visions rising, legion after legion,
   Bring the unreal world too strangely near.

I'll walk, but not in old heroic traces,
   And not in paths of high morality,   10
And not among the half-distinguished faces,
   The clouded forms of long-past history.

I'll walk where my own nature would be leading:
   It vexes me to choose another guide:
Where the gray flocks in ferny glens are feeding;
   Where the wild wind blows on the mountain side.

What have those lonely mountains worth revealing?
   More glory and more grief than I can tell:
The earth that wakes *one* human heart to feeling
   Can centre both the worlds of Heaven and Hell.   20

                              (1850)

EDWARD LEAR

1812–1888

(i)

THERE was an Old Man who supposed,
That the street door was partially closed;
But some very large rats, ate his coats and his hats,
While that futile old gentleman dozed.

(ii)

THERE was a Young Lady whose eyes,
Were unique as to colour and size;
When she opened them wide, people all turned aside,
And started away in surprise.

(iii)

THERE was an Old Man on some rocks,
Who shut his wife up in a box,
When she said, 'Let me out,' he exclaimed, 'Without doubt,
You will pass all your life in that box.'

(iv)

THERE was an old man who screamed out
Whenever they knocked him about;
So they took off his boots, And fed him with fruits,
And continued to knock him about.

(i–iii, 1846; iv, 1872)

174 *The Dong with a Luminous Nose*

WHEN awful darkness and silence reign
Over the great Gromboolian plain,
  Through the long, long wintry nights;—
When the angry breakers roar
As they beat on the rocky shore;—
  When Storm-clouds brood on the towering heights
Of the Hills of the Chankly Bore:—

Then, through the vast and gloomy dark,
There moves what seems a fiery spark,
  A lonely spark with silvery rays   10
  Piercing the coal-black night,—
  A Meteor strange and bright:—
Hither and thither the vision strays,
  A single lurid light.

Slowly it wanders,—pauses,—creeps,—
Anon it sparkles,—flashes and leaps;
And ever as onward it gleaming goes
A light on the Bong-tree stems it throws.
And those who watch at that midnight hour
From Hall or Terrace, or lofty Tower,   20
Cry, as the wild light passes along,—
      'The Dong!—the Dong!
  'The wandering Dong through the forest goes!
      'The Dong! the Dong!
  'The Dong with a luminous Nose!'

    Long years ago
  The Dong was happy and gay,
Till he fell in love with a Jumbly Girl
Who came to those shores one day,
For the Jumblies came in a sieve, they did,— 30
Landing at eve near the Zemmery Fidd
    Where the Oblong Oysters grow,
  And the rocks are smooth and gray.
And all the woods and the valleys rang
With the Chorus they daily and nightly sang,—
      'Far and few, far and few,
      Are the lands where the Jumblies live;
      Their heads are green, and their hands are blue
      And they went to sea in a sieve.'

Happily, happily passed those days!   40
  While the cheerful Jumblies staid;
 They danced in circlets all night long,
 To the plaintive pipe of the lively Dong,
  In moonlight, shine, or shade.
For day and night he was always there
By the side of the Jumbly Girl so fair,
With her sky-blue hands, and her sea-green hair.
Till the morning came of that hateful day
When the Jumblies sailed in their sieve away,
And the Dong was left on the cruel shore 50
Gazing—gazing for evermore,—
Ever keeping his weary eyes on
That pea-green sail on the far horizon,—
Singing the Jumbly Chorus still
As he sate all day on the grassy hill,—
   'Far and few, far and few,
   Are the lands where the Jumblies live;
   Their heads are green, and their hands are blue,
   And they went to sea in a sieve.'

But when the sun was low in the West,   60
 The Dong arose and said,—
—'What little sense I once possessed
 Has quite gone out of my head!'—
And since that day he wanders still
By lake and forest, marsh and hill,
Singing—'O somewhere, in valley or plain
'Might I find my Jumbly Girl again!
'For ever I'll seek by lake and shore
'Till I find my Jumbly Girl once more!'

  Playing a pipe with silvery squeaks, 70
  Since then his Jumbly Girl he seeks,
  And because by night he could not see,
  He gathered the bark of the Twangum Tree
   On the flowery plain that grows.
   And he wove him a wondrous Nose,—
  A Nose as strange as a Nose could be!
Of vast proportions and painted red,
And tied with cords to the back of his head.
   —In a hollow rounded space it ended
  With a luminous Lamp within suspended, 80
    All fenced about
    With a bandage stout
   To prevent the wind from blowing it out;—

And with holes all round to send the light,
In gleaming rays on the dismal night.

And now each night, and all night long,
Over those plains still roams the Dong;
And above the wail of the Chimp and Snipe
You may hear the squeak of his plaintive pipe
While ever he seeks, but seeks in vain   90
To meet with his Jumbly Girl again;
Lonely and wild—all night he goes,—
The Dong with a luminous Nose!
And all who watch at the midnight hour,
From Hall or Terrace, or lofty Tower,
Cry, as they trace the Meteor bright,
Moving along through the dreary night,—
    'This is the hour when forth he goes,
    'The Dong with a luminous Nose!
    'Yonder—over the plain he goes;   100
       'He goes!
       'He goes;
    'The Dong with a luminous Nose!'

(1877)

175   *The New Vestments*

THERE lived an old man in the Kingdom of Tess,
Who invented a purely original dress;
And when it was perfectly made and complete,
He opened the door, and walked into the street.

By way of a hat, he'd a loaf of Brown Bread,
In the middle of which he inserted his head;—
His Shirt was made up of no end of dead Mice,
The warmth of whose skins was quite fluffy and nice;—
His Drawers were of Rabbit-skins;—so were his Shoes;—
His Stockings were skins,—but it is not known whose;—   10
His Waistcoat and Trowsers were made of Pork Chops;—
His Buttons were Jujubes, and Chocolate Drops;—
His Coat was all Pancakes with Jam for a border,
And a girdle of Biscuits to keep it in order;
And he wore over all, as a screen from bad weather,
A Cloak of green Cabbage-leaves stitched all together.

He had walked a short way, when he heard a great noise,
Of all sorts of Beasticles, Birdlings, and Boys;—

And from every long street and dark lane in the town
Beasts, Birdles, and Boys in a tumult rushed down. 20
Two Cows and a half ate his Cabbage-leaf Cloak;—
Four Apes seized his Girdle, which vanished like smoke;—
Three Kids ate up half of his Pancaky Coat,—
And the tails were devour'd by an ancient He Goat;—
An army of Dogs in a twinkling tore *up* his
Pork Waistcoat and Trowsers to give to their Puppies;—
And while they were growling, and mumbling the Chops,
Ten Boys prigged the Jujubes and Chocolate Drops.—
He tried to run back to his house, but in vain,
For Scores of fat Pigs came again and again;— 30
They rushed out of stables and hovels and doors,—
They tore off his stockings, his shoes, and his drawers;—
And now from the housetops with screechings descend,
Striped, spotted, white, black, and gray Cats without end,
They jumped on his shoulders and knocked off his hat,—
When Crows, Ducks, and Hens made a mincemeat of that;—
They speedily flew at his sleeves in a trice,
And utterly tore up his Shirt of dead Mice;—
They swallowed the last of his Shirt with a squall,—
Whereon he ran home with no clothes on at all. 40

And he said to himself as he bolted the door,
'I will not wear a similar dress any more,
'Any more, any more, any more, never more!'

(1877)

176   'How pleasant to know Mr Lear!'
     Who has written such volumes of stuff!
Some think him ill-tempered and queer,
     But a few think him pleasant enough.

His mind is concrete and fastidious,
     His nose is remarkably big;
His visage is more or less hideous,
     His beard it resembles a wig.

He has ears, and two eyes, and ten fingers,
     Leastways if you reckon two thumbs; 10
Long ago he was one of the singers,
     But now he is one of the dumbs.

He sits in a beautiful parlour,
　　With hundreds of books on the wall;
He drinks a great deal of Marsala,
　　But never gets tipsy at all.

He has many friends, laymen and clerical,
　　Old Foss is the name of his cat:
His body is perfectly spherical,
　　He weareth a runcible hat.　　　　　　　　　　　20

When he walks in a waterproof white,
　　The children run after him so!
Calling out, 'He's come out in his night-
　　gown, that crazy old Englishman, oh!'

He weeps by the side of the ocean,
　　He weeps on the top of the hill;
He purchases pancakes and lotion,
　　And chocolate shrimps from the mill.

He reads but he cannot speak Spanish,
　　He cannot abide ginger-beer:　　　　　　　　　30
Ere the days of his pilgrimage vanish,
　　How pleasant to know Mr Lear!

　　　　　　　　　　　　(Wr. 1879; pub. 1894)

CHARLES KINGSLEY

1819–1875

177　　　WHEN I was a greenhorn and young,
　　　　And wanted to be and to do,
　　　　I puzzled my brains about choosing my line,
　　　　Till I found out the way that things go.

　　　　The same piece of clay makes a tile,
　　　　A pitcher, a taw, or a brick:
　　　　Dan Horace knew life; you may cut out a saint,
　　　　Or a bench, from the self-same stick.

The urchin who squalls in a gaol,
By circumstance turns out a rogue;   10
While the castle-bred brat is a senator born,
Or a saint, if religion's in vogue.

We fall on our legs in this world,
Blind kittens, tossed in neck and heels:
'Tis Dame Circumstance licks Nature's cubs into shape,
She's the mill-head, if we are the wheels.

Then why puzzle and fret, plot and dream?
He that's wise will just follow his nose;
Contentedly fish, while he swims with the stream;
'Tis no business of his where it goes.   20

(Wr. 1846–7; pub. 1848)

178   *The Invitation*

                        To Tom Hughes

                COME away with me, Tom,
                Term and talk are done;
                My poor lads are reaping,
                Busy every one.
                Curates mind the parish,
                Sweepers mind the court;
                We'll away to Snowdon
                For our ten days' sport;
                Fish the August evening
                Till the eve is past,   10
                Whoop like boys, at pounders
                Fairly played and grassed.
                When they cease to dimple,
                Lunge, and swerve, and leap,
                Then up over Siabod,
                Choose our nest, and sleep.
                Up a thousand feet, Tom,
                Round the lion's head,
                Find soft stones to leeward
                And make up our bed.   20
                Eat our bread and bacon,
                Smoke the pipe of peace,
                And, ere we be drowsy,
                Give our boots a grease.

Homer's heroes did so,
Why not such as we?
What are sheets and servants?
Superfluity!
Pray for wives and children
Safe in slumber curled,   30
Then to chat till midnight
O'er this babbling world—
Of the workmen's college,
Of the price of grain,
Of the tree of knowledge,
Of the chance of rain;
If Sir A. goes Romeward,
If Miss B. sings true,
If the fleet comes homeward,
If the mare will do,—   40
Anything and everything—
Up there in the sky
Angels understand us,
And no 'saints' are by.
Down, and bathe at day-dawn,
Tramp from lake to lake,
Washing brain and heart clean
Every step we take.
Leave to Robert Browning
Beggars, fleas, and vines;   50
Leave to mournful Ruskin
Popish Apennines,
Dirty Stones of Venice
And his Gas-lamps Seven—
We've the stones of Snowdon
And the lamps of heaven.
Where's the mighty credit
In admiring Alps?
Any goose sees 'glory'
In their 'snowy scalps.'   60
Leave such signs and wonders
For the dullard brain,
As æsthetic brandy,
Opium and cayenne.
Give me Bramshill common
(St John's harriers by),
Or the vale of Windsor,
England's golden eye.
Show me life and progress,
Beauty, health, and man;   70

Houses fair, trim gardens,
Turn where'er I can.
Or, if bored with 'High Art,'
And such popish stuff,
One's poor ear need airing,
Snowdon's high enough.
While we find God's signet
Fresh on English ground,
Why go gallivanting
With the nations round?   80
Though we try no ventures
Desperate or strange;
Feed on commonplaces
In a narrow range;
Never sought for Franklin
Round the frozen Capes;
Even, with Macdougall,
Bagged our brace of apes;
Never had our chance, Tom,
In that black Redan;   90
Can't avenge poor Brereton
Out in Sakarran;
Tho' we earn our bread, Tom,
By the dirty pen,
What we can we will be,
Honest Englishmen.
Do the work that's nearest,
Though it's dull at whiles,
Helping, when we meet them,
Lame dogs over stiles;   100
See in every hedgerow
Marks of angels' feet,
Epics in each pebble
Underneath our feet;
Once a year, like schoolboys,
Robin-Hooding go,
Leaving fops and fogies
A thousand feet below.

(Wr. 1856; pub. 1884)

ARTHUR HUGH CLOUGH
1819–1861

Natura Naturans

BESIDE me,—in the car,—she sat,
　She spake not, no, nor looked to me:
From her to me, from me to her,
　What passed so subtly stealthily?
As rose to rose that by it blows
　Its interchanged aroma flings;
Or wake to sound of one sweet note
　The virtues of disparted strings.

Beside me, nought but this!—but this,
　That influent as within me dwelt   10
Her life, mine too within her breast,
　Her brain, her every limb she felt:
We sat; while o'er and in us, more
　And more, a power unknown prevailed,
Inhaling, and inhaled,—and still
　'Twas one, inhaling or inhaled.

Beside me, nought but this;—and passed;
　I passed; and know not to this day
If gold or jet her girlish hair,
　If black, or brown, or lucid-grey   20
Her eye's young glance: the fickle chance
　That joined us, yet may join again;
But I no face again could greet
　As hers, whose life was in me then.

As unsuspecting mere a maid
　As, fresh in maidhood's bloomiest bloom,
In casual second-class did e'er
　By casual youth her seat assume;
Or vestal, say, of saintliest clay,
　For once by balmiest airs betrayed   30
Unto emotions too too sweet
　To be unlingeringly gainsaid:

Unowning then, confusing soon
　　With dreamier dreams that o'er the glass
Of shyly ripening woman-sense
　　Reflected, scarce reflected, pass,
A wife may-be, a mother she
　　In Hymen's shrine recalls not now,
She first in hour, ah, not profane,
　　With me to Hymen learnt to bow.　　　　　　40

Ah no!—Yet owned we, fused in one,
　　The Power which e'en in stones and earths
By blind elections felt, in forms
　　Organic breeds to myriad births;
By lichen small on granite wall
　　Approved, its faintest feeblest stir
Slow-spreading, strengthening long, at last
　　Vibrated full in me and her.

In me and her—sensation strange!
　　The lily grew to pendent head,　　　　　　50
To vernal airs and mossy bank
　　Its sheeny primrose spangles spread,
In roof o'er roof of shade sun-proof
　　Did cedar strong itself outclimb,
And altitude of aloe proud
　　Aspire in floreal crown sublime;

Flashed flickering forth fantastic flies,
　　Big bees their burly bodies swung,
Rooks roused with civic din the elms,
　　And lark its wild reveillez rung;　　　　　　60
In Libyan dell the light gazelle,
　　The leopard lithe in Indian glade,
And dolphin, brightening tropic seas,
　　In us were living, leapt and played:

Their shells did slow crustacea build,
　　Their gilded skins did snakes renew,
While mightier spines for loftier kind
　　Their types in amplest limbs outgrew;
Yea, close comprest in human breast,
　　What moss, and tree, and livelier thing,　　　　　　70
What Earth, Sun, Star of force possest,
　　Lay budding, burgeoning forth for Spring.

Such sweet preluding sense of old
 Led on in Eden's sinless place
The hour when bodies human first
 Combined the primal prime embrace,
Such genial heat the blissful seat
 In man and woman owned unblamed,
When, naked both, its garden paths
 They walked unconscious, unashamed: 80

Ere, clouded yet in mistiest dawn,
 Above the horizon dusk and dun,
One mountain crest with light had tipped
 That Orb that is the Spirit's Sun;
Ere dreamed young flowers in vernal showers
 Of fruit to rise the flower above,
Or ever yet to young Desire
 Was told the mystic name of Love.

(Wr. 1847?; pub. 1849)

180   S AY not the struggle nought availeth,
    The labour and the wounds are vain,
   The enemy faints not, nor faileth,
    And as things have been, things remain.

   If hopes were dupes, fears may be liars;
    It may be, in yon smoke concealed,
   Your comrades chase e'en now the fliers,
    And, but for you, possess the field.

   For while the tired waves, vainly breaking,
    Seem here no painful inch to gain,   10
   Far back through creeks and inlets making
    Came, silent, flooding in, the main,

   And not by eastern windows only,
    When daylight comes, comes in the light,
   In front the sun climbs slow, how slowly,
    But westward, look, the land is bright.

(Wr. from 1849; pub. 1855)

181

To spend uncounted years of pain,
Again, again, and yet again,
In working out in heart and brain
   The problem of our being here;
To gather facts from far and near,
Upon the mind to hold them clear,
And, knowing more may yet appear,
Unto one's latest breath to fear
The premature result to draw—
Is this the object, end and law,   10
   And purpose of our being here?

(Wr. from 1851; pub. 1853)

182   *Amours de Voyage*

Oh, you are sick of self-love, Malvolio,
And taste with a distempered appetite!
SHAKSPEARE

Il doutait de tout, même de l'amour.
FRENCH NOVEL

Solvitur ambulando.
SOLUTIO SOPHISMATUM

Flevit amores
Non elaboratum ad pedem.
HORACE

CANTO I

Over the great windy waters, and over the clear crested summits,
   Unto the sun and the sky, and unto the perfecter earth,
Come, let us go,—to a land wherein gods of the old time wandered,
   Where every breath even now changes to ether divine.
Come, let us go; though withal a voice whisper, 'The world that we live in,
   Whithersoever we turn, still is the same narrow crib;
'Tis but to prove limitation, and measure a cord, that we travel;
   Let who would 'scape and be free go to his chamber and think;
'Tis but to change idle fancies for memories wilfully falser;
   'Tis but to go and have been.'—Come, little bark! let us go.   10

I. CLAUDE TO EUSTACE

DEAR EUSTATIO, I write that you may write me an answer,
Or at the least to put us again *en rapport* with each other.
Rome disappoints me much,—St Peter's, perhaps, in especial;

229

Only the Arch of Titus and view from the Lateran please me:
This, however, perhaps, is the weather, which truly is horrid.
Greece must be better, surely; and yet I am feeling so spiteful,
That I could travel to Athens, to Delphi, and Troy, and Mount Sinai,
Though but to see with my eyes that these are vanity also.
  Rome disappoints me much; I hardly as yet understand, but
Rubbishy seems the word that most exactly would suit it.   20
All the foolish destructions, and all the sillier savings,
All the incongruous things of past incompatible ages,
Seem to be treasured up here to make fools of present and future.
Would to Heaven the old Goths had made a cleaner sweep of it!
Would to Heaven some new ones would come and destroy these
    churches!
However, one can live in Rome as also in London.
Rome is better than London, because it is other than London.
It is a blessing, no doubt, to be rid, at least for a time, of
All one's friends and relations,—yourself (forgive me!) included,—
All the *assujettissement* of having been what one has been,   30
What one thinks one is, or thinks that others suppose one;
Yet, in despite of all, we turn like fools to the English.
Vernon has been my fate; who is here the same that you knew him,—
Making the tour, it seems, with friends of the name of Trevellyn.

II. CLAUDE TO EUSTACE

ROME disappoints me still; but I shrink and adapt myself to it.
Somehow a tyrannous sense of a superincumbent oppression
Still, wherever I go, accompanies ever, and makes me
Feel like a tree (shall I say?) buried under a ruin of brick-work.
Rome, believe me, my friend, is like its own Monte Testaceo,
Merely a marvellous mass of broken and castaway wine-pots.   40
Ye gods! what do I want with this rubbish of ages departed,
Things that Nature abhors, the experiments that she has failed in?
What do I find in the Forum? An archway and two or three pillars.
Well, but St Peter's? Alas, Bernini has filled it with sculpture!
No one can cavil, I grant, at the size of the great Coliseum.
Doubtless the notion of grand and capacious and massive amusement,
This the old Romans had; but tell me, is this an idea?
Yet of solidity much, but of splendour little is extant:
'Brickwork I found thee, and marble I left thee!' their Emperor
    vaunted;
'Marble I thought thee, and brickwork I find thee!' the Tourist may
    answer.   50

III. GEORGINA TREVELLYN TO LOUISA

AT last, dearest Louisa, I take up my pen to address you.
Here we are, you see, with the seven-and-seventy boxes,
Courier, Papa and Mamma, the children, and Mary and Susan:
Here we all are at Rome, and delighted of course with St Peter's,
And very pleasantly lodged in the famous Piazza di Spagna.
Rome is a wonderful place, but Mary shall tell you about it;
Not very gay, however; the English are mostly at Naples;
There are the A.s, we hear, and most of the W. party.
George, however, is come; did I tell you about his mustachios?
Dear, I must really stop, for the carriage, they tell me, is waiting.　60
Mary will finish; and Susan is writing, they say, to Sophia.
Adieu, dearest Louise,—evermore your faithful Georgina.
Who can a Mr Claude be whom George has taken to be with?
Very stupid, I think, but George says so *very* clever.

IV. CLAUDE TO EUSTACE

NO, the Christian faith, as at any rate I understood it,
With its humiliations and exaltations combining,
Exaltations sublime, and yet diviner abasements,
Aspirations from something most shameful here upon earth and
In our poor selves to something most perfect above in the heavens,—
No, the Christian faith, as I, at least, understood it,　70
Is not here, O Rome, in any of these thy churches;
Is not here, but in Freiburg, or Rheims, or Westminster Abbey.
What in thy Dome I find, in all thy recenter efforts,
Is a something, I think, more *rational* far, more earthly,
Actual, less ideal, devout not in scorn and refusal,
But in a positive, calm, Stoic-Epicurean acceptance.
This I begin to detect in St Peter's and some of the churches,
Mostly in all that I see of the sixteenth-century masters;
Overlaid of course with infinite gauds and gewgaws,
Innocent, playful follies, the toys and trinkets of childhood,　80
Forced on maturer years, as the serious one thing needful,
By the barbarian will of the rigid and ignorant Spaniard.
　Curious work, meantime, re-entering society; how we
Walk a livelong day, great Heaven, and watch our shadows!
What our shadows seem, forsooth, we will ourselves be.
Do I look like that? you think me that: then I am that.

V. CLAUDE TO EUSTACE

LUTHER, they say, was unwise; like a half-taught German, he could
　not

See that old follies were passing most tranquilly out of remembrance;
Leo the Tenth was employing all efforts to clear out abuses;
Jupiter, Juno, and Venus, Fine Arts, and Fine Letters, the Poets,   90
Scholars, and Sculptors, and Painters, were quietly clearing away the
Martyrs, and Virgins, and Saints, or at any rate Thomas Aquinas:
He must forsooth make a fuss and distend his huge Wittenberg lungs,
    and
Bring back Theology once yet again in a flood upon Europe:
Lo you, for forty days from the windows of heaven it fell; the
Waters prevail on the earth yet more for a hundred and fifty;
Are they abating at last? the doves that are sent to explore are
Wearily fain to return, at the best with a leaflet of promise,—
Fain to return, as they went, to the wandering wave-tost vessel,—
Fain to re-enter the roof which covers the clean and the unclean,—   100
Luther, they say, was unwise; he didn't see how things were going;
Luther was foolish,—but, O great God! what call you Ignatius?
O my tolerant soul, be still! but you talk of barbarians,
Alaric, Attila, Genseric;—why, they came, they killed, they
Ravaged, and went on their way; but these vile, tyrannous Spaniards,
These are here still,—how long, O ye Heavens, in the country of
    Dante?
These, that fanaticized Europe, which now can forget them, release not
This, their choicest of prey, this Italy; here you see them,—
Here, with emasculate pupils, and gimcrack churches of Gesu,
Pseudo-learning and lies, confessional-boxes and postures,—   110
Here, with metallic beliefs and regimental devotions,—
Here, overcrusting with slime, perverting, defacing, debasing,
Michel Angelo's dome, that had hung the Pantheon in heaven,
Raphael's Joys and Graces, and thy clear stars, Galileo!

VI. CLAUDE TO EUSTACE

WHICH of three Misses Trevellyn is it that Vernon shall marry
Is not a thing to be known; for our friend is one of those natures
Which have their perfect delight in the general tender-domestic,
So that he trifles with Mary's shawl, ties Susan's bonnet,
Dances with all, but at home is most, they say, with Georgina,
Who is, however, *too* silly in my apprehension for Vernon.   120
I, as before when I wrote, continue to see them a little;
Not that I like them much or care a *bajocco* for Vernon,
But I am slow at Italian, have not many English acquaintance,
And I am asked, in short, and am not good at excuses.
Middle-class people these, bankers very likely, not wholly
Pure of the taint of the shop; will at table d'hôte and restaurant
Have their shilling's worth, their penny's pennyworth even:
Neither man's aristocracy this, nor God's, God knoweth!

Yet they are fairly descended, they give you to know, well connected;
Doubtless somewhere in some neighbourhood have, and are careful
    to keep, some   130
Threadbare-genteel relations, who in their turn are enchanted
Grandly among county people to introduce at assemblies
To the unpennied cadets our cousins with excellent fortunes.
Neither man's aristocracy this, nor God's, God knoweth!

VII. CLAUDE TO EUSTACE

AH, what a shame, indeed, to abuse these most worthy people!
Ah, what a sin to have sneered at their innocent rustic pretensions!
Is it not laudable really, this reverent worship of station?
Is it not fitting that wealth should tender this homage to culture?
Is it not touching to witness these efforts, if little availing,
Painfully made, to perform the old ritual service of manners?   140
Shall not devotion atone for the absence of knowledge? and fervour
Palliate, cover, the fault of a superstitious observance?
Dear, dear, what do I say? but, alas! just now, like Iago,
I can be nothing at all, if it is not critical wholly;
So in fantastic height, in coxcomb exaltation,
Here in the Garden I can walk, can freely concede to the Maker
That the works of his hand are all very good: his creatures,
Beast of the field and fowl, he brings them before me; I name them;
That which I name them, they are,—the bird, the beast, and the cattle.
But for Adam,—alas, poor critical coxcomb Adam!   150
But for Adam there is not found an help-meet for him.

VIII. CLAUDE TO EUSTACE

NO, great dome of Agrippa, thou art not Christian! canst not,
Strip and replaster and daub and do what they will with thee, be so!
Here underneath the great porch of colossal Corinthian columns,
Here as I walk, do I dream of the Christian belfries above them?
Or on a bench as I sit and abide for long hours, till thy whole vast
Round grows dim as in dreams to my eyes, I repeople thy niches,
Not with the Martyrs, and Saints, and Confessors, and Virgins, and
    children,
But with the mightier forms of an older, austerer worship;
And I recite to myself, how   160
                Eager for battle here
        Stood Vulcan, here matronal Juno,
          And with the bow to his shoulder faithful
        He who with pure dew laveth of Castaly
        His flowing locks, who holdeth of Lycia

The oak forest and the wood that bore him,
Delos' and Patara's own Apollo.[1]

IX. CLAUDE TO EUSTACE

YET it is pleasant, I own it, to be in their company; pleasant,
Whatever else it may be, to abide in the feminine presence.
Pleasant, but wrong, will you say? But this happy, serene coexistence 170
Is to some poor soft souls, I fear, a necessity simple,
Meat and drink and life, and music, filling with sweetness,
Thrilling with melody sweet, with harmonies strange overwhelming,
All the long-silent strings of an awkward, meaningless fabric.
Yet as for that, I could live, I believe, with children; to have those
Pure and delicate forms encompassing, moving about you,
This were enough, I could think; and truly with glad resignation
Could from the dream of romance, from the fever of flushed
    adolescence,
Look to escape and subside into peaceful avuncular functions.
Nephews and nieces! alas, for as yet I have none! and, moreover, 180
Mothers are jealous, I fear me, too often, too rightfully; fathers
Think they have title exclusive to spoiling their own little darlings;
And by the law of the land, in despite of Malthusian doctrine,
No sort of proper provision is made for that most patriotic,
Most meritorious subject, the childless and bachelor uncle.

X. CLAUDE TO EUSTACE

YE, too, marvellous Twain, that erect on the Monte Cavallo
Stand by your rearing steeds in the grace of your motionless movement,
Stand with your upstretched arms and tranquil regardant faces,
Stand as instinct with life in the might of immutable manhood,—
O ye mighty and strange, ye ancient divine ones of Hellas, 190
Are ye Christian too? to convert and redeem and renew you,
Will the brief form have sufficed, that a Pope has set up on the apex
Of the Egyptian stone that o'ertops you, the Christian symbol?
And ye, silent, supreme in serene and victorious marble,
Ye that encircle the walls of the stately Vatican chambers,
Juno and Ceres, Minerva, Apollo, the Muses and Bacchus,
Ye unto whom far and near come posting the Christian pilgrims,

[1]   Hic avidus stetit
        Vulcanus, hic matrona Juno, et
            Nunquam humeris positurus arcum,
        Qui rore puro Castaliæ lavit
        Crines solutos, qui Lyciæ tenet
            Dumeta natalemque silvam,
                Delius et Patareus Apollo.   [C.'s note]

Ye that are ranged in the halls of the mystic Christian pontiff,
Are ye also baptized? are ye of the Kingdom of Heaven?
Utter, O some one, the word that shall reconcile Ancient and Modern!   200
Am I to turn me for this unto thee, great Chapel of Sixtus?

XI. CLAUDE TO EUSTACE

THESE are the facts. The uncle, the elder brother, the squire (a
Little embarrassed, I fancy), resides in a family place in
Cornwall, of course; 'Papa is in business,' Mary informs me;
He's a good sensible man, whatever his trade is. The mother
Is—shall I call it fine?—herself she would tell you refined, and
Greatly, I fear me, looks down on my bookish and maladroit manners;
Somewhat affecteth the blue; would talk to me often of poets;
Quotes, which I   hate,   Childe   Harold;   but   also   appreciates
    Wordsworth;
Sometimes adventures on Schiller; and then to religion diverges;   210
Questions me much about Oxford; and yet, in her loftiest flights, still
Grates the fastidious ear with the slightly mercantile accent.

   Is it contemptible, Eustace,—I'm perfectly ready to think so,—
Is it,—the horrible pleasure of pleasing inferior people?
I am ashamed my own self; and yet true it is, if disgraceful,
That for the first time in life I am living and moving with freedom.
I, who never could talk to the people I meet with my uncle,—
I, who have always failed,—I, trust me, can suit the Trevellyns;
I, believe me,—great conquest,—am liked by the country bankers.
And I am glad to be liked, and like in return very kindly.   220
So it proceeds; *Laissez faire, laissez aller,*—such is the watchword.
Well, I know there are thousands as pretty and hundreds as pleasant,
Girls by the dozen as good, and girls in abundance with polish
Higher and manners more perfect than Susan or Mary Trevellyn.
Well, I know, after all, it is only juxtaposition,—
Juxtaposition, in short; and what is juxtaposition?

XII. CLAUDE TO EUSTACE

BUT I am in for it now,—*laissez faire,* of a truth, *laissez aller.*
Yes, I am going,—I feel it, I feel and cannot recall it,—
Fusing with this thing and that, entering into all sorts of relations,
Tying I know not what ties, which, whatever they are, I know one thing,   230
Will, and must, woe is me, be one day painfully broken,—
Broken with painful remorses, with shrinkings of soul, and relentings,
Foolish delays, more foolish evasions, most foolish renewals.
But I have made the step, have quitted the ship of Ulysses;
Quitted the sea and the shore, passed into the magical island;

Yet on my lips is the *moly*, medicinal, offered of Hermes.
I have come into the precinct, the labyrinth closes around me,
Path into path rounding slyly; I pace slowly on, and the fancy,
Struggling awhile to sustain the long sequences, weary, bewildered,
Fain must collapse in despair; I yield, I am lost and know nothing;   240
Yet in my bosom unbroken remaineth the clew; I shall use it.
Lo, with the rope on my loins I descend through the fissure; I sink, yet
Inly secure in the strength of invisible arms up above me;
Still, wheresoever I swing, wherever to shore, or to shelf, or
Floor of cavern untrodden, shell-sprinkled, enchanting, I know I
Yet shall one time feel the strong cord tighten about me,—
Feel it relentless, upbear me from spots I would rest in; and though the
Rope sway wildly, I faint, crags wound me, from crag unto crag re-
Bounding, or, wide in the void, I die ten deaths, ere the end I
Yet shall plant firm foot on the broad lofty spaces I quit, shall   250
Feel underneath me again the great massy strengths of abstraction,
Look yet abroad from the height o'er the sea whose salt wave I have
    tasted.

XIII. GEORGINA TREVELLYN TO LOUISA ——

DEAREST LOUISA,—Inquire, if you please, about Mr Claude ——.
He has been once at R., and remembers meeting the H.s.
Harriet L., perhaps, may be able to tell you about him.
It is an awkward youth, but still with very good manners;
Not without prospects, we hear; and, George says, highly connected.
Georgy declares it absurd, but Mamma is alarmed, and insists he has
Taken up strange opinions and may be turning a Papist.
Certainly once he spoke of a daily service he went to.   260
'Where?' we asked, and he laughed and answered, 'At the Pantheon.'
This was a temple, you know, and now is a Catholic church; and
Though it is said that Mazzini has sold it for Protestant service,
Yet I suppose the change can hardly as yet be effected.
Adieu again,—evermore, my dearest, your loving Georgina.

P.S. BY MARY TREVELLYN

I AM to tell you, you say, what I think of our last new acquaintance.
Well, then, I think that George has a very fair right to be jealous.
I do not like him much, though I do not dislike being with him.
He is what people call, I suppose, a superior man, and
Certainly seems so to me; but I think he is frightfully selfish.   270

Alba, thou findest me still, and, Alba, thou findest me ever,
*   Now from the Capitol steps, now over Titus's Arch,*
Here from the large grassy spaces that spread from the Lateran portal,
*   Towering o'er aqueduct lines lost in perspective between,*

Or from a Vatican window, or bridge, or the high Coliseum,
  Clear by the garlanded line cut of the Flavian ring.
Beautiful can I not call thee, and yet thou hast power to o'ermaster,
  Power of mere beauty; in dreams, Alba, thou hauntest me still.
Is it religion? I ask me; or is it a vain superstition?
  Slavery abject and gross? service, too feeble, of truth?   280
Is it an idol I bow to, or is it a god that I worship?
  Do I sink back on the old, or do I soar from the mean?
So through the city I wander and question, unsatisfied ever,
  Reverent so I accept, doubtful because I revere.

CANTO II

Is it illusion? or does there a spirit from perfecter ages,
  Here, even yet, amid loss, change, and corruption, abide?
Does there a spirit we know not, though seek, though we find, comprehend not
  Here to entice and confuse, tempt and evade us, abide?
Lives in the exquisite grace of the column disjointed and single,
  Haunts the rude masses of brick garlanded gayly with vine,
E'en in the turret fantastic surviving that springs from the ruin,
  E'en in the people itself? is it illusion or not?
Is it illusion or not that attracteth the pilgrim transalpine,
  Brings him a dullard and dunce hither to pry and to stare?   10
Is it illusion or not that allures the barbarian stranger,
  Brings him with gold to the shrine, brings him in arms to the gate?

I. CLAUDE TO EUSTACE

WHAT do the people say, and what does the government do?—you
Ask, and I know not at all. Yet fortune will favour your hopes; and
I, who avoided it all, am fated, it seems, to describe it.
I, who nor meddle nor make in politics,—I who sincerely
Put not my trust in leagues nor any suffrage by ballot,
Never predicted Parisian millenniums, never beheld a
New Jerusalem coming down dressed like a bride out of heaven
Right on the Place de la Concorde,—I, nevertheless, let me say it,   20
Could in my soul of souls, this day, with the Gaul at the gates, shed
One true tear for thee, thou poor little Roman republic!
France, it is foully done! and you, my stupid old England,—
You, who a twelvemonth ago said nations must choose for themselves,
      you
Could not, of course, interfere,—you, now, when a nation has
      chosen—
Pardon this folly! *The Times* will, of course, have announced the
      occasion,
Told you the news of to-day; and although it was slightly in error

When it proclaimed as a fact the Apollo was sold to a Yankee,
You may believe when it tells you the French are at Civita Vecchia.

II. CLAUDE TO EUSTACE

DULCE it is, and *decorum*, no doubt, for the country to fall,—to   30
Offer one's blood an oblation to Freedom, and die for the Cause; yet
Still, individual culture is also something, and no man
Finds quite distinct the assurance that he of all others is called on,
Or would be justified, even, in taking away from the world that
Precious creature, himself. Nature sent him here to abide here;
Else why sent him at all? Nature wants him still, it is likely.
On the whole, we are meant to look after ourselves; it is certain
Each has to eat for himself, digest for himself, and in general
Care for his own dear life, and see to his own preservation;
Nature's intentions, in most things uncertain, in this most plain are
    decisive;   40
These, on the whole, I conjecture the Romans will follow, and I shall.
  So we cling to our rocks like limpets; Ocean may bluster,
Over and under and round us; we open our shells to imbibe our
Nourishment, close them again, and are safe, fulfilling the purpose
Nature intended,—a wise one, of course, and a noble, we doubt not.
Sweet it may be and decorous, perhaps, for the country to die; but,
On the whole, we conclude the Romans won't do it, and I sha'n't.

III. CLAUDE TO EUSTACE

WILL they fight? They say so. And will the French? I can hardly,
Hardly think so; and yet—He is come, they say, to Palo,
He is passed from Monterone, at Santa Severa   50
He hath laid up his guns. But the Virgin, the Daughter of Roma,
She hath despised thee and laughed thee to scorn,—the Daughter of
    Tiber,
She hath shaken her head and built barricades against thee!
Will they fight? I believe it. Alas! 'tis ephemeral folly,
Vain and ephemeral folly, of course, compared with pictures,
Statues, and antique gems!—Indeed: and yet indeed too,
Yet methought, in broad day did I dream—tell it not in St James's,
Whisper it not in thy courts, O Christ Church!—yet did I, waking,
Dream of a cadence that sings, *Si tombent nos jeunes héros, la*
Terre en produit de nouveaux contre vous tous prêts à se battre;   60
Dreamt of great indignations and angers transcendental,
Dreamt of a sword at my side and a battle-horse underneath me.

IV. CLAUDE TO EUSTACE

NOW supposing the French or the Neapolitan soldier
Should by some evil chance come exploring the Maison Serny

(Where the family English are all to assembly for safety),
Am I prepared to lay down my life for the British female?
Really, who knows? One has bowed and talked, till, little by little,
All the natural heat has escaped of the chivalrous spirit.
Oh, one conformed, of course; but one doesn't die for good manners,
Stab or shoot, or be shot, by way of graceful attention. 70
No, if it should be at all, it should be on the barricades there;
Should I incarnadine ever this inky pacifical finger,
Sooner far should it be for this vapour of Italy's freedom,
Sooner far by the side of the d——d and dirty plebeians.
Ah, for a child in the street I could strike; for the full-blown lady—
Somehow, Eustace, alas! I have not felt the vocation.
Yet these people of course will expect, as of course, my protection,
Vernon in radiant arms stand forth for the lovely Georgina,
And to appear, I suppose, were but common civility. Yes, and
Truly I do not desire they should either be killed or offended. 80
Oh, and of course you will say, 'When the times comes, you will be
    ready.'
Ah, but before it comes, am I to presume it will be so?
What I cannot feel now, am I to suppose that I shall feel?
Am I not free to attend for the ripe and indubious instinct?
Am I forbidden to wait for the clear and lawful perception?
Is it the calling of man to surrender his knowledge and insight,
For the mere venture of what may, perhaps, be the virtuous action?
Must we, walking our earth, discerning a little, and hoping
Some plain visible task shall yet for our hands be assigned us,—
Must we abandon the future for fear of omitting the present, 90
Quit our own fireside hopes at the alien call of a neighbour,
To the mere possible shadow of Deity offer the victim?
And is all this, my friend, but a weak and ignoble refining,
Wholly unworthy the head or the heart of Your Own Correspondent?

V. CLAUDE TO EUSTACE

YES, we are fighting at last, it appears. This morning as usual,
Murray, as usual, in hand, I enter the Caffè Nuovo;
Seating myself with a sense as it were of a change in the weather,
Not understanding, however, but thinking mostly of Murray,
And, for to-day is their day, of the Campidoglio Marbles,
Caffè-latte! I call to the waiter,—and *Non c' è latte*, 100
This is the answer he makes me, and this the sign of a battle.
So I sit; and truly they seem to think any one else more
Worthy than me of attention. I wait for my milkless *nero*,
Free to observe undistracted all sorts and sizes of persons,
Blending civilian and soldier in strangest costume, coming in, and
Gulping in hottest haste, still standing, their coffee,—withdrawing

Eagerly, jangling a sword on the steps, or jogging a musket
Slung to the shoulder behind. They are fewer, moreover, than usual,
Much, and silenter far; and so I begin to imagine
Something is really afloat. Ere I leave, the Caffè is empty,   110
Empty too the streets, in all its length the Corso
Empty, and empty I see to my right and left the Condotti.

    Twelve o'clock, on the Pincian Hill, with lots of English,
Germans, Americans, French,—the Frenchmen, too, are protected,—
So we stand in the sun, but afraid of a probable shower;
So we stand and stare, and see, to the left of St Peter's,
Smoke, from the cannon, white,—but that is at intervals only,—
Black, from a burning house, we suppose, by the Cavalleggieri;
And we believe we discern some lines of men descending
Down through the vineyard-slopes, and catch a bayonet gleaming.   120
Every ten minutes, however,—in this there is no misconception,—
Comes a great white puff from behind Michel Angelo's dome, and
After a space the report of a real big gun,—not the Frenchman's?—
That must be doing some work. And so we watch and conjecture.

    Shortly, an Englishman comes, who says he has been to St Peter's,
Seen the Piazza and troops, but that is all he can tell us;
So we watch and sit, and, indeed, it begins to be tiresome.—
All this smoke is outside; when it has come to the inside,
It will be time, perhaps, to descend and retreat to our houses.

    Half past one, or two. The report of small arms frequent,   130
Sharp and savage indeed; that cannot all be for nothing:
So we watch and wonder; but guessing is tiresome, very.
Weary of wondering, watching, and guessing, and gossiping idly,
Down I go, and pass through the quiet streets with the knots of
National Guards patrolling, and flags hanging out at the windows,
English, American, Danish,—and, after offering to help an
Irish family moving *en masse* to the Maison Serny,
After endeavouring idly to minister balm to the trembling
Quinquagenarian fears of two lone British spinsters,
Go to make sure of my dinner before the enemy enter.   140
But by this there are signs of stragglers returning; and voices
Talk, though you don't believe it, of guns and prisoners taken;
And on the walls you read the first bulletin of the morning.—
This is all that I saw, and all I know of the battle.

VI. CLAUDE TO EUSTACE

VICTORY! Victory!—Yes! ah, yes, thou republican Zion,
Truly the kings of the earth are gathered and gone by together;
Doubtless they marvelled to witness such things, were astonished, and
    so forth.
Victory! Victory! Victory!—Ah, but it is, believe me,

Easier, easier far, to intone the chant of the martyr
Than to indite any pæan of any victory. Death may   150
Sometimes be noble; but life, at the best, will appear an illusion.
While the great pain is upon us, it is great; when it is over,
Why, it is over. The smoke of the sacrifice rises to heaven,
Of a sweet savour, no doubt, to Somebody; but on the altar,
Lo, there is nothing remaining but ashes and dirt and ill odour.
   So it stands, you perceive; the labial muscles, that swelled with
Vehement evolution of yesterday Marseillaises,
Articulations sublime of defiance and scorning, to-day col-
Lapse and languidly mumble, while men and women and papers
Scream and re-scream to each other the chorus of Victory. Well, but 160
I am thankful they fought, and glad that the Frenchmen were beaten.

VII. CLAUDE TO EUSTACE

So, I have seen a man killed! An experience that, among others!
Yes, I suppose I have; although I can hardly be certain,
And in a court of justice could never declare I had seen it.
But a man was killed, I am told, in a place where I saw
Something; a man was killed, I am told, and I saw something.
   I was returning home from St Peter's; Murray, as usual,
Under my arm, I remember; had crossed the St Angelo bridge; and
Moving towards the Condotti, had got to the first barricade, when
Gradually, thinking still of St Peter's, I became conscious   170
Of a sensation of movement opposing me,—tendency this way
(Such as one fancies may be in a stream when the wave of the tide is
Coming and not yet come,—a sort of poise and retention);
So I turned, and, before I turned, caught sight of stragglers
Heading a crowd, it is plain, that is coming behind that corner.
Looking up, I see windows filled with heads; the Piazza,
Into which you remember the Ponte St Angelo enters,
Since I passed, has thickened with curious groups; and now the
Crowd is coming, has turned, has crossed that last barricade, is
Here at my side. In the middle they drag at something. What is it? 180
Ha! bare swords in the air, held up! There seem to be voices
Pleading and hands putting back; official, perhaps; but the swords are
Many, and bare in the air. In the air? They descend; they are smiting
Hewing, chopping—At what? In the air once more upstretched! And
Is it blood that's on them? Yes, certainly blood! Of whom, then?
Over whom is the cry of this furor of exultation?
   While they are skipping and screaming, and dancing their caps on
      the points of
Swords and bayonets, I to the outskirts back, and ask a
Mercantile-seeming by-stander, 'What is it?' and he, looking always
That way, makes me answer, 'A Priest, who was trying to fly to   190

The Neapolitan army,'—and thus explains the proceeding.
    You didn't see the dead man? No;—I began to be doubtful;
I was in black myself, and didn't know what mightn't happen;—
But a National Guard close by me, outside of the hubbub,
Broke his sword with slashing a broad hat covered with dust,—and
Passing away from the place with Murray under my arm, and
Stooping, I saw through the legs of the people the legs of a body.
    You are the first, do you know, to whom I have mentioned the matter.
Whom should I tell it to, else?—these girls?—the Heavens forbid it!—
Quidnuncs at Monaldini's?—idlers upon the Pincian?   200
    If I rightly remember, it happened on that afternoon when
Word of the nearer approach of a new Neapolitan army
First was spread. I began to bethink me of Paris Septembers,
Thought I could fancy the look of the old 'Ninety-two. On that evening
Three or four, or, it may be, five, of these people were slaughtered.
Some declare they had, one of them, fired on a sentinel; others
Say they were only escaping; a Priest, it is currently stated,
Stabbed a National Guard on the very Piazza Colonna:
History, Rumour of Rumours, I leave it to thee to determine!
    But I am thankful to say the government seems to have strength to   210
Put it down; it has vanished, at least; the place is most peaceful.
Through the Trastevere walking last night, at nine of the clock, I
Found no sort of disorder; I crossed by the Island-bridges,
So by the narrow streets to the Ponte Rotto, and onwards
Thence, by the Temple of Vesta, away to the great Coliseum,
Which at the full of the moon is an object worthy a visit.

VIII. GEORGINA TREVELLYN TO LOUISA ——

ONLY think, dearest Louisa, what fearful scenes we have witnessed!

         *   *   *

George has just seen Garibaldi, dressed up in a long white cloak, on
Horseback, riding by, with his mounted negro behind him:
This is a man, you know, who came from America with him,   220
Out of the woods, I suppose, and uses a *lasso* in fighting,
Which is, I don't quite know, but a sort of noose, I imagine;
This he throws on the heads of the enemy's men in a battle,
Pulls them into his reach, and then most cruelly kills them:
Mary does not believe, but we heard it from an Italian.
Mary allows she was wrong about Mr Claude *being selfish*;
He was *most* useful and kind on the terrible thirtieth of April.
Do not write here any more; we are starting directly for Florence:
We should be off to-morrow, if only Papa could get horses;
All have been seized everywhere for the use of this dreadful Mazzini.   230
P.S.
    Mary has seen thus far.—I am really so angry, Louisa,—

Quite out of patience, my dearest! What can the man be intending!
I am quite tired; and Mary, who might bring him to in a moment,
Lets him go on as he likes, and neither will help nor dismiss him.

IX. CLAUDE TO EUSTACE

IT is most curious to see what a power a few calm words (in
Merely a brief proclamation) appear to possess on the people.
Order is perfect, and peace; the city is utterly tranquil;
And one cannot conceive that this easy and *nonchalant* crowd, that
Flows like a quiet stream through street and market-place, entering
Shady recesses and bays of church, *osteria*, and *caffè*,   240
Could in a moment be changed to a flood as of molten lava,
Boil into deadly wrath and wild homicidal delusion.
    Ah, 'tis an excellent race,—and even in old degradation,
Under a rule that enforces to flattery, lying, and cheating,
E'en under Pope and Priest, a nice and natural people.
Oh, could they but be allowed this chance of redemption!—but clearly
That is not likely to be. Meantime, notwithstanding all journals,
Honour for once to the tongue and the pen of the eloquent writer!
Honour to speech! and all honour to thee, thou noble Mazzini!

X. CLAUDE TO EUSTACE

I AM in love, meantime, you think; no doubt you would think so.   250
I am in love, you say; with those letters, of course, you would say so.
I am in love, you declare. I think not so; yet I grant you
It is a pleasure, indeed, to converse with this girl. Oh, rare gift,
Rare felicity, this! she can talk in a rational way, can
Speak upon subjects that really are matters of mind and of thinking,
Yet in perfection retain her simplicity; never, one moment,
Never, however you urge it, however you tempt her, consents to
Step from ideas and fancies and loving sensations to those vain
Conscious understandings that vex the minds of man-kind.
No, though she talk, it is music; her fingers desert not the keys; 'tis 260
Song, though you hear in the song the articulate vocables sounded,
Syllabled singly and sweetly the words of melodious meaning.
    I am in love, you say; I do not think so exactly.

XI. CLAUDE TO EUSTACE

THERE are two different kinds, I believe, of human attraction:
One which simply disturbs, unsettles, and makes you uneasy,
And another that poises, retains, and fixes and holds you.
I have no doubt, for myself, in giving my voice for the latter.
I do not wish to be moved, but growing where I was growing,
There more truly to grow, to live where as yet I had languished.
I do not like being moved: for the will is excited; and action   270

Is a most dangerous thing; I tremble for something factitious,
Some malpractice of heart and illegitimate process;
We are so prone to these things with our terrible notions of duty.

XII. CLAUDE TO EUSTACE

AH, let me look, let me watch, let me wait, unhurried, unprompted!
Bid me not venture on aught that could alter or end what is present!
Say not, Time flies, and Occasion, that never returns, is departing!
Drive me not out, ye ill angels with fiery swords, from my Eden,
Waiting, and watching, and looking! Let love be its own inspiration!
Shall not a voice, if a voice there must be, from the airs that environ,
Yea, from the conscious heavens, without our knowledge or effort,   280
Break into audible words? and love be its own inspiration?

XIII. CLAUDE TO EUSTACE

WHEREFORE and how I am certain, I hardly can tell; but it *is* so.
She doesn't like me, Eustace; I think she never will like me.
Is it my fault, as it is my misfortune, my ways are not her ways?
Is it my fault, that my habits and modes are dissimilar wholly?
'Tis not her fault, 'tis her nature, her virtue, to misapprehend them:
'Tis not her fault, 'tis her beautiful nature, not ever to know me.
Hopeless it seems,—yet I cannot, though hopeless, determine to leave
    it:
She goes,—therefore I go; she moves,—I move, not to lose her.

XIV. CLAUDE TO EUSTACE

OH, 'tisn't manly, of course, 'tisn't manly, this method of wooing;   290
'Tisn't the way very likely to win. For the woman, they tell you,
Ever prefers the audacious, the wilful, the vehement hero;
She has no heart for the timid, the sensitive soul; and for knowledge,—
Knowledge, O ye Gods!—when did they appreciate knowledge?
Wherefore should they, either? I am sure I do not desire it.
  Ah, and I feel too, Eustace, she cares not a tittle about me!
(Care about me, indeed! and do I really expect it?)
But my manner offends; my ways are wholly repugnant;
Every word that I utter estranges, hurts, and repels her;
Every moment of bliss that I gain, in her exquisite presence,   300
Slowly, surely, withdraws her, removes her, and severs her from me.
Not that I care very much!—any way, I escape from the boy's own
Folly, to which I am prone, of loving where it is easy.
Not that I mind very much! Why should I? I am not in love, and
Am prepared, I think, if not by previous habit,
Yet in the spirit beforehand for this and all that is like it;
It is an easier matter for us contemplative creatures,
Us, upon whom the pressure of action is laid so lightly;

We discontented indeed with things in particular, idle,
Sickly, complaining, by faith in the vision of things in general,　　310
Manage to hold on our way without, like others around us,
Seizing the nearest arm to comfort, help, and support us.
Yet, after all, my Eustace, I know but little about it.
All I can say for myself, for present alike and for past, is,
Mary Trevellyn, Eustace, is certainly worth your acquaintance.
You couldn't come, I suppose, as far as Florence, to see her?

XV.　GEORGINA TREVELLYN TO LOUISA ——

．　．　．　．　．　．　TO-MORROW we're starting for Florence,
Truly rejoiced, you may guess, to escape from republican terrors;
Mr C. and Papa to escort us; we by *vettura*
Through Siena, and Georgy to follow and join us by Leghorn.　　320
Then——Ah, what shall I say, my dearest? I tremble in thinking!
You will imagine my feelings,—the blending of hope and of sorrow!
How can I bear to abandon Papa and Mamma and my Sisters?
Dearest Louisa, indeed it is very alarming; but trust me
Ever, whatever may change, to remain your loving Georgina.

P.S.　BY MARY TREVELLYN

．　．　．　．　．　．　'DO I like Mr Claude any better?'
I am to tell you,—and, 'Pray, is it Susan or I that attract him?'
This he never has told, but Georgina could certainly ask him.
All I can say for myself is, alas! that he rather repels me.
There! I think him agreeable, but also a little repulsive.　　330
So be content, dear Louisa; for one satisfactory marriage
Surely will do in one year for the family you would establish;
Neither Susan nor I shall afford you the joy of a second.

P.S.　BY GEORGINA TREVELLYN

MR CLAUDE, you must know, is behaving a little bit better;
He and Papa are great friends; but he really is too *shilly-shally,*—
So unlike George! Yet I hope that the matter is going on fairly.
I shall, however, get George, before he goes, to say something.
Dearest Louisa, how delightful, to bring young people together!

———————

Is it to Florence we follow, or are we to tarry yet longer,
　E'en amid clamour of arms, here in the city of old,　　340
Seeking from clamour of arms in the Past and the Arts to be hidden,
　Vainly 'mid Arts and the Past seeking one life to forget?
Ah, fair shadow, scarce seen, go forth! for anon he shall follow,—
　He that beheld thee, anon, whither thou leadest, must go!

Go, and the wise, loving Muse, she also will follow and find thee!
She, should she linger in Rome, were not dissevered from thee!

CANTO III

Yet to the wondrous St Peter's, and yet to the solemn Rotonda,
  Mingling with heroes and gods, yet to the Vatican walls,
Yet may we go, and recline, while a whole mighty world seems above us
  Gathered and fixed to all time into one roofing supreme;
Yet may we, thinking on these things, exclude what is meaner around us;
  Yet, at the worst of the worst, books and a chamber remain;
Yet may we think, and forget, and possess our souls in resistance.—
  Ah, but away from the stir, shouting, and gossip of war,
Where, upon Apennine slope, with the chestnut the oak-trees immingle,
  Where amid odorous copse bridle-paths wander and wind,   10
Where under mulberry-branches the diligent rivulet sparkles,
  Or amid cotton and maize peasants their waterworks ply,
Where, over fig-tree and orange in tier upon tier still repeated,
  Garden on garden upreared, balconies step to the sky,—
Ah, that I were, far away from the crowd and the streets of the city,
  Under the vine-trellis laid, O my beloved, with thee!

I. MARY TREVELLYN TO MISS ROPER,—*on the way to Florence*

WHY doesn't Mr Claude come with us? you ask.— We don't know.
You should know better than we. He talked of the Vatican marbles;
But I can't wholly believe that this was the actual reason,—
He was so ready before, when we asked him to come and escort us.   20
Certainly he is odd, my dear Miss Roper. To change so
Suddenly, just for a whim, was not quite fair to the party,—
Not quite right. I declare, I really almost am offended:
I, his great friend, as you say, have doubtless a title to be so.
Not that I greatly regret it, for dear Georgina distinctly
Wishes for nothing so much as to show her adroitness. But, oh, my
Pen will not write any more;—let us say nothing further about it.

*   *   *

Yes, my dear Miss Roper, I certainly called him repulsive;
So I think him, but cannot be sure I have used the expression
Quite as your pupil should; yet he does most truly repel me.   30
Was it to you I made use of the word? or who was it told you?
Yes, repulsive; observe, it is but when he talks of ideas,
That he is quite unaffected, and free, and expansive, and easy;
I could pronounce him simply a cold intellectual being.—
When does he make advances?—He thinks that women should woo
    him;

Yet, if a girl should do so, would be but alarmed and disgusted.
She that should love him must look for small love in return,—like the
    ivy
On the stone wall, must expect but a rigid and niggard support, and
E'en to get that must go searching all round with her humble embraces.

II. CLAUDE TO EUSTACE,—*from Rome*

TELL me, my friend, do you think that the grain would sprout in the
    furrow,   40
Did it not truly accept as its *summum* and *ultimum bonum*
That mere common and may-be indifferent soil it is set in?
Would it have force to develop and open its young cotyledons,
Could it compare, and reflect, and examine one thing with another?
Would it endure to accomplish the round of its natural functions,
Were it endowed with a sense of the general scheme of existence?
    While from Marseilles in the steamer we voyaged to Civita Vecchia,
Vexed in the squally seas as we lay by Capraja and Elba,
Standing, uplifted, alone on the heaving poop of the vessel,
Looking around on the waste of the rushing incurious billows,   50
'This is Nature,' I said: 'we are born as it were from her waters,
Over her billows that buffet and beat us, her offspring uncared-for,
Casting one single regard of a painful victorious knowledge,
Into her billows that buffet and beat us we sink and are swallowed.'
This was the sense in my soul, as I swayed with the poop of the steamer;
And as unthinking I sat in the hall of the famed Ariadne,
Lo, it looked at me there from the face of a Triton in marble.
It is the simpler thought, and I can believe it the truer.
Let us not talk of growth; we are still in our Aqueous Ages.

III. CLAUDE TO EUSTACE

FAREWELL, Politics, utterly! What can I do? I cannot   60
Fight, you know; and to talk I am wholly ashamed. And although I
Gnash my teeth when I look in your French or your English papers,
What is the good of that? Will swearing, I wonder, mend matters?
Cursing and scolding repel the assailants? No, it is idle;
No, whatever befalls, I will hide, will ignore or forget it.
Let the tail shift for itself; I will bury my head. And what's the
Roman Republic to me, or I to the Roman Republic?
    Why not fight?—In the first place, I haven't so much as a musket.
In the next, if I had, I shouldn't know how I should use it.
In the third, just at present I'm studying ancient marbles.   70
In the fourth, I consider I owe my life to my country.
In the fifth,—I forget, but four good reasons are ample.
Meantime, pray, let 'em fight, and be killed. I delight in devotion.

So that I 'list not, hurrah for the glorious army of martyrs!
Sanguis martyrum semen Ecclesiæ; though it would seem this
Church is indeed of the purely Invisible, Kingdom-come kind:
Militant here on earth! Triumphant, of course, then, elsewhere!
Ah, good Heaven, but I would I were out far away from the pother!

IV. CLAUDE TO EUSTACE

NOT, as we read in the words of the olden-time inspiration,
Are there two several trees in the place we are set to abide in; 80
But on the apex most high of the Tree of Life in the Garden,
Budding, unfolding, and falling, decaying and flowering ever,
Flowering is set and decaying the transient blossom of Knowledge,—
Flowering alone, and decaying, the needless, unfruitful blossom.
  Or as the cypress-spires by the fair-flowing stream Hellespontine,
Which from the mythical tomb of the godlike Protesilaüs
Rose sympathetic in grief to his lovelorn Laodamia,
Evermore growing, and, when in their growth to the prospect attaining,
Over the low sea-banks, of the fatal Ilian city,
Withering still at the sight which still they upgrow to encounter. 90
  Ah, but ye that extrude from the ocean your helpless faces,
Ye over stormy seas leading long and dreary processions,
Ye, too, brood of the wind, whose coming is whence we discern not,
Making your nest on the wave, and your bed on the crested billow,
Skimming rough waters, and crowding wet sands that the tide shall
    return to,
Cormorants, ducks, and gulls, fill ye my imagination!
Let us not talk of growth; we are still in our Aqueous Ages.

V. MARY TREVELLYN TO MISS ROPER,—*from Florence*

DEAREST MISS ROPER,—Alas! we are all at Florence quite safe, and
You, we hear, are shut up! indeed, it is sadly distressing!
We were most lucky, they say, to get off when we did from the troubles. 100
Now you are really besieged! they tell us it soon will be over;
Only I hope and trust without any fight in the city.
Do you see Mr Claude?—I thought he might do something for you.
I am quite sure on occasion he really would wish to be useful.
What is he doing? I wonder;—still studying Vatican marbles?
Letters, I hope, pass through. We trust your brother is better.

VI. CLAUDE TO EUSTACE

JUXTAPOSITION, in fine; and what is juxtaposition?
Look you, we travel along in the railway-carriage, or steamer,
And, *pour passer le temps*, till the tedious journey be ended,
Lay aside paper or book, to talk with the girl that is next one; 110
And, *pour passer le temps*, with the terminus all but in prospect,

Talk of eternal ties and marriages made in heaven.
  Ah, did we really accept with a perfect heart the illusion!
Ah, did we really believe that the Present indeed is the Only!
Or through all transmutation, all shock and convulsion of passion,
Feel we could carry undimmed, unextinguished, the light of our
      knowledge!
  But for his funeral train which the bridegroom sees in the distance,
Would he so joyfully, think you, fall in with the marriage-procession?
But for that final discharge, would he dare to enlist in that service?
But for that certain release, ever sign to that perilous contract?   120
But for that exit secure, ever bend to that treacherous doorway?—
Ah, but the bride, meantime,—do you think she sees it as he does?
  But for the steady fore-sense of a freer and larger existence,
Think you that man could consent to be circumscribed here into
      action?
But for assurance within of a limitless ocean divine, o'er
Whose great tranquil depths unconscious the wind-tost surface
Breaks into ripples of trouble that come and change and endure not,—
But that in this, of a truth, we have our being, and know it,
Think you we men could submit to live and move as we do here?
Ah, but the women,—God bless them!—they don't think at all about it. 130
  Yet we must eat and drink, as you say. And as limited beings
Scarcely can hope to attain upon earth to an Actual Abstract,
Leaving to God contemplation, to His hands knowledge confiding,
Sure that in us if it perish, in Him it abideth and dies not,
Let us in His sight accomplish our petty particular doings,—
Yes, and contented sit down to the victual that He has provided.
Allah is great, no doubt, and Juxtaposition his prophet.
Ah, but the women, alas! they don't look at it in that way.
  Juxtaposition is great;—but, my friend, I fear me, the maiden
Hardly would thank or acknowledge the lover that sought to obtain her, 140
Not as the thing he would wish, but the thing he must even put up
      with,—
Hardly would tender her hand to the wooer that candidly told her
That she is but for a space, an *ad-interim* solace and pleasure,—
That in the end she shall yield to a perfect and absolute something,
Which I then for myself shall behold, and not another,—
Which, amid fondest endearments, meantime I forget not, forsake not.
Ah, ye feminine souls, so loving and so exacting,
Since we cannot escape, must we even submit to deceive you?
Since, so cruel is truth, sincerity shocks and revolts you,
Will you have us your slaves to lie to you, flatter and—leave you?   150

VII. CLAUDE TO EUSTACE

JUXTAPOSITION is great,—but, you tell me, affinity greater.
Ah, my friend, there are many affinities, greater and lesser,

Stronger and weaker; and each, by the favour of juxtaposition,
Potent, efficient, in force,—for a time; but none, let me tell you,
Save by the law of the land and the ruinous force of the will, ah,
None, I fear me, at last quite sure to be final and perfect.
Lo, as I pace in the street, from the peasant-girl to the princess,
Homo sum, nihil humani a me alienum puto,—
*Vir sum, nihil fœminei,—*and e'en to the uttermost circle,
All that is Nature's is I, and I all things that are Nature's.   160
Yes, as I walk, I behold, in a luminous, large intuition,
That I can be and become anything that I meet with or look at:
I am the ox in the dray, the ass with the garden-stuff panniers;
I am the dog in the doorway, the kitten that plays in the window,
On sunny slab of the ruin the furtive and fugitive lizard,
Swallow above me that twitters, and fly that is buzzing about me;
Yea, and detect, as I go, by a faint but a faithful assurance,
E'en from the stones of the street, as from rocks or trees of the forest,
Something of kindred, a common, though latent vitality, greet me;
And, to escape from our strivings, mistakings, misgrowths, and
    perversions,   170
Fain could demand to return to that perfect and primitive silence,
Fain be enfolded and fixed, as of old, in their rigid embraces.

VIII. CLAUDE TO EUSTACE

AND as I walk on my way, I behold them consorting and coupling;
Faithful it seemeth, and fond, very fond, very probably faithful;
All as I go on my way, with a pleasure sincere and unmingled.
  Life is beautiful, Eustace, entrancing, enchanting to look at;
As are the streets of a city we pace while the carriage is changing,
As a chamber filled-in with harmonious, exquisite pictures,
Even so beautiful Earth; and could we eliminate only
This vile hungering impulse, this demon within us of craving,   180
Life were beatitude, living a perfect divine satisfaction.

IX. CLAUDE TO EUSTACE

MILD monastic faces in quiet collegiate cloisters:
So let me offer a single and celibatarian phrase, a
Tribute to those whom perhaps you do not believe I can honour.
But, from the tumult escaping, 'tis pleasant, of drumming and
    shouting,
Hither, oblivious awhile, to withdraw, of the fact or the falsehood,
And amid placid regards and mildly courteous greetings
Yield to the calm and composure and gentle abstraction that reign o'er
Mild monastic faces in quiet collegiate cloisters.
  Terrible word, Obligation! You should not, Eustace, you should not,   190
No, you should not have used it. But, O great Heavens! I repel it.

Oh, I cancel, reject, disavow, and repudiate wholly
Every debt in this kind, disclaim every claim, and dishonour,
Yea, my own heart's own writing, my soul's own signature! Ah, no!
I will be free in this; you shall not, none shall, bind me.
No, my friend, if you wish to be told, it was this above all things,
This that charmed me, ah, yes, even this, that she held me to nothing.
No, I could talk as I pleased; come close; fasten ties, as I fancied;
Bind and engage myself deep;—and lo, on the following morning
It was all e'en as before, like losings in games played for nothing.   200
Yes, when I came, with mean fears in my soul, with a semi-
     performance
At the first step breaking down in its pitiful rôle of evasion,
When to shuffle I came, to compromise, not meet, engagements,
Lo, with her calm eyes there she met me and knew nothing of it,—
Stood unexpecting, unconscious. *She* spoke not of obligations,
Knew not of debt,—ah, no, I believe you, for excellent reasons.

X. CLAUDE TO EUSTACE

HANG this thinking, at last! what good is it? oh, and what evil!
Oh, what mischief and pain! like a clock in a sick man's chamber,
Ticking and ticking, and still through each covert of slumber pursuing.
     What shall I do to thee, O thou Preserver of Men? Have compassion;   210
Be favourable, and hear! Take from me this regal knowledge;
Let me, contented and mute, with the beasts of the field, my brothers,
Tranquilly, happily lie,—and eat grass, like Nebuchadnezzar!

XI. CLAUDE TO EUSTACE

TIBUR is beautiful, too, and the orchard slopes, and the Anio
Falling, falling yet, to the ancient lyrical cadence;
Tibur and Anio's tide; and cool from Lucretilis ever,
With the Digentian stream, and with the Bandusian fountain,
Folded in Sabine recesses, the valley and villa of Horace:—
So not seeing I sung; so seeing and listening say I,
Here as I sit by the stream, as I gaze at the cell of the Sibyl,   220
Here with Albunea's home and the grove of Tiburnus beside me;[1]
Tivoli beautiful is, and musical, O Teverone,
Dashing from mountain to plain, thy parted impetuous waters!
Tivoli's waters and rocks; and fair under Monte Gennaro
(Haunt even yet, I must think, as I wander and gaze, of the shadows,
Faded and pale, yet immortal, of Faunus, the Nymphs, and the
     Graces),

[1]   ——domus Albuneæ resonantis,
      Et præceps Anio, et Tiburni lucus, et uda
      Mobilibus pomaria rivis.   [C.'s note]

Fair in itself, and yet fairer with human completing creations,
Folded in Sabine recesses the valley and villa of Horace:—
So not seeing I sung; so now—Nor seeing, nor hearing,
Neither by waterfall lulled, nor folded in sylvan embraces,   230
Neither by cell of the Sibyl, nor stepping the Monte Gennaro,
Seated on Anio's bank, nor sipping Bandusian waters,
But on Montorio's height, looking down on the tile-clad streets, the
    Cupolas, crosses, and domes, the bushes and kitchen-gardens,
Which, by the grace of the Tiber, proclaim themselves Rome of the
    Romans,—
But on Montorio's height, looking forth to the vapoury mountains,
Cheating the prisoner Hope with illusions of vision and fancy,—
But on Montorio's height, with these weary soldiers by me,
Waiting till Oudinot enter, to reinstate Pope and Tourist.

XII. MARY TREVELLYN TO MISS ROPER

DEAR MISS ROPER,—It seems, George Vernon, before we left
    Rome, said   240
Something to Mr Claude about what they call his attentions.
Susan, two nights ago, for the first time, heard this from Georgina.
It is *so* disagreeable and *so* annoying to think of!
If it could only be known, though we may never meet him again, that
It was all George's doing, and we were entirely unconscious,
It would extremely relieve—Your ever affectionate Mary.

P.S. (1)

Here is your letter arrived this moment, just as I wanted.
So you have seen him,—indeed,—and guessed,—how dreadfully
    clever!
What did he really say? and what was your answer exactly?
Charming!—but wait for a moment, I haven't read through the letter.   250

P.S. (2)

Ah, my dearest Miss Roper, do just as you fancy about it.
If you think it sincerer to tell him I know of it, do so.
Though I should most extremely dislike it, I know I could manage.
It is the simplest thing, but surely wholly uncalled for.
Do as you please; you know I trust implicitly to you.
Say whatever is right and needful for ending the matter.
Only don't tell Mr Claude, what I will tell you as a secret,
That I should like very well to show him myself I forget it.

P.S. (3)

I am to say that the wedding is finally settled for Tuesday.
Ah, my dear Miss Roper, you surely, surely can manage   260

Not to let it appear that I know of that odious matter.
It would be pleasanter far for myself to treat it exactly
As if it had not occurred; and I do not think he would like it.
I must remember to add, that as soon as the wedding is over
We shall be off, I believe, in a hurry, and travel to Milan,
There to meet friends of Papa's, I am told, at the Croce di Malta;
Then I cannot say whither, but not at present to England.

XIII. CLAUDE TO EUSTACE

YES, on Montorio's height for a last farewell of the city,—
So it appears; though then I was quite uncertain about it.
So, however, it was. And now to explain the proceeding.   270
   I was to go, as I told you, I think, with the people to Florence.
Only the day before, the foolish family Vernon
Made some uneasy remarks, as we walked to our lodging together,
As to intentions, forsooth, and so forth. I was astounded,
Horrified quite; and obtaining just then, as it happened, an offer
(No common favour) of seeing the great Ludovisi collection,
Why, I made this a pretence, and wrote that they must excuse me.
How could I go? Great Heaven! to conduct a permitted flirtation
Under those vulgar eyes, the observed of such observers!
Well, but I now, by a series of fine diplomatic inquiries,   280
Find from a sort of relation, a good and sensible woman,
Who is remaining at Rome with a brother too ill for removal,
That it was wholly unsanctioned, unknown,—not, I think, by
      Georgina:
She, however, ere this,—and that is the best of the story,—
She and the Vernon, thank Heaven, are wedded and gone—
      honey-mooning.
So—on Montorio's height for a last farewell of the city.
Tibur I have not seen, nor the lakes that of old I had dreamt of;
Tiber I shall not see, nor Anio's waters, nor deep en-
Folded in Sabine recesses the valley and villa of Horace;
Tibur I shall not see;—but something better I shall see.   290
   Twice I have tried before, and failed in getting the horses;
Twice I have tried and failed: this time it shall not be a failure.

Therefore farewell, ye hills, and ye, ye envineyarded ruins.
   Therefore farewell, ye walls, palaces, pillars, and domes!
Therefore farewell, far seen, ye peaks of the mythic Albano,
   Seen from Montorio's height, Tibur and Æsula's hills!
Ah, could we once, ere we go, could we stand, while, to ocean descending,
   Sinks o'er the yellow dark plain slowly the yellow broad sun,
Stand, from the forest emerging at sunset, at once in the champaign,
   Open, but studded with trees, chestnuts umbrageous and old,   300

E'en in those fair open fields that incurve to thy beautiful hollow,
  Nemi, imbedded in wood, Nemi, inurned in the hill!—
Therefore farewell, ye plains, and ye hills, and the City Eternal!
  Therefore farewell! We depart, but to behold you again!

CANTO IV

Eastward, or Northward, or West? I wander and ask as I wander,
  Weary, yet eager and sure, Where shall I come to my love?
Whitherward hasten to seek her? Ye daughters of Italy, tell me,
  Graceful and tender and dark, is she consorting with you?
Thou that out-climbest the torrent, that tendest thy goats to the summit,
  Call to me, child of the Alp, has she been seen on the heights?
Italy, farewell I bid thee! for whither she leads me, I follow.
  Farewell the vineyard! for I, where I but guess her, must go.
Weariness welcome, and labour, wherever it be, if at last it
  Bring me in mountain or plain into the sight of my love.   10

I. CLAUDE TO EUSTACE,—*from Florence*

GONE from Florence; indeed; and that is truly provoking;—
Gone to Milan, it seems; then I go also to Milan.
Five days now departed; but they can travel but slowly;—
I quicker far; and I know, as it happens, the house they will go to.—
Why, what else should I do? Stay here and look at the pictures,
Statues, and churches? Alack, I am sick of the statues and pictures!—
No, to Bologna, Parma, Piacenza, Lodi, and Milan,
Off go we to-night,—and the Venus go to the Devil!

II. CLAUDE TO EUSTACE,—*from Bellaggio*

GONE to Como, they said; and I have posted to Como.
There was a letter left; but the *cameriere* had lost it.   20
Could it have been for me? They came, however, to Como,
And from Como went by the boat,—perhaps to the Splügen,—
Or to the Stelvio, say, and the Tyrol; also it might be
By Porlezza across to Lugano, and so to the Simplon
Possibly, or the St Gothard,—or possibly, too, to Baveno,
Orta, Turin, and elsewhere. Indeed, I am greatly bewildered.

III. CLAUDE TO EUSTACE,—*from Bellaggio*

I HAVE been up the Splügen, and on the Stelvio also:
Neither of these can I find they have followed; in no one inn, and
This would be odd, have they written their names. I have been to
    Porlezza;
There they have not been seen, and therefore not at Lugano.   30

What shall I do? Go on through the Tyrol, Switzerland, Deutschland,
Seeking, an inverse Saul, a kingdom, to find only asses?
  There is a tide, at least in the *love* affairs of mortals,
Which, when taken at flood, leads on to the happiest fortune,—
Leads to the marriage-morn and the orange-flowers and the altar,
And the long lawful line of crowned joys to crowned joys succeeding.—
Ah, it has ebbed with me! Ye gods, and when it was flowing,
Pitiful fool that I was, to stand fiddle-faddling in that way!

IV. CLAUDE TO EUSTACE,—*from Bellaggio*

I HAVE returned and found their names in the book at Como.
Certain it is I was right, and yet I am also in error.   40
Added in feminine hand, I read, *By the boat to Bellaggio.*—
So to Bellaggio again, with the words of her writing to aid me.
Yet at Bellaggio I find no trace, no sort of remembrance.
So I am here, and wait, and know every hour will remove them.

V. CLAUDE TO EUSTACE,—*from Bellaggio*

I HAVE but one chance left,—and that is going to Florence.
But it is cruel to turn. The mountains seem to demand me,—
Peak and valley from far to beckon and motion me onward.
Somewhere amid their folds she passes whom fain I would follow;
Somewhere among those heights she haply calls me to seek her.
Ah, could I hear her call! could I catch the glimpse of her raiment! 50
Turn, however, I must, though it seem I turn to desert her;
For the sense of the thing is simply to hurry to Florence,
Where the certainty yet may be learnt, I suppose, from the Ropers.

VI. MARY TREVELLYN, *from Lucerne*
TO MISS ROPER, *at Florence*

DEAR MISS ROPER,—By this you are safely away, we are hoping,
Many a league from Rome; erelong we trust we shall see you.
How have you travelled? I wonder;—was Mr Claude your companion?
As for ourselves, we went from Como straight to Lugano;
So by the Mount St Gothard; we meant to go by Porlezza,
Taking the steamer, and stopping, as you had advised, at Bellaggio,
Two or three days or more; but this was suddenly altered, 60
After we left the hotel, on the very way to the steamer.
So we have seen, I fear, not one of the lakes in perfection.
  Well, he is not come; and now, I suppose, he will not come.
What will you think, meantime?—and yet I must really confess it;—
What will you say? I wrote him a note. We left in a hurry,
Went from Milan to Como, three days before we expected.
But I thought, if he came all the way to Milan, he really

Ought not to be disappointed; and so I wrote three lines to
Say I had heard he was coming, desirous of joining our party;—
If so, then I said, we had started for Como, and meant to   70
Cross the St Gothard, and stay, we believed, at Lucerne, for the
   summer.
Was it wrong? and why, if it was, has it failed to bring him?
Did he not think it worth while to come to Milan? He knew (you
Told him) the house we should go to. Or may it, perhaps, have
   miscarried?
Any way, now, I repent, and am heartily vexed that I wrote it.

There is a home on the shore of the Alpine sea, that upswelling
   High up the mountain-sides spreads in the hollow between;
Wilderness, mountain, and snow from the land of the olive conceal it;
   Under Pilatus's hill low by its river it lies:
Italy, utter the word, and the olive and vine will allure not,—   80
   Wilderness, forest, and snow will not the passage impede;
Italy, unto thy cities receding, the clew to recover,
   Hither, recovered the clew, shall not the traveller haste?

CANTO V

There is a city, upbuilt on the quays of the turbulent Arno,
   Under Fiesole's heights,—thither are we to return?
There is a city that fringes the curve of the inflowing waters,
   Under the perilous hill fringes the beautiful bay,—
Parthenope do they call thee?—the Siren, Neapolis, seated
   Under Vesevus's hill,—are we receding to thee?—
Sicily, Greece, will invite, and the Orient;—or are we to turn to
   England, which may after all be for its children the best?

I. MARY TREVELLYN, *at Lucerne,* TO MISS ROPER, *at Florence*

So you are really free, and living in quiet at Florence;
That is delightful news;—you travelled slowly and safely;   10
Mr Claude got you out; took rooms at Florence before you;
Wrote from Milan to say so; had left directly for Milan,
Hoping to find us soon;—*if he could, he would, you are certain.*—
Dear Miss Roper, your letter has made me exceedingly happy.
   You are quite sure, you say, he asked you about our intentions;
You had not heard as yet of Lucerne, but told him of Como.—
Well, perhaps he will come;—however, I will not expect it.
Though you say you are sure,—*if he can, he will, you are certain.*
O my dear, many thanks from your ever affectionate Mary.

ARTHUR HUGH CLOUGH

II. CLAUDE TO EUSTACE

Florence.

ACTION will furnish belief,—but will that belief be the true one?   20
This is the point, you know. However, it doesn't much matter.
What one wants, I suppose, is to predetermine the action,
So as to make it entail, not a chance-belief, but the true one.
Out of the question, you say; *if a thing isn't wrong, we may do it.*
Ah! but this *wrong*, you see—but I do not know that it matters.
     Eustace, the Ropers are gone, and no one can tell me about them.

Pisa.

Pisa, they say they think; and so I follow to Pisa,
Hither and thither inquiring, I weary of making inquiries;
I am ashamed, I declare, of asking people about it.—
Who are your friends? You said you had friends who would certainly
     know them.   30

Florence.

But it is idle, moping, and thinking, and trying to fix her
Image more and more in, to write the old perfect inscription
Over and over again upon every page of remembrance.
     I have settled to stay at Florence to wait for your answer.
Who are your friends? Write quickly and tell me. I wait for your answer.

III. MARY TREVELLYN TO MISS ROPER, *at Lucca Baths*

YOU are at Lucca Baths, you tell me, to stay for the summer;
Florence was quite too hot; you can't move further at present.
Will you not come, do you think, before the summer is over?
     Mr C. got you out with very considerable trouble;
And he was useful and kind, and seemed so happy to serve you;   40
Didn't stay with you long, but talked very openly to you;
Made you almost his confessor, without appearing to know it,—
What about?—and you say you didn't need his confessions.
O my dear Miss Roper, I dare not trust what you tell me!
     Will he come, do you think? I am really so sorry for him!
They didn't give him my letter at Milan, I feel pretty certain.
You had told him Bellaggio. We didn't go to Bellaggio;
So he would miss our track, and perhaps never come to Lugano,
Where we were written in full, *To Lucerne across the St Gothard.*
But he could write to you;—you would tell him where you were going.   50

IV. CLAUDE TO EUSTACE

LET me, then, bear to forget her. I will not cling to her falsely;
Nothing factitious or forced shall impair the old happy relation.
I will let myself go, forget, not try to remember;
I will walk on my way, accept the chances that meet me,
Freely encounter the world, imbibe these alien airs, and
Never ask if new feelings and thoughts are of her or of others.
Is she not changing, herself—the old image would only delude me.
I will be bold, too, and change,—if it must be. Yet if in all things,
Yet if I do but aspire evermore to the Absolute only,
I shall be doing, I think, somehow, what she will be doing;—   60
I shall be thine, O my child, some way, though I know not in what way.
Let me submit to forget her; I must; I already forget her.

V. CLAUDE TO EUSTACE

UTTERLY vain is, alas! this attempt at the Absolute,—wholly!
I, who believed not in her, because I would fain believe nothing,
Have to believe as I may, with a wilful, unmeaning acceptance.
I, who refused to enfasten the roots of my floating existence
In the rich earth, cling now to the hard, naked rock that is left me.—
Ah! she was worthy, Eustace,—and that, indeed, is my comfort,—
Worthy a nobler heart than a fool such as I could have given.

———————

YES, it relieves me to write, though I do not send, and the chance that   70
Takes may destroy my fragments. But as men pray, without asking
Whether One really exist to hear or do anything for them,—
Simply impelled by the need of the moment to turn to a Being
In a conception of whom there is freedom from all limitation,—
So in your image I turn to an *ens rationis* of friendship.
Even so write in your name I know not to whom nor in what wise.

———————

THERE was a time, methought it was but lately departed,
When, if a thing was denied me, I felt I was bound to attempt it;
Choice alone should take, and choice alone should surrender.
There was a time, indeed, when I had not retired thus early,   80
Languidly thus, from pursuit of a purpose I once had adopted.
But it is over, all that! I have slunk from the perilous field in
Whose wild struggle of forces the prizes of life are contested.
It is over, all that! I am a coward, and know it.
Courage in me could be only factitious, unnatural, useless.

———————

COMFORT has come to me here in the dreary streets of the city,
Comfort—how do you think?—with a barrel-organ to bring it.

Moping along the streets, and cursing my day as I wandered,
All of a sudden my ear met the sound of an English psalm-tune.
Comfort me it did, till indeed I was very near crying.   90
Ah, there is some great truth, partial, very likely, but needful,
Lodged, I am strangely sure, in the tones of the English psalm-tune.
Comfort it was at least; and I must take without question
Comfort, however it come, in the dreary streets of the city.

WHAT with trusting myself, and seeking support from within me,
Almost I could believe I had gained a religious assurance,
Formed in my own poor soul a great moral basis to rest on.
Ah, but indeed I see, I feel it factitious entirely;
I refuse, reject, and put it utterly from me;
I will look straight out, see things, not try to evade them;   100
Fact shall be fact for me; and the Truth the Truth as ever,
Flexible, changeable, vague, and multiform, and doubtful.—
Off, and depart to the void, thou subtle, fanatical tempter!

I SHALL behold thee again (is it so?) at a new visitation,
O ill genius thou! I shall, at my life's dissolution,
(When the pulses are weak, and the feeble light of the reason
Flickers, an unfed flame retiring slow from the socket),
Low on a sick-bed laid, hear one, as it were, at the doorway,
And, looking up, see thee, standing by, looking emptily at me;
I shall entreat thee then, though now I dare to refuse thee,—   110
Pale and pitiful now, but terrible then to the dying.—
Well, I will see thee again, and while I can, will repel thee.

VI. CLAUDE TO EUSTACE

ROME is fallen, I hear, the gallant Medici taken,
Noble Manara slain, and Garibaldi has lost *il Moro*;—
Rome is fallen; and fallen, or falling, heroical Venice.
I, meanwhile, for the loss of a single small chit of a girl, sit
Moping and mourning here,—for her, and myself much smaller.
   Whither depart the souls of the brave that die in the battle,
Die in the lost, lost fight, for the cause that perishes with them?
Are they upborne from the field on the slumberous pinions of
       angels   120
Unto a far-off home, where the weary rest from their labour,
And the deep wounds are healed, and the bitter and burning moisture
Wiped from the generous eyes? or do they linger, unhappy,
Pining, and haunting the grave of their by-gone hope and endeavour?
   All declamation, alas! though I talk, I care not for Rome, nor
Italy; feebly and faintly, and but with the lips, can lament the

Wreck of the Lombard youth and the victory of the oppressor.
Whither depart the brave?—God knows; I certainly do not.

VII. MARY TREVELLYN TO MISS ROPER

HE has not come as yet; and now I must not expect it.
You have written you say, to friends at Florence, to see him,   130
If he perhaps should return;—but that is surely unlikely.
Has he not written to you?—he did not know your direction.
Oh, how strange never once to have told him where you were going!
Yet if he only wrote to Florence, that would have reached you.
If what you say he said was true, why has he not done so?
Is he gone back to Rome, do you think, to his Vatican marbles?—
O my dear Miss Roper, forgive me! do not be angry!—
You have written to Florence;—your friends would certainly find him.
Might you not write to him?—but yet it is so little likely!
I shall expect nothing more.—Ever yours, your affectionate Mary.   140

VIII. CLAUDE TO EUSTACE

I CANNOT stay at Florence, not even to wait for a letter.
Galleries only oppress me. Remembrance of hope I had cherished
(Almost more than as hope, when I passed through Florence the first
      time)
Lies like a sword in my soul. I am more a coward than ever,
Chicken-hearted, past thought. The *caffès* and waiters distress me.
All is unkind, and, alas! I am ready for any one's kindness.
Oh, I knew it of old, and knew it, I thought, to perfection,
If there is any one thing in the world to preclude all kindness,
It is the need of it,—it is this sad, self-defeating dependence.
Why is this, Eustace? Myself, were I stronger, I think I could tell you.   150
But it is odd when it comes. So plumb I the deeps of depression,
Daily in deeper, and find no support, no will, no purpose.
All my old strengths are gone. And yet I shall have to do something.
Ah, the key of our life, that passes all wards, opens all locks,
Is not *I will*, but *I must*. I must,—I must,—and I do it.

———

AFTER all, do I know that I really cared so about her?
Do whatever I will, I cannot call up her image;
For when I close my eyes, I see, very likely, St Peter's,
Or the Pantheon façade, or Michel Angelo's figures,
Or, at a wish, when I please, the Alban hills and the Forum,—   160
But that face, those eyes,—ah no, never anything like them;
Only, try as I will, a sort of featureless outline,
And a pale blank orb, which no recollection will add to.

After all perhaps there was something factitious about it:
I have had pain, it is true, I have wept; and so have the actors.

———————

AT the last moment I have your letter, for which I was waiting.
I have taken my place, and see no good in inquiries.
Do nothing more, good Eustace, I pray you. It only will vex me.
Take no measures. Indeed, should we meet, I could not be certain;
All might be changed, you know. Or perhaps there was nothing to be
    changed.   170
It is a curious history, this; and yet I foresaw it;
I could have told it before. The Fates, it is clear, are against us;
For it is certain enough that I met with the people you mention;
They were at Florence the day I returned there, and spoke to me even;
Stayed a week, saw me often; departed, and whither I know not.
Great is Fate, and is best. I believe in Providence partly.
What is ordained is right, and all that happens is ordered.
Ah, no, that isn't it. But yet I retain my conclusion.
I will go where I am led, and will not dictate to the chances.
Do nothing more, I beg. If you love me, forbear interfering.   180

IX. CLAUDE TO EUSTACE

SHALL we come out of it all, some day, as one does from a tunnel?
Will it be all at once, without our doing or asking,
We shall behold clear day, the trees and meadows about us,
And the faces of friends, and the eyes we loved looking at us?
Who knows? Who can say? It will not do to suppose it.

X. CLAUDE TO EUSTACE,—*from Rome*

ROME will not suit me, Eustace; the priests and soldiers possess it;
Priests and soldiers;—and, ah! which is worst, the priest or the soldier?
   Politics, farewell, however! For what could I do? with inquiring,
Talking, collating the journals, go fever my brain about things o'er
Which I can have no control. No, happen whatever may happen,   190
Time, I suppose, will subsist; the earth will revolve on its axis;
People will travel; the stranger will wander as now in the city;
Rome will be here, and the Pope the *custode* of Vatican marbles.
   I have no heart, however, for any marble or fresco;
I have essayed it in vain; 'tis vain as yet to essay it:
But I may haply resume some day my studies in this kind;
Not as the Scripture says, is, I think, the fact. Ere our death-day,
Faith, I think, does pass, and Love; but Knowledge abideth.
Let us seek Knowledge;—the rest must come and go as it happens.
Knowledge is hard to seek, and harder yet to adhere to.   200
Knowledge is painful often; and yet when we know, we are happy.

Seek it, and leave mere Faith and Love to come with the chances.
As for Hope,—to-morrow I hope to be starting for Naples.
Rome will not do, I see, for many very good reasons.
    Eastward, then, I suppose, with the coming of winter, to Egypt.

XI. MARY TREVELLYN TO MISS ROPER

YOU have heard nothing; of course, I know you can have heard
    nothing.
Ah, well, more than once I have broken my purpose, and sometimes,
Only too often, have looked for the little lake-steamer to bring him.
But it is only fancy,—I do not really expect it.
Oh, and you see I know so exactly how he would take it: 210
Finding the chances prevail against meeting again, he would banish
Forthwith every thought of the poor little possible hope, which
I myself could not help, perhaps, thinking only too much of;
He would resign himself, and go. I see it exactly.
So I also submit, although in a different manner.
    Can you not really come? We go very shortly to England.

———

So go forth to the world, to the good report and the evil?
  Go, little book! thy tale, is it not evil and good?
Go, and if strangers revile, pass quietly by without answer.
  Go, and if curious friends ask of thy rearing and age,   220
Say, 'I am flitting about many years from brain unto brain of
  Feeble and restless youths born to inglorious days;
But,' so finish the word, 'I was writ in a Roman chamber,
  When from Janiculan heights thundered the cannon of France.'

(Wr. from 1849; pub. 1858)

183   *The Latest Decalogue*

THOU shalt have one God only; who
Would be at the expense of two?
No graven images may be
Worshipped, except the currency:
Swear not at all; for for thy curse
Thine enemy is none the worse:
At church on Sunday to attend
Will serve to keep the world thy friend:
Honour thy parents; that is, all
From whom advancement may befall: 10
Thou shalt not kill; but needst not strive
Officiously to keep alive:

Do not adultery commit;
Advantage rarely comes of it:
Thou shalt not steal; an empty feat,
When it's so lucrative to cheat:
Bear not false witness; let the lie
Have time on its own wings to fly:
Thou shalt not covet; but tradition
Approves all forms of competition.   20

The sum of all is, thou shalt love,
If any body, God above:
At any rate shall never labour
More than thyself to love thy neighbour.

(1862)

from *Dipsychus* (184–185)

184   As I sat at the café, I said to myself,
They may talk as they please about what they call pelf,
They may sneer as they like about eating and drinking,
But help it I cannot, I cannot help thinking
   How pleasant it is to have money, heigh ho!
   How pleasant it is to have money.

I sit at my table *en grand seigneur*,
And when I have done, throw a crust to the poor;
Not only the pleasure, one's self, of good living,
But also the pleasure of now and then giving.   10
   So pleasant it is to have money, heigh ho!
   So pleasant it is to have money.

It was but last winter I came up to Town,
But already I'm getting a little renown;
I make new acquaintance where'er I appear;
I am not too shy, and have nothing to fear.
   So pleasant it is to have money, heigh ho!
   So pleasant it is to have money.

I drive through the streets, and I care not a d—mn;
The people they stare, and they ask who I am;   20
And if I should chance to run over a cad,
I can pay for the damage if ever so bad.
   So pleasant it is to have money, heigh ho!
   So pleasant it is to have money.

We stroll to our box and look down on the pit,
And if it weren't low should be tempted to spit;
We loll and we talk until people look up,
And when it's half over we go out and sup.
  So pleasant it is to have money, heigh ho!
  So pleasant it is to have money.   30

The best of the table and best of the fare—
And as for the others, the devil may care;
It isn't our fault if they dare not afford
To sup like a prince and be drunk as a lord.
  So pleasant it is to have money, heigh ho!
  So pleasant it is to have money.

We sit at our tables and tipple champagne;
Ere one bottle goes, comes another again;
The waiters they skip and they scuttle about,
And the landlord attends us so civilly out.   40
  So pleasant it is to have money, heigh ho!
  So pleasant it is to have money.

It was but last winter I came up to Town,
But already I'm getting a little renown;
I get to good houses without much ado,
Am beginning to see the nobility too.
  So pleasant it is to have money, heigh ho!
  So pleasant it is to have money.

O dear! what a pity they ever should lose it!
For they are the gentry that know how to use it;   50
So grand and so graceful, such manners, such dinners,
But yet, after all, it is we are the winners.
  So pleasant it is to have money, heigh ho!
  So pleasant it is to have money.

Thus I sat at my table *en grand seigneur*,
And when I had done threw a crust to the poor;
Not only the pleasure, one's self, of good eating,
But also the pleasure of now and then treating.
  So pleasant it is to have money, heigh ho!
  So pleasant it is to have money.   60

They may talk as they please about what they call pelf,
And how one ought never to think of one's self,
And how pleasures of thought surpass eating and drinking—
My pleasure of thought is the pleasure of thinking
   How pleasant it is to have money, heigh ho!
   How pleasant it is to have money.

A gondola here, and a gondola there,
'Tis the pleasantest fashion of taking the air.
To right and to left; stop, turn, and go yonder,
And let us repeat, o'er the tide as we wander,   70
   How pleasant it is to have money, heigh ho!
   How pleasant it is to have money.

                      (Scene V)

185   'THERE is no God,' the wicked saith,
          'And truly it's a blessing,
       For what he might have done with us
          It's better only guessing.'

       'There is no God,' a youngster thinks,
          'Or really, if there may be,
       He surely didn't mean a man
          Always to be a baby.'

       'There is no God, or if there is,'
          The tradesman thinks, ''twere funny   10
       If he should take it ill in me
          To make a little money.'

       'Whether there be,' the rich man says,
          'It matters very little,
       For I and mine, thank somebody,
          Are not in want of victual.'

       Some others, also, to themselves
          Who scarce so much as doubt it,
       Think there is none, when they are well,
          And do not think about it.   20

       But country folks who live beneath
          The shadow of the steeple;
       The parson and the parson's wife,
          And mostly married people;

Youths green and happy in first love,
   So thankful for illusion;
And men caught out in what the world
   Calls guilt, in first confusion;

And almost every one when age,
   Disease, or sorrows strike him,   30
Inclines to think there is a God,
   Or something very like Him.

                (Scene VI; wr. from 1850; pub. 1865)

186   I DREAMED a dream: I dreamt that I espied,
Upon a stone that was not rolled aside,
A shadow sitting by a grave—a Shade,
As thin, as unsubstantial, as of old
Came, the Greek poet told,
To lick the life-blood in the trench Ulysses made—
As pale, as thin, and said:
'I am the resurrection of the dead.
The night is past, the morning is at hand,
And I must in my proper semblance stand,   10
Appear brief space and vanish,—hear me, this is true,
I am that Jesus whom they slew.'

And shadows dim, I dreamed, the dead apostles came,
And bent their heads for sorrow and for shame—
Sorrow for their great loss, and shame
For what they did in that vain name.

And in long ranges far behind there seemed
Pale vapoury angel forms; or was it cloud? that kept
Strange watch; the women also stood beside and wept.
   And Peter spoke the word: 20
'O my own Lord,
What is it we must do?
Is it then all untrue?
Did we not see, and hear, and handle thee,
Yea, for whole hours
Upon the Mount in Galilee,
On the lake shore, and here at Bethany,
When thou ascended to thy God and ours?'
    And paler still became the distant cloud,
    The women wept aloud.   30

And the Shade answered, 'What ye say I know not;
    But it is true
    I am that Jesus whom they slew,
Whom ye have preached, but in what way I know not.'

*

And the great World, it chanced, came by that way,
And stopped, and looked, and spoke to the police,
And said the thing, for order's sake and peace,
Most certainly must be suppressed, the nuisance cease.
His wife and daughter must have where to pray,
And whom to pray to, at the least one day   40
In seven, and something definite to say.
Whether the fact so many years ago
Had, or not, happened, how was he to know?
Yet he had always heard that it was so.
As for himself, perhaps it was all one;
And yet he found it not unpleasant, too,
On Sunday morning in the roomy pew,
To see the thing with such decorum done.
As for himself, perhaps it was all one;
Yet on one's death-bed all men always said   50
It was a comfortable thing to think upon
The Atonement and the Resurrection of the dead.
So the great world as having said his say,
Unto his country-house pursued his way.
And on the grave the Shadow sat all day.

*

And the poor Pope was sure it must be so,
Else wherefore did the people kiss his toe?
The subtle Jesuit cardinal shook his head,
And mildly looked and said,
It mattered not a jot   60
Whether the thing, indeed, were so or not;
Religion must be kept up, and the Church preserved,
And for the people this best served,
And then he turned, and added most demurely,
'Whatever may befall,
We Catholics need no evidence at all,
The holy father is infallible, surely!'

An English canon heard,
And [quietly demurred.]
Religion rests on evidence, of course,   70
And on inquiry we must put no force.

Difficulties still, upon whatever ground,
Are likely, almost certain, to be found.
The Theist scheme, the Pantheist, one and all,
Must with, or e'en before, the Christian fall.
And till the thing were plainer to our eyes,
To disturb faith was surely most unwise.
As for the Shade, who trusted such narrations?
Except, of course, in ancient revelations.

And dignitaries of the Church came by.   80
It had been worth to some of them, they said,
Some £100,000 a year a head.
If it fetched so much in the market, truly,
'Twas not a thing to be given up unduly.
It had been proved by Butler in one way,
By Paley better in a later day;
It had been proved in twenty ways at once,
By many a doctor plain to any a dunce;
There was no question but it must be so.
   And the Shade answered, that he did not know;   90
He had no reading, and might be deceived,
But still He was the Christ, as he believed.

And women, mild and pure,
Forth from still homes and village schools did pass,
And asked, if this indeed were thus, alas,
What should they teach their children and the poor?
   The Shade replied, he could not know,
But it was truth, the fact was so.

                    *   *   *

Who had kept all commandments from his youth
Yet still found one thing lacking—even Truth: 100
And the Shade only answered, 'Go, make haste,
Enjoy thy great possessions as thou may'st.'

                                        (1869)

187   THAT there are powers above us I admit;
         It may be true too
         That while we walk the troublous tossing sea,
         That when we see the o'ertopping waves advance,
         And when [we] feel our feet beneath us sink,
         There are who walk beside us; and the cry
         That rises so spontaneous to the lips,

The 'Help us or we perish,' is not nought,
An evanescent spectrum of disease.
It may be that in deed and not in fancy,   10
A hand that is not ours upstays our steps,
A voice that is not ours commands the waves,
Commands the waves, and whispers in our ear,
O thou of little faith, why didst thou doubt?
At any rate—
That there are beings above us, I suppose,
(Hypothesis the soul of science is),
And when we lift up holy hands of prayer,
I will not say they will not give us aid.

(1869)

DANTE GABRIEL ROSSETTI
1828–1882

188   *The Blessed Damozel*

THE blessed damozel leaned out
  From the gold bar of Heaven;
Her eyes were deeper than the depth
  Of waters stilled at even;
She had three lilies in her hand,
  And the stars in her hair were seven.

Her robe, ungirt from clasp to hem,
  No wrought flowers did adorn,
But a white rose of Mary's gift,
  For service meetly worn;   10
Her hair that lay along her back
  Was yellow like ripe corn.

Herseemed she scarce had been a day
  One of God's choristers;
The wonder was not yet quite gone
  From that still look of hers;
Albeit, to them she left, her day
  Had counted as ten years.

(To one, it is ten years of years.
   . . . Yet now, and in this place,   20
Surely she leaned o'er me—her hair
   Fell all about my face . . .
Nothing: the autumn-fall of leaves.
   The whole year sets apace.)

It was the rampart of God's house
   That she was standing on;
By God built over the sheer depth
   The which is Space begun;
So high, that looking downward thence
   She scarce could see the sun.   30

It lies in Heaven, across the flood
   Of ether, as a bridge.
Beneath, the tides of day and night
   With flame and darkness ridge
The void, as low as where this earth
   Spins like a fretful midge.

Around her, lovers, newly met
   'Mid deathless love's acclaims,
Spoke evermore among themselves
   Their heart-remembered names;   40
And the souls mounting up to God
   Went by her like thin flames.

And still she bowed herself and stooped
   Out of the circling charm;
Until her bosom must have made
   The bar she leaned on warm,
And the lilies lay as if asleep
   Along her bended arm.

From the fixed place of Heaven she saw
   Time like a pulse shake fierce   50
Through all the worlds. Her gaze still strove
   Within the gulf to pierce
Its path; and now she spoke as when
   The stars sang in their spheres.

The sun was gone now; the curled moon
   Was like a little feather
Fluttering far down the gulf; and now
   She spoke through the still weather.
Her voice was like the voice the stars
   Had when they sang together.   60

(Ah sweet! Even now, in that bird's song,
    Strove not her accents there,
Fain to be hearkened? When those bells
    Possessed the mid-day air,
Strove not her steps to reach my side
    Down all the echoing stair?)

'I wish that he were come to me,
    For he will come,' she said.
'Have I not prayed in Heaven?—on earth,
    Lord, Lord, has he not pray'd?   70
Are not two prayers a perfect strength?
    And shall I feel afraid?

'When round his head the aureole clings,
    And he is clothed in white,
I'll take his hand and go with him
    To the deep wells of light;
As unto a stream we will step down,
    And bathe there in God's sight.

'We two will stand beside that shrine,
    Occult, withheld, untrod,   80
Whose lamps are stirred continually
    With prayer sent up to God;
And see our old prayers, granted, melt
    Each like a little cloud.

'We two will lie i' the shadow of
    That living mystic tree
Within whose secret growth the Dove
    Is sometimes felt to be,
While every leaf that His plumes touch
    Saith His Name audibly.   90

'And I myself will teach to him,
    I myself, lying so,
The songs I sing here; which his voice
    Shall pause in, hushed and slow,
And find some knowledge at each pause,
    Or some new thing to know.'

(Alas! we two, we two, thou say'st!
    Yea, one wast thou with me
That once of old. But shall God lift
    To endless unity   100
The soul whose likeness with thy soul
    Was but its love for thee?)

'We two,' she said, 'will seek the groves
  Where the lady Mary is,
With her five handmaidens, whose names
  Are five sweet symphonies,
Cecily, Gertrude, Magdalen,
  Margaret and Rosalys.

'Circlewise sit they, with bound locks
  And foreheads garlanded;   110
Into the fine cloth white like flame
  Weaving the golden thread,
To fashion the birth-robes for them
  Who are just born, being dead.

'He shall fear, haply, and be dumb:
  Then will I lay my cheek
To his, and tell about our love,
  Not once abashed or weak:
And the dear Mother will approve
  My pride, and let me speak.   120

'Herself shall bring us, hand in hand,
  To Him round whom all souls
Kneel, the clear-ranged unnumbered heads
  Bowed with their aureoles:
And angels meeting us shall sing
  To their citherns and citoles.

'There will I ask of Christ the Lord
  Thus much for him and me:—
Only to live as once on earth
  With Love,—only to be,   130
As then awhile, for ever now
  Together, I and he.'

She gazed and listened and then said,
  Less sad of speech than mild,—
'All this is when he comes.' She ceased.
  The light thrilled towards her, fill'd
With angels in strong level flight.
  Her eyes prayed, and she smil'd.

(I saw her smile.) But soon their path
  Was vague in distant spheres: 140
And then she cast her arms along
  The golden barriers,
And laid her face between her hands,
  And wept. (I heard her tears.)

(Wr. 1847; pub. 1850)

272

189 ## *A Half-Way Pause*

THE turn of noontide has begun.
  In the weak breeze the sunshine yields.
  There is a bell upon the fields.
On the long hedgerow's tangled run
  A low white cottage intervenes:
  Against the wall a blind man leans,
And sways his face to have the sun.

Our horses' hoofs stir in the road,
  Quiet and sharp. Light hath a song
  Whose silence, being heard, seems long.   10
The point of noon maketh abode,
  And will not be at once gone through.
  The sky's deep colour saddens you,
And the heat weighs a dreamy load.

                        (Wr. 1849; pub. 1886)

190 ## *Autumn Idleness*

THIS sunlight shames November where he grieves
  In dead red leaves, and will not let him shun
  The day, though bough with bough be over-run.
But with a blessing every glade receives
High salutation; while from hillock-eaves
  The deer gaze calling, dappled white and dun,
  As if, being foresters of old, the sun
Had marked them with the shade of forest-leaves.

Here dawn to-day unveiled her magic glass;
  Here noon now gives the thirst and takes the dew;   10
Till eve bring rest when other good things pass.
  And here the lost hours the lost hours renew
While I still lead my shadow o'er the grass,
  Nor know, for longing, that which I should do.

                        (Wr. 1850; pub. 1870)

191 *Sudden Light*

I HAVE been here before,
    But when or how I cannot tell:
I know the grass beyond the door,
    The sweet, keen smell,
The sighing sound, the lights around the shore.

You have been mine before,—
    How long ago I may not know:
But just when at that swallow's soar
    Your neck turned so,
Some veil did fall,—I knew it all of yore.   10

Has this been thus before?
    And shall not thus time's eddying flight
Still with our lives our love restore
    In death's despite,
And day and night yield one delight once more?

                        (Wr. 1854; pub. 1863)

192 *A Match with the Moon*

WEARY already, weary miles to-night
    I walked for bed: and so, to get some ease,
    I dogged the flying moon with similes.
And like a wisp she doubled on my sight
In ponds; and caught in tree-tops like a kite;
    And in a globe of film all liquorish
    Swam full-faced like a silly silver fish;—
Last like a bubble shot the welkin's height
Where my road turned, and got behind me, and sent
    My wizened shadow craning round at me,   10
    And jeered, 'So, step the measure,—one two three!'
And if I faced on her, looked innocent.
But just at parting, halfway down a dell,
She kissed me for good-night. So you'll not tell.

                        (Wr. 1854; pub. 1870)

193 *The Woodspurge*

THE wind flapped loose, the wind was still,
Shaken out dead from tree and hill:
I had walked on at the wind's will,—
I sat now, for the wind was still.

Between my knees my forehead was,—
My lips drawn in, said not Alas!
My hair was over in the grass,
My naked ears heard the day pass.

My eyes, wide open, had the run
Of some ten weeds to fix upon;   10
Among those few, out of the sun,
The woodspurge flowered, three cups in one.

From perfect grief there need not be
Wisdom or even memory:
One thing then learnt remains to me,—
The woodspurge has a cup of three.

(Wr. 1856; pub. 1870)

194 *Even So*

So it is, my dear.
All such things touch secret strings
For heavy hearts to hear.
So it is, my dear.

Very like indeed:
Sea and sky, afar, on high,
Sand and strewn seaweed,—
Very like indeed.

But the sea stands spread
As one wall with the flat skies,   10
Where the lean black craft like flies
Seem well-nigh stagnated,
Soon to drop off dead.

Seemed it so to us
When I was thine and thou wast mine,
And all these things were thus,
But all our world in us?

Could we be so now?
Not if all beneath heaven's pall
Lay dead but I and thou,   20
Could we be so now!

(Wr. 1859; pub. 1870)

195   *Nuptial Sleep*

AT length their long kiss severed, with sweet smart:
    And as the last slow sudden drops are shed
    From sparkling eaves when all the storm has fled,
So singly flagged the pulses of each heart.
Their bosoms sundered, with the opening start
    Of married flowers to either side outspread
    From the knit stem; yet still their mouths, burnt red,
Fawned on each other where they lay apart.

Sleep sank them lower than the tide of dreams,
    And their dreams watched them sink, and slid away.   10
Slowly their souls swam up again, through gleams
    Of watered light and dull drowned waifs of day;
Till from some wonder of new woods and streams
    He woke, and wondered more: for there she lay.

(Wr. 1869; pub. 1870)

196   *Smithereens*

UNCERTAIN-AGED Miss Thereabouts,
    Tough fossil of her teens,
Has lifted up with saving hand
    The ruined Smithereens.

Down the dark steps of debt that hand
    Sped like an angel's wing,
Deep-dowered with gold, and for itself
    Brought back a golden ring.

Ah lovely Lucy Lovandove,
    That ring's a snake, and means   10
Woe without end: therein lies crushed
    Thy heart—to smithereens.

(Wr. 1871; pub. 1911)

CHRISTINA G. ROSSETTI

1830–1894

197   *Song*

WHEN I am dead, my dearest,
   Sing no sad songs for me;
Plant thou no roses at my head,
   Nor shady cypress tree:
Be the green grass above me
   With showers and dewdrops wet;
And if thou wilt, remember,
   And if thou wilt, forget.

I shall not see the shadows,
   I shall not feel the rain;   10
I shall not hear the nightingale
   Sing on, as if in pain:
And dreaming through the twilight
   That doth not rise nor set,
Haply I may remember,
   And haply may forget.

(Wr. 1848; pub. 1862)

198   *Song*

OH roses for the flush of youth,
   And laurel for the perfect prime;
But pluck an ivy branch for me
   Grown old before my time.

Oh violets for the grave of youth,
   And bay for those dead in their prime;
Give me the withered leaves I chose
   Before in the old time.

(Wr. 1849; pub. 1850)

199   *Remember*

REMEMBER me when I am gone away,
  Gone far away into the silent land;
  When you can no more hold me by the hand,
Nor I half turn to go yet turning stay.
Remember me when no more day by day
  You tell me of our future that you planned:
  Only remember me; you understand
It will be late to counsel then or pray.
Yet if you should forget me for a while
  And afterwards remember, do not grieve: 10
  For if the darkness and corruption leave
  A vestige of the thoughts that once I had,
Better by far you should forget and smile
  Than that you should remember and be sad.

                              (Wr. 1849; pub. 1862)

200   *One Sea-Side Grave*

UNMINDFUL of the roses,
  Unmindful of the thorn,
A reaper tired reposes
  Among his gathered corn:
  So might I, till the morn!

Cold as the cold Decembers,
  Past as the days that set,
While only one remembers
  And all the rest forget,—
  But one remembers yet.   10

                              (Wr. 1853; pub. 1884)

201   *Echo*

COME to me in the silence of the night;
  Come in the speaking silence of a dream;
Come with soft rounded cheeks and eyes as bright
  As sunlight on a stream;
    Come back in tears,
O memory, hope, love of finished years.

Oh dream how sweet, too sweet, too bitter sweet,
　　Whose wakening should have been in Paradise,
Where souls brimfull of love abide and meet;
　　Where thirsting longing eyes　　　　　　　　　10
　　　　Watch the slow door
That opening, letting in, lets out no more.

Yet come to me in dreams, that I may live
　　My very life again tho' cold in death:
Come back to me in dreams, that I may give
　　Pulse for pulse, breath for breath:
　　　　Speak low, lean low,
As long ago, my love, how long ago.

(Wr. 1854; pub. 1862)

202　　　　　　　　*The Bourne*

UNDERNEATH the growing grass,
　　Underneath the living flowers,
　　Deeper than the sound of showers:
　　There we shall not count the hours
By the shadows as they pass.

Youth and health will be but vain,
　　Beauty reckoned of no worth:
　　There a very little girth
　　Can hold round what once the earth
Seemed too narrow to contain.　　　　　　　　10

(Wr. 1854; pub. 1863)

203　　　　　　　　*From the Antique*

IT'S a weary life, it is, she said:—
　　Doubly blank in a woman's lot:
I wish and I wish I were a man:
　　Or, better than any being, were not:

Were nothing at all in all the world,
　　Not a body and not a soul:
Not so much as a grain of dust
　　Or drop of water from pole to pole.

Still the world would wag on the same,
  Still the seasons go and come: 10
Blossoms bloom as in days of old,
  Cherries ripen and wild bees hum.

None would miss me in all the world,
  How much less would care or weep:
I should be nothing, while all the rest
  Would wake and weary and fall asleep.

(Wr. 1854; pub. 1896)

204   *May*

I CANNOT tell you how it was;
But this I know: it came to pass
Upon a bright and breezy day
When May was young; ah pleasant May!
As yet the poppies were not born
Between the blades of tender corn;
The last eggs had not hatched as yet,
Nor any bird foregone its mate.

I cannot tell you what it was;
But this I know: it did but pass.   10
It passed away with sunny May,
With all sweet things it passed away,
And left me old, and cold, and grey.

(Wr. 1855; pub. 1862)

205   *A Birthday*

MY heart is like a singing bird
  Whose nest is in a watered shoot;
My heart is like an apple tree
  Whose boughs are bent with thickset fruit;
My heart is like a rainbow shell
  That paddles in a halcyon sea;
My heart is gladder than all these
  Because my love is come to me.

Raise me a dais of silk and down;
    Hang it with vair and purple dyes;   10
Carve it in doves and pomegranates,
    And peacocks with a hundred eyes;
Work it in gold and silver grapes,
    In leaves and silver fleurs-de-lys;
Because the birthday of my life
    Is come, my love is come to me.

(Wr. 1857; pub. 1861)

206   *Winter: My Secret*

I TELL my secret? No indeed, not I:
Perhaps some day, who knows?
But not today; it froze, and blows, and snows,
And you're too curious: fie!
You want to hear it? well:
Only, my secret's mine, and I won't tell.

Or, after all, perhaps there's none:
Suppose there is no secret after all,
But only just my fun.
Today's a nipping day, a biting day;   10
In which one wants a shawl,
A veil, a cloak, and other wraps:
I cannot ope to every one who taps,
And let the draughts come whistling thro' my hall;
Come bounding and surrounding me,
Come buffeting, astounding me,
Nipping and clipping thro' my wraps and all.
I wear my mask for warmth: who ever shows
His nose to Russian snows
To be pecked at by every wind that blows?   20
You would not peck? I thank you for good will,
Believe, but leave that truth untested still.

Spring's an expansive time: yet I don't trust
March with its peck of dust,
Nor April with its rainbow-crowned brief showers,
Nor even May, whose flowers
One frost may wither thro' the sunless hours.

281

Perhaps some languid summer day,
When drowsy birds sing less and less,
And golden fruit is ripening to excess,   30
If there's not too much sun nor too much cloud,
And the warm wind is neither still nor loud,
Perhaps my secret I may say,
Or you may guess.

(Wr. 1857; pub. 1862)

207   *A Better Resurrection*

I HAVE no wit, no words, no tears;
    My heart within me like a stone
Is numbed too much for hopes or fears;
    Look right, look left, I dwell alone;
I lift mine eyes, but dimmed with grief
    No everlasting hills I see;
My life is in the falling leaf:
    O Jesus, quicken me.

My life is like a faded leaf,
    My harvest dwindled to a husk;   10
Truly my life is void and brief
    And tedious in the barren dusk;
My life is like a frozen thing,
    No bud nor greenness can I see:
Yet rise it shall—the sap of Spring;
    O Jesus, rise in me.

My life is like a broken bowl,
    A broken bowl that cannot hold
One drop of water for my soul
    Or cordial in the searching cold;   20
Cast in the fire the perished thing,
    Melt and remould it, till it be
A royal cup for Him my King:
    O Jesus, drink of me.

(Wr. 1857; pub. 1862)

208   *By the Sea*

WHY does the sea moan evermore?
  Shut out from heaven it makes its moan,
It frets against the boundary shore;
  All earth's full rivers cannot fill
  The sea, that drinking thirsteth still.

Sheer miracles of loveliness
  Lie hid in its unlooked-on bed:
Anemones, salt, passionless,
  Blow flower-like; just enough alive
  To blow and multiply and thrive.   10

Shells quaint with curve, or spot, or spike,
  Encrusted live things argus-eyed,
All fair alike, yet all unlike,
  Are born without a pang, and die
  Without a pang, and so pass by.

                              (Wr. 1858; pub. 1866)

209   THEY lie at rest, our blessed dead;
                       The dews drop cool above their head,
                       They knew not when fleet summer fled.

                       Together all, yet each alone;
                       Each laid at rest beneath his own
                       Smooth turf or white allotted stone.

                       When shall our slumber sink so deep,
                       And eyes that wept and eyes that weep
                       Weep not in the sufficient sleep?

                       God be with you, our great and small,   10
                       Our loves, our best beloved of all,
                       Our own beyond the salt sea-wall.

                              (Wr. 1858; pub. 1885)

Goblin Market

MORNING and evening
Maids heard the goblins cry:
'Come buy our orchard fruits,
Come buy, come buy:
Apples and quinces,
Lemons and oranges,
Plump unpecked cherries,
Melons and raspberries,
Bloom-down-cheeked peaches,
Swart-headed mulberries,   10
Wild free-born cranberries,
Crab-apples, dewberries,
Pine-apples, blackberries,
Apricots, strawberries;—
All ripe together
In summer weather,—
Morns that pass by,
Fair eves that fly;
Come buy, come buy:
Our grapes fresh from the vine,   20
Pomegranates full and fine,
Dates and sharp bullaces,
Rare pears and greengages,
Damsons and bilberries,
Taste them and try:
Currants and gooseberries,
Bright-fire-like barberries,
Figs to fill your mouth,
Citrons from the South,
Sweet to tongue and sound to eye;   30
Come buy, come buy.'

Evening by evening
Among the brookside rushes,
Laura bowed her head to hear,
Lizzie veiled her blushes:
Crouching close together
In the cooling weather,
With clasping arms and cautioning lips,
With tingling cheeks and finger tips.
'Lie close,' Laura said,   40
Pricking up her golden head:

'We must not look at goblin men,
We must not buy their fruits:
Who knows upon what soil they fed
Their hungry thirsty roots?'
'Come buy,' call the goblins
Hobbling down the glen.
'Oh,' cried Lizzie, 'Laura, Laura,
You should not peep at goblin men.'
Lizzie covered up her eyes,   50
Covered close lest they should look;
Laura reared her glossy head,
And whispered like the restless brook:
'Look, Lizzie, look, Lizzie,
Down the glen tramp little men.
One hauls a basket,
One bears a plate,
One lugs a golden dish
Of many pounds weight.
How fair the vine must grow   60
Whose grapes are so luscious;
How warm the wind must blow
Thro' those fruit bushes.'
'No,' said Lizzie: 'No, no, no;
Their offers should not charm us,
Their evil gifts would harm us.'
She thrust a dimpled finger
In each ear, shut eyes and ran:
Curious Laura chose to linger
Wondering at each merchant man.   70
One had a cat's face,
One whisked a tail,
One tramped at a rat's pace,
One crawled like a snail,
One like a wombat prowled obtuse and furry,
One like a ratel tumbled hurry skurry.
She heard a voice like voice of doves
Cooing all together:
They sounded kind and full of loves
In the pleasant weather.   80

Laura stretched her gleaming neck
Like a rush-imbedded swan,
Like a lily from the beck,
Like a moonlit poplar branch,
Like a vessel at the launch
When its last restraint is gone.

Backwards up the mossy glen
Turned and trooped the goblin men,
With their shrill repeated cry,
'Come buy, come buy.'   90
When they reached where Laura was
They stood stock still upon the moss,
Leering at each other,
Brother with queer brother;
Signalling each other,
Brother with sly brother.
One set his basket down,
One reared his plate;
One began to weave a crown
Of tendrils, leaves and rough nuts brown   100
(Men sell not such in any town);
One heaved the golden weight
Of dish and fruit to offer her:
'Come buy, come buy,' was still their cry.

Laura stared but did not stir,
Longed but had no money:
The whisk-tailed merchant bade her taste
In tones as smooth as honey,
The cat-faced purr'd,
The rat-paced spoke a word   110
Of welcome, and the snail-paced even was heard;
One parrot-voiced and jolly
Cried 'Pretty Goblin' still for 'Pretty Polly;'—
One whistled like a bird.

But sweet-tooth Laura spoke in haste:
'Good folk, I have no coin;
To take were to purloin:
I have no copper in my purse,
I have no silver either,
And all my gold is on the furze   120
That shakes in windy weather
Above the rusty heather.'
'You have much gold upon your head,'
They answered all together:
'Buy from us with a golden curl.'
She clipped a precious golden lock,
She dropped a tear more rare than pearl,
Then sucked their fruit globes fair or red:
Sweeter than honey from the rock,
Stronger than man-rejoicing wine,   130

Clearer than water flowed that juice;
She never tasted such before,
How should it cloy with length of use?
She sucked and sucked and sucked the more
Fruits which that unknown orchard bore;
She sucked until her lips were sore;
Then flung the emptied rinds away
But gathered up one kernel-stone,
And knew not was it night or day
As she turned home alone.   140

Lizzie met her at the gate
Full of wise upbraidings:
'Dear, you should not stay so late,
Twilight is not good for maidens;
Should not loiter in the glen
In the haunts of goblin men.
Do you not remember Jeanie,
How she met them in the moonlight,
Took their gifts both choice and many,
Ate their fruits and wore their flowers   150
Plucked from bowers
Where summer ripens at all hours?
But ever in the noonlight
She pined and pined away;
Sought them by night and day,
Found them no more but dwindled and grew grey;
Then fell with the first snow,
While to this day no grass will grow
Where she lies low:
I planted daisies there a year ago   160
That never blow.
You should not loiter so.'
'Nay, hush,' said Laura:
'Nay, hush, my sister:
I ate and ate my fill,
Yet my mouth waters still;
Tomorrow night I will
Buy more:' and kissed her:
'Have done with sorrow;
I'll bring you plums tomorrow   170
Fresh on their mother twigs,
Cherries worth getting;
You cannot think what figs
My teeth have met in,
What melons icy-cold

Piled on a dish of gold
Too huge for me to hold,
What peaches with a velvet nap,
Pellucid grapes without one seed:
Odorous indeed must be the mead   180
Whereon they grow, and pure the wave they drink
With lilies at the brink,
And sugar-sweet their sap.'

Golden head by golden head,
Like two pigeons in one nest
Folded in each other's wings,
They lay down in their curtained bed:
Like two blossoms on one stem,
Like two flakes of new-fall'n snow,
Like two wands of ivory   190
Tipped with gold for awful kings.
Moon and stars gazed in at them,
Wind sang to them lullaby,
Lumbering owls forbore to fly,
Not a bat flapped to and fro
Round their rest:
Cheek to cheek and breast to breast
Locked together in one nest.

Early in the morning
When the first cock crowed his warning,   200
Neat like bees, as sweet and busy,
Laura rose with Lizzie:
Fetched in honey, milked the cows,
Aired and set to rights the house,
Kneaded cakes of whitest wheat,
Cakes for dainty mouths to eat,
Next churned butter, whipped up cream,
Fed their poultry, sat and sewed;
Talked as modest maidens should:
Lizzie with an open heart,   210
Laura in an absent dream,
One content, one sick in part;
One warbling for the mere bright day's delight,
One longing for the night.

At length slow evening came:
They went with pitchers to the reedy brook;
Lizzie most placid in her look,
Laura most like a leaping flame.

They drew the gurgling water from its deep;
Lizzie plucked purple and rich golden flags,   220
Then turning homewards said: 'The sunset flushes
Those furthest loftiest crags;
Come, Laura, not another maiden lags,
No wilful squirrel wags,
The beasts and birds are fast asleep.'
But Laura loitered still among the rushes
And said the bank was steep.

And said the hour was early still,
The dew not fall'n, the wind not chill:
Listening ever, but not catching   230
The customary cry,
'Come buy, come buy,'
With its iterated jingle
Of sugar-baited words:
Not for all her watching
Once discerning even one goblin
Racing, whisking, tumbling, hobbling;
Let alone the herds
That used to tramp along the glen,
In groups or single,   240
Of brisk fruit-merchant men.
Till Lizzie urged, 'O Laura, come;
I hear the fruit-call but I dare not look:
You should not loiter longer at this brook:
Come with me home.
The stars rise, the moon bends her arc,
Each glowworm winks her spark,
Let us get home before the night grows dark:
For clouds may gather
Tho' this is summer weather,   250
Put out the lights and drench us thro';
Then if we lost our way what should we do?'

Laura turned cold as stone
To find her sister heard that cry alone,
That goblin cry,
'Come buy our fruits, come buy.'
Must she then buy no more such dainty fruit?
Must she no more such succous pasture find,
Gone deaf and blind?
Her tree of life drooped from the root: 260
She said not one word in her heart's sore ache;
But peering thro' the dimness, nought discerning,

Trudged home, her pitcher dripping all the way;
So crept to bed, and lay
Silent till Lizzie slept;
Then sat up in a passionate yearning,
And gnashed her teeth for baulked desire, and wept
As if her heart would break.

Day after day, night after night,
Laura kept watch in vain   270
In sullen silence of exceeding pain.
She never caught again the goblin cry:
'Come buy, come buy;'—
She never spied the goblin men
Hawking their fruits along the glen:
But when the noon waxed bright
Her hair grew thin and gray;
She dwindled, as the fair full moon doth turn
To swift decay and burn
Her fire away.   280

One day remembering her kernel-stone
She set it by a wall that faced the south;
Dewed it with tears, hoped for a root,
Watched for a waxing shoot,
But there came none;
It never saw the sun,
It never felt the trickling moisture run:
While with sunk eyes and faded mouth
She dreamed of melons, as a traveller sees
False waves in desert drouth   290
With shade of leaf-crowned trees,
And burns the thirstier in the sandful breeze.

She no more swept the house,
Tended the fowls or cows,
Fetched honey, kneaded cakes of wheat,
Brought water from the brook:
But sat down listless in the chimney-nook
And would not eat.

Tender Lizzie could not bear
To watch her sister's cankerous care   300
Yet not to share.
She night and morning
Caught the goblins' cry:
'Come buy our orchard fruits,

Come buy, come buy:'—
Beside the brook, along the glen,
She heard the tramp of goblin men,
The voice and stir
Poor Laura could not hear;
Longed to buy fruit to comfort her,   310
But feared to pay too dear.
She thought of Jeanie in her grave,
Who should have been a bride;
But who for joys brides hope to have
Fell sick and died
In her gay prime,
In earliest Winter time,
With the first glazing rime,
With the first snow-fall of crisp Winter time.

Till Laura dwindling   320
Seemed knocking at Death's door:
Then Lizzie weighed no more
Better and worse;
But put a silver penny in her purse,
Kissed Laura, crossed the heath with clumps of furze
At twilight, halted by the brook:
And for the first time in her life
Began to listen and look.

Laughed every goblin
When they spied her peeping: 330
Came towards her hobbling,
Flying, running, leaping,
Puffing and blowing,
Chuckling, clapping, crowing,
Clucking and gobbling,
Mopping and mowing,
Full of airs and graces,
Pulling wry faces,
Demure grimaces,
Cat-like and rat-like,   340
Ratel- and wombat-like,
Snail-paced in a hurry,
Parrot-voiced and whistler,
Helter skelter, hurry skurry,
Chattering like magpies,
Fluttering like pigeons,
Gliding like fishes,—
Hugged her and kissed her,

Squeezed and caressed her:
Stretched up their dishes,   350
Panniers, and plates:
'Look at our apples
Russet and dun,
Bob at our cherries,
Bite at our peaches,
Citrons and dates,
Grapes for the asking,
Pears red with basking
Out in the sun,
Plums on their twigs;   360
Pluck them and suck them,
Pomegranates, figs.'—

'Good folk,' said Lizzie,
Mindful of Jeanie:
'Give me much and many:'—
Held out her apron,
Tossed them her penny.
'Nay, take a seat with us,
Honour and eat with us,'
They answered grinning: 370
'Our feast is but beginning.
Night yet is early,
Warm and dew-pearly,
Wakeful and starry:
Such fruits as these
No man can carry;
Half their bloom would fly,
Half their dew would dry,
Half their flavour would pass by.
Sit down and feast with us,   380
Be welcome guest with us,
Cheer you and rest with us.'—
'Thank you,' said Lizzie: 'But one waits
At home alone for me:
So without further parleying,
If you will not sell me any
Of your fruits tho' much and many,
Give me back my silver penny
I tossed you for a fee.'—
They began to scratch their pates,   390
No longer wagging, purring,
But visibly demurring,
Grunting and snarling.

One called her proud,
Cross-grained, uncivil;
Their tones waxed loud,
Their looks were evil.
Lashing their tails
They trod and hustled her,
Elbowed and jostled her,   400
Clawed with their nails,
Barking, mewing, hissing, mocking,
Tore her gown and soiled her stocking,
Twitched her hair out by the roots,
Stamped upon her tender feet,
Held her hands and squeezed their fruits
Against her mouth to make her eat.

White and golden Lizzie stood,
Like a lily in a flood,—
Like a rock of blue-veined stone   410
Lashed by tides obstreperously,—
Like a beacon left alone
In a hoary roaring sea,
Sending up a golden fire,—
Like a fruit-crowned orange-tree
White with blossoms honey-sweet
Sore beset by wasp and bee,—
Like a royal virgin town
Topped with gilded dome and spire
Close beleaguered by a fleet   420
Mad to tug her standard down.

One may lead a horse to water,
Twenty cannot make him drink.
Tho' the goblins cuffed and caught her,
Coaxed and fought her,
Bullied and besought her,
Scratched her, pinched her black as ink,
Kicked and knocked her,
Mauled and mocked her,
Lizzie uttered not a word;   430
Would not open lip from lip
Lest they should cram a mouthful in:
But laughed in heart to feel the drip
Of juice that syrupped all her face,
And lodged in dimples of her chin,
And streaked her neck which quaked like curd.
At last the evil people
Worn out by her resistance

Flung back her penny, kicked their fruit
Along whichever road they took,   440
Not leaving root or stone or shoot;
Some writhed into the ground,
Some dived into the brook
With ring and ripple,
Some scudded on the gale without a sound,
Some vanished in the distance.

In a smart, ache, tingle,
Lizzie went her way;
Knew not was it night or day;
Sprang up the bank, tore thro' the furze,   450
Threaded copse and dingle,
And heard her penny jingle
Bouncing in her purse,
Its bounce was music to her ear.
She ran and ran
As if she feared some goblin man
Dogged her with gibe or curse
Or something worse:
But not one goblin skurried after,
Nor was she pricked by fear;   460
The kind heart made her windy-paced
That urged her home quite out of breath with haste
And inward laughter.

She cried 'Laura,' up the garden,
'Did you miss me?
Come and kiss me.
Never mind my bruises,
Hug me, kiss me, suck my juices
Squeezed from goblin fruits for you,
Goblin pulp and goblin dew.   470
Eat me, drink me, love me;
Laura, make much of me:
For your sake I have braved the glen
And had to do with goblin merchant men.'

Laura started from her chair,
Flung her arms up in the air,
Clutched her hair:
'Lizzie, Lizzie, have you tasted
For my sake the fruit forbidden?
Must your light like mine be hidden,   480
Your young life like mine be wasted,

Undone in mine undoing
And ruined in my ruin,
Thirsty, cankered, goblin-ridden?'—
She clung about her sister,
Kissed and kissed and kissed her:
Tears once again
Refreshed her shrunken eyes,
Dropping like rain
After long sultry drouth;   490
Shaking with aguish fear, and pain,
She kissed and kissed her with a hungry mouth.

Her lips began to scorch,
That juice was wormwood to her tongue,
She loathed the feast:
Writhing as one possessed she leaped and sung,
Rent all her robe, and wrung
Her hands in lamentable haste,
And beat her breast.
Her locks streamed like the torch   500
Borne by a racer at full speed,
Or like the mane of horses in their flight,
Or like an eagle when she stems the light
Straight toward the sun,
Or like a caged thing freed,
Or like a flying flag when armies run.

Swift fire spread thro' her veins, knocked at her heart,
Met the fire smouldering there
And overbore its lesser flame;
She gorged on bitterness without a name: 510
Ah! fool, to choose such part
Of soul-consuming care!
Sense failed in the mortal strife:
Like the watch-tower of a town
Which an earthquake shatters down,
Like a lightning-stricken mast,
Like a wind-uprooted tree
Spun about,
Like a foam-topped waterspout
Cast down headlong in the sea,   520
She fell at last;
Pleasure past and anguish past,
Is it death or is it life?

Life out of death.
That night long Lizzie watched by her,

Counted her pulse's flagging stir,
Felt for her breath,
Held water to her lips, and cooled her face
With tears and fanning leaves:
But when the first birds chirped about their eaves, 530
And early reapers plodded to the place
Of golden sheaves,
And dew-wet grass
Bowed in the morning winds so brisk to pass,
And new buds with new day
Opened of cup-like lilies on the stream,
Laura awoke as from a dream,
Laughed in the innocent old way,
Hugged Lizzie but not twice or thrice;
Her gleaming locks showed not one thread of grey, 540
Her breath was sweet as May
And light danced in her eyes.

Days, weeks, months, years
Afterwards, when both were wives
With children of their own;
Their mother-hearts beset with fears,
Their lives bound up in tender lives;
Laura would call the little ones
And tell them of her early prime,
Those pleasant days long gone 550
Of not-returning time:
Would talk about the haunted glen,
The wicked, quaint fruit-merchant men,
Their fruits like honey to the throat
But poison in the blood;
(Men sell not such in any town:)
Would tell them how her sister stood
In deadly peril to do her good,
And win the fiery antidote:
Then joining hands to little hands 560
Would bid them cling together,
'For there is no friend like a sister
In calm or stormy weather;
To cheer one on the tedious way,
To fetch one if one goes astray,
To lift one if one totters down,
To strengthen whilst one stands.'

(Wr. 1859; pub. 1862)

211   *Promises Like Pie-Crust*

PROMISE me no promises,
    So will I not promise you:
Keep we both our liberties,
    Never false and never true:
Let us hold the die uncast,
    Free to come as free to go:
For I cannot know your past,
    And of mine what can you know?

You, so warm, may once have been
    Warmer towards another one: 10
I, so cold, may once have seen
    Sunlight, once have felt the sun:
Who shall show us if it was
    Thus indeed in time of old?
Fades the image from the glass,
    And the fortune is not told.

If you promised, you might grieve
    For lost liberty again:
If I promised, I believe
    I should fret to break the chain.   20
Let us be the friends we were,
    Nothing more but nothing less:
Many thrive on frugal fare
    Who would perish of excess.

                    (Wr. 1861; pub. 1896)

212   *Somewhere or Other*

SOMEWHERE or other there must surely be
    The face not seen, the voice not heard,
The heart that not yet—never yet—ah me!
    Made answer to my word.

Somewhere or other, may be near or far;
    Past land and sea, clean out of sight;
Beyond the wandering moon, beyond the star
    That tracks her night by night.

Somewhere or other, may be far or near;
With just a wall, a hedge, between;   10
With just the last leaves of the dying year
Fallen on a turf grown green.

(Wr. 1863; pub. 1866)

213   *The Lowest Place*

GIVE me the lowest place: not that I dare
  Ask for that lowest place, but Thou hast died
That I might live and share
  Thy glory by Thy side.

Give me the lowest place: or if for me
  That lowest place too high, make one more low
Where I may sit and see
  My God and love Thee so.

(Wr. 1863; pub. 1866)

214   *Grown and Flown*

I LOVED my love from green of Spring
  Until sere Autumn's fall;
But now that leaves are withering
  How should one love at all?
  One heart's too small
For hunger, cold, love, everything.

I loved my love on sunny days
  Until late Summer's wane;
But now that frost begins to glaze
  How should one love again?   10
  Nay, love and pain
Walk wide apart in diverse ways.

I loved my love—alas to see
  That this should be, alas!
I thought that this could scarcely be,
  Yet has it come to pass:
  Sweet sweet love was,
Now bitter bitter grown to me.

(Wr. 1864; pub. 1866)

215   *A Dirge*

WHY were you born when the snow was falling?
You should have come to the cuckoo's calling,
Or when grapes are green in the cluster,
Or, at least, when lithe swallows muster
        For their far off flying
        From summer dying.

Why did you die when the lambs were cropping?
You should have died at the apples' dropping,
When the grasshopper comes to trouble,
And the wheat-fields are sodden stubble,   10
        And all winds go sighing
        For sweet things dying.

                              (Wr. 1865; pub. 1874)

216   *A Christmas Carol*

IN the bleak mid-winter
    Frosty wind made moan,
Earth stood hard as iron,
    Water like a stone;
Snow had fallen, snow on snow,
    Snow on snow,
In the bleak mid-winter
    Long ago.

Our God, Heaven cannot hold Him
    Nor earth sustain;   10
Heaven and earth shall flee away
    When He comes to reign:
In the bleak mid-winter
    A stable-place sufficed
The Lord God Almighty
    Jesus Christ.

Enough for Him whom cherubim
    Worship night and day,
A breastful of milk
    And a mangerful of hay;   20
Enough for Him whom angels
    Fall down before,
The ox and ass and camel
    Which adore.

299

Angels and archangels
　May have gathered there,
Cherubim and seraphim
　Throng'd the air,
But only His mother
　In her maiden bliss　　　　　　　　　　30
Worshipped the Beloved
　With a kiss.

What can I give Him,
　Poor as I am?
If I were a shepherd
　I would bring a lamb,
If I were a wise man
　I would do my part,—
Yet what I can I give Him,
　Give my heart.　　　　　　　　　　　　40

(1872)

217　　　　　　　　*'Summer is Ended'*

To think that this meaningless thing was ever a rose,
　　Scentless, colourless, *this*!
　Will it ever be thus (who knows?)
　　　Thus with our bliss,
　　If we wait till the close?

Tho' we care not to wait for the end, there comes the end
　　Sooner, later, at last,
　Which nothing can mar, nothing mend:
　　　An end locked fast,
　Bent we cannot re-bend.　　　　　　　　　10

(1881)

218　　　　　　　　*'Endure hardness'*

A COLD wind stirs the blackthorn
　To burgeon and to blow,
Besprinkling half-green hedges
　With flakes and sprays of snow.

Thro' coldness and thro' keenness,
　Dear hearts, take comfort so:
Somewhere or other doubtless
　These make the blackthorn blow.

(1885)

219   LORD Jesus, who would think that I am Thine?
     Ah, who would think
Who sees me ready to turn back or sink,
     That Thou art mine?

I cannot hold Thee fast tho' Thou art mine:
     Hold Thou me fast,
So earth shall know at last and heaven at last
     That I am Thine.

(1885)

220   *A Frog's Fate*

CONTEMPTUOUS of his home beyond
The village and the village-pond,
A large-souled Frog who spurned each byeway
Hopped along the imperial highway.

Nor grunting pig nor barking dog
Could disconcert so great a Frog.
The morning dew was lingering yet,
His sides to cool, his tongue to wet:
The night-dew, when the night should come,
A travelled Frog would send him home.   10

Not so, alas! The wayside grass
Sees him no more: not so, alas!
A broad-wheeled waggon unawares
Ran him down, his joys, his cares.
From dying choke one feeble croak
The Frog's perpetual silence broke:—
'Ye buoyant Frogs, ye great and small,
Even I am mortal after all!
My road to fame turns out a wry way;
I perish on the hideous highway;   20
Oh for my old familiar byeway!'

The choking Frog sobbed and was gone;
The Waggoner strode whistling on.
Unconscious of the carnage done,
Whistling that Waggoner strode on—
Whistling (it may have happened so)
'A froggy would a-wooing go.'
A hypothetic frog trolled he,
Obtuse to a reality.

O rich and poor, O great and small,　　　　30
Such oversights beset us all.
The mangled Frog abides incog,
The uninteresting actual frog:
The hypothetic frog alone
Is the one frog we dwell upon.

(1885)

EBENEZER ELLIOTT
1781–1849

221　　　　*Epigram*

'PREPARE to meet the King of Terrors,' cried
To prayerless Want, his plunderer ferret-eyed:
'I am the King of Terrors,' Want replied.

(1850)

222　　　　*Song*

1

DONOUGHT would have everything;
Eat the lark, and use its wing;
Sip the sweet, and be the sting:
Donought is the only King.

2

Donought is an alchemist;
Hencock is a communist;
Idle head is heavy fist;
Will's a right line—with a twist.

3

Hark! the throstle! what sings he?
'Worm, my Beauty, come to me!'　　　　10
Yet all lovely things are free:
'Chain'd and happy, cannot be.'

4

'See the daisies, how they grow!'
When they list, the breezes blow:
Why can't weary man do so?
All enjoy, and nothing owe?

5

'Mouth, keep open! Eyes, be shut!'
Take no care for back or gut:
Best of women is the slut:
Hey, for cattle cook'd and cut!   20

(1850)

223   *Epigram*

WHAT is a communist? One who hath yearnings
For equal division of unequal earnings:
Idler, or bungler, or both, he is willing
To fork out his penny, and pocket your shilling.*

* And he has two names, Legion and Danger.

(1850)

MATTHEW ARNOLD
1822–1888

224   *To Marguerite—Continued*

YES! in the sea of life enisled,
With echoing straits between us thrown,
Dotting the shoreless watery wild,
We mortal millions live *alone*.
The islands feel the enclasping flow,
And then their endless bounds they know.

But when the moon their hollows lights,
And they are swept by balms of spring,
And in their glens, on starry nights,
The nightingales divinely sing;   10
And lovely notes, from shore to shore,
Across the sounds and channels pour—

Oh! then a longing like despair
Is to their farthest caverns sent;
For surely once, they feel, we were
Parts of a single continent!
Now round us spreads the watery plain—
Oh might our marges meet again!

Who order'd, that their longing's fire
Should be, as soon as kindled, cool'd?   20
Who renders vain their deep desire?—
A God, a God their severance ruled!
And bade betwixt their shores to be
The unplumb'd, salt, estranging sea.

(Wr. 1849?; pub. 1852)

225   *Destiny*

WHY each is striving, from of old,
To love more deeply than he can?
Still would be true, yet still grows cold?
—Ask of the Powers that sport with man!

They yok'd in him, for endless strife,
A heart of ice, a soul of fire;
And hurl'd him on the Field of Life,
An aimless unallay'd Desire.

(Wr. 1849–50?; pub. 1852)

226   *Dover Beach*

THE sea is calm to-night.
The tide is full, the moon lies fair
Upon the straits;—on the French coast the light
Gleams and is gone; the cliffs of England stand,
Glimmering and vast, out in the tranquil bay.
Come to the window, sweet is the night-air!

Only, from the long line of spray
Where the sea meets the moon-blanch'd land,
Listen! you hear the grating roar
Of pebbles which the waves draw back, and fling,   10
At their return, up the high strand,
Begin, and cease, and then again begin,
With tremulous cadence slow, and bring
The eternal note of sadness in.

Sophocles long ago
Heard it on the Ægæan, and it brought
Into his mind the turbid ebb and flow
Of human misery; we
Find also in the sound a thought,
Hearing it by this distant northern sea.   20

The Sea of Faith
Was once, too, at the full, and round earth's shore
Lay like the folds of a bright girdle furl'd.
But now I only hear
Its melancholy, long, withdrawing roar,
Retreating, to the breath
Of the night-wind, down the vast edges drear
And naked shingles of the world.

Ah, love, let us be true
To one another! for the world, which seems   30
To lie before us like a land of dreams,
So various, so beautiful, so new,
Hath really neither joy, nor love, nor light,
Nor certitude, nor peace, nor help for pain;
And we are here as on a darkling plain
Swept with confused alarms of struggle and flight,
Where ignorant armies clash by night.

                              (Wr. 1851?; pub. 1867)

227   *The Scholar-Gipsy*

Go, for they call you, shepherd, from the hill;
    Go, shepherd, and untie the wattled cotes!
        No longer leave thy wistful flock unfed,
    Nor let thy bawling fellows rack their throats,
        Nor the cropp'd herbage shoot another head.
            But when the fields are still,
        And the tired men and dogs all gone to rest,
            And only the white sheep are sometimes seen
            Cross and recross the strips of moon-blanch'd green,
        Come, shepherd, and again begin the quest!   10

Here, where the reaper was at work of late—
    In this high field's dark corner, where he leaves
        His coat, his basket, and his earthen cruse,
    And in the sun all morning binds the sheaves,
        Then here, at noon, comes back his stores to use—
            Here will I sit and wait,
        While to my ear from uplands far away
            The bleating of the folded flocks is borne,
            With distant cries of reapers in the corn—
        All the live murmur of a summer's day.   20

Screen'd is this nook o'er the high, half-reap'd field,
  And here till sun-down, shepherd! will I be.
    Through the thick corn the scarlet poppies peep,
  And round green roots and yellowing stalks I see
    Pale pink convolvulus in tendrils creep;
      And air-swept lindens yield
Their scent, and rustle down their perfumed showers
  Of bloom on the bent grass where I am laid,
  And bower me from the August sun with shade;
And the eye travels down to Oxford's towers.   30

And near me on the grass lies Glanvil's book—
  Come, let me read the oft-read tale again!
    The story of the Oxford scholar poor,
  Of pregnant parts and quick inventive brain,
    Who, tired of knocking at preferment's door,
      One summer-morn forsook
His friends, and went to learn the gipsy-lore,
  And roam'd the world with that wild brotherhood,
  And came, as most men deem'd, to little good,
But came to Oxford and his friends no more.   40

But once, years after, in the country-lanes,
  Two scholars, whom at college erst he knew,
    Met him, and of his way of life enquired;
  Whereat he answer'd, that the gipsy-crew,
    His mates, had arts to rule as they desired
      The workings of men's brains,
And they can bind them to what thoughts they will.
  'And I,' he said, 'the secret of their art,
  When fully learn'd, will to the world impart;
But it needs heaven-sent moments for this skill.'   50

This said, he left them, and return'd no more.—
  But rumours hung about the country-side,
    That the lost Scholar long was seen to stray,
  Seen by rare glimpses, pensive and tongue-tied,
    In hat of antique shape, and cloak of grey,
      The same the gipsies wore.
Shepherds had met him on the Hurst in spring;
  At some lone alehouse in the Berkshire moors,
  On the warm ingle-bench, the smock-frock'd boors
Had found him seated at their entering,   60

But, 'mid their drink and clatter, he would fly.
  And I myself seem half to know thy looks,
    And put the shepherds, wanderer! on thy trace;
  And boys who in lone wheatfields scare the rooks
    I ask if thou hast pass'd their quiet place;
      Or in my boat I lie
  Moor'd to the cool bank in the summer-heats,
    'Mid wide grass meadows which the sunshine fills,
    And watch the warm, green-muffled Cumner hills,
  And wonder if thou haunt'st their shy retreats.   70

For most, I know, thou lov'st retired ground!
  Thee at the ferry Oxford riders blithe,
    Returning home on summer-nights, have met
  Crossing the stripling Thames at Bab-lock-hithe,
    Trailing in the cool stream thy fingers wet,
      As the punt's rope chops round;
  And leaning backward in a pensive dream,
    And fostering in thy lap a heap of flowers
    Pluck'd in shy fields and distant Wychwood bowers,
  And thine eyes resting on the moonlit stream.   80

And then they land, and thou art seen no more!—
  Maidens, who from the distant hamlets come
    To dance around the Fyfield elm in May,
  Oft through the darkening fields have seen thee roam,
    Or cross a stile into the public way.
      Oft thou hast given them store
  Of flowers—the frail-leaf'd, white anemony,
    Dark bluebells drench'd with dews of summer eves,
    And purple orchises with spotted leaves—
  But none hath words she can report of thee.   90

And, above Godstow Bridge, when hay-time's here
  In June, and many a scythe in sunshine flames,
    Men who through those wide fields of breezy grass
  Where black-wing'd swallows haunt the glittering Thames,
    To bathe in the abandon'd lasher pass,
      Have often pass'd thee near
  Sitting upon the river bank o'ergrown;
    Mark'd thine outlandish garb, thy figure spare,
    Thy dark vague eyes, and soft abstracted air—
  But, when they came from bathing, thou wast gone!   100

At some lone homestead in the Cumner hills,
    Where at her open door the housewife darns,
        Thou hast been seen, or hanging on a gate
To watch the threshers in the mossy barns.
        Children, who early range these slopes and late
            For cresses from the rills,
Have known thee eying, all an April-day,
    The springing pastures and the feeding kine;
    And mark'd thee, when the stars come out and shine,
Through the long dewy grass move slow away.   110

In autumn, on the skirts of Bagley Wood—
    Where most the gipsies by the turf-edged way
        Pitch their smoked tents, and every bush you see
With scarlet patches tagg'd and shreds of grey,
        Above the forest-ground called Thessaly—
            The blackbird, picking food,
Sees thee, nor stops his meal, nor fears at all;
    So often has he known thee past him stray,
    Rapt, twirling in thy hand a wither'd spray,
And waiting for the spark from heaven to fall.   120

And once, in winter, on the causeway chill
    Where home through flooded fields foot-travellers go,
        Have I not pass'd thee on the wooden bridge,
Wrapt in thy cloak and battling with the snow,
        Thy face tow'rd Hinksey and its wintry ridge?
            And thou hast climb'd the hill,
And gain'd the white brow of the Cumner range;
    Turn'd once to watch, while thick the snowflakes fall,
    The line of festal light in Christ-Church hall—
Then sought thy straw in some sequester'd grange.   130

But what—I dream! Two hundred years are flown
    Since first thy story ran through Oxford halls,
        And the grave Glanvil did the tale inscribe
That thou wert wander'd from the studious walls
        To learn strange arts, and join a gipsy-tribe;
            And thou from earth art gone
Long since, and in some quiet churchyard laid—
    Some country-nook, where o'er thy unknown grave
    Tall grasses and white flowering nettles wave,
Under a dark, red-fruited yew-tree's shade.   140

—No, no, thou hast not felt the lapse of hours!
  For what wears out the life of mortal men?
    'Tis that from change to change their being rolls;
  'Tis that repeated shocks, again, again,
    Exhaust the energy of strongest souls
      And numb the elastic powers.
Till having used our nerves with bliss and teen,
  And tired upon a thousand schemes our wit,
  To the just-pausing Genius we remit
Our worn-out life, and are—what we have been.   150

Thou hast not lived, why should'st thou perish, so?
  Thou hadst *one* aim, *one* business, *one* desire;
    Else wert thou long since number'd with the dead!
  Else hadst thou spent, like other men, thy fire!
    The generations of thy peers are fled,
      And we ourselves shall go;
But thou possessest an immortal lot,
    And we imagine thee exempt from age
    And living as thou liv'st on Glanvil's page,
Because thou hadst—what we, alas! have not.   160

For early didst thou leave the world, with powers
  Fresh, undiverted to the world without,
    Firm to their mark, not spent on other things;
  Free from the sick fatigue, the languid doubt,
    Which much to have tried, in much been baffled, brings.
      O life unlike to ours!
Who fluctuate idly without term or scope,
  Of whom each strives, nor knows for what he strives,
    And each half lives a hundred different lives;
Who wait like thee, but not, like thee, in hope.   170

Thou waitest for the spark from heaven! and we,
  Light half-believers of our casual creeds,
    Who never deeply felt, nor clearly will'd,
  Whose insight never has borne fruit in deeds,
    Whose vague resolves never have been fulfill'd;
      For whom each year we see
Breeds new beginnings, disappointments new;
    Who hesitate and falter life away,
    And lose to-morrow the ground won to-day—
Ah! do not we, wanderer! await it too?   180

Yes, we await it!—but it still delays,
    And then we suffer! and amongst us one,
      Who most has suffer'd, takes dejectedly
His seat upon the intellectual throne;
      And all his store of sad experience he
        Lays bare of wretched days;
Tells us his misery's birth and growth and signs,
    And how the dying spark of hope was fed,
    And how the breast was soothed, and how the head,
And all his hourly varied anodynes.   190

This for our wisest! and we others pine,
    And wish the long unhappy dream would end,
      And waive all claim to bliss, and try to bear;
With close-lipp'd patience for our only friend,
      Sad patience, too near neighbour to despair—
        But none has hope like thine!
Thou through the fields and through the woods dost stray,
    Roaming the country-side, a truant boy,
    Nursing thy project in unclouded joy,
And every doubt long blown by time away.   200

O born in days when wits were fresh and clear,
    And life ran gaily as the sparkling Thames;
      Before this strange disease of modern life,
With its sick hurry, its divided aims,
      Its heads o'ertax'd, its palsied hearts, was rife—
        Fly hence, our contact fear!
Still fly, plunge deeper in the bowering wood!
    Averse, as Dido did with gesture stern
    From her false friend's approach in Hades turn,
Wave us away, and keep thy solitude!   210

Still nursing the unconquerable hope,
    Still clutching the inviolable shade,
      With a free, onward impulse brushing through,
By night, the silver'd branches of the glade—
      Far on the forest-skirts, where none pursue,
        On some mild pastoral slope
Emerge, and resting on the moonlit pales
    Freshen thy flowers as in former years
    With dew, or listen with enchanted ears,
From the dark dingles, to the nightingales!   220

But fly our paths, our feverish contact fly!
  For strong the infection of our mental strife,
    Which, though it gives no bliss, yet spoils for rest;
  And we should win thee from thy own fair life,
    Like us distracted, and like us unblest.
      Soon, soon thy cheer would die,
  Thy hopes grow timorous, and unfix'd thy powers,
    And thy clear aims be cross and shifting made;
    And then thy glad perennial youth would fade,
Fade, and grow old at last, and die like ours.   230

Then fly our greetings, fly our speech and smiles!
  —As some grave Tyrian trader, from the sea,
    Descried at sunrise an emerging prow
Lifting the cool-hair'd creepers stealthily,
    The fringes of a southward-facing brow
      Among the Ægæan isles;
  And saw the merry Grecian coaster come,
    Freighted with amber grapes, and Chian wine,
    Green, bursting figs, and tunnies steep'd in brine—
And knew the intruders on his ancient home,   240

The young light-hearted masters of the waves—
  And snatch'd his rudder, and shook out more sail;
    And day and night held on indignantly
O'er the blue Midland waters with the gale,
    Betwixt the Syrtes and soft Sicily,
      To where the Atlantic raves
Outside the western straits; and unbent sails
    There, where down cloudy cliffs, through sheets of foam, ·
    Shy traffickers, the dark Iberians come;
And on the beach undid his corded bales.   250

(Wr. 1852–3?; pub. 1853)

228   *Growing Old*

WHAT is it to grow old?
Is it to lose the glory of the form,
The lustre of the eye?
Is it for beauty to forego her wreath?
—Yes, but not this alone.

Is it to feel our strength—
Not our bloom only, but our strength—decay?
Is it to feel each limb
Grow stiffer, every function less exact,
Each nerve more loosely strung?   10

Yes, this, and more; but not
Ah, 'tis not what in youth we dream'd 'twould be!
'Tis not to have our life
Mellow'd and soften'd as with sunset-glow,
A golden day's decline.

'Tis not to see the world
As from a height, with rapt prophetic eyes,
And heart profoundly stirr'd;
And weep, and feel the fulness of the past,
The years that are no more.   20

It is to spend long days
And not once feel that we were ever young;
It is to add, immured
In the hot prison of the present, month
To month with weary pain.

It is to suffer this,
And feel but half, and feebly, what we feel.
Deep in our hidden heart
Festers the dull remembrance of a change,
But no emotion—none.   30

It is—last stage of all—
When we are frozen up within, and quite
The phantom of ourselves,
To hear the world applaud the hollow ghost
Which blamed the living man.

                              (Wr. 1864–7?; pub. 1867)

229   *The Progress of Poesy*

                            A Variation

            YOUTH rambles on life's arid mount,
            And strikes the rock, and finds the vein,
            And brings the water from the fount,
            The fount which shall not flow again.

The man mature with labour chops
For the bright stream a channel grand,
And sees not that the sacred drops
Ran off and vanish'd out of hand.

And then the old man totters nigh,
And feebly rakes among the stones.   10
The mount is mute, the channel dry;
And down he lays his weary bones.

(Wr. 1864–7?; pub. 1867)

230   BELOW the surface-stream, shallow and light,
Of what we *say* we feel—below the stream,
As light, of what we *think* we feel—there flows
With noiseless current strong, obscure and deep,
The central stream of what we feel indeed.

(Wr. and pub. 1869)

231   *Geist's Grave*

FOUR years!—and didst thou stay above
The ground, which hides thee now, but four?
And all that life, and all that love,
Were crowded, Geist! into no more?

Only four years those winning ways,
Which make me for thy presence yearn,
Call'd us to pet thee or to praise,
Dear little friend! at every turn?

That loving heart, that patient soul,
Had they indeed no longer span,   10
To run their course, and reach their goal,
And read their homily to man?

That liquid, melancholy eye,
From whose pathetic, soul-fed springs
Seem'd surging the Virgilian cry,
The sense of tears in mortal things—

313

That steadfast, mournful strain, consoled
By spirits gloriously gay,
And temper of heroic mould—
What, was four years their whole short day? 20

Yes, only four!—and not the course
Of all the centuries yet to come,
And not the infinite resource
Of Nature, with her countless sum

Of figures, with her fulness vast
Of new creation evermore,
Can ever quite repeat the past,
Or just thy little self restore.

Stern law of every mortal lot!
Which man, proud man, finds hard to bear, 30
And builds himself I know not what
Of second life I know not where.

But thou, when struck thine hour to go,
On us, who stood despondent by,
A meek last glance of love didst throw,
And humbly lay thee down to die.

Yet would we keep thee in our heart—
Would fix our favourite on the scene,
Nor let thee utterly depart
And be as if thou ne'er hadst been. 40

And so there rise these lines of verse
On lips that rarely form them now;
While to each other we rehearse:
Such ways, such arts, such looks hadst thou!

We stroke thy broad brown paws again,
We bid thee to thy vacant chair,
We greet thee by the window-pane,
We hear thy scuffle on the stair.

We see the flaps of thy large ears
Quick raised to ask which way we go; 50
Crossing the frozen lake, appears
Thy small black figure on the snow!

Nor to us only art thou dear
Who mourn thee in thine English home;
Thou hast thine absent master's tear,
Dropt by the far Australian foam.

Thy memory lasts both here and there,
And thou shalt live as long as we.
And after that—thou dost not care!
In us was all the world to thee.   60

Yet, fondly zealous for thy fame,
Even to a date, beyond our own
We strive to carry down thy name,
By mounded turf, and graven stone.

We lay thee, close within our reach,
Here, where the grass is smooth and warm,
Between the holly and the beech,
Where oft we watch'd thy couchant form,

Asleep, yet lending half an ear
To travellers on the Portsmouth road;—   70
There build we thee, O guardian dear,
Mark'd with a stone, thy last abode!

Then some, who through this garden pass,
When we too, like thyself, are clay,
Shall see thy grave upon the grass,
And stop before the stone, and say:

People who lived here long ago
Did by this stone, it seems, intend
To name for future times to know
The dachs-hound, Geist, their little friend.   80

(Wr. 1880; pub. 1881)

WILLIAM ALLINGHAM
1824–1889

232   *A Dream*

I HEARD the dogs howl in the moonlight night;
I went to the window to see the sight;
All the Dead that ever I knew
Going one by one and two by two.

On they pass'd, and on they pass'd;
Townsfellows all, from first to last;
Born in the moonlight of the lane,
Quench'd in the heavy shadow again.

Schoolmates, marching as when we play'd
At soldiers once—but now more staid;   10
Those were the strangest sight to me
Who were drown'd, I knew, in the awful sea.

Straight and handsome folk; bent and weak too;
Some that I loved, and gasp'd to speak to;
Some but a day in their churchyard bed;
Some that I had not known were dead.

A long, long crowd—where each seem'd lonely,
Yet of them all there was one, one only,
Raised a head or look'd my way:
She linger'd a moment,—she might not stay.   20

How long since I saw that fair pale face!
Ah! Mother dear! might I only place
My head on thy breast, a moment to rest,
While thy hand on my tearful cheek were prest!

On, on, a moving bridge they made
Across the moon-stream, from shade to shade,
Young and old, women and men;
Many long-forgot, but remember'd then.

And first there came a bitter laughter;
A sound of tears the moment after;   30
And then a music so lofty and gay,
That every morning, day by day,
I strive to recall it if I may.

(1850)

316

The Fairies

Up the airy mountain,
  Down the rushy glen,
We daren't go a-hunting
  For fear of little men;
Wee folk, good folk,
  Trooping all together;
Green jacket, red cap,
  And white owl's feather!

Down along the rocky shore
  Some make their home,   10
They live on crispy pancakes
  Of yellow tide-foam;
Some in the reeds
  Of the black mountain lake,
With frogs for their watch-dogs,
  All night awake.

High on the hill-top
  The old King sits;
He is now so old and gray
  He's nigh lost his wits.   20
With a bridge of white mist
  Columbkill he crosses,
On his stately journeys
  From Slieveleague to Rosses;
Or going up with music
  On cold starry nights,
To sup with the Queen
  Of the gay Northern Lights.

They stole little Bridget
  For seven years long;   30
When she came down again
  Her friends were all gone.
They took her lightly back,
  Between the night and morrow,
They thought that she was fast asleep,
  But she was dead with sorrow.
They have kept her ever since
  Deep within the lake,
On a bed of flag-leaves,
  Watching till she wake.   40

By the craggy hill-side,
    Through the mosses bare,
They have planted thorn-trees
    For pleasure here and there.
Is any man so daring
    As dig them up in spite,
He shall find their sharpest thorns
    In his bed at night.

Up the airy mountain,
    Down the rushy glen,   50
We daren't go a-hunting
    For fear of little men;
Wee folk, good folk,
    Trooping all together;
Green jacket, red cap,
    And white owl's feather!

(1850)

The Witch-Bride

234

A FAIR witch crept to a young man's side,
And he kiss'd her and took her for his bride.

But a Shape came in at the dead of night,
And fill'd the room with snowy light.

And he saw how in his arms there lay
A thing more frightful than mouth may say.

And he rose in haste, and follow'd the Shape
Till morning crown'd an eastern cape.

And he girded himself, and follow'd still
When sunset sainted the western hill.   10

But, mocking and thwarting, clung to his side,
Weary day!—the foul Witch-Bride.

(1850)

235

THE Boy from his bedroom-window
    Look'd over the little town,
And away to the bleak black upland
    Under a clouded moon.

The moon came forth from her cavern,
   He saw the sudden gleam
Of a tarn in the swarthy moorland;
   Or perhaps the whole was a dream.

For I never could find that water
   In all my walks and rides:
Far-off, in the Land of Memory,
   That midnight pool abides.

Many fine things had I glimpse of,
   And said, 'I shall find them one day.'
Whether within or without me
   They were, I cannot say.

(1877)

10

236

FOUR ducks on a pond,
A grass-bank beyond,
A blue sky of spring,
White clouds on the wing;
What a little thing
To remember for years—
To remember with tears!

(1882)

237

EVERYTHING passes and vanishes;
   Everything leaves its trace;
And often you see in a footstep
   What you could not see in a face.

(1882)

238

Writing

A MAN who keeps a diary, pays
Due toll to many tedious days;
But life becomes eventful—then
His busy hand forgets the pen.
Most books, indeed, are records less
Of fulness than of emptiness.

(1884)

239

An Evening

A SUNSET'S mounded cloud;
A diamond evening-star;
Sad blue hills afar;
Love in his shroud.

Scarcely a tear to shed;
Hardly a word to say;
The end of a summer day;
Sweet Love dead.

(1888)

240

Express

(*From Liverpool, Southwards*)

WE move in elephantine row,
The faces of our friends retire,
The roof withdraws, and curtsying flow
The message-bearing lines of wire;
With doubling, redoubling beat,
Smoother we run and more fleet.

By flow'r-knots, shrubs, and slopes of grass,
Cut walls of rock with ivy-stains,
Thro' winking arches swift we pass,
And flying, meet the flying trains,   10
Whirr—whirr—gone!
And still we hurry on;

By orchards, kine in pleasant leas,
A hamlet-lane, a spire, a pond,
Long hedgerows, counter-changing trees,
With blue and steady hills beyond;
(House, platform, post,
Flash—and are lost!)

Smooth-edged canals, and mills on brooks;
Old farmsteads, busier than they seem,   20
Rose-crusted or of graver looks,
Rich with old tile and motley beam;
Clay-cutting, slope, and ridge,
The hollow rumbling bridge.

Gray vapour-surges, whirl'd in the wind
Of roaring tunnels, dark and long,
Then sky and landscape unconfined,
    Then streets again where workers throng
        Come—go. The whistle shrill
        Controls us to its will.   30

Broad vents, and chimneys tall as masts,
    With heavy flags of streaming smoke;
Brick mazes, fiery furnace-blasts,
    Walls, waggons, gritty heaps of coke;
        Through these our ponderous rank
        Glides in with hiss and clank.

So have we sped our wondrous course
    Amid a peaceful busy land,
Subdued by long and painful force
    Of planning head and plodding hand.   40
        How much by labour can
        The feeble race of man!

                        (1889)

241   No funeral gloom, my dears, when I am gone,
      Corpse-gazing, tears, black raiment, graveyard grimness;
      Think of me as withdrawn into the dimness,
      Yours still, you mine; remember all the best
      Of our past moments, and forget the rest;
          And so, to where I wait, come gently on.

                        (1890)

COVENTRY PATMORE

1823–1896

from *The Angel in the House* (242–244)

242   *Love at Large*

WHENE'ER I come where ladies are,
    How sad soever I was before,
Though like a ship frost-bound and far
    Withheld in ice from the ocean's roar,

Third-winter'd in that dreadful dock,
   With stiffen'd cordage, sails decay'd,
And crew that care for calm and shock
   Alike, too dull to be dismay'd,
Yet, if I come where ladies are,
   How sad soever I was before,   10
Then is my sadness banish'd far,
   And I am like that ship no more;
Or like that ship if the ice-field splits,
   Burst by the sudden polar Spring,
And all thank God with their warming wits,
   And kiss each other and dance and sing,
And hoist fresh sails, that make the breeze
   Blow them along the liquid sea,
Out of the North, where life did freeze,
   Into the haven where they would be.   20

              (Wr. from 1850; pub. 1854)

243   *The Kiss*

'I SAW you take his kiss!' ''Tis true.'
 'O, modesty!' ''Twas strictly kept:
'He thought me asleep; at least, I knew
 'He thought I thought he thought I slept.'

              (Wr. from 1850; pub. 1856)

244   *Constancy rewarded*

I VOW'D unvarying faith, and she,
   To whom in full I pay that vow,
Rewards me with variety
   Which men who change can never know.

              (Wr. from 1850; pub. 1856)

245   *The Rosy Bosom'd Hours*

A FLORIN to the willing Guard
   Secured, for half the way,
(He lock'd us in, ah, lucky-starr'd,)
   A curtain'd, front coupé.

The sparkling sun of August shone;
  The wind was in the West;
Your gown and all that you had on
  Was what became you best;
And we were in that seldom mood
  When soul with soul agrees,   10
Mingling, like flood with equal flood,
  In agitated ease.
Far round, each blade of harvest bare
  Its little load of bread;
Each furlong of that journey fair
  With separate sweetness sped.
The calm of use was coming o'er
  The wonder of our wealth,
And now, maybe, 'twas not much more
  Than Eden's common health.   20
We paced the sunny platform, while
  The train at Havant changed:
What made the people kindly smile,
  Or stare with looks estranged?
Too radiant for a wife you seem'd,
  Serener than a bride;
Me happiest born of men I deem'd,
  And show'd perchance my pride.
I loved that girl, so gaunt and tall,
  Who whispered loud, 'Sweet Thing!'   30
Scanning your figure, slight yet all
  Round as your own gold ring.
At Salisbury you stray'd alone
  Within the shafted glooms,
Whilst I was by the Verger shown
  The brasses and the tombs.
At tea we talk'd of matters deep,
  Of joy that never dies;
We laugh'd, till love was mix'd with sleep
  Within your great sweet eyes.   40
The next day, sweet with luck no less
  And sense of sweetness past,
The full tide of our happiness
  Rose higher than the last.
At Dawlish, 'mid the pools of brine,
  You stept from rock to rock,
One hand quick tightening upon mine,
  One holding up your frock.
On starfish and on weeds alone
  You seem'd intent to be: 50

Flash'd those great gleams of hope unknown
    From you, or from the sea?
Ne'er came before, ah, when again
    Shall come two days like these:
Such quick delight within the brain,
    Within the heart such peace?
I thought, indeed, by magic chance,
    A third from Heaven to win,
But as, at dusk, we reach'd Penzance,
    A drizzling rain set in.   60

                (1876)

246   *The Toys*

MY little Son, who look'd from thoughtful eyes
And moved and spoke in quiet grown-up wise,
Having my law the seventh time disobey'd,
I struck him, and dismiss'd
With hard words and unkiss'd,
His Mother, who was patient, being dead.
Then, fearing lest his grief should hinder sleep,
I visited his bed,
But found him slumbering deep,
With darken'd eyelids, and their lashes yet   10
From his late sobbing wet.
And I, with moan,
Kissing away his tears, left others of my own;
For, on a table drawn beside his head,
He had put, within his reach,
A box of counters and a red-vein'd stone,
A piece of glass abraded by the beach
And six or seven shells,
A bottle with bluebells
And two French copper coins, ranged there with careful art,   20
To comfort his sad heart.
So when that night I pray'd
To God, I wept, and said:
Ah, when at last we lie with tranced breath,
Not vexing Thee in death,
And Thou rememberest of what toys
We made our joys,
How weakly understood,
Thy great commanded good,

Then, fatherly not less   30
Than I whom Thou hast moulded from the clay,
Thou'lt leave Thy wrath, and say,
'I will be sorry for their childishness.'

                                                    (1876)

247   *Magna est Veritas*

HERE, in this little Bay,
Full of tumultuous life and great repose,
Where, twice a day,
The purposeless, glad ocean comes and goes,
Under high cliffs, and far from the huge town,
I sit me down.
For want of me the world's course will not fail:
When all its work is done, the lie shall rot;
The truth is great, and shall prevail,
When none cares whether it prevail or not.   10

                                                    (1877)

248   *Arbor Vitæ*

WITH honeysuckle, over-sweet, festoon'd;
With bitter ivy bound;
Terraced with funguses unsound;
Deform'd with many a boss
And closed scar, o'ercushion'd deep with moss;
Bunch'd all about with pagan mistletoe;
And thick with nests of the hoarse bird
That talks, but understands not his own word;
Stands, and so stood a thousand years ago,
A single tree.   10
Thunder has done its worst among its twigs,
Where the great crest yet blackens, never pruned,
But in its heart, alway
Ready to push new verdurous boughs, whene'er
The rotting saplings near it fall and leave it air,
Is all antiquity and no decay.
Rich, though rejected by the forest-pigs,
Its fruit, beneath whose rough, concealing rind
They that will break it find

Heart-succouring savour of each several meat,   20
And kernell'd drink of brain-renewing power,
With bitter condiment and sour,
And sweet economy of sweet,
And odours that remind
Of haunts of childhood and a different day.
Beside this tree,
Praising no Gods nor blaming, sans a wish,
Sits, Tartar-like, the Time's civility,
And eats its dead-dog off a golden dish.

(1878)

ERNEST JONES

1819–1869

249   *The Song of the Low*

(*To a Popular Melody*)

WE'RE low—we're low—we're very very low,
   As low as low can be;
The rich are high—for we make them so—
   And a miserable lot are we!
   And a miserable lot are we! are we!
     And a miserable lot are we!

We plough and sow—we're so very very low,
   That we delve in the dirty clay,
Till we bless the plain with the golden grain,
   And the vale with the fragrant hay.   10
Our place we know—we're so very low,
   'Tis down at the landlords' feet:
We're not too low—the bread to grow,
   But too low the bread to eat.
     We're low, we're low, etc.

Down, down we go—we're so very very low,
   To the hell of the deep sunk mines.
But we gather the proudest gems that glow,
   When the crown of a despot shines;

And whenever he lacks—upon our backs   20
　Fresh loads he deigns to lay,
We're far too low to vote the tax,
　But not too low to pay.
　　　　We're low, we're low, etc.

We're low, we're low—mere rabble, we know,
　But at our plastic power,
The mould at the lordling's feet will grow
　Into palace and church and tower—
Then prostrate fall—in the rich man's hall,
　And cringe at the rich man's door,   30
We're not too low to build the wall,
　But too low to tread the floor.
　　　　We're low, we're low, etc.

We're low, we're low—we're very very low,
　Yet from our fingers glide
The silken flow—and the robes that glow,
　Round the limbs of the sons of pride.
And what we get—and what we give,
　We know—and we know our share.
We're not too low the cloth to weave—   40
　But too low the cloth to wear.
　　　　We're low, we're low, etc.

We're low, we're low—we're very very low,
　And yet when the trumpets ring,
The thrust of a poor man's arm will go
　Through the heart of the proudest king!
We're low, we're low—our place we know,
　We're only the rank and file,
We're not too low—to kill the foe,
　But too low to touch the spoil.   50
　　　　We're low, we're low, etc.

　　　　　　　(Wr. and pub. 1852)

WILLIAM MAKEPEACE THACKERAY
1811–1863

250

Sorrows of Werther

WERTHER had a love for Charlotte
    Such as words could never utter;
Would you know how first he met her?
    She was cutting bread-and-butter.

Charlotte was a married lady,
    And a moral man was Werther,
And, for all the wealth of Indies,
    Would do nothing for to hurt her.

So he sighed and pined and ogled,
    And his passion boiled and bubbled,
Till he blew his silly brains out,
    And no more was by it troubled.

Charlotte, having seen his body
    Borne before her on a shutter,
Like a well-conducted person,
    Went on cutting bread-and-butter.

(1853)

JAMES HENRY
1798–1876

251

Out of the Frying Pan into the Fire

I DREAMT one night—it was a horrid dream—
That I was dead, and made was the division
Between the innocent flesh and guilty spirit,
And that the former, with a white sheet wrapt round
And nailed up in a box, was to the bottom
Sunk of a deep and narrow pit, which straight
Was filled to overheaping with a mixture
Of damp clay, rotting flesh and mouldering bones,
And lidded with a weighty stone whereon

Was writ my name and on what days precise   10
I first and last drew breath; while up the latter
Flew, without help of wings or fins or members,
By its mere lightness, through the air, to heaven;
And there being placed before the judgment-seat
Of its Maker, and most unsatisfactory
Answer returning to the question:—'Wherefore
Wast thou as I made thee?' was sent down
Tumbling by its own weight, down down to Hell,
To sink or swim or wade as best it might,
In sulphurous fires unquenchable for ever,   20
With Socrates and Plato, Aristides
Falsely surnamed the just, and Zoroaster,
Titus the good, and Cato and divine
Homer and Virgil, and so many millions
And millions more of wrongfully called good
And wise and virtuous, that for want of sulphur
And fire and snakes and instruments of torture
And room in Hell, the Universal Maker
Was by his own inherent justice forced,
That guilt might not go scot-free and unpunished,   30
To set apart so large a share of Heaven
For penal colonies and jails and treadmills,
That mutinies for want of flying-space
Began t' arise among the cherubim
And blessed spirits, and a Proclamation
Of Martial Law in Heaven was just being read
When, in a sweat of agony and fear,
I woke, and found myself in Germany,
In the close prison of a German bed,
And at my bedside Mr Oberkellner   40
With printed list of questions in his hand:
My name and age and birthplace and religion,
Trade or profession, wherefore I had come,
How long to stay, whither next bound, and so forth;
All at my peril to be truly answered,
And upon each a sixpence to the State,
Which duly paid I should obtain permission
To stay where I was so long as the State pleased,
Without being prosecuted as a felon,
Spy, or disturber of the public peace.   50

(Wr. and pub. 1854)

329

252   *Pain*

'PAIN, who made thee?' thus I said once
To the grim unpitying monster,
As, one sleepless night, I watched him
Heating in the fire his pincers.

'God Almighty; who dare doubt it?'
With a hideous grin he answered:
'I'm his eldest best-beloved son,
Cut from my dead mother's bowels.'

'Wretch, thou liest;' shocked and shuddering
To the monster I replied then;   10
'God is good, and kind, and gracious;
Never made a thing so ugly.'

'Tell me then, since thou know'st better,
Whose I am, by whom begotten;'
'Hell's thy birth-place, and the Devil
Both thy father and thy mother.'

'Be it so; to me the same 'tis
Whether I'm God's son or grandson,
And to thee not great the difference
Once thy flesh between my tongs is.'   20

'Spare me, spare me, Pain;' I shrieked out,
As the red-hot pincers caught me;
'Thou art God's son; aye thou 'rt God's self;
Only take thy fingers off me.'

                                    (Wr. and pub. 1854)

253   *Old Man*

AT six years old I had before mine eyes
A picture painted, like the rainbow, bright,
But far, far off in th' unapproachable distance.
With all my childish heart I longed to reach it,
And strove and strove the livelong day in vain,
Advancing with slow step some few short yards
But not perceptibly the distance lessening.
At threescore years old, when almost within
Grasp of my outstretched arms the selfsame picture

With all its beauteous colors painted bright,   10
I'm backward from it further borne each day
By an invisible, compulsive force,
Gradual but yet so steady, sure, and rapid,
That at threescore and ten I'll from the picture
Be even more distant than I was at six.

(Wr. and pub. 1854)

254   *Very Old Man*

I WELL remember how some threescore years
And ten ago, a helpless babe, I toddled
From chair to chair about my mother's chamber,
Feeling, as 'twere, my way in the new world
And foolishly afraid of, or, as 't might be,
Foolishly pleased with, th' unknown objects round me.
And now with stiffened joints I sit all day
In one of those same chairs, as foolishly
Hoping or fearing something from me hid
Behind the thick, dark veil which I see hourly   10
And minutely on every side round closing
And from my view all objects shutting out.

(Wr. and pub. 1854)

255   ANOTHER and another and another
And still another sunset and sunrise,
The same yet different, different yet the same,
Seen by me now in my declining years
As in my early childhood, youth and manhood;
And by my parents and my parents' parents,
And by the parents of my parents' parents,
And by their parents counted back for ever,
Seen, all their lives long, even as now by me;
And by my children and my children's children   10
And by the children of my children's children
And by their children counted on for ever
Still to be seen as even now seen by me;
Clear and bright sometimes, sometimes dark and clouded
But still the same sunsetting and sunrise;
The same for ever to the never ending
Line of observers, to the same observer
Through all the changes of his life the same:

331

Sunsetting and sunrising and sunsetting,
And then again sunrising and sunsetting,   20
Sunrising and sunsetting evermore.

(Wr. and pub. 1854)

256   *My Stearine Candles*

HE'S gone to bed at last, that flaring, glaring,
Round, red-faced, bold, monopolizing Sun,
And I may venture from their hiding-place
To bring my pair of stearine candles forth
And set them, firmly stayed, upon my table,
To illuminate and cheer my studious evening.
Thou hast my praise, Prometheus, for thy theft,
And, were I to idolatry addicted,
Shouldst be my God in preference to Buddh,
Brahma, or Thor, or Odin, or Jove's self.   10
Her of the olive branch I'd hold to thee
The next in honor, and before her shrine
In gratitude would keep for ever burning
A lamp of such Athenian oil as Plato,
Demosthenes, Pythagoras, and Solon
Were wont in bed to read by, after midnight.
The third, last person of my Trinity
Should be th' inventor of the stearine candle;
He that enabled me to sit, the long
Midwinter nights, in study, by a light   20
Which neither flickers nor offends the nostrils,
Nor from the distance of a thousand miles,
Or thousand years, or both perhaps, keeps ever
And anon calling me—like some bold child
The mother's hand—to come and snuff and snub it;
But steady, cleanly, bright and inodorous,
Than tallow more humane, than wax less costly,
Gives me just what I want, and asks back nothing.

(Wr. and pub. 1854)

257   ONCE on a time a thousand different men
Together knelt before as many Gods
Each from the other different as themselves
Were different each from each, yet didn't fall out,
Or cut each others' throats amidst their prayers—

'Stop there! that never happened, or, if it did,
'Twas by a miracle; or if it happened
Really and in the way of nature, tell me
How, where, and when, what kind of men they were,
What kind of Gods—didn't even the Gods fall out?'   10
Not even the Gods; I'll tell thee how it was;
But art thou trusty? canst thou keep the secret?
'Yes yes.' Then in thine ear: the thousand Gods
Had all the selfsame name; so every God,
Hearing no name invoked except his own,
Believed that every man of all the thousand
Worshipped him only; while each one of all
The thousand worshippers, hearing no name
Except his own God's name invoked, believed
That every one of all the whole nine hundred   20
Ninety and nine worshipped no God but his;
So all the thousand men together lived
In love and peace, as holding the same faith,
And of the thousand Gods not one was jealous.

(Wr. 1856; pub. 1866)

258   *Two hundred men and eighteen killed
    For want of a second door!
Ay, for with two doors, each ton coal
    Had cost one penny more.

And what is it else makes England great,
    At home, by land, by sea,
But her cheap coal, and eye's tail turned
    Toward strict economy?

* At ten o'clock on the morning of Thursday, January 16, 1862, the great iron beam of the steam-engine which worked the pumps of the Hester coal pit near Hartley in Northumberland, snapped across, and a portion of the beam, 40 tons in weight, fell into the shaft, tearing away the boarded lining so that the earthy sides collapsed and fell in, filling up the shaft in such a manner as not only to cut off all communication between the interior of the pit and the outer world, but entirely to obstruct all passage of pure air into, and of foul air out of, the pit. All the persons who were at work below at the time, two hundred and eighteen in number, were of course suffocated, nor was it until the seventh day after the accident that access could be had to the interior of the pit, or anything, beyond the mere fact of their entombment, ascertained concerning the helpless and unfortunate victims of that 'auri sacra fames' which so generally, so heartlessly, so pertinaciously refuses the poor workers in the coal mines of England, even the sad resource of a second staple or air shaft. See the Illustrated London News of Jan. 25, and Febr. 1, 1862.

But if a slate falls off the roof
   And kills a passer-by,   10
Or if a doctor's dose too strong
   Makes some half-dead man die,

We have coroners and deodands
   And inquests, to no end,
And every honest Englishman's
   The hapless sufferer's friend,

And householder's or doctor's foe,
   For he has nought to lose,
And fain will, if he can, keep out
   Of that poor dead man's shoes.   20

But if of twice a hundred men,
   And eighteen more, the breath
Is stopped at once in a coal pit,
   It's quite a natural death;

For, God be praised! the chance is small
   That either you or I
Should come, for want of a second door,
   In a coal pit to die.

Besides, 'twould cost a thousand times
   As much, or something more,   30
To make to every pit of coal
   A second, or safety door,

As all the shrouds and coffins cost
   For those who perish now
For want of a second door, and that's
   No trifle, you'll allow;

And trade must live, though now and then
   A man or two may die;
So merry sing 'God bless the Queen,'
   And long live you and I;   40

And, Jenny, let each widow have
   A cup of congo strong,
And every orphan half a cup,
   And so I end my song,

With prayer to God to keep coal cheap,
  Both cheap and plenty too,
And if the pit's a whole mile deep,
  What is it to me or you?

For though we're mortal too, no doubt,
  And Death for us his sithe   50
Has ready still, the chance is small
  We ever die of stithe.

And if we do, our gracious Queen
  Will, sure, a telegram send,
To say how sore she grieves for us
  And our untimely end;

And out of her own privy purse
  A sovereign down will pay,
To have us decently interred
  And put out of the way;   60

And burial service shall for us
  In the churchyard be read,
And more bells rung and more hymns sung
  Than if we had died in bed:

For such an accident as this
  May never occur again,
And till it does, one door's enough
  For pumps, air, coal, and men;

And should it occur—which God forbid!—
  And stifle every soul,   70
Remember well, good Christians all,
  Not one whit worse the coal.

                  (Wr. 1862; pub. 1866)

WILLIAM BELL SCOTT

1811–1890

A Rhyme of the Sun-Dial

THE dial is dark, 'tis but half-past one:
But the crow is abroad, and the day's begun.

The dial is dim, 'tis but half-past two:
Fit the small foot with its neat first shoe.

The light gains fast, it is half-past three:
Now the blossom appears all over the tree.

The gnomon tells it is but half-past four:
Shut upon him the old school-door.

The sun is strong, it is half-past five:
Through this and through that let him hustle and strive.   10

Ha, thunder and rain! it is half-past six:
Hither and thither, go, wander and fix.

The shadows are sharp, it is half-past seven:
The Titan dares to scale even heaven!

The rain soon dries, it is half-past eight:
Time faster flies, but it is not late!

The sky now is clear, it is half-past nine:
Draw all the threads and make them entwine.

Clearer and calmer, 'tis half-past ten:
Count we the gains? not yet: try again.   20

The shadows lengthen, half-past eleven:
He looks back, alas! let the man be shriven!

The mist falls cold, it is half-past twelve:
Hark, the bell tolls! up, sexton and delve!

(1854)

260

Death

    I AM the one whose thought
Is as the deed; I have no brother, and
    No father; years
Have never seen my power begin. A chain
Doth bind all things to me. In my hand, man,—
Infinite thinker,—vanishes as doth
The worm that he creates, as doth the moth
That it creates, as doth the limb minute
That stirs upon that moth. My being is
    Inborn with all things, and   10
    With all things doth expand.

    But fear me not; I am
The hoary dust, the shut ear, the profound,
    The deep of night,
When Nature's universal heart doth cease
To beat; communicating nothing; dark
And tongueless, negative of all things. Yet
Fear me not, man; I am the blood that flows
Within thee,—I am change; and it is I
Creates a joy within thee, when thou feel'st   20
Manhood and new untried superior powers
Rising before thee: I it is can make
    Old things give place
    To thy free race.

    All things are born for me.
His father and his mother,—yet man hates
    Me foolishly.
An easy spirit and a free lives on,
But he who fears the ice doth stumble. Walk
Straight onward peacefully,—I am a friend   30
Will pass thee graciously: but grudge and weep
And cark,—I'll be a cold chain round thy neck
Into the grave, each day a link drawn in,
Untill thy face shall be upon the turf,
    And the hair from thy crown
    Be blown like thistle-down.

                (1854)

The Witch's Ballad

O, I HAE come from far away,
  From a warm land far away,
A southern land across the sea,
With sailor-lads about the mast,
Merry and canny, and kind to me.

And I hae been to yon town,
  To try my luck in yon town;
Nort, and Mysie, Elspie too.
Right braw we were to pass the gate,
Wi' gowden clasps on girdles blue.   10

Mysie smiled wi' miminy mouth,
  Innocent mouth, miminy mouth;
Elspie wore her scarlet gown,
Nort's grey eyes were unco' gleg,
My Castile comb was like a crown.

We walked abreast all up the street,
  Into the market up the street;
Our hair with marygolds was wound,
Our bodices with love-knots laced,
Our merchandise with tansy bound.   20

Nort had chickens, I had cocks,
  Gamesome cocks, loud-crowing cocks;
Mysie ducks, and Elspie drakes,—
For a wee groat or a pound:
We lost nae time wi' gives and takes.

Lost nae time, for well we knew,
  In our sleeves full well we knew,
When the gloaming came that night,
Duck nor drake nor hen nor cock
Would be found by candle-light.   30

And when our chaffering all was done,
  All was paid for, sold and done,
We drew a glove on ilka hand,
We sweetly curtsied each to each,
And deftly danced a saraband.

The market lasses looked and laughed,
　Left their gear and looked and laughed;
They made as they would join the game,
But soon their mithers, wild and wud,
With whack and screech they stopped the same.　　40

Sae loud the tongues o' randies grew,
　The flitin' and the skirlin' grew,
At all the windows in the place,
Wi' spoons or knives, wi' needle or awl,
Was thrust out every hand and face.

And down each stair they thronged anon,
　Gentle, semple, thronged anon;
Souter and tailor, frowsy Nan,
The ancient widow young again,
Simpering behind her fan.　　50

Without a choice, against their will,
　Doited, dazed, against their will,
The market lassie and her mither,
The farmer and his husbandman,
Hand in hand dance a' thegether.

Slow at first, but faster soon,
　Still increasing wild and fast,
Hoods and mantles, hats and hose,
Blindly doffed and cast away,
Left them naked, heads and toes.　　60

They would have torn us limb from limb,
　Dainty limb from dainty limb;
But never one of them could win
Across the line that I had drawn
With bleeding thumb a-widdershin.

But there was Jeff the provost's son,
　Jeff the provost's only son;
There was Father Auld himsel',
The Lombard frae the hostelry,
And the lawyer Peter Fell.　　70

All goodly men we singled out,
　Waled them well, and singled out,
And drew them by the left hand in;
Mysie the priest, and Elspie won
The Lombard, Nort the lawyer carle,
I mysel' the provost's son.

Then, with cantrip kisses seven,
  Three times round with kisses seven,
Warped and woven there spun we,
Arms and legs and flaming hair,   80
Like a whirlwind on the sea.

Like the wind that sucks the sea,
  Over and in and on the sea,
Good sooth it was a mad delight;
And every man of all the four
Shut his eyes and laughed outright.

Laughed as long as they had breath,
  Laughed while they had sense or breath;
And close about us coiled a mist
Of gnats and midges, wasps and flies,   90
Like the whirlwind shaft it rist.

Drawn up I was right off my feet,
  Into the mist and off my feet;
And, dancing on each chimney-top,
I saw a thousand darling imps
Keeping time with skip and hop.

And on the provost's brave ridge-tile,
  On the provost's grand ridge-tile,
The Blackamoor first to master me
I saw,—I saw that winsome smile,   100
The mouth that did my heart beguile,
And spoke the great Word over me,
In the land beyond the sea.

I called his name, I called aloud,
  Alas! I called on him aloud;
And then he filled his hand with stour,
And threw it towards me in the air;
My mouse flew out, I lost my pow'r!

My lusty strength, my power, were gone;
  Power was gone, and all was gone.   110
He will not let me love him more!
Of bell and whip and horse's tail
He cares not if I find a store.

But I am proud if he is fierce!
  I am as proud as he is fierce;
I'll turn about and backward go,
If I meet again that Blackamoor,
And he'll help us then, for he shall know
I seek another paramour.

And we'll gang once more to yon town,   120
  Wi' better luck to yon town;
We'll walk in silk and cramoisie,
And I shall wed the provost's son;
My-lady of the town I'll be!

For I was born a crowned king's child,
  Born and nursed a king's child,
King o' a land ayont the sea,
Where the Blackamoor kissed me first,
And taught me art and glamourie.

Each one in her wame shall hide   130
  Her hairy mouse, her wary mouse,
Fed on madwort and agramie,—
Wear amber beads between her breasts,
And blind-worm's skin about her knee.

The Lombard shall be Elspie's man,
  Elspie's gowden husband-man;
Nort shall take the lawyer's hand;
The priest shall swear another vow:
We'll dance again the saraband!

(1875)

262   *Music*

            LISTLESS the silent ladies sit
            About the room so gaily lit;
            Madame Ions likes the cups or ray,
            But thinks it scarce enough to say:
            Mistress Cox is gone astray
            To the night-light in her own nursery,
            Wonders if little Maude was led
            Without long coaxing into bed:

Miss Jemima Applewhite,
On a low stool by the fire,   10
Concentrates her confused desire,—
Perhaps will do so all the night,
On an unused rhyme for 'scan,'
And can but find the stiff word *man*:
Miss Temple pets the little hound,
That has a tendency to whine,
To-night its cushion can't be found;
And wonders when they'll leave the wine
Few take, but which men still combine
To linger over when they dine.   20
Indeed a frightful interval!
Madame Ions wants her game,
Or she must have her usual wink;
But now satiric Bertha Stahl
Jumps upon the music-stool,
And breaks into a sportive flame;
But what of all things do you think
She plays, that laughter-loving fool?
The funeral march, Dead March of Saul!

Oh, Lord of Hosts! their mailéd tread,   30
Bearing along the mailéd dead,
Makes me bow my stubborn head.
Never underneath the sun
With this heart-fathoming march be done;
Still, Lord of Hosts! to Thee we cry,
When our great ones, loved ones, die,
Still some grand lament we crave,
When we descend into the grave.

I turn, afraid that I may weep,—
Jemima's pestered wits still ran   40
After the unused rhyme for 'scan,'
Dear old Ions was asleep.

(1882)

MORTIMER COLLINS

1827–1876

Lotos Eating

I

WHO would care to pass his life away
  Of the Lotos-land a dreamful denizen—
Lotos-islands in a waveless bay,
      Sung by Alfred Tennyson?

II

Who would care to be a dull new-comer
  Far across the wild sea's wide abysses,
Where, about the earth's 3000th summer
      Passed divine Ulysses?

III

Rather give me coffee, art, a book,
  From my windows a delicious sea-view,   10
Southdown mutton, somebody to cook—
      'Music?' I believe you.

IV

Strawberry icebergs in the summer time—
  But of elmwood many a massive splinter,
Good ghost stories, and a classic rhyme,
      For the nights of winter.

V

Now and then a friend and some sauterne,
  Now and then a haunch of Highland venison:
And for Lotos-lands I'll never yearn
      Maugre Alfred Tennyson.   20

                                    (1855)

264 *To F. C.*

20th February 1875

FAST falls the snow, O lady mine,
Sprinkling the lawn with crystals fine,
But by the gods we won't repine
    While we're together,
We'll chat and rhyme and kiss and dine,
    Defying weather.

So stir the fire and pour the wine,
And let those sea-green eyes divine
Pour their love-madness into mine:
    I don't care whether   10
'Tis snow or sun or rain or shine
    If we're together.

(Wr. 1875; pub. 1876)

SHIRLEY BROOKS
1816–1874

265   *Poem by a Perfectly Furious Academician*

I TAKES and paints,
Hears no complaints,
And sells before I'm dry;
Till savage Ruskin
He sticks his tusk in,
Then nobody will buy.

N.B.—Confound Ruskin; only that won't come into the poetry—but it's true.

(1856)

EDWARD FITZGERALD

1809–1883

Rubáiyát of Omar Khayyám

I

AWAKE! for Morning in the Bowl of Night
Has flung the Stone that puts the Stars to Flight:
  And Lo! the Hunter of the East has caught
The Sultán's Turret in a Noose of Light.

II

Dreaming when Dawn's Left Hand was in the Sky
I heard a Voice within the Tavern cry,
  'Awake, my Little ones, and fill the Cup
'Before Life's Liquor in its Cup be dry.'

III

And, as the Cock crew, those who stood before
The Tavern shouted—'Open then the Door!   10
  'You know how little while we have to stay,
'And, once departed, may return no more.'

IV

Now the New Year reviving old Desires,
The thoughtful Soul to Solitude retires,
  Where the WHITE HAND OF MOSES on the Bough
Puts out, and Jesus from the Ground suspires.

V

Irám indeed is gone with all its Rose,
And Jamshýd's Sev'n-ring'd Cup where no one knows;
  But still the Vine her ancient Ruby yields,
And still a Garden by the Water blows.   20

VI

And David's Lips are lock't; but in divine
High piping Péhlevi, with 'Wine! Wine! Wine!
  '*Red* Wine!'—the Nightingale cries to the Rose
That yellow Cheek of her's to'incarnadine.

VII

Come, fill the Cup, and in the Fire of Spring
The Winter Garment of Repentance fling:
    The Bird of Time has but a little way
To fly—and Lo! the Bird is on the Wing.

VIII

And look—a thousand Blossoms with the Day
Woke—and a thousand scatter'd into Clay;   30
    And this first Summer Month that brings the Rose
Shall take Jamshýd and Kaikobád away.

IX

But come with old Khayyám, and leave the Lot
Of Kaikobád and Kaikhosrú forgot:
    Let Rustum lay about him as he will,
Or Hátim Tai cry Supper—heed them not.

X

With me along some Strip of Herbage strown
That just divides the desert from the sown,
    Where name of Slave and Sultán scarce is known,
And pity Sultán Máhmúd on his Throne.   40

XI

Here with a Loaf of Bread beneath the Bough,
A Flask of Wine, a Book of Verse—and Thou
    Beside me singing in the Wilderness—
And Wilderness is Paradise enow.

XII

'How sweet is mortal Sovranty!'—think some:
Others—'How blest the Paradise to come!'
    Ah, take the Cash in hand and waive the Rest;
Oh, the brave Music of a *distant* Drum!

XIII

Look to the Rose that blows about us—'Lo,
'Laughing,' she says, 'into the World I blow: 50
    'At once the silken Tassel of my purse
'Tear, and its Treasure on the Garden throw.'

XIV

The Worldly Hope men set their Hearts upon
Turns Ashes—or it prospers; and anon,
   Like Snow upon the Desert's dusty Face
Lighting a little Hour or two—is gone.

XV

And those who husbanded the Golden Grain,
And those who flung it to the Winds like Rain,
   Alike to no such aureate Earth are turn'd
As, buried once, Men want dug up again.   60

XVI

Think, in this batter'd Caravanserai
Whose Doorways are alternate Night and Day,
   How Sultán after Sultán with his Pomp
Abode his Hour or two, and went his way.

XVII

They say the Lion and the Lizard keep
The Courts where Jamshýd gloried and drank deep:
   And Bahrám, that great Hunter—the Wild Ass
Stamps o'er his Head, and he lies fast asleep.

XVIII

I sometimes think that never blows so red
The Rose as where some buried Cæsar bled;   70
   That every Hyacinth the Garden wears
Dropt in its Lap from some once lovely Head.

XIX

And this delightful Herb whose tender Green
Fledges the River's Lip on which we lean—
   Ah, lean upon it lightly! for who knows
From what once lovely Lip it springs unseen!

XX

Ah, my Belovéd, fill the Cup that clears
To-day of past Regrets and future Fears—
   To-morrow?—Why, To-morrow I may be
Myself with Yesterday's Sev'n Thousand Years.   80

XXI

Lo! some we loved, the loveliest and best
That Time and Fate of all their Vintage prest,
  Have drunk their Cup a Round or two before,
And one by one crept silently to Rest.

XXII

And we, that now make merry in the Room
They left, and Summer dresses in new Bloom,
  Ourselves must we beneath the Couch of Earth
Descend, ourselves to make a Couch—for whom?

XXIII

Ah, make the most of what we yet may spend,
Before we too into the Dust descend;   90
  Dust into Dust, and under Dust, to lie,
Sans Wine, sans Song, sans Singer, and—sans End!

XXIV

Alike for those who for TO-DAY prepare,
And those that after a TO-MORROW stare,
  A Muezzín from the Tower of Darkness cries
'Fools! your Reward is neither Here nor There!'

XXV

Why, all the Saints and Sages who discuss'd
Of the Two Worlds so learnedly, are thrust
  Like foolish Prophets forth; their Words to Scorn
Are scatter'd, and their Mouths are stopt with Dust.   100

XXVI

Oh, come with old Khayyám, and leave the Wise
To talk; one thing is certain, that Life flies;
  One thing is certain, and the Rest is Lies;
The Flower that once has blown for ever dies.

XXVII

Myself when young did eagerly frequent
Doctor and Saint, and heard great Argument
  About it and about: but evermore
Came out by the same Door as in I went.

XXVIII

With them the Seed of Wisdom did I sow,
And with my own hand labour'd it to grow:
   And this was all the Harvest that I reap'd—
'I came like Water, and like Wind I go.'   110

XXIX

Into this Universe, and *why* not knowing,
Nor *whence*, like Water willy-nilly flowing:
   And out of it, as Wind along the Waste,
I know not *whither*, willy-nilly blowing.

XXX

What, without asking, hither hurried *whence?*
And, without asking, *whither* hurried hence!
   Another and another Cup to drown
The Memory of this Impertinence!   120

XXXI

Up from Earth's Centre through the Seventh Gate
I rose, and on the Throne of Saturn sate,
   And many Knots unravel'd by the Road;
But not the Knot of Human Death and Fate.

XXXII

There was a Door to which I found no Key:
There was a Veil past which I could not see:
   Some little Talk awhile of ME and THEE
There seemed—and then no more of THEE and ME.

XXXIII

Then to the rolling Heav'n itself I cried,
Asking, 'What Lamp had Destiny to guide   130
   'Her little Children stumbling in the Dark?'
And—'A blind Understanding!' Heav'n replied.

XXXIV

Then to this earthen Bowl did I adjourn
My Lip the secret Well of Life to learn:
   And Lip to Lip it murmur'd—'While you live
'Drink!—for once dead you never shall return.'

349

XXXV

I think the Vessel, that with fugitive
Articulation answer'd, once did live,
   And merry-make; and the cold Lip I kiss'd
How many Kisses might it take—and give!   140

XXXVI

For in the Market-place, one Dusk of Day,
I watch'd the Potter thumping his wet Clay:
   And with its all obliterated Tongue
It murmur'd—'Gently, Brother, gently, pray!'

XXXVII

Ah, fill the Cup:—what boots it to repeat
How Time is slipping underneath our Feet:
   Unborn TO-MORROW, and dead YESTERDAY,
Why fret about them if TO-DAY be sweet!

XXXVIII

One Moment in Annihilation's Waste,
   One Moment, of the Well of Life to taste—   150
   The Stars are setting and the Caravan
Starts for the Dawn of Nothing—Oh, make haste!

XXXIX

How long, how long, in infinite Pursuit
Of This and That endeavour and dispute?
   Better be merry with the fruitful Grape
Than sadden after none, or bitter, Fruit.

XL

You know, my Friends, how long since in my House
For a new Marriage I did make Carouse:
   Divorced old barren Reason from by Bed,
And took the Daughter of the Vine to Spouse.   160

XLI

For 'Is' and 'IS-NOT' though *with* Rule and Line,
And 'UP-AND-DOWN' *without*, I could define,
   I yet in all I only cared to know,
Was never deep in anything but—Wine.

XLII

And lately, by the Tavern Door agape,
Came stealing through the Dusk an Angel Shape
  Bearing a Vessel on his Shoulder; and
He bid me taste of it; and 'twas—the Grape!

XLIII

The Grape that can with Logic absolute
The Two-and-Seventy jarring Sects confute: 170
  The subtle Alchemist that in a Trice
Life's leaden Metal into Gold transmute.

XLIV

The mighty Mahmúd, the victorious Lord,
That all the misbelieving and black Horde
  Of Fears and Sorrows that infest the Soul
Scatters and slays with his enchanted Sword.

XLV

But leave the Wise to wrangle, and with me
The Quarrel of the Universe let be:
  And, in some corner of the Hubbub coucht,
Make Game of that which makes as much of Thee.   180

XLVI

For in and out, above, about, below,
'Tis nothing but a Magic Shadow-show,
  Play'd in a Box whose Candle is the Sun,
Round which we Phantom Figures come and go.

XLVII

And if the Wine you drink, the Lip you press,
End in the Nothing all Things end in—Yes—
  Then fancy while Thou art, Thou art but what
Thou shalt be—Nothing—Thou shalt not be less.

XLVIII

While the Rose blows along the River Brink,
With old Khayyám the Ruby Vintage drink: 190
  And when the Angel with his darker Draught
Draws up to Thee—take that, and do not shrink.

XLIX

'Tis all a Chequer-board of Nights and Days
Where Destiny with Men for Pieces plays:
   Hither and thither moves, and mates, and slays,
And one by one back in the Closet lays.

L

The Ball no Question makes of Ayes and Noes,
But Right or Left as strikes the Player goes;
   And He that toss'd Thee down into the Field,
He knows about it all—HE knows—HE knows!   200

LI

The Moving Finger writes; and, having writ,
Moves on: nor all thy Piety nor Wit
   Shall lure it back to cancel half a Line,
Nor all thy Tears wash out a Word of it.

LII

And that inverted Bowl we call The Sky,
Whereunder crawling coop't we live and die,
   Lift not thy hands to *It* for help—for It
Rolls impotently on as Thou or I.

LIII

With Earth's first Clay They did the Last Man's knead,
And then of the Last Harvest sow'd the Seed: 210
   Yea, the first Morning of Creation wrote
What the Last Dawn of Reckoning shall read.

LIV

I tell Thee this—When, starting from the Goal,
Over the shoulders of the flaming Foal
   Of Heav'n Parwín and Mushtara they flung,
In my predestin'd Plot of Dust and Soul

LV

The Vine had struck a Fibre; which about
If clings my Being—let the Súfi flout;
   Of my Base Metal may be filed a Key,
That shall unlock the Door he howls without.   220

LVI

And this I know: whether the one True Light,
Kindle to Love, or Wrath consume me quite,
   One Glimpse of It within the Tavern caught
Better than in the Temple lost outright.

LVII

Oh Thou, who didst with Pitfall and with Gin
Beset the Road I was to wander in,
   Thou wilt not with Predestination round
Enmesh me, and impute my Fall to Sin?

LVIII

Oh, Thou, who Man of baser Earth didst make,
And who with Eden didst devise the Snake;   230
   For all the Sin wherewith the Face of Man
Is blacken'd, Man's Forgiveness give—and take!

*   *   *

KÚZA-NÁMA

LIX

Listen again. One Evening at the Close
Of Ramazán, ere the better Moon arose,
   In that old Potter's Shop I stood alone
With the clay Population round in Rows.

LX

And, strange to tell, among that Earthen Lot
Some could articulate, while others not:
   And suddenly one more impatient cried—
'Who *is* the Potter, pray, and who the Pot?'   240

LXI

Then said another—'Surely not in vain
'My Substance from the common Earth was ta'en,
   'That He who subtly wrought me into Shape
'Should stamp me back to common Earth again.'

LXII

Another said—'Why, ne'er a peevish Boy,
'Would break the Bowl from which he drank in Joy;
   'Shall He that *made* the Vessel in pure Love
'And Fansy, in an after Rage destroy!'

LXIII

None answer'd this; but after Silence spake
A Vessel of a more ungainly Make:
   'They sneer at me for leaning all awry;
'What! did the Hand then of the Potter shake?'

250

LXIV

Said one—'Folks of a surly Tapster tell,
'And daub his Visage with the Smoke of Hell;
   'They talk of some strict Testing of us—Pish!
'He's a Good Fellow, and 'twill all be well.'

LXV

Then said another with a long-drawn Sigh,
'My Clay with long oblivion is gone dry:
   'But, fill me with the old familiar Juice,
'Methinks I might recover by-and-bye!'

260

LXVI

So while the Vessels one by one were speaking,
One spied the little Crescent all were seeking:
   And then they jogg'd each other, 'Brother! Brother!
'Hark to the Porter's Shoulder-knot a-creaking!'

*   *   *

LXVII

Ah, with the Grape my fading Life provide,
And wash my Body whence the Life has died,
   And in a Windingsheet of Vine-leaf wrapt,
So bury me by some sweet Garden-side.

LXVIII

That ev'n my buried Ashes such a Snare
Of Perfume shall fling up into the Air,
   As not a True Believer passing by
But shall be overtaken unaware.

270

LXIX

Indeed the Idols I have loved so long
Have done my Credit in Men's Eye much wrong:
   Have drown'd my Honour in a shallow Cup,
And sold my Reputation for a Song.

LXX

Indeed, indeed, Repentance oft before
I swore—but was I sober when I swore?
   And then and then came Spring, and Rose-in-hand
My thread-bare Penitence apieces tore.   280

LXXI

And much as Wine has play'd the Infidel,
And robb'd me of my Robe of Honour—well,
   I often wonder what the Vintners buy
One half so precious as the Goods they sell.

LXXII

Alas, that Spring should vanish with the Rose!
That Youth's sweet-scented Manuscript should close!
   The Nightingale that in the Branches sang,
Ah, whence, and whither flown again, who knows!

LXXIII

Ah Love! could thou and I with Fate conspire
To grasp this sorry Scheme of Things entire,   290
   Would not we shatter it to bits—and then
Re-mould it nearer to the Heart's Desire!

LXXIV

Ah, Moon of my Delight who know'st no wane,
The Moon of Heav'n is rising once again:
   How oft hereafter rising shall she look
Through this same Garden after me—in vain!

LXXV

And when Thyself with shining Foot shall pass
Among the Guests Star-scatter'd on the Grass,
   And in thy joyous Errand reach the Spot
Where I made one—turn down an empty Glass!   300

TAMÁM SHUD

                                    (Wr. from 1856; pub. 1859)

ELIZABETH SIDDAL
(later ROSSETTI)
1829–1862

267 *A Silent Wood*

O SILENT wood, I enter thee
With a heart so full of misery
For all the voices from the trees
And the ferns that cling about my knees.

In thy darkest shadow let me sit
When the grey owls about thee flit;
There will I ask of thee a boon,
That I may not faint or die or swoon.

Gazing through the gloom like one
Whose life and hopes are also done,   10
Frozen like a thing of stone
I sit in thy shadow—but not alone.

Can God bring back the day when we two stood
Beneath the clinging trees in that dark wood?

(Wr. 1857?; pub. 1903)

268 *Dead Love*

OH never weep for love that's dead
    Since love is seldom true
But changes his fashion from blue to red,
    From brightest red to blue,
And love was born to an early death
    And is so seldom true.

Then harbour no smile on your bonny face
    To win the deepest sigh.
The fairest words on truest lips
    Pass on and surely die,   10
And you will stand alone, my dear,
    When wintry winds draw nigh.

Sweet, never weep for what cannot be,
   For this God has not given.
If the merest dream of love were true
   Then, sweet, we should be in heaven,
And this is only earth, my dear,
   Where true love is not given.

(Wr. 1859?; pub. 1899)

WILLIAM MORRIS
1834–1896

269   *Summer Dawn*

PRAY but one prayer for me 'twixt thy closed lips,
   Think but one thought of me up in the stars.
The summer night waneth, the morning light slips,
   Faint & grey 'twixt the leaves of the aspen, betwixt the cloud-bars,
That are patiently waiting there for the dawn:
   Patient and colourless, though Heaven's gold
Waits to float through them along with the sun.
Far out in the meadows, above the young corn,
   The heavy elms wait, and restless and cold
The uneasy wind rises; the roses are dun;   10
Through the long twilight they pray for the dawn,
Round the lone house in the midst of the corn.
   Speak but one word to me over the corn,
   Over the tender, bow'd locks of the corn.

(1858)

270   *For the Briar Rose*

THE BRIARWOOD

THE fateful slumber floats and flows
About the tangle of the rose;
But lo! the fated hand and heart
To rend the slumbrous curse apart!

THE COUNCIL ROOM

The threat of war, the hope of peace,
The Kingdom's peril and increase
Sleep on and bide the latter day,
When fate shall take her chain away.

357

THE GARDEN COURT

The maiden pleasance of the land
Knoweth no stir of voice or hand,
No cup the sleeping waters fill,
The restless shuttle lieth still.

THE ROSEBOWER

Here lies the hoarded love, the key
To all the treasure that shall be;
Come fated hand the gift to take,
And smite this sleeping world awake.

(1890)

271   *Another for the Briar Rose*

O TREACHEROUS scent, O thorny sight,
O tangle of world's wrong and right,
What art thou 'gainst my armour's gleam
But dusky cobwebs of a dream?

Beat down, deep sunk from every gleam
Of hope, they lie and dully dream;
Men once, but men no more, that Love
Their waste defeated hearts should move.

Here sleeps the world that would not love!
Let it sleep on, but if He move
Their hearts in humble wise to wait
On his new-wakened fair estate.

O won at last is never late!
Thy silence was the voice of fate;
Thy still hands conquered in the strife;
Thine eyes were light; thy lips were life.

(1891)

272

Pomona

I AM the ancient Apple-Queen,
As once I was so am I now.
For evermore a hope unseen,
Betwixt the blossom and the bough.

Ah, where's the river's hidden Gold!
And where the windy grave of Troy?
Yet come I as I came of old,
From out the heart of Summer's joy.

(1891)

273

The End of May

How the wind howls this morn
About the end of May,
And drives June on apace
To mock the world forlorn
And the world's joy passed away
And my unlonged-for face!
The world's joy passed away;
For no more may I deem
That any folk are glad
To see the dawn of day   10
Sunder the tangled dream
Wherein no grief they had.
Ah, through the tangled dream
Where others have no grief
Ever it fares with me
That fears and treasons stream
And dumb sleep slays belief
Whatso therein may be.
Sleep slayeth all belief
Until the hopeless light   20
Wakes at the birth of June
More lying tales to weave,
More love in woe's despite,
More hope to perish soon.

(1891)

359

THOMAS ASHE

1836–1889

Corpse-Bearing

I REMEMBER, they sent
  Some one to me, who said,
'You were his friend while he lived:
  Be so now he is dead.'

So I went next day to the house;
  And a woman nodded to me,
As I sat alone in thought:—
  Said, 'Sir, would you like to see

The poor dead body upstairs,
  Before we rivet the lid?'   10
But I said, 'I would rather not:
  For the look would never be hid

'From my sight, day after day,
  From my soul, year after year.
Enough to look on the pall:
  Enough to follow the bier.'

So the mourners gather'd at last;
  And the poor dead body was put
In a hearse with mournful plumes,
  And the door of the hearse was shut.   20

And when the mourners were all
  In the coaches, ready to start,
The sorrowing parent came
  To me, and whisper'd apart.

He smiled as well as he could;
  And the import of what he said
Was, that I should bear at the feet,
  And his son would bear at the head.

He was ever my friend;
  And I was happy to be   30
Of ever so small use still
  To one who had so loved me.

But, what a weight, O God!
  Was that one coffin to bear!
Like a coffin of lead!
  And I carry it everywhere

About, wherever I go!
  If I lift the slightest thing,
That requires an effort to lift,
  The effort at once will bring   40

The whole weight into my hands,
  And I carry the corpse at the feet;
And feel as if it would drop,
  And slip out of its winding-sheet.

I have made a vow in my heart,
  Whatever the friends may say,
Never to carry a corpse
  Again, to my dying day.

          (Wr. 1859–60; pub. 1871)

275   *To Two Bereaved*

YOU must be sad; for though it is to Heaven,
'Tis hard to yield a little girl of seven.
Alas, for me, 'tis hard my grief to rule,
Who only met her as she went to school;
Who never heard the little lips so sweet
Say even 'Good morning,' though our eyes would meet
As whose would fain be friends! How must you sigh,
Sick for your loss, when even so sad am I,
Who never clasp'd the small hands any day!
Fair flowers thrive round the little grave, I pray.   10

          (Wr. 1874; pub. 1876)

T. L. PEACOCK

1785–1866

276 *Love and Age*

I PLAYED with you 'mid cowslips blowing,
When I was six and you were four;
When garlands weaving, flower-balls throwing,
Were pleasures soon to please no more.
Through groves and meads, o'er grass and heather,
With little playmates, to and fro,
We wandered hand in hand together;
But that was sixty years ago.

You grew a lovely roseate maiden,
And still our early love was strong; 10
Still with no care our days were laden,
They glided joyously along;
And I did love you, very dearly,
How dearly words want power to show;
I thought your heart was touched as nearly;
But that was fifty years ago.

Then other lovers came around you,
Your beauty grew from year to year,
And many a splendid circle found you
The centre of its glittering sphere. 20
I saw you then, first vows forsaking,
On rank and wealth your hand bestow;
Oh, then I thought my heart was breaking,—
But that was forty years ago.

And I lived on, to wed another:
No cause she gave me to repine;
And when I heard you were a mother,
I did not wish the children mine.
My own young flock, in fair progression,
Made up a pleasant Christmas row: 30
My joy in them was past expression;—
But that was thirty years ago.

You grew a matron plump and comely,
You dwelt in fashion's brightest blaze;
My earthly lot was far more homely;
But I too had my festal days.

No merrier eyes have ever glistened
Around the hearth-stone's wintry glow,
Than when my youngest child was christened:—
But that was twenty years ago.   40

Time passed. My eldest girl was married,
And I am now a grandsire grey;
One pet of four years old I've carried
Among the wild-flowered meads to play.
In our old fields of childish pleasure,
Where now, as then, the cowslips blow,
She fills her basket's ample measure,—
And that is not ten years ago.

But though first love's impassioned blindness
Has passed away in colder light,   50
I still have thought of you with kindness,
And shall do, till our last good-night.
The ever-rolling silent hours
Will bring a time we shall not know,
When our young days of gathering flowers
Will be an hundred years ago.

(Wr. and pub. 1860)

ADELAIDE ANNE PROCTER

1825–1864

277   *Envy*

HE was the first always: Fortune
    Shone bright in his face.
I fought for years; with no effort
    He conquered the place:
We ran; my feet were all bleeding,
    But he won the race.

Spite of his many successes
    Men loved him the same;
My one pale ray of good fortune
    Met scoffing and blame.   10
When we erred, they gave him pity,
    But me—only shame.

My home was still in the shadow,
　　His lay in the sun:
I longed in vain: what he asked for
　　It straightway was done.
Once I staked all my heart's treasure,
　　We played—and he won.

Yes; and just now I have seen him,
　　Cold, smiling, and blest,　　　　　　　　　　20
Laid in his coffin. God help me!
　　While he is at rest,
I am cursed still to live:—even
　　Death loved him the best.

(1861)

RICHARD WATSON DIXON

1833–1900

278　　　　　　*Dream*

I

WITH camel's hair I clothed my skin,
　　I fed my mouth with honey wild;
And set me scarlet wool to spin,
　　And all my breast with hyssop filled;
Upon my brow and cheeks and chin
　　A bird's blood spilled.

I took a broken reed to hold,
　　I took a sponge of gall to press;
I took weak water-weeds to fold
　　About my sacrificial dress.　　　　　　　　　10

I took the grasses of the field,
　　The flax was bolled upon my crine;
And ivy thorn and wild grapes healed
　　To make good wine.

I took my scrip of manna sweet,
　　My cruse of water did I bless;
I took the white dove by the feet,
　　And flew into the wilderness.

II

The tiger came and played;
Uprose the lion in his mane;   20
The jackal's tawny nose
And sanguine dripping tongue
Out of the desert rose
And plunged its sands among;
The bear came striding o'er the desert plain.

Uprose the horn and eyes
And quivering flank of the great unicorn,
And galloped round and round;
Uprose the gleaming claw
Of the leviathan, and wound   30
In steadfast march did draw
Its course away beyond the desert's bourn.

I stood within a maze
Woven round about me by a magic art,
And ordered circle-wise:
The bear more near did tread,
And with two fiery eyes,
And with a wolfish head,
Did close the circle round in every part.

III

With scarlet corded horn,   40
With frail wrecked knees and stumbling pace,
The scapegoat came:
His eyes took flesh and spirit dread in flame
At once, and he died looking towards my face.

(1861)

279   *The Wizard's Funeral*

For me, for me, two horses wait,
Two horses stand before my gate:
Their vast black plumes on high are cast,
Their black manes swing in the midnight blast,
Red sparkles from their eyes fly fast.
But can they drag the hearse behind,
Whose black plumes mystify the wind?

What a thing for this heap of bones and hair!
Despair, despair!
Yet think of half the world's winged shapes   10
Which have come to thee wondering:
At thee the terrible idiot gapes,
At thee the running devil japes,
And angels stoop to thee and sing
From the soft midnight that enwraps
Their limbs, so gently, sadly fair;—
Thou seest the stars shine through their hair.
The blast again, ho, ho, the blast!
I go to a mansion that shall outlast;
And the stoled priest who steps before   20
Shall turn and welcome me at the door.

                                        (1861)

280   *Dawning*

OVER the hill I have watched the dawning,
I have watched the dawn of morning light,
Because I cannot well sleep by night,
Every day I have watched the dawning.
And to-day very early my window shook
With the cold wind fresh from the ghastly brook,
And I left my bed to watch the dawning.
Very cold was the light, very pale, very still,
And the wind blew great clouds over the hill
Towards the wet place of the dying dawning;   10
It blew them over towards the east
In heavier charge as the light increased,
From the very death of the dying dawning.
Whence did the clouds come over the hill?
I cannot tell, for no clouds did fill
The clear space opposite the dawning
Right over the hill, long, low, and pearl-grey,
Set in the wind to live as it may;
And as the light increased from the dawning,
The cold, cold brook unto my seeming   20
Did intermit its ghastly gleaming
And ran forth brighter in the dawning.
The wall-fruit stretched along the wall,
The pear-tree waved its banners tall;
Then close beside me in the dawning,
I saw thy face so stonily grey,
And the close lips no word did say,

The eyes confessed not in the dawning.
I saw a man ride through the light
Upon the hill-top, out of sight   30
Of me and thee and all the dawning.

(1861)

GEORGE MEREDITH

1828–1909

from *Modern Love* (281–297)

281   I

BY this he knew she wept with waking eyes:
That, at his hand's light quiver by her head,
The strange low sobs that shook their common bed,
Were called into her with a sharp surprise,
And strangled mute, like little gaping snakes,
Dreadfully venomous to him. She lay
Stone-still, and the long darkness flowed away
With muffled pulses. Then, as midnight makes
Her giant heart of Memory and Tears
Drink the pale drug of silence, and so beat   10
Sleep's heavy measure, they from head to feet
Were moveless, looking through their dead black years,
By vain regret scrawled over the blank wall.
Like sculptured effigies they might be seen
Upon their marriage-tomb, the sword between;
Each wishing for the sword that severs all.

282   V

A MESSAGE from her set his brain aflame.
A world of household matters filled her mind,
Wherein he saw hypocrisy designed:
She treated him as something that is tame,
And but at other provocation bites.
Familiar was her shoulder in the glass,
Through that dark rain: yet it may come to pass
That a changed eye finds such familiar sights

More keenly tempting than new loveliness.
The 'What has been' a moment seemed his own: 10
The splendours, mysteries, dearer because known,
Nor less divine: Love's inmost sacredness,
Called to him, 'Come!'—In his restraining start,
Eyes nurtured to be looked at, scarce could see
A wave of the great waves of Destiny
Convulsed at a checked impulse of the heart.

283   VI

IT chanced his lips did meet her forehead cool.
She had no blush, but slanted down her eye.
Shamed nature, then, confesses love can die:
And most she punishes the tender fool
Who will believe what honours her the most!
Dead! is it dead? She has a pulse, and flow
Of tears, the price of blood-drops, as I know,
For whom the midnight sobs around Love's ghost,
Since then I heard her, and so will sob on.
The love is here; it has but changed its aim.   10
O bitter barren woman! what's the name?
The name, the name, the new name thou hast won?
Behold me striking the world's coward stroke!
That will I not do, though the sting is dire.
—Beneath the surface this, while by the fire
They sat, she laughing at a quiet joke.

284   VII

SHE issues radiant from her dressing-room,
Like one prepared to scale an upper sphere:
—By stirring up a lower, much I fear!
How deftly that oiled barber lays his bloom!
That long-shanked dapper Cupid with frisked curls,
Can make known women torturingly fair;
The gold-eyed serpent dwelling in rich hair,
Awakes beneath his magic whisks and twirls.
His art can take the eyes from out my head,
Until I see with eyes of other men;   10
While deeper knowledge crouches in its den,
And sends a spark up:—is it true we are wed?

Yea! filthiness of body is most vile,
But faithlessness of heart I do hold worse.
The former, it were not so great a curse
To read on the steel-mirror of her smile.

285

IX

HE felt the wild beast in him betweenwhiles
So masterfully rude, that he would grieve
To see the helpless delicate thing receive
His guardianship through certain dark defiles.
Had he not teeth to rend, and hunger too?
But still he spared her. Once: 'Have you no fear?'
He said: 'twas dusk; she in his grasp; none near.
She laughed: 'No, surely; am I not with you?'
And uttering that soft starry 'you,' she leaned
Her gentle body near him, looking up;   10
And from her eyes, as from a poison-cup,
He drank until the flittering eyelids screened.
Devilish malignant witch! and oh, young beam
Of heaven's circle-glory! Here thy shape
To squeeze like an intoxicating grape—
I might, and yet thou goest safe, supreme.

286

XVI

IN our old shipwrecked days there was an hour,
When in the firelight steadily aglow,
Joined slackly, we beheld the red chasm grow
Among the clicking coals. Our library-bower
That eve was left to us: and hushed we sat
As lovers to whom Time is whispering.
From sudden-opened doors we heard them sing:
The nodding elders mixed good wine with chat.
Well knew we that Life's greatest treasure lay
With us, and of it was our talk. 'Ah, yes!   10
Love dies!' I said: I never thought it less.
She yearned to me that sentence to unsay.
Then when the fire domed blackening, I found
Her cheek was salt against my kiss, and swift
Up the sharp scale of sobs her breast did lift:—
Now am I haunted by that taste! that sound!

287

XVII

AT dinner, she is hostess, I am host.
Went the feast ever cheerfuller? She keeps
The Topic over intellectual deeps
In buoyancy afloat. They see no ghost.
With sparkling surface-eyes we ply the ball:
It is in truth a most contagious game:
HIDING THE SKELETON, shall be its name.
Such play as this, the devils might appal!
But here's the greater wonder; in that we
Enamoured of an acting nought can tire,   10
Each other, like true hypocrites, admire;
Warm-lighted looks, Love's ephemerioe,
Shoot gaily o'er the dishes and the wine.
We waken envy of our happy lot.
Fast, sweet, and golden, shows the marriage-knot.
Dear guests, you now have seen Love's corpse-light shine.

288

XXI

WE three are on the cedar-shadowed lawn;
My friend being third. He who at love once laughed,
Is in the weak rib by a fatal shaft
Struck through, and tells his passion's bashful dawn
And radiant culmination, glorious crown,
When 'this' she said: went 'thus': most wondrous she.
Our eyes grow white, encountering: that we are three,
Forgetful; then together we look down.
But he demands our blessing; is convinced
That words of wedded lovers must bring good.   10
We question; if we dare! or if we should!
And pat him, with light laugh. We have not winced.
Next, she has fallen. Fainting points the sign
To happy things in wedlock. When she wakes,
She looks the star that thro' the cedar shakes:
Her lost moist hand clings mortally to mine.

289

XXIII

'TIS Christmas weather, and a country house
Receives us: rooms are full: we can but get
An attic-crib. Such lovers will not fret
At that, it is half-said. The great carouse

Knocks hard upon the midnight's hollow door,
But when I knock at hers, I see the pit.
Why did I come here in that dullard fit?
I enter, and lie couched upon the floor.
Passing, I caught the coverlet's quick beat:—
Come, Shame, burn to my soul! and Pride, and Pain—   10
Foul demons that have tortured me, enchain!
Out in the freezing darkness the lambs bleat.
The small bird stiffens in the low starlight.
I know not how, but shuddering as I slept,
I dreamed a banished angel to me crept:
My feet were nourished on her breasts all night.

290   XXV

YOU like not that French novel? Tell me why.
You think it quite unnatural. Let us see.
The actors are, it seems, the usual three:
Husband, and wife, and lover. She—but fie!
In England we'll not hear of it. Edmond,
The lover, her devout chagrin doth share;
Blanc-mange and absinthe are his penitent fare,
Till his pale aspect makes her over-fond:
So, to preclude fresh sin, he tries rosbif.
Meantime the husband is no more abused: 10
Auguste forgives her ere the tear is used.
Then hangeth all on one tremendous IF:—
_If_ she will choose between them. She does choose;
And takes her husband, like a proper wife.
Unnatural? My dear, these things are life:
And life, some think, is worthy of the Muse.

291   XXXI

THIS golden head has wit in it. I live
Again, and a far higher life, near her.
Some women like a young philosopher;
Perchance because he is diminutive.
For woman's manly god must not exceed
Proportions of the natural nursing size.
Great poets and great sages draw no prize
With women: but the little lap-dog breed,

371

Who can be hugged, or on a mantel-piece
Perched up for adoration, these obtain   10
Her homage. And of this we men are vain?
Of this! 'Tis ordered for the world's increase!
Small flattery! Yet she has that rare gift
To beauty, Common Sense. I am approved.
It is not half so nice as being loved,
And yet I do prefer it. What's my drift?

292   XXXIV

MADAM would speak with me. So, now it comes:
The Deluge or else Fire! She's well; she thanks
My husbandship. Our chain on silence clanks.
Time leers between, above his twiddling thumbs.
Am I quite well? Most excellent in health!
The journals, too, I diligently peruse.
Vesuvius is expected to give news:
Niagara is no noisier. By stealth
Our eyes dart scrutinizing snakes. She's glad
I'm happy, says her quivering under-lip.   10
'And are not you?' 'How can I be?' 'Take ship!
For happiness is somewhere to be had.'
'Nowhere for me!' Her voice is barely heard.
I am not melted, and make no pretence.
With commonplace I freeze her, tongue and sense.
Niagara or Vesuvius is deferred.

293   XXXVI

MY Lady unto Madam makes her bow.
The charm of women is, that even while
You're probed by them for tears, you yet may smile,
Nay, laugh outright, as I have done just now.
The interview was gracious: they anoint
(To me aside) each other with fine praise:
Discriminating compliments they raise,
That hit with wondrous aim on the weak point:
My Lady's nose of Nature might complain.
It is not fashioned aptly to express   10
Her character of large-browed steadfastness.
But Madam says: Thereof she may be vain!

Now, Madam's faulty feature is a glazed
And inaccessible eye, that has soft fires,
Wide gates, at love-time only. This admires
My Lady. At the two I stand amazed.

294

XXXVII

ALONG the garden terrace, under which
A purple valley (lighted at its edge
By smoky torch-flame on the long cloud-ledge
Whereunder dropped the chariot), glimmers rich,
A quiet company we pace, and wait
The dinner-bell in prae-digestive calm.
So sweet up violet banks the Southern balm
Breathes round, we care not if the bell be late:
Though here and there grey seniors question Time
In irritable coughings. With slow foot   10
The low rosed moon, the face of Music mute,
Begins among her silent bars to climb.
As in and out, in silvery dusk, we thread,
I hear the laugh of Madam, and discern
My Lady's heel before me at each turn.
Our tragedy, is it alive or dead?

295

XLII

I AM to follow her. There is much grace
In women when thus bent on martyrdom.
They think that dignity of soul may come,
Perchance, with dignity of body. Base!
But I was taken by that air of cold
And statuesque sedateness, when she said
'I'm going'; lit a taper, bowed her head,
And went, as with the stride of Pallas bold.
Fleshly indifference horrible! The hands
Of Time now signal: O, she's safe from me!   10
Within those secret walls what do I see?
Where first she set the taper down she stands:
Not Pallas: Hebe shamed! Thoughts black as death,
Like a stirred pool in sunshine break. Her wrists
I catch: she faltering, as she half resists,
'You love . . .? love . . .? love . . .?' all on an indrawn breath.

373

296

XLVII

WE saw the swallows gathering in the sky,
And in the osier-isle we heard them noise.
We had not to look back on summer joys,
Or forward to a summer of bright dye:
But in the largeness of the evening earth
Our spirits grew as we went side by side.
The hour became her husband and my bride.
Love that had robbed us so, thus blessed our dearth!
The pilgrims of the year waxed very loud
In multitudinous chatterings, as the flood   10
Full brown came from the West, and like pale blood
Expanded to the upper crimson cloud.
Love that had robbed us of immortal things,
This little moment mercifully gave,
Where I have seen across the twilight wave
The swan sail with her young beneath her wings.

297

L

THUS piteously Love closed what he begat:
The union of this ever-diverse pair!
These two were rapid falcons in a snare,
Condemned to do the flitting of the bat.
Lovers beneath the singing sky of May,
They wandered once; clear as the dew on flowers:
But they fed not on the advancing hours:
Their hearts held cravings for the buried day.
Then each applied to each that fatal knife,
Deep questioning, which probes to endless dole.   10
Ah, what a dusty answer gets the soul
When hot for certainties in this our life!—
In tragic hints here see what evermore
Moves dark as yonder midnight ocean's force,
Thundering like ramping hosts of warrior horse,
To throw that faint thin line upon the shore!

(Wr. 1861–2; pub. 1862)

298   *When I Would Image*

WHEN I would image her features,
      Comes up a shrouded head:
I touch the outlines, shrinking;
      She seems of the wandering dead.

But when love asks for nothing,
      And lies on his bed of snow,
The face slips under my eyelids,
      All in its living glow.

Like a dark cathedral city,
      Whose spires, and domes, and towers   10
Quiver in violet lightnings,
      My soul basks on for hours.

                              (1862)

299   *Lucifer in Starlight*

ON a starred night Prince Lucifer uprose.
Tired of his dark dominion swung the fiend
Above the rolling ball in cloud part screened,
Where sinners hugged their spectre of repose.
Poor prey to his hot fit of pride were those.
And now upon his western wing he leaned,
Now his huge bulk o'er Afric's sands careened,
Now the black planet shadowed Arctic snows.
Soaring through wider zones that pricked his scars
With memory of the old revolt from Awe,   10
He reached a middle height, and at the stars,
Which are the brain of heaven, he looked, and sank.
Around the ancient track marched, rank on rank,
The army of unalterable law.

                              (1883)

J. STANYAN BIGG
1828–1865

300

An Irish Picture

A SMOKING swamp before a cottage door;
A drowned dog bobbing to a soleless shoe;
A broken wash-tub, with its ragged staves
Swimming and ducking to a battered hat,
Whenever the wind stirs the reedy slime;
A tumbled peat-stack, dripping in the rain;
A long, lank pig, with dissipated eyes,
Leading a vagrant life among the moors;
A rotting paling, and a plot of ground,
With fifteen cabbage-stalks amid lush weeds;   10
A moss-grown pathway, and a worn-out gate,
Its broken bars down-dangling from the nails;
A windy cottage, with a leaky thatch,
And two dim windows set like eyes asquint;
A bulging doorway, with a drunken lean;
Two half-nude children dabbling in the mire,
And scrambling eagerly for bottle-necks;
A man akimbo at the open door,
His battered hat slouched o'er his sottish eyes,
Smoking contented in the falling rain.   20

(1862)

ALGERNON CHARLES SWINBURNE
1837–1909

301

Before Parting

A MONTH or twain to live on honeycomb
Is pleasant; but one tires of scented time,
Cold sweet recurrence of accepted rhyme,
And that strong purple under juice and foam
Where the wine's heart has burst;
Nor feel the latter kisses like the first.

Once yet, this poor one time; I will not pray
Even to change the bitterness of it,
The bitter taste ensuing on the sweet,
To make your tears fall where your soft hair lay   10
All blurred and heavy in some perfumed wise
Over my face and eyes.

And yet who knows what end the scythèd wheat
Makes of its foolish poppies' mouths of red?
These were not sown, these are not harvested,
They grow a month and are cast under feet
And none has care thereof,
As none has care of a divided love.

I know each shadow of your lips by rote,
Each change of love in eyelids and eyebrows;   20
The fashion of fair temples tremulous
With tender blood, and colour of your throat;
I know not how love is gone out of this,
Seeing that all was his.

Love's likeness there endures upon all these:
But out of these one shall not gather love.
Day hath not strength nor the night shade enough
To make love whole and fill his lips with ease,
As some bee-builded cell
Feels at filled lips the heavy honey swell.   30

I know not how this last month leaves your hair
Less full of purple colour and hid spice,
And that luxurious trouble of closed eyes
Is mixed with meaner shadow and waste care;
And love, kissed out by pleasure, seems not yet
Worth patience to regret.

(1862)

302   *After Death*

THE four boards of the coffin lid
Heard all the dead man did.

The first curse was in his mouth,
Made of grave's mould and deadly drouth.

The next curse was in his head,
Made of God's work discomfited.

377

The next curse was in his hands,
Made out of two grave-bands.

The next curse was in his feet,
Made out of a grave-sheet.   10

'I had fair coins red and white,
And my name was as great light;

I had fair clothes green and red,
And strong gold bound round my head.

But no meat comes in my mouth,
Now I fare as the worm doth;

And no gold binds in my hair,
Now I fare as the blind fare.

My live thews were of great strength,
Now am I waxen a span's length;   20

My live sides were full of lust,
Now are they dried with dust.'

The first board spake and said:
'Is it best eating flesh or bread?'

The second answered it:
'Is wine or honey the more sweet?'

The third board spake and said:
'Is red gold worth a girl's gold head?'

The fourth made answer thus:
'All these things are as one with us.'   30

The dead man asked of them:
'Is the green land stained brown with flame?

Have they hewn my son for beasts to eat,
And my wife's body for beasts' meat?

Have they boiled my maid in a brass pan,
And built a gallows to hang my man?'

The boards said to him:
'This is a lewd thing that ye deem.

Your wife has gotten a golden bed,
All the sheets are sewn with red.   40

Your son has gotten a coat of silk,
The sleeves are soft as curded milk.

Your maid has gotten a kirtle new,
All the skirt has braids of blue.

Your man has gotten both ring and glove,
Wrought well for eyes to love.'

The dead man answered thus:
'What good gift shall God give us?'

The boards answered him anon:
'Flesh to feed hell's worm upon.'   50

(1862)

303   *A Leave-Taking*

LET us go hence, my songs; she will not hear.
Let us go hence together without fear;
Keep silence now, for singing-time is over,
And over all old things and all things dear.
She loves not you nor me as all we love her.
Yea, though we sang as angels in her ear,
          She would not hear.

Let us rise up and part; she will not know.
Let us go seaward as the great winds go,
Full of blown sand and foam; what help is here?   10
There is no help, for all these things are so,
And all the world is bitter as a tear.
And how these things are, though ye strove to show,
          She would not know.

Let us go home and hence; she will not weep.
We gave love many dreams and days to keep,
Flowers without scent, and fruits that would not grow,
Saying 'If thou wilt, thrust in thy sickle and reap.'
All is reaped now; no grass is left to mow;
And we that sowed, though all we fell on sleep,   20
          She would not weep.

Let us go hence and rest; she will not love.
She shall not hear us if we sing hereof,
Nor see love's ways, how sore they are and steep.
Come hence, let be, lie still; it is enough.
Love is a barren sea, bitter and deep;
And though she saw all heaven in flower above,
    She would not love.

Let us give up, go down; she will not care.
Though all the stars made gold of all the air,   30
And the sea moving saw before it move
One moon-flower making all the foam-flowers fair;
Though all those waves went over us, and drove
Deep down the stifling lips and drowning hair,
    She would not care.

Let us go hence, go hence; she will not see.
Sing all once more together; surely she,
She too, remembering days and words that were,
Will turn a little toward us, sighing; but we,
We are hence, we are gone, as though we had not been there.   40
Nay, and though all men seeing had pity on me,
    She would not see.

                             (1866)

304   *Ilicet*

THERE is an end of joy and sorrow;
Peace all day long, all night, all morrow,
   But never a time to laugh or weep.
The end is come of pleasant places,
The end of tender words and faces,
   The end of all, the poppied sleep.

No place for sound within their hearing,
No room for hope, no time for fearing,
   No lips to laugh, no lids for tears.
The old years have run out all their measure;   10
No chance of pain, no chance of pleasure,
   No fragment of the broken years.

Outside of all the worlds and ages,
There where the fool is as the sage is,
   There where the slayer is clean of blood,
No end, no passage, no beginning,
There where the sinner leaves off sinning,
   There where the good man is not good.

There is not one thing with another,
But Evil saith to Good: My brother,   20
    My brother, I am one with thee:
They shall not strive nor cry for ever:
No man shall choose between them: never
    Shall this thing end and that thing be.

Wind wherein seas and stars are shaken
Shall shake them, and they shall not waken;
    None that has lain down shall arise;
The stones are sealed across their places;
One shadow is shed on all their faces,
    One blindness cast on all their eyes.   30

Sleep, is it sleep perchance that covers
Each face, as each face were his lover's?
    Farewell; as men that sleep fare well.
The grave's mouth laughs unto derision
Desire and dread and dream and vision,
    Delight of heaven and sorrow of hell.

No soul shall tell nor lip shall number
The names and tribes of you that slumber;
    No memory, no memorial.
'Thou knowest'—who shall say thou knowest?   40
There is none highest and none lowest:
    An end, an end, an end of all.

Good night, good sleep, good rest from sorrow
To these that shall not have good morrow;
    The gods be gentle to all these.
Nay, if death be not, how shall they be?
Nay, is there help in heaven? it may be
    All things and lords of things shall cease.

The stooped urn, filling, dips and flashes;
The bronzèd brims are deep in ashes;   50
    The pale old lips of death are fed.
Shall this dust gather flesh hereafter?
Shall one shed tears or fall to laughter,
    At sight of all these poor old dead?

Nay, as thou wilt; these know not of it;
Thine eyes' strong weeping shall not profit,
    Thy laughter shall not give thee ease;
Cry aloud, spare not, cease not crying,
Sigh, till thou cleave thy sides with sighing,
    Thou shalt not raise up one of these.   60

Burnt spices flash, and burnt wine hisses,
The breathing flame's mouth curls and kisses
   The small dried rows of frankincense;
All round the sad red blossoms smoulder,
Flowers coloured like the fire, but colder,
   In sign of sweet things taken hence;

Yea, for their sake and in death's favour
Things of sweet shape and of sweet savour
   We yield them, spice and flower and wine;
Yea, costlier things than wine or spices,   70
Whereof none knoweth how great the price is,
   And fruit that comes not of the vine.

From boy's pierced throat and girl's pierced bosom
Drips, reddening round the blood-red blossom,
   The slow delicious bright soft blood,
Bathing the spices and the pyre,
Bathing the flowers and fallen fire,
   Bathing the blossom by the bud.

Roses whose lips the flame has deadened
Drink till the lapping leaves are reddened   80
   And warm wet inner petals weep;
The flower whereof sick sleep gets leisure,
Barren of balm and purple pleasure,
   Fumes with no native steam of sleep.

Why will ye weep? what do ye weeping?
For waking folk and people sleeping,
   And sands that fill and sands that fall,
The days rose-red, the poppied hours,
Blood, wine, and spice and fire and flowers,
   There is one end of one and all.   90

Shall such an one lend love or borrow?
Shall these be sorry for thy sorrow?
   Shall these give thanks for words or breath?
Their hate is as their loving-kindness;
The frontlet of their brows is blindness,
   The armlet of their arms is death.

Lo, for no noise or light of thunder
Shall these grave-clothes be rent in sunder;
   He that hath taken, shall he give?
He hath rent them: shall he bind together?   100
He hath bound them: shall he break the tether?
   He hath slain them: shall he bid them live?

A little sorrow, a little pleasure,
Fate metes us from the dusty measure
   That holds the date of all of us;
We are born with travail and strong crying,
And from the birth-day to the dying
   The likeness of our life is thus.

One girds himself to serve another,
Whose father was the dust, whose mother   110
   The little dead red worm therein;
They find no fruit of things they cherish;
The goodness of a man shall perish,
   It shall be one thing with his sin.

In deep wet ways by grey old gardens
Fed with sharp spring the sweet fruit hardens;
   They know not what fruits wane or grow;
Red summer burns to the utmost ember;
They know not, neither can remember,
   The old years and flowers they used to know.   120

Ah, for their sakes, so trapped and taken,
For theirs, forgotten and forsaken,
   Watch, sleep not, gird thyself with prayer.
Nay, where the heart of wrath is broken,
Where long love ends as a thing spoken,
   How shall thy crying enter there?

Though the iron sides of the old world falter,
The likeness of them shall not alter
   For all the rumour of periods,
The stars and seasons that come after,   130
The tears of latter men, the laughter
   Of the old unalterable gods.

Far up above the years and nations,
The high gods, clothed and crowned with patience,
   Endure through days of deathlike date;
They bear the witness of things hidden;
Before their eyes all life stands chidden,
   As they before the eyes of Fate.

Not for their love shall Fate retire,
Nor they relent for our desire,   140
   Nor the graves open for their call.
The end is more than joy and anguish,
Than lives that laugh and lives that languish,
   The poppied sleep, the end of all.

          (1866)

305 *A Match*

IF love were what the rose is,
  And I were like the leaf,
Our lives would grow together
In sad or singing weather,
Blown fields or flowerful closes,
  Green pleasure or grey grief;
If love were what the rose is,
  And I were like the leaf.

If I were what the words are,
  And love were like the tune,   10
With double sound and single
Delight our lips would mingle,
With kisses glad as birds are
  That get sweet rain at noon;
If I were what the words are,
  And love were like the tune.

If you were life, my darling,
  And I your love were death,
We'd shine and snow together
Ere March made sweet the weather   20
With daffodil and starling
  And hours of fruitful breath;
If you were life, my darling,
  And I your love were death.

If you were thrall to sorrow,
  And I were page to joy,
We'd play for lives and seasons
With loving looks and treasons
And tears of night and morrow
  And laughs of maid and boy;   30
If you were thrall to sorrow,
  And I were page to joy.

If you were April's lady,
  And I were lord in May,
We'd throw with leaves for hours
And draw for days with flowers,
Till day like night were shady
  And night were bright like day;
If you were April's lady,
  And I were lord in May.   40

If you were queen of pleasure,
    And I were king of pain,
We'd hunt down love together,
Pluck out his flying-feather,
And teach his feet a measure,
    And find his mouth a rein;
If you were queen of pleasure,
    And I were king of pain.

(1866)

306   *The Leper*

NOTHING is better, I well think,
    Than love; the hidden well-water
Is not so delicate to drink:
    This was well seen of me and her.

I served her in a royal house;
    I served her wine and curious meat.
For will to kiss between her brows,
    I had no heart to sleep or eat.

Mere scorn God knows she had of me,
    A poor scribe, nowise great or fair,   10
Who plucked his clerk's hood back to see
    Her curled-up lips and amorous hair.

I vex my head with thinking this.
    Yea, though God always hated me,
And hates me now that I can kiss
    Her eyes, plait up her hair to see

How she then wore it on the brows,
    Yet am I glad to have her dead
Here in this wretched wattled house
    Where I can kiss her eyes and head.   20

Nothing is better, I well know,
    Than love; no amber in cold sea
Or gathered berries under snow:
    That is well seen of her and me.

385

Three thoughts I make my pleasure of:
  First I take heart and think of this:
That knight's gold hair she chose to love,
  His mouth she had such will to kiss.

Then I remember that sundawn
  I brought him by a privy way   30
Out at her lattice, and thereon
  What gracious words she found to say.

(Cold rushes for such little feet—
  Both feet could lie into my hand.
A marvel was it of my sweet
  Her upright body could so stand.)

'Sweet friend, God give you thank and grace;
  Now am I clean and whole of shame,
Nor shall men burn me in the face
  For my sweet fault that scandals them.'   40

I tell you over word by word.
  She, sitting edgewise on her bed,
Holding her feet, said thus. The third,
  A sweeter thing than these, I said.

God, that makes time and ruins it
  And alters not, abiding God,
Changed with disease her body sweet,
  The body of love wherein she abode.

Love is more sweet and comelier
  Than a dove's throat strained out to sing.   50
All they spat out and cursed at her
  And cast her forth for a base thing.

They cursed her, seeing how God had wrought
  This curse to plague her, a curse of his.
Fools were they surely, seeing not
  How sweeter than all sweet she is.

He that had held her by the hair,
  With kissing lips blinding her eyes,
Felt her bright bosom, strained and bare,
  Sigh under him, with short mad cries   60

Out of her throat and sobbing mouth
   And body broken up with love,
With sweet hot tears his lips were loth
   Her own should taste the savour of,

Yea, he inside whose grasp all night
   Her fervent body leapt or lay,
Stained with sharp kisses red and white,
   Found her a plague to spurn away.

I hid her in this wattled house,
   I served her water and poor bread.   70
For joy to kiss between her brows
   Time upon time I was nigh dead.

Bread failed; we got but well-water
   And gathered grass with dropping seed.
I had such joy of kissing her,
   I had small care to sleep or feed.

Sometimes when service made me glad
   The sharp tears leapt between my lids,
Falling on her, such joy I had
   To do the service God forbids.   80

'I pray you let me be at peace,
   Get hence, make room for me to die.'
She said that: her poor lip would cease,
   Put up to mine, and turn to cry.

I said, 'Bethink yourself how love
   Fared in us twain, what either did;
Shall I unclothe my soul thereof?
   That I should do this, God forbid.'

Yea, though God hateth us, he knows
   That hardly in a little thing   90
Love faileth of the work it does
   Till it grow ripe for gathering.

Six months, and now my sweet is dead
   A trouble takes me; I know not
If all were done well, all well said,
   No word or tender deed forgot.

Too sweet, for the least part in her,
  To have shed life out by fragments; yet,
Could the close mouth catch breath and stir,
  I might see something I forget.   100

Six months, and I sit still and hold
  In two cold palms her cold two feet.
Her hair, half grey half ruined gold,
  Thrills me and burns me in kissing it.

Love bites and stings me through, to see
  Her keen face made of sunken bones.
Her worn-off eyelids madden me,
  That were shot through with purple once.

She said, 'Be good with me; I grow
  So tired for shame's sake, I shall die   110
If you say nothing:' even so.
  And she is dead now, and shame put by.

Yea, and the scorn she had of me
  In the old time, doubtless vexed her then.
I never should have kissed her. See
  What fools God's anger makes of men!

She might have loved me a little too,
  Had I been humbler for her sake.
But that new shame could make love new
  She saw not—yet her shame did make.   120

I took too much upon my love,
  Having for such mean service done
Her beauty and all the ways thereof,
  Her face and all the sweet thereon.

Yea, all this while I tended her,
  I know the old love held fast his part:
I know the old scorn waxed heavier,
  Mixed with sad wonder, in her heart.

It may be all my love went wrong—
  A scribe's work writ awry and blurred,   130
Scrawled after the blind evensong—
  Spoilt music with no perfect word.

But surely I would fain have done
    All things the best I could. Perchance
Because I failed, came short of one,
    She kept at heart that other man's.

I am grown blind with all these things:
    It may be now she hath in sight
Some better knowledge; still there clings
    The old question. Will not God do right?   140

                    (1866)

307   *The Garden of Proserpine*

HERE, where the world is quiet;
Here, where all trouble seems
Dead winds' and spent waves' riot
In doubtful dreams of dreams;
I watch the green field growing
For reaping folk and sowing,
For harvest-time and mowing,
A sleepy world of streams.

I am tired of tears and laughter,
And men that laugh and weep;   10
Of what may come hereafter
For men that sow to reap:
I am weary of days and hours,
Blown buds of barren flowers,
Desires and dreams and powers
And everything but sleep.

Here life has death for neighbour,
And far from eye or ear
Wan waves and wet winds labour,
Weak ships and spirits steer;   20
They drive adrift, and whither
They wot not who make thither;
But no such winds blow hither,
And no such things grow here.

389

No growth of moor or coppice,
No heather-flower or vine,
But bloomless buds of poppies,
Green grapes of Proserpine,
Pale beds of blowing rushes
Where no leaf blooms or blushes   30
Save this whereout she crushes
For dead men deadly wine.

Pale, without name or number,
In fruitless fields of corn,
They bow themselves and slumber
All night till light is born;
And like a soul belated,
In hell and heaven unmated,
By cloud and mist abated
Comes out of darkness morn.   40

Though one were strong as seven,
He too with death shall dwell,
Nor wake with wings in heaven,
Nor weep for pains in hell;
Though one were fair as roses,
His beauty clouds and closes;
And well though love reposes,
In the end it is not well.

Pale, beyond porch and portal,
Crowned with calm leaves, she stands   50
Who gathers all things mortal
With cold immortal hands;
Her languid lips are sweeter
Than love's who fears to greet her
To men that mix and meet her
From many times and lands.

She waits for each and other,
She waits for all men born;
Forgets the earth her mother,
The life of fruits and corn;   60
And spring and seed and swallow
Take wing for her and follow
Where summer song rings hollow
And flowers are put to scorn.

There go the loves that wither,
The old loves with wearier wings;
And all dead years draw thither,
And all disastrous things;
Dead dreams of days forsaken,
Blind buds that snows have shaken,   70
Wild leaves that winds have taken,
Red strays of ruined springs.

We are not sure of sorrow,
And joy was never sure;
To-day will die to-morrow;
Time stoops to no man's lure;
And love, grown faint and fretful,
With lips but half regretful
Sighs, and with eyes forgetful
Weeps that no loves endure.   80

From too much love of living,
From hope and fear set free,
We thank with brief thanksgiving
Whatever gods may be
That no life lives for ever;
That dead men rise up never;
That even the weariest river
Winds somewhere safe to sea.

Then star nor sun shall waken,
Nor any change of light: 90
Nor sound of waters shaken,
Nor any sound or sight:
Nor wintry leaves nor vernal,
Nor days nor things diurnal;
Only the sleep eternal
In an eternal night.

                          (1866)

308
WHY grudge them lotus-leaf and laurel,
O toothless mouth or swinish maw,
Who never grudged you bells and coral,
Who never grudged you troughs and straw?

Lie still in kennel, sleek in stable,
Good creatures of the stall or sty;
Shove snouts for crumbs below the table;
Lie still; and rise not up to lie.

(Wr. and pub. 1866)

309   *A Forsaken Garden*

IN a coign of the cliff between lowland and highland,
  At the sea-down's edge between windward and lee,
Walled round with rocks as an inland island,
  The ghost of a garden fronts the sea.
A girdle of brushwood and thorn encloses
  The steep square slope of the blossomless bed
Where the weeds that grew green from the graves of its roses
      Now lie dead.

The fields fall southward, abrupt and broken,
  To the low last edge of the long lone land.   10
If a step should sound or a word be spoken,
  Would a ghost not rise at the strange guest's hand?
So long have the grey bare walks lain guestless,
  Through branches and briars if a man make way,
He shall find no life but the sea-wind's, restless
      Night and day.

The dense hard passage is blind and stifled
  That crawls by a track none turn to climb
To the strait waste place that the years have rifled
  Of all but the thorns that are touched not of time. 20
The thorns he spares when the rose is taken;
  The rocks are left when he wastes the plain.
The wind that wanders, the weeds wind-shaken,
      These remain.

Not a flower to be pressed of the foot that falls not;
  As the heart of a dead man the seed-plots are dry;
From the thicket of thorns whence the nightingale calls not,
  Could she call, there were never a rose to reply.

Over the meadows that blossom and wither
  Rings but the note of a sea-bird's song;   30
Only the sun and the rain come hither
      All year long.

The sun burns sere and the rain dishevels
  One gaunt bleak blossom of scentless breath.
Only the wind here hovers and revels
  In a round where life seems barren as death.
Here there was laughing of old, there was weeping,
  Haply, of lovers none ever will know,
Whose eyes went seaward a hundred sleeping
      Years ago.   40

Heart handfast in heart as they stood, 'Look thither,'
  Did he whisper? 'look forth from the flowers to the sea;
For the foam-flowers endure when the rose-blossoms wither,
  And men that love lightly may die—but we?'
And the same wind sang and the same waves whitened,
  And or ever the garden's last petals were shed,
In the lips that had whispered, the eyes that had lightened,
      Love was dead.

Or they loved their life through, and then went whither?
  And were one to the end—but what end who knows?   50
Love deep as the sea as a rose must wither,
  As the rose-red seaweed that mocks the rose.
Shall the dead take thought for the dead to love them?
  What love was ever as deep as a grave?
They are loveless now as the grass above them
      Or the wave.

All are at one now, roses and lovers,
  Not known of the cliffs and the fields and the sea.
Not a breath of the time that has been hovers
  In the air now soft with a summer to be.   60
Not a breath shall there sweeten the seasons hereafter
  Of the flowers or the lovers that laugh now or weep,
When as they that are free now of weeping and laughter
      We shall sleep.

Here death may deal not again for ever;
  Here change may come not till all change end.
From the graves they have made they shall rise up never,
  Who have left nought living to ravage and rend.

Earth, stones, and thorns of the wild ground growing,
    While the sun and the rain live, these shall be;   70
Till a last wind's breath upon all these blowing
        Roll the sea.

Till the slow sea rise and the sheer cliff crumble,
    Till terrace and meadow the deep gulfs drink,
Till the strength of the waves of the high tides humble
    The fields that lessen, the rocks that shrink,
Here now in his triumph where all things falter,
    Stretched out on the spoils that his own hand spread,
As a god self-slain on his own strange altar,
        Death lies dead.   80

(1876)

JOHN LEICESTER WARREN, LORD DE TABLEY

1835–1895

310   *Philoctetes*

SILENCE on silence treads at each low morn.
Pain and new pain, some glimpse of painless sleep,
And waking to old anguish and new day:
Blasted of glory, sundered from my kind:
My hearth, my realm, the lips that love me, lost:
So runs it. 'Tis some courage to keep life
Where life is worthless, and on feeble stay
To dwell in hope of better till we die.

I hate this island steep, this seam of beach.
This ample desolation of gray rock   10
Man tills not: and man reaps not, woe is me!
No voices, save stress-landed mariners
Leaning in ring with eyebrow-level wrists
To watch the scummy rack and buzzing waves,
Toss me a word in pity: stare and pass
Grinding a clumsy jest or surly sneer.
Yet in their talk I gather waifs and strays
Of that great Trojan battle how it goes;
Of beardless youths who gain down heaven with deeds,
And all the noise and turmoil of the thing,   20

394

Deed quenching deed, and echo's swollen boast,
While I am rotting here and touch no praise.

Ye have done well to leave me. 'Tis most wise,
And friendly too, expedient, generous:
Why this is bounty's crown; I have deserved
No less than a sick hound: full thanks for all.
My kings and comrades, ye are wise and brave,
As wise as brave, and brave your chiefest voice
Of foxy Ithaca: 'twas nobly said,
'Pack out the carrion on this leeward Isle.   30
We need no wounded leaders, no, nor fear.
His men and ships *are* needed; they sail on:
They cannot heal him, and our need is great.'
Why, man, this is true valour and no theft:
I could not quit thee, and kings cannot steal.
But if I meet thy foxship afterdays,
With half an arm to raise and half a spear,
I'll mar that serpent face and false gray smile,
And leave thy surgy rock without a king.

Alas, alas, how mean a thing am I   40
To rail and threat and bluster like a God.
The old pain trembles thro' me marrow-deep,
A quivering mass of earth, than earth no more,
Earth gifted with a cunning power of pain,
Full knowledge of its fall and loathsomeness,
Craving for enterprize in impotence,
Some little sleep and all the rest a pain—
Shall such a thing have pride or hoard revenge?

I loathe the glancing sameness of this brine,
Its hissing suck of waves, its equal face.   50
I loathe the toss of sails, the pass of clouds,
The white wings curving on the tawny rocks,
The evening and the dawning and the day.
We thrive by action, I am chained from all,
And I forget the pleasure of this earth,
Of all but pain and slow time dispossess'd.

Yet is there hope; slow hope yet comfort sure,
I had forgot it in my wrath and pain.
Is there no oracle? Troy cannot fall.
I guard thine arrows, Heracles divine,   60
And Troy falls not without them year on year.
I hoard them as the marrow of my bones,

395

Sweet nurses to revenge. Oh, fate is just.
Ye reap, my kings, wound-harvest and much dead,
Thinn'd troops, and kingdoms waned to wrack at home,
And gloomy faces by a gloomy sea,
And firm-braced Troy before, the sponge of toil,
And all your warring as an idle dream.

I can abide my hour it is so sure,
I lean on this unstumbling oracle,   70
And nourish hope, till worn with many woes
The haught Kings fall in thinking on the wreck
They left by Lemnos and the archer hand
Once fellowless in Hellas. They shall come,
By Zeus I swear it, they shall come in shame,
And stand in shame before the man they wrong'd
And weeded out as refuse. See, they bend,
Pestilent faces crusted in meek smiles,
And supple eyes and all the fawn of need:
And one mouths out on justice, gratitude,   80
The cause of Hellas. Then another smooths
My name with praise, and all the worthy ring
Lisp sympathy with dew on glassy cheeks.

Sweet oracle, thou climax of revenge,
I will wear out my painful coil in joy,
Voiceless of all complaining, firm and sure
The Gods are just, and compensation comes.

(1863)

311   *The Power of Interval*

A FAIR girl tripping out to meet her love,
Trimmed in her best, fresh as a clover bud.
An old crone leaning at an ember'd fire,
Short-breath'd in sighs and moaning to herself—
And all the interval of stealing years
To make that this, and one by one detach
Some excellent condition; till Despair
Faint at the vision, sadly, fiercely blinds
Her burning eyes on her forgetful hands.

(1863)

312   *The Knight in the Wood*

THE thing itself was rough and crudely done,
Cut in coarse stone, spitefully placed aside
As merest lumber, where the light was worst
On a back staircase. Overlooked it lay
In a great Roman palace crammed with art.
It had no number in the list of gems,
Weeded away long since, pushed out and banished,
Before insipid Guidos over-sweet
And Dolce's rose sensationalities,
And curly chirping angels spruce as birds.   10
And yet the motive of this thing ill-hewn
And hardly seen *did* touch me. O, indeed,
The skill-less hand that carved it had belonged
To a most yearning and bewildered brain:
There was such desolation in the work;
And through its utter failure the thing spoke
With more of human message, heart to heart,
Than all these faultless, smirking, skin-deep saints,
In artificial troubles picturesque,
And martyred sweetly, not one curl awry—   20
Listen; a clumsy knight, who rode alone
Upon a stumbling jade in a great wood
Belated. The poor beast with head low-bowed
Snuffing the treacherous ground. The rider leant
Forward to sound the marish with his lance.
You saw the place was deadly; that doomed pair,
The wretched rider and the hide-bound steed,
Feared to advance, feared to return—That's all!

                                        (1870)

313   *Nuptial Song*
                 'Sigh, Heart, Break Not'

SIGH, heart, and break not; rest, lark, and wake not!
    Day I hear coming to draw my Love away.
As mere-waves whisper, and clouds grow crisper,
    Ah, like a rose he will waken up with day.

In moon-light lonely, he is my Love only,
    I share with none when Luna rides in grey.
As dawn-beams quicken, my rivals thicken,
    The light and deed and turmoil of the day.

To watch my sleeper to me is sweeter,
　　Than any waking words my Love can say;　　　10
In dream he finds me and closer winds me!
　　Let him rest by me a little more and stay.

Ah, mine eyes, close not: and, tho' he knows not,
　　My lips, on his be tender while you may;
Ere leaves are shaken, and ring-doves waken,
　　And infant buds begin to scent new day.

Fair Darkness, measure thine hours, as treasure
　　Shed each one slowly from thine urn, I pray;
Hoard in and cover each from my lover;
　　I cannot lose him yet; dear night, delay.　　　20

Each moment dearer, true-love, lie nearer,
　　My hair shall blind thee lest thou see the ray;
My locks encumber thine ears in slumber,
　　Lest any bird dare give thee note of day.

He rests so calmly; we lie so warmly;
　　Hand within hand, as children after play;—
In shafted amber on roof and chamber
　　Dawn enters; my Love wakens; here is day.

(1873)

314　　　　*The Churchyard on the Sands*

My Love lies in the gates of foam,
　　The last dear wreck of shore;
The naked sea-marsh binds her home,
　　The sand her chamber door.

The grey gull flaps the written stones,
　　The ox-birds chase the tide;
And near that narrow field of bones
　　Great ships at anchor ride.

Black piers with crust of dripping green,
　　One foreland, like a hand,　　　10
O'er intervals of grass between
　　Dim lonely dunes of sand.

A church of silent weathered looks,
    A breezy reddish tower,
A yard whose mounded resting-nooks
    Are tinged with sorrel flower.

In peace the swallow's eggs are laid
    Along the belfry walls;
The tempest does not reach her shade,
    The rain her silent halls.   20

But sails are sweet in summer sky,
    The lark throws down a lay;
The long salt levels steam and dry,
    The cloud-heart melts away.

But patches of the sea-pink shine,
    The pied crows poise and come;
The mallow hangs, the bindweeds twine,
    Where her sweet lips are dumb.

The passion of the wave is mute;
    No sound or ocean shock;   30
No music save the trilling flute
    That marks the curlew flock.

But yonder when the wind is keen,
    And rainy air is clear,
The merchant city's spires are seen,
    The toil of men grows near.

Along the coast-way grind the wheels
    Of endless carts of coal;
And on the sides of giant keels
    The shipyard hammers roll.   40

The world creeps here upon the shout,
    And stirs my heart in pain;
The mist descends and blots it out,
    And I am strong again.

Strong and alone, my dove, with thee;
    And, tho' mine eyes be wet,
There's nothing in the world to me
    So dear as my regret.

I would not change my sorrow, sweet,
    For others' nuptial hours;   50
I love the daisies at thy feet
    More than their orange flowers.

My hand alone shall tend thy tomb
    From leaf-bud to leaf-fall,
And wreathe around each season's bloom
    Till autumn ruins all.

Let snowdrops, early in the year,
    Droop o'er her silent breast;
And bid the later cowslip rear
    The amber of its crest.   60

Come hither, linnets tufted-red,
    Drift by, O wailing tern;
Set pure vale lilies at her head,
    At her feet lady-fern.

Grow, samphire, at the tidal brink,
    Wave, pansies of the shore,
To whisper how alone I think
    Of her for evermore.

Bring blue sea-hollies thorny, keen,
    Long lavender in flower;   70
Grey wormwood like a hoary queen,
    Stanch mullein like a tower.

O sea-wall mounded long and low,
    Let iron bounds be thine;
Nor let the salt wave overflow
    That breast I held divine.

Nor float its sea-weed to her hair,
    Nor dim her eyes with sands:
No fluted cockle burrow where
    Sleep folds her patient hands.   80

Tho' thy crest feel the wild sea's breath,
    Tho' tide-weight tear thy root,
Oh, guard the treasure house, where Death
    Has bound my darling mute.

Tho' cold her pale lips to reward
    With Love's own mysteries,
Ah, rob no daisy from her sward,
    Rough gale of eastern seas!

Ah, render sere no silken bent,
    That by her head-stone waves;   90
Let noon and golden summer blent
    Pervade these ocean graves.

And, ah, dear heart, in thy still nest,
    Resign this earth of woes,
Forget the ardours of the west,
    Neglect the morning glows.

Sleep, and forget all things but one,
    Heard in each wave of sea,—
How lonely all the years will run
    Until I rest by thee.   100

                    (1873)

315   *Circe*

THIS the house of Circe, queen of charms—
A kind of beacon-cauldron poised on high,
Hooped round with ember-clasping iron bars,
Sways in her palace porch, and smoulderingly
Drips out in blots of fire and ruddy stars;
But out behind that trembling furnace air,
The lands are ripe and fair,
Hush are the hills and quiet to the eye.
The river's reach goes by
With lamb and holy tower and squares of corn,   10
And shelving interspace
Of holly bush and thorn,
And hamlets happy in an Alpine morn,
And deep-bowered lanes with grace
Of woodbine newly born.
But inward o'er the hearth a torch-head stands
Inverted, slow green flames of fulvous hue,
Echoed in wave-like shadows over her.
A censer's swing-chain set in her fair hands
Dances up wreaths of intertwisted blue   20
In clouds of fragrant frankincense and myrrh.
A giant tulip head and two pale leaves

                    401

Grew in the midmost of her chamber there,
A flaunting bloom, naked and undivine,
Rigid and bare,
Gaunt as a tawny bond-girl born to shame,
With freckled cheeks and splotched side serpentine,
A gipsy among flowers,
Unmeet for bed or bowers,
Virginal where pure-handed damsels sleep: 30
Let it not breathe a common air with them,
Lest when the night is deep,
And all things have their quiet in the moon,
Some birth of poison from its leaning stem
Waft in between their slumber-parted lips,
And they cry out or swoon,
Deeming some vampire sips,
Where riper Love may come for nectar boon!

And near this tulip, reared across a loom,
Hung a fair web of tapestry half done, 40
Crowding with folds and fancies half the room:
Men eyed as gods and damsels still as stone,
Pressing their brows alone,
In amethystine robes,
Or reaching at the polished orchard globes,
Or rubbing parted love-lips on their rind,
While the wind
Sows with sere apple leaves their breast and hair.
And all the margin there
Was arabesqued and bordered intricate 50
With hairy spider things
That catch and clamber,
And salamander in his dripping cave
Satanic ebon-amber;
Blind worm, and asp, and eft of cumbrous gait,
And toads who love rank grasses near a grave,
And the great goblin moth, who bears
Between his wings the ruined eyes of death;
And the enamelled sails
Of butterflies, who watch the morning's breath. 60
And many an emerald lizard with quick ears
Asleep in rocky dales.
And for an outer fringe embroidered small,
A ring of many locusts, horny-coated,
A round of chirping tree-frogs merry-throated,
And sly, fat fishes sailing, watching all.

(1893)

316   *The Study of a Spider*

FROM holy flower to holy flower
Thou weavest thine unhallowed bower.
The harmless dewdrops, beaded thin,
Ripple along thy ropes of sin.
Thy house a grave, a gulf thy throne
Affright the fairies every one.
Thy winding sheets are grey and fell,
Imprisoning with nets of hell
The lovely births that winnow by,
Winged sisters of the rainbow sky: 10
Elf-darlings, fluffy, bee-bright things,
And owl-white moths with mealy wings,
And tiny flies, as gauzy thin
As e'er were shut electrum in.
These are thy death spoils, insect ghoul,
With their dear life thy fangs are foul.
Thou felon anchorite of pain
Who sittest in a world of slain.
Hermit, who tunest song unsweet
To heaving wing and writhing feet.   20
A glutton of creation's sighs,
Miser of many miseries.
Toper, whose lonely feasting chair
Sways in inhospitable air.
The board is bare, the bloated host
Drinks to himself toast after toast.
His lip requires no goblet brink,
But like a weasel must he drink.
The vintage is as old as time
And bright as sunset, pressed and prime.   30

Ah, venom mouth and shaggy thighs
And paunch grown sleek with sacrifice,
Thy dolphin back and shoulders round
Coarse-hairy, as some goblin hound
Whom a hag rides to sabbath on,
While shuddering stars in fear grow wan.
Thou palace priest of treachery,
Thou type of selfish lechery,
I break the toils around thy head
And from their gibbets take thy dead.   40

(1893)

317   *A Croon on Hennacliff*

THUS said the rushing raven,
  Unto his hungry mate:
'Ho! gossip! for Bude Haven:
  There be corpses six or eight.
Cawk! cawk! the crew and skipper
  Are wallowing in the sea:
So there's a savoury supper
  For my old dame and me.'

'Cawk! gaffer! thou art dreaming,
  The shore hath wreckers bold;   10
Would rend the yelling seamen,
  From the clutching billows' hold.
Cawk! cawk! they'd bound for booty
  Into the dragon's den:
And shout, for "death or duty,"
  If the prey were drowning men.'

Loud laughed the listening surges,
  At the guess our grandame gave:
You might call them Boanerges,
  From the thunder of their wave.   20
And mockery followed after
  The sea-bird's jeering brood:
That filled the skies with laughter,
  From Lundy Light to Bude.

'Cawk! cawk!' then said the raven,
  'I am fourscore years and ten:
Yet never in Bude Haven,
  Did I croak for rescued men.—
They will save the Captain's girdle,
  And shirt, if shirt there be: 30
But leave their blood to curdle,
  For my old dame and me.'

So said the rushing raven,
    Unto his hungry mate:
'Ho! gossip! for Bude Haven:
    There be corpses six or eight.
Cawk! cawk! the crew and skipper
    Are wallowing in the sea:
O what a savoury supper
    For my old dame and me.'   40

(1864)

CHARLES TURNER
(formerly TENNYSON)
1808–1879

318   *The Lion's Skeleton*

How long, O lion, hast thou fleshless lain?
What rapt thy fierce and thirsty eyes away?
First came the vulture: worms, heat, wind, and rain
Ensued, and ardors of the tropic day.
I know not—if they spared it thee—how long
The canker sate within thy monstrous mane,
Till it fell piecemeal, and bestrew'd the plain;
Or, shredded by the storming sands, was flung
Again to earth; but now thine ample front,
Whereon the great frowns gather'd, is laid bare;   10
The thunders of thy throat, which erst were wont
To scare the desert, are no longer there;
Thy claws remain, but worms, wind, rain, and heat
Have sifted out the substance of thy feet.

(1864)

319   *A Brilliant Day*

O KEEN pellucid air! nothing can lurk
Or disavow itself on this bright day;
The small rain-plashes shine from far away,
The tiny emmet glitters at his work;
The bee looks blithe and gay, and as she plies
Her task, and moves and sidles round the cup
Of this spring flower, to drink its honey up,
Her glassy wings, like oars that dip and rise,

Gleam momently. Pure-bosom'd, clear of fog,
The long lake glistens, while the glorious beam   10
Bespangles the wet joints and floating leaves
Of water-plants, whose every point receives
His light; and jellies of the spawning frog,
Unmark'd before, like piles of jewels seem!

(1868)

320   *On a Vase of Gold-Fish*

THE tortured mullet served the Roman's pride
By darting round the crystal vase, whose heat
Ensured his woe and beauty till he died:
These unharm'd gold-fish yield as rich a treat;
Seen thus, in parlour-twilight, they appear
As though the hand of Midas, hovering o'er,
Wrought on the waters, as his touch drew near,
And set them glancing with his golden power,
The flash of transmutation! In their glass
They float and glitter, by no anguish rackt;   10
And, though we see them swelling as they pass,
'Tis but a painless and phantasmal act,
The trick of their own bellying walls, which charms
All eyes—themselves it vexes not, nor harms.

(1868)

321   *From Harvest to January*

THE hay has long been built into the stack
And now the grain; anon the hunter's moon
Shall wax and wane in cooler skies, and soon
Again re-orb'd, speed on her wonted track,
To spend her snowy light upon the rack
Of dark November, while her brother Sun
Shall get up later for his eight-hours' run
In that cold section of the Zodiac:
Far from the Lion, from the Virgin far!
Then onward through the last dim month shall go   10
The two great lights, to where the kalendar
Splits the mid-winter; and the feathery snow
Ushering another spring, with falling flakes
Shall nurse the soil for next year's scythes and rakes.

(1868)

322 *Gout and Wings*

THE pigeons flutter'd fieldward, one and all,
I saw the swallows wheel, and soar, and dive;
The little bees hung poised before the hive,
Even Partlet hoised herself across the wall:
I felt my earth-bound lot in every limb,
And, in my envious mood, I half-rebell'd;
When lo! an insect cross'd the page I held,
A little helpless minim, slight and slim;
Ah! sure, there was no room for envy there,
But gracious aid and condescending care;   10
Alas! my pride and pity were misspent,
The atom knew his strength, and rose in air!
My gout came tingling back, as off he went,
A wing was open'd at me everywhere!

(1873)

323 *On Seeing a Little Child Spin a Coin of
Alexander the Great*

THIS is the face of him, whose quick resource
Of eye and hand subdued Bucephalus,
And made the shadow of a startled horse
A foreground for his glory. It is thus
They hand him down; this coin of Philip's son
Recalls his life, his glories, and misdeeds;
And that abortive court of Babylon,
Where the world's throne was left among the reeds.
His dust is lost among the ancient dead,
A coin his only presence: he is gone: 10
And all but this half mythic image fled—
A simple child may do him shame and slight;
'Twixt thumb and finger take the golden head,
And spin the horns of Ammon out of sight.

(1880)

324 *Letty's Globe*

WHEN Letty had scarce pass'd her third glad year,
And her young, artless words began to flow,
One day we gave the child a colour'd sphere
Of the wide earth, that she might mark and know,

By tint and outline, all its sea and land.
She patted all the world; old empires peep'd
Between her baby fingers; her soft hand
Was welcome at all frontiers. How she leap'd,
And laugh'd, and prattled in her world-wide bliss;
But when we turned her sweet unlearned eye   10
On our own isle, she raised a joyous cry,
'Oh! yes, I see it, Letty's home is there!'
And, while she hid all England with a kiss,
Bright over Europe fell her golden hair.

(1880)

325   *On Shooting a Swallow in Early Youth*

I HOARD a little spring of secret tears,
For thee, poor bird; thy death-blow was my crime:
From the far past it has flow'd on for years;
It never dries; it brims at swallow-time.
No kindly voice within me took thy part,
Till I stood o'er thy last faint flutterings;
Since then, methinks, I have a gentler heart,
And gaze with pity on all wounded wings.
Full oft the vision of thy fallen head,
Twittering in highway dust, appeals to me;   10
Thy helpless form, as when I struck thee dead,
Drops out from every swallow-flight I see.
I would not have thine airy spirit laid,
I seem to love the little ghost I made.

(1880)

326   *Calvus to a Fly*

AH! little fly, alighting fitfully
In the dim dawn on this bare head of mine,
Which spreads a white and gleaming track for thee,
When chairs and dusky wardrobes cease to shine.
Though thou art irksome, let me not complain;
Thy foolish passion for my hairless head
Will spend itself, when these dark hours are sped,
And thou shalt seek the sunlight on the pane.
But still beware! thou art on dangerous ground:
An angry sonnet, or a hasty hand,   10
May slander thee, or crush thee: thy shrill sound

And constant touch may shake my self-command:
And thou mayst perish in that moment's spite,
And die a martyr to thy love of light.

(1880)

327   *A Country Dance*

HE has not woo'd, but he has lost his heart.
That country dance is a sore test for him;
He thinks her cold; his hopes are faint and dim;
But though with seeming mirth she takes her part
In all the dances and the laughter there,
And though to many a youth, on brief demand,
She gives a kind assent and courteous hand,
She loves but him, for him is all her care.
With jealous heed her lessening voice he hears
Down that long vista, where she seems to move   10
Among fond faces and relays of love,
And sweet occasion, full of tender fears:
Down those long lines he watches from above,
Till with the refluent dance she reappears.

(1880)

GERARD M. HOPKINS

1844–1889

328   IT was a hard thing to undo this knot.
The rainbow shines, but only in the thought
Of him that looks. Yet not in that alone,
For who makes rainbows by invention?
And many standing round a waterfall
See one bow each, yet not the same to all,
But each a hand's breadth further than the next.
The sun on falling waters writes the text
Which yet is in the eye or in the thought.
It was a hard thing to undo this knot.   10

(Wr. 1864; pub. 1937)

329   *The Habit of Perfection*

ELECTED Silence, sing to me
And beat upon my whorlèd ear,
Pipe me to pastures still and be
The music that I care to hear.

Shape nothing, lips; be lovely-dumb:
It is the shut, the curfew sent
From there where all surrenders come
Which only makes you eloquent.

Be shellèd, eyes, with double dark
And find the uncreated light: 10
This ruck and reel which you remark
Coils, keeps, and teases simple sight.

Palate, the hutch of tasty lust,
Desire not to be rinsed with wine:
The can must be so sweet, the crust
So fresh that come in fasts divine!

Nostrils, your careless breath that spend
Upon the stir and keep of pride,
What relish shall the censers send
Along the sanctuary side!   20

O feel-of-primrose hands, O feet
That want the yield of plushy sward,
But you shall walk the golden street
And you unhouse and house the Lord.

And, Poverty, be thou the bride
And now the marriage feast begun,
And lily-coloured clothes provide
Your spouse not laboured-at nor spun.

                              (Wr. 1866; pub. 1893)

330 ## *The Wreck of the Deutschland*

To the
happy memory of five Franciscan nuns
exiles by the Falck Laws
drowned between midnight and morning of
Dec. 7th, 1875

PART THE FIRST

1

THOU mastering me
God! giver of breath and bread;
World's strand, sway of the sea;
Lord of living and dead;
Thou hast bound bones and veins in me, fastened me flesh,
And after it almost unmade, what with dread,
Thy doing: and dost thou touch me afresh?
Over again I feel thy finger and find thee.

2

I did say yes
O at lightning and lashed rod;   10
Thou heardst me truer than tongue confess
Thy terror, O Christ, O God;
Thou knowest the walls, altar and hour and night:
The swoon of a heart that the sweep and the hurl of thee trod
Hard down with a horror of height:
And the midriff astrain with leaning of, laced with fire of stress.

3

The frown of his face
Before me, the hurtle of hell
Behind, where, where was a, where was a place?
I whirled out wings that spell   20
And fled with a fling of the heart to the heart of the Host.
My heart, but you were dovewinged, I can tell,
Carrier-witted, I am bold to boast,
To flash from the flame to the flame then, tower from the grace to the
grace.

4

I am soft sift
In an hourglass—at the wall
Fast, but mined with a motion, a drift,
    And it crowds and it combs to the fall;
I steady as a water in a well, to a poise, to a pane,
But roped with, always, all the way down from the tall   30
    Fells or flanks of the voel, a vein
Of the gospel proffer, a pressure, a principle, Christ's gift.

5

I kiss my hand
To the stars, lovely-asunder
Starlight, wafting him out of it; and
    Glow, glory in thunder;
Kiss my hand to the dappled-with-damson west:
Since, tho' he is under the world's splendour and wonder,
    His mystery must be instressed, stressed;
For I greet him the days I meet him, and bless when I understand.   40

6

Not out of his bliss
Springs the stress felt
Nor first from heaven (and few know this)
    Swings the stroke dealt—
Stroke and a stress that stars and storms deliver,
That guilt is hushed by, hearts are flushed by and melt—
    But it rides time like riding a river
(And here the faithful waver, the faithless fable and miss).

7

It dates from day
Of his going in Galilee;   50
Warm-laid grave of a womb-life grey;
    Manger, maiden's knee;
The dense and the driven Passion, and frightful sweat:
Thence the discharge of it, there its swelling to be,
    Though felt before, though in high flood yet—
What none would have known of it, only the heart, being hard at bay,

8

Is out with it! Oh,
We lash with the best or worst
Word last! How a lush-kept plush-capped sloe
Will, mouthed to flesh-burst,   60
Gush!—flush the man, the being with it, sour or sweet,
Brim, in a flash, full!—Hither then, last or first,
To hero of Calvary, Christ,'s feet—
Never ask if meaning it, wanting it, warned of it—men go.

9

Be adored among men,
God, three-numberèd form;
Wring thy rebel, dogged in den,
Man's malice, with wrecking and storm.
Beyond saying sweet, past telling of tongue,
Thou art lightning and love, I found it, a winter and warm;   70
Father and fondler of heart thou hast wrung:
Hast thy dark descending and most art merciful then.

10

With an anvil-ding
And with fire in him forge thy will
Or rather, rather then, stealing as Spring
Through him, melt him but master him still:
Whether at once, as once at a crash Paul,
Or as Austin, a lingering-out swéet skíll,
Make mercy in all of us, out of us all
Mastery, but be adored, but be adored King.   80

PART THE SECOND

11

'Some find me a sword; some
The flange and the rail; flame,
Fang, or flood' goes Death on drum,
And storms bugle his fame.
But wé dream we are rooted in earth—Dust!
Flesh falls within sight of us, we, though our flower the same,
Wave with the meadow, forget that there must
The sour scythe cringe, and the blear share come.

12

On Saturday sailed from Bremen,
American-outward-bound,
Take settler and seamen, tell men with women,   10
Two hundred souls in the round—
O Father, not under thy feathers nor ever as guessing
The goal was a shoal, of a fourth the doom to be drowned;
Yet did the dark side of the bay of thy blessing
Not vault them, the million of rounds of thy mercy not reeve even them
in?

13

Into the snows she sweeps,
Hurling the haven behind,
The Deutschland, on Sunday; and so the sky keeps,
For the infinite air is unkind,   20
And the sea flint-flake, black-backed in the regular blow,
Sitting Eastnortheast, in cursed quarter, the wind;
Wiry and white-fiery and whirlwind-swivellèd snow
Spins to the widow-making unchilding unfathering deeps.

14

She drove in the dark to leeward,
She struck—not a reef or a rock
But the combs of a smother of sand: night drew her
Dead to the Kentish Knock;
And she beat the bank down with her bows and the ride of her
keel:
The breakers rolled on her beam with ruinous shock;   30
And canvas and compass, the whorl and the wheel
Idle for ever to waft her or wind her with, these she endured.

15

Hope had grown grey hairs,
Hope had mourning on,
Trenched with tears, carved with cares,
Hope was twelve hours gone;
And frightful a nightfall folded rueful a day
Nor rescue, only rocket and lightship, shone,
And lives at last were washing away:
To the shrouds they took,—they shook in the hurling and horrible airs.   40

16

One stirred from the rigging to save
The wild woman-kind below,
With a rope's end round the man, handy and brave—
He was pitched to his death at a blow,
For all his dreadnought breast and braids of thew:
They could tell him for hours, dandled the to and fro
Through the cobbled foam-fleece. What could he do
With the burl of the fountains of air, buck and the flood of the wave?

17

They fought with God's cold—
And they could not and fell to the deck   50
(Crushed them) or water (and drowned them) or rolled
With the sea-romp over the wreck.
Night roared, with the heart-break hearing a heart-broke rabble,
The woman's wailing, the crying of child without check—
Till a lioness arose breasting the babble,
A prophetess towered in the tumult, a virginal tongue told.

18

Ah, touched in your bower of bone,
Are you! turned for an exquisite smart,
Have you! make words break from me here all alone,
Do you!—mother of being in me, heart.   60
O unteachably after evil, but uttering truth,
Why, tears! is it? tears; such a melting, a madrigal start!
Never-eldering revel and river of youth,
What can it be, this glee? the good you have there of your own?

19

Sister, a sister calling
A master, her master and mine!—
And the inboard seas run swirling and hawling;
The rash smart sloggering brine
Blinds her; but she that weather sees one thing, one;
Has one fetch in her: she rears herself to divine   70
Ears, and the call of the tall nun
To the men in the tops and the tackle rode over the storm's brawling.

20

She was first of a five and came
Of a coifèd sisterhood.
(O Deutschland, double a desperate name!
O world wide of its good!
But Gertrude, lily, and Luther, are two of a town,
Christ's lily and beast of the waste wood:
From life's dawn it is drawn down,
Abel is Cain's brother and breasts they have sucked the same.)   80

21

Loathed for a love men knew in them,
Banned by the land of their birth,
Rhine refused them, Thames would ruin them;
Surf, snow, river and earth
Gnashed: but thou art above, thou Orion of light;
Thy unchancelling poising palms were weighing the worth,
Thou martyr-master: in thy sight
Storm flakes were scroll-leaved flowers, lily showers—sweet heaven
was astrew in them.

22

Five! the finding and sake
And cipher of suffering Christ.   90
Mark, the mark is of man's make
And the word of it Sacrificed.
But he scores it in scarlet himself on his own bespoken,
Before-time-taken, dearest prizèd and priced—
Stigma, signal, cinquefoil token
For lettering of the lamb's fleece, ruddying of the rose-flake.

23

Joy fall to thee, father Francis,
Drawn to the Life that died;
With the gnarls of the nails in thee, niche of the lance, his
Lovescape crucified   100
And seal of his seraph-arrival! and these thy daughters
And five-livèd and leavèd favour and pride,
Are sisterly sealed in wild waters,
To bathe in his fall-gold mercies, to breathe in his all-fire glances.

24

Away in the loveable west,
  On a pastoral forehead of Wales,
I was under a roof here, I was at rest,
  And they the prey of the gales;
She to the black-about air, to the breaker, the thickly
Falling flakes, to the throng that catches and quails   110
  Was calling 'O Christ, Christ, come quickly':
The cross to her she calls Christ to her, christens her wild-worst Best.

25

The majesty! what did she mean?
  Breathe, arch and original Breath.
Is it love in her of the being as her lover had been?
  Breathe, body of lovely Death.
They were else-minded then, altogether, the men
Woke thee with a *We are perishing* in the weather of Gennesareth.
  Or is it that she cried for the crown then,
The keener to come at the comfort for feeling the combating keen? 120

26

For how to the heart's cheering
  The down-dugged ground-hugged grey
Hovers off, the jay-blue heavens appearing
  Of pied and peeled May!
Blue-beating and hoary-glow height; or night, still higher,
With belled fire and the moth-soft Milky Way,
  What by your measure is the heaven of desire,
The treasure never eyesight got, nor was ever guessed what for the
    hearing?

27

No, but it was not these.
  The jading and jar of the cart,   130
Time's tasking, it is fathers that asking for ease
  Of the sodden-with-its-sorrowing heart,
Not danger, electrical horror; then further it finds
The appealing of the Passion is tenderer in prayer apart:
  Other, I gather, in measure her mind's
Burden, in wind's burly and beat of endragonèd seas.

28

But how shall I . . . make me room there:
    Reach me a . . . Fancy, come faster—
Strike you the sight of it? look at it loom there,
    Thing that she . . . There then! the Master,   140
Ipse, the only one, Christ, King, Head:
    He was to cure the extremity where he had cast her;
    Do, deal, lord it with living and dead;
Let him ride, her pride, in his triumph, despatch and have done with
    his doom there.

29

Ah! there was a heart right!
    There was single eye!
Read the unshapeable shock night
    And knew the who and the why;
Wording it how but by him that present and past,
    Heaven and earth are word of, worded by?—   150
    The Simon Peter of a soul! to the blast
Tarpeïan-fast, but a blown beacon of light.

30

Jesu, heart's light,
    Jesu, maid's son,
What was the feast followed the night
    Thou hadst glory of this nun?—
Feast of the one woman without stain.
    For so conceivèd, so to conceive thee is done;
    But here was heart-throe, birth of a brain,
Word, that heard and kept thee and uttered thee outright.   160

31

Well, she has thee for the pain, for the
    Patience; but pity of the rest of them!
Heart, go and bleed at a bitterer vein for the
    Comfortless unconfessed of them—
No not uncomforted: lovely-felicitous Providence
    Finger of a tender of, O of a feathery delicacy, the breast of the
        Maiden could obey so, be a bell to, ring of it, and
Startle the poor sheep back! is the shipwrack then a harvest, does
    tempest carry the grain for thee?

32

I admire thee, master of the tides,
 Of the Yore-flood, of the year's fall;   170
 The recurb and the recovery of the gulf's sides,
  The girth of it and the wharf of it and the wall;
Stanching, quenching ocean of a motionable mind;
Ground of being, and granite of it: past all
  Grasp God, throned behind
Death with a sovereignty that heeds but hides, bodes but abides;

33

With a mercy that outrides
 The all of water, an ark
 For the listener; for the lingerer with a love glides
  Lower than death and the dark;   180
A vein for the visiting of the past-prayer, pent in prison,
The-last-breath penitent spirits—the uttermost mark
  Our passion-plungèd giant risen,
The Christ of the Father compassionate, fetched in the storm of his
  strides.

34

Now burn, new born to the world,
 Double-naturèd name,
 The heaven-flung, heart-fleshed, maiden-furled
  Miracle-in-Mary-of-flame,
Mid-numberèd he in three of the thunder-throne!
Not a dooms-day dazzle in his coming nor dark as he came; 190
  Kind, but royally reclaiming his own;
A released shower, let flash to the shire, not a lightning of fire
  hard-hurled.

35

Dame, at our door
 Drowned, and among our shoals,
 Remember us in the roads, the heaven-haven of the reward:
  Our King back, Oh, upon English souls!
Let him easter in us, be a dayspring to the dimness of us, be a
 crimson-cresseted east,
More brightening her, rare-dear Britain, as his reign rolls,
  Pride, rose, prince, hero of us, high-priest,
Our heart's charity's hearth's fire, our thoughts' chivalry's throng's
  Lord.   200

(Wr. 1876; pub. 1918)

331 *Moonrise*

I AWOKE in the Midsummer not-to-call night, | in the white and the
    walk of the morning:
The moon, dwindled and thinned to the fringe | of a fingernail held to
    the candle,
Or paring of paradisaïcal fruit, | lovely in waning but lustreless,
Stepped from the stool, drew back from the barrow, | of dark Maenefa
    the mountain;
A cusp still clasped him, a fluke yet fanged him, | entangled him, not
    quit utterly.
This was the prized, the desirable sight, | unsought, presented so easily,
Parted me leaf and leaf, divided me, | eyelid and eyelid of slumber.

(Wr. 1876; pub. 1918)

332 *God's Grandeur*

THE world is charged with the grandeur of God.
  It will flame out, like shining from shook foil;
  It gathers to a greatness, like the ooze of oil
Crushed. Why do men then now not reck his rod?
Generations have trod, have trod, have trod;
  And all is seared with trade; bleared, smeared with toil;
  And wears man's smudge and shares man's smell: the soil
Is bare now, nor can foot feel, being shod.

And for all this, nature is never spent;
  There lives the dearest freshness deep down things;   10
And though the last lights off the black West went
  Oh, morning, at the brown brink eastwards, springs—
Because the Holy Ghost over the bent
  World broods with warm breast and with ah! bright wings.

(Wr. 1877; pub. 1895)

333 *Spring*

NOTHING is so beautiful as Spring—
    When weeds, in wheels, shoot long and lovely and lush;
    Thrush's eggs look little low heavens, and thrush
  Through the echoing timber does so rinse and wring

The ear, it strikes like lightnings to hear him sing;
   The glassy peartree leaves and blooms, they brush
   The descending blue; that blue is all in a rush
With richness; the racing lambs too have fair their fling.

What is all this juice and all this joy?
   A strain of the earth's sweet being in the beginning   10
In Eden garden.—Have, get, before it cloy,

   Before it cloud, Christ, lord, and sour with sinning,
Innocent mind and Mayday in girl and boy,
   Most, O maid's child, thy choice and worthy the winning.

                       (Wr. 1877; pub. 1893)

334   *In the Valley of the Elwy*

   I REMEMBER a house where all were good
      To me, God knows, deserving no such thing:
      Comforting smell breathed at very entering,
   Fetched fresh, as I suppose, off some sweet wood.

   That cordial air made those kind people a hood
      All over, as a bevy of eggs the mothering wing
      Will, or mild nights the new morsels of Spring:
   Why, it seemed of course; seemed of right it should.

   Lovely the woods, waters, meadows, combes, vales,
      All the air things wear that build this world of Wales;   10
      Only the inmate does not correspond:

   God, lover of souls, swaying considerate scales,
   Complete thy creature dear O where it fails,
      Being mighty a master, being a father and fond.

                       (Wr. 1877; pub. 1916)

335   *The Windhover:*

            To Christ our Lord

I CAUGHT this morning morning's minion, king-
   dom of daylight's dauphin, dapple-dawn-drawn Falcon, in his riding
   Of the rolling level underneath him steady air, and striding
High there, how he rung upon the rein of a wimpling wing

In his ecstasy! then off, off forth on swing,
   As a skate's heel sweeps smooth on a bow-bend: the hurl and gliding
   Rebuffed the big wind. My heart in hiding
Stirred for a bird,—the achieve of, the mastery of the thing!

Brute beauty and valour and act, oh, air, pride, plume, here
   Buckle! AND the fire that breaks from thee then, a billion   10
Times told lovelier, more dangerous, O my chevalier!

   No wonder of it: shéer plód makes plough down sillion
Shine, and blue-bleak embers, ah my dear,
   Fall, gall themselves, and gash gold-vermilion.

(Wr. 1877; pub. 1918)

336   *Pied Beauty*

GLORY be to God for dappled things—
   For skies of couple-colour as a brinded cow;
      For rose-moles all in stipple upon trout that swim;
Fresh-firecoal chestnut-falls; finches' wings;
   Landscape plotted and pieced—fold, fallow, and plough;
      And áll trádes, their gear and tackle and trim.

All things counter, original, spare, strange;
   Whatever is fickle, freckled (who knows how?)
      With swift, slow; sweet, sour; adazzle, dim;
He fathers-forth whose beauty is past change: 10
           Praise him.

(Wr. 1877; pub. 1918)

337   As kingfishers catch fire, dragonflies draw flame;
   As tumbled over rim in roundy wells
      Stones ring; like each tucked string tells, each hung bell's
Bow swung finds tongue to fling out broad its name;
Each mortal thing does one thing and the same:
   Deals out that being indoors each one dwells;
      Selves—goes its self; *myself* it speaks and spells,
Crying *What I do is me: for that I came.*

Í say more: the just man justices;
   Keeps gráce: thát keeps all his goings graces;   10

GERARD M. HOPKINS

Acts in God's eye what in God's eye he is—
    Chríst. For Christ plays in ten thousand places,
Lovely in limbs, and lovely in eyes not his
    To the Father through the features of men's faces.

(Wr. 1881–2?; pub. 1918)

338   *The Leaden Echo and the Golden Echo*

(Maidens' song from St Winefred's Well)

THE LEADEN ECHO

How to kéep—is there ány any, is there none such, nowhere known
    some, bow or brooch or braid or brace, láce, latch or catch or key
    to keep
Back beauty, keep it, beauty, beauty, beauty, . . . from vanishing away?
Ó is there no frowning of these wrinkles, rankèd wrinkles deep,
Dówn? no waving off of these most mournful messengers, still
    messengers, sad and stealing messengers of grey?—
No there's none, there's none, O no there's none,
Nor can you long be, what you now are, called fair,
Do what you may do, what, do what you may,
And wisdom is early to despair:
Be beginning; since, no, nothing can be done
To keep at bay   10
Age and age's evils, hoar hair,
Ruck and wrinkle, drooping, dying, death's worst, winding sheets,
    tombs and worms and tumbling to decay;
So be beginning, be beginning to despair.
O there's none; no no no there's none:
Be beginning to despair, to despair,
Despair, despair, despair, despair.

THE GOLDEN ECHO

                    Spare!
There ís one, yes I have one (Hush there!),
Only not within seeing of the sun.
Not within the singeing of the strong sun,
Tall sun's tingeing, or treacherous the tainting of the earth's air,
Somewhere elsewhere there is ah well where! one,
Óne. Yes I cán tell such a key, I dó know such a place,
Where whatever's prizèd and passes of us, everything that's fresh and
    fast flying of us, seems to us sweet of us and swiftly away with,
    done away with, undone,

Undone, done with, soon done with, and yet dearly and dangerously
    sweet
Of us, the wimpled-water-dimpled, not-by-morning-matchèd face,   10
The flower of beauty, fleece of beauty, too too apt to, ah! to fleet,
Never fleets móre, fastened with the tenderest truth
To its own best being and its loveliness of youth: it is an ever-
    lastingness of, O it is an all youth!
Come then, your ways and airs and looks, locks, maidengear, gallantry
    and gaiety and grace,
Winning ways, airs innocent, maiden manners, sweet looks, loose
    locks, long locks, lovelocks, gaygear, going gallant, girlgrace—
Resign them, sign them, seal them, send them, motion them with
    breath,
And with sighs soaring, soaring síghs, deliver
Them; beauty-in-the-ghost, deliver it, early now, long before death
Give beauty back, beauty, beauty, beauty, back to God, beauty's self
    and beauty's giver.
See; not a hair is, not an eyelash, not the least lash lost; every hair   20
Is, hair of the head, numbered.
Nay, what we had lighthanded left in surly the mere mould
Will have waked and have waxed and have walked with the wind what
    while we slept,
This side, that side hurling a heavyheaded hundredfold
What while we, while we slumbered.
O then, weary then whý should we tread? O why are we so haggard at
    the heart, so care-coiled, care-killed, so fagged, so fashed, so
    cogged, so cumbered,
When the thing we freely fórfeit is kept with fonder a care,
Fonder a care kept than we could have kept it, kept
Far with fonder a care (and we, we should have lost it) finer, fonder
A care kept.—Where kept? do but tell us where kept, where.—   30
Yonder.—What high as that! We follow, now we follow.—Yonder, yes
    yonder, yonder,
Yonder.

                              (Wr. 1882; pub. 1918)

339   *The Blessed Virgin compared to the Air we Breathe*

WILD air, world-mothering air,
Nestling me everywhere,
That each eyelash or hair
Girdles; goes home betwixt
The fleeciest, frailest-flixed
Snowflake; that's fairly mixed

With, riddles, and is rife
In every least thing's life;
This needful, never spent,
And nursing element;   10
My more than meat and drink,
My meal at every wink;
This air, which, by life's law,
My lung must draw and draw
Now but to breathe its praise,
Minds me in many ways
Of her who not only
Gave God's infinity
Dwindled to infancy
Welcome in womb and breast,   20
Birth, milk, and all the rest
But mothers each new grace
That does now reach our race—
Mary Immaculate,
Merely a woman, yet
Whose presence, power is
Great as no goddess's
Was deemèd, dreamèd; who
This one work has to do—
Let all God's glory through,   30
God's glory which would go
Through her and from her flow
Off, and no way but so.
    I say that we are wound
With mercy round and round
As if with air: the same
Is Mary, more by name.
She, wild web, wondrous robe,
Mantles the guilty globe,
Since God has let dispense   40
Her prayers his providence:
Nay, more than almoner,
The sweet alms' self is her
And men are meant to share
Her life as life does air.
    If I have understood,
She holds high motherhood
Towards all our ghostly good
And plays in grace her part
About man's beating heart,   50
Laying, like air's fine flood,
The deathdance in his blood;

Yet no part but what will
Be Christ our Saviour still.
Of her flesh he took flesh:
He does take fresh and fresh,
Though much the mystery how,
Not flesh but spirit now
And makes, O marvellous!
New Nazareths in us,   60
Where she shall yet conceive
Him, morning, noon, and eve;
New Bethlems, and he born
There, evening, noon, and morn—
Bethlem or Nazareth,
Men here may draw like breath
More Christ and baffle death;
Who, born so, comes to be
New self and nobler me
In each one and each one   70
More makes, when all is done,
Both God's and Mary's Son.
  Again, look overhead
How air is azurèd;
Oh how! Nay do but stand
Where you can lift your hand
Skywards: rich, rich it laps
Round the four fingergaps.
Yet such a sapphire-shot,
Charged, steepèd sky will not   80
Stain light. Yea, mark you this:
It does no prejudice.
The glass-blue days are those
When every colour glows,
Each shape and shadow shows.
Blue be it: this blue heaven
The seven or seven times seven
Hued sunbeam will transmit
Perfect, not alter it.
Or if there does some soft,   90
On things aloof, aloft,
Bloom breathe, that one breath more
Earth is the fairer for.
Whereas did air not make
This bath of blue and slake
His fire, the sun would shake,
A blear and blinding ball
With blackness bound, and all

The thick stars round him roll
Flashing like flecks of coal,   100
Quartz-fret, or sparks of salt,
In grimy vasty vault.
    So God was god of old:
A mother came to mould
Those limbs like ours which are
What must make our daystar
Much dearer to mankind;
Whose glory bare would blind
Or less would win man's mind.
Through her we may see him   110
Made sweeter, not made dim,
And her hand leaves his light
Sifted to suit our sight.
    Be thou then, O thou dear
Mother, my atmosphere;
My happier world, wherein
To wend and meet no sin;
Above me, round me lie
Fronting my froward eye
With sweet and scarless sky;   120
Stir in my ears, speak there
Of God's love, O live air,
Of patience, penance, prayer:
World-mothering air, air wild,
Wound with thee, in thee isled,
Fold home, fast fold thy child.

                    (Wr. 1883; pub. 1895)

340   *'The Child is Father to the Man'*

                        (*Wordsworth*)

    'THE child is father to the man.'
How can he be? The words are wild.
Suck any sense from that who can:
'The child is father to the man.'
No; what the poet did write ran,
'The man is father to the child.'
'The child is father to the man!'
How *can* he be? The words are wild.

                        (1883)

341   *Spelt from Sibyl's Leaves*

EARNEST, earthless, equal, attuneable, ˈ vaulty, voluminous, . . .
    stupendous
Evening strains to be tíme's vást, ˈ womb-of-all, home-of-all, hearse-
    of-all night.
Her fond yellow hornlight wound to the west, ˈ her wild hollow
    hoarlight hung to the height
Waste; her earliest stars, earlstars, ˈ stárs principal, overbend us,
Fíre-féaturing heaven. For earth ˈ her being has unbound; her dapple
    is at an end, as-
tray or aswarm, all throughther, in throngs; ˈ self ín self steepèd and
    páshed—qúite
Disremembering, dísmémbering ˈ áll now. Heart, you round me right
With: Óur évening is over us; óur night ˈ whélms, whélms, ánd will end
    us.
Only the beakleaved boughs dragonish ˈ damask the tool-smooth bleak
    light; black,
Ever so black on it. Óur tale, O óur oracle! ˈ Lét life, wáned, ah lét life
    wind   10
Off hér once skéined stained véined varíety ˈ upon, áll on twó spools;
    párt, pen, páck
Now her áll in twó flocks, twó folds—black, white; ˈ right, wrong;
    reckon but, reck but, mind
But thése two; wáre of a wórld where bút these ˈ twó tell, each off the
    óther; of a rack
Where, selfwrung, selfstrung, sheathe- and shelterless, ˈ thóughts
    agaínst thoughts ín groans grínd.

                                                        (Wr. 1885; pub. 1918)

342   NO worst, there is none. Pitched past pitch of grief,
         More pangs will, schooled at forepangs, wilder wring.
         Comforter, where, where is your comforting?
         Mary, mother of us, where is your relief?
         My cries heave, herds-long; huddle in a main, a chief-
         woe, world-sorrow; on an age-old anvil wince and sing—
         Then lull, then leave off. Fury had shrieked 'No ling-
         ering! Let me be fell: force I must be brief'.
         O the mind, mind has mountains; cliffs of fall
         Frightful, sheer, no-man-fathomed. Hold them cheap   10

May who ne'er hung there. Nor does long our small
Durance deal with that steep or deep. Here! creep,
Wretch, under a comfort serves in a whirlwind: all
Life death does end and each day dies with sleep.

(Wr. 1885; pub. 1918)

343   To seem the stranger lies my lot, my life
       Among strangers. Father and mother dear,
       Brothers and sisters are in Christ not near
       And he my peace/my parting, sword and strife.

       England, whose honour O all my heart woos, wife
       To my creating thought, would neither hear
       Me, were I pleading, plead nor do I: I wear-
       y of idle a being but by where wars are rife.

       I am in Ireland now; now I am at a thírd
       Remove. Not but in all removes I can   10
       Kind love both give and get. Only what word

       Wisest my heart breeds dark heaven's baffling ban
       Bars or hell's spell thwarts. This to hoard unheard,
       Heard unheeded, leaves me a lonely began.

(Wr. 1885?; pub. 1893)

344   I WAKE and feel the fell of dark, not day.
       What hours, O what black hoürs we have spent
       This night! what sights you, heart, saw; ways you went!
       And more must, in yet longer light's delay.

       With witness I speak this. But where I say
       Hours I mean years, mean life. And my lament
       Is cries countless, cries like dead letters sent
       To dearest him that lives alas! away.

       I am gall, I am heartburn. God's most deep decree
       Bitter would have me taste: my taste was me;   10
       Bones built in me, flesh filled, blood brimmed the curse.

       Selfyeast of spirit a dull dough sours. I see
       The lost are like this, and their scourge to be
       As I am mine, their sweating selves; but worse.

(Wr. 1885?; pub. 1918)

345   PATIENCE, hard thing! the hard thing but to pray,
       But bid for, Patience is! Patience who asks
       Wants war, wants wounds; weary his times, his tasks;
       To do without, take tosses, and obey.

       Rare patience roots in these, and, these away,
       Nowhere. Natural heart's ivy, Patience masks
       Our ruins of wrecked past purpose. There she basks
       Purple eyes and seas of liquid leaves all day.

       We hear our hearts grate on themselves: it kills
       To bruise them dearer. Yet the rebellious wills   10
       Of us we do bid God bend to him even so.

       And where is he who more and more distills
       Delicious kindness?—He is patient. Patience fills
       His crisp combs, and that comes those ways we know.

                                    (Wr. 1885?; pub. 1918)

346   MY own heart let me more have pity on; let
       Me live to my sad self hereafter kind,
       Charitable; not live this tormented mind
       With this tormented mind tormenting yet.

       I cast for comfort I can no more get
       By groping round my comfortless, than blind
       Eyes in their dark can day or thirst can find
       Thirst's all-in-all in all a world of wet.

       Soul, self; come, poor Jackself, I do advise
       You, jaded, let be; call off thoughts awhile   10
       Elsewhere; leave comfort root-room; let joy size

       At God knows when to God knows what; whose smile
       's not wrung, see you; unforeseen times rather—as skies
       Betweenpie mountains—lights a lovely mile.

                                    (Wr. 1885?; pub. 1918)

347 *Justus quidem tu es, Domine, si disputem tecum; verumtamen*
justa loquar ad te: Quare via impiorum prosperatur? &c.

THOU art indeed just, Lord, if I contend
With thee; but, sir, so what I plead is just.
Why do sinners' ways prosper? and why must
Disappointment all I endeavour end?

Wert thou my enemy, O thou my friend,
How wouldst thou worse, I wonder, than thou dost
Defeat, thwart me? Oh, the sots and thralls of lust
Do in spare hours more thrive than I that spend,

Sir, life upon thy cause. See, banks and brakes
Now, leavèd how thick! lacèd they are again   10
With fretty chervil, look, and fresh wind shakes

Them; birds build—but not I build; no, but strain,
Time's eunuch, and not breed one work that wakes.
Mine, O thou lord of life, send my roots rain.

(Wr. 1889; pub. 1893)

JOHN HENRY NEWMAN
1801–1890

348   from *The Dream of Gerontius*
              Fifth Choir of Angelicals

PRAISE to the Holiest in the height,
    And in the depth be praise:
In all His words most wonderful;
    Most sure in all His ways!

O loving wisdom of our God!
    When all was sin and shame,
A second Adam to the fight
    And to the rescue came.

O wisest love! that flesh and blood
    Which did in Adam fail,   10
Should strive afresh against their foe,
    Should strive and should prevail;

And that a higher gift than grace
    Should flesh and blood refine,
God's Presence and His very Self,
    And Essence all-divine.

O generous love! that He who smote
    In man for man the foe,
The double agony in man
    For man should undergo;   20

And in the garden secretly,
    And on the cross on high,
Should teach His brethren and inspire
    To suffer and to die.

                            (Wr. and pub. 1865)

ARTHUR MUNBY

1828–1910

349   *The Serving Maid*

WHEN you go out at early morn,
    Your busy hands, sweet drudge, are bare;
    For you must work, and none are there
To see with scorn—to feel with scorn.

And when the weekly wars begin,
    Your arms are naked to the hilt,
    And many a sturdy pail's a-tilt
To sheathe them in—to plunge them in.

For you at least can understand
    That daily work is hard and stern,
    That those who toil for bread must learn   10
To bare the hand—to spoil the hand.

But in the evening, when they dine,
    And you behind each frequent chair
    Are flitting lightly here and there
To bring them wine—to pour them wine;

Oh then, from every dainty eye
  That may not so be shock'd or grieved,
  Your hands are hid, your arms are sleeved:
We ask not why—we tell not why.   20

Ah fools! Though you for workday scours,
  And they for show, unveil their charms,
  Love is not bound to snowy arms,
He thinks of yours—he speaks of yours:

To me his weighted shaft has come;
  Though hand and arm are both unseen,
  Your rosy wrist peeps out between
And sends it home—and speeds it home.

(1865)

350   *One Way of Looking at It*

I THOUGHT you always knew it well
  (Although indeed you never said so)—
I thought you knew I dared not tell,
  And that was why you toss'd your head so:

For I have often heard you say
  You hate to see a fellow sighing,
To hear him stammer all the day,
  And hint mysteriously at dying.

And if I *have* adored you so,
  I thought you knew I couldn't help it;   10
I could no more escape my woe
  Than Joseph could his empty well-pit.

It wasn't fair of you at all:
  You moved so light and play'd so neatly,
And set your foot upon the ball,
  And croquet'd me, I know, completely!

Why did you let me look such things,
  And whisper o'er our melting ices,
If converse with you only brings
  This most objectionable crisis?   20

433

I wish I had not loved, for then
   Perhaps you would not be offended,
Nor fling me back my heart again,
   Nor tell me thus that all is ended!

Oh yes! Sir John's a charming catch—
   His stud, his balance at his banker's,
Unlike himself, are hard to match;
   And I have but one horse at Spanker's!

He will not house you in some den,
   Served by a footman single-handed—   30
He has such store of maids and men
   As your position, love, demanded:

And so, I quite approve your choice;
   I won't regret my wasted wooing;
I'll think your sweet soprano voice
   Has warn'd me from my own undoing:

And yet I know, that when too late—
   Just as the spectre came to Priam—
You'll learn to rue your splendid fate,
   And wish yourself as free as I am.   40

(1865)

351   *Post Mortem*

I LAY in my coffin under the sod;
But the rooks they caw'd, and the sheep they trod
And munch'd and bleated, and made such a noise—
What with the feet of the charity boys
Trampling over the old grave-stones—
That it loosen'd my inarticulate bones,
   And chased my sleep away.

So I turn'd (for the coffin is not so full
As it was, you know) my aching skull;
And said to my wife—and it's not my fault   10
If she *does* lie next to me in the vault—
Said to her kindly, 'My love, my dear,
How do you like these sounds we hear
   Over our heads to-day?'

My wife had always a good strong voice;
But I'm not so sure that I did rejoice
When I found it as strong as it used to be,
And so unexpectedly close to me:
I thought, if her temper *should* set in,
Why, the boards between us are very thin,   20
And whenever the bearers come one by one
To deposit the corpse of my eldest son,
Who is spending the earnings of his papa
With such sumptuous ease and such great *éclât*,
They may think it more pleasant, perhaps, than I did,
To find that in death we were not divided.
However, I trusted to time and the worms;
And I kept myself to the mildest terms
    Of a conjugal How d'ye do.

'John,' said my wife, 'you're a Body, like me;   30
At least if you ain't, why you ought to be;
And I really don't think, when I reflect,
That I ought to pay as much respect
To a rattling prattling skeleton
As I did to a man of sixteen stone.
However (says she), I shall just remark
That this here place is so cool and dark,
I'm certain sure, if you hadn't have spoke,
My slumber'd never have thus been broke;
So I wish you'd keep your—voice in your head;   40
For I don't see the good of being dead,
    If one mayn't be quiet too.'

She spoke so clear and she spoke so loud,
I thank'd my stars that a linen shroud
And a pair of boards (though they *were* but thin)
Kept out some part of that well-known din:
And, talking of shrouds, the very next word
That my empty echoing orbits heard
Was, 'Gracious me, I can tell by the feel
That I'm all over rags from head to heel!   50
Here's jobs for needle and thread without ending,
For there's ever-so-many holes wants mending!'
'My love,' I ventured to say, 'I fear
It's not much use, your mending 'em here;
For, as fast as you do, there's worse than moth,
And worse than mice, or rats, or both,

Will eat up the work of your cotton ball
And leave you never a shroud at all—
  No more than they have to me.'

Now, whether it was that she took it ill   60
My seeming to question her feminine skill,
Or whether 'twas simply that we were wedded—
The very thing happen'd that most I dreaded:
For, by way of reply, on the coffin-side,
Just where the planks had started wide,
There came a blow so straight and true
That it shook my vertebral column in two;
And what more might have follow'd I cannot tell,
But that very minute ('twas just as well)
The flagstone was lifted overhead,   70
And the red-nosed buriers of the dead
Let down a load on my coffin-plate
That stunn'd me quite with the shock of its weight.
'Twas the corpse, of course, of my eldest son,
Who had injured his brain (a little one)
By many a spirituous brain-dissolver,
And finish'd it off with a Colt's revolver.
Well—when they had gone and the noise had ceased,
I look'd for one other attack, at least:
But, would you believe it? The place was quiet,   80
And the worms had resumed their usual diet!
Nay, everything else was silent too;
The rooks they neither caw'd nor flew,
And the sheep slept sound by footstone and head,
And the charity boys had been whipp'd to bed.
So I turn'd again, and I said to myself—
'Now, as sure as I'm laid on this sordid shelf
Away from the living that smile or weep,
I'll sleep if I can, and let *her* too sleep:
And I will not once, for pleasure or pain,   90
Unhinge my jaws to speak again,
  No, not if she speaks to me.'

(1865)

SEBASTIAN EVANS

1830–1909

The Fifteen Days of Judgment

'THEN there shall be signs in Heaven.'—
Thus much in the text is given,
Worthy of the sinner's heeding:
But the other signs preceding
Earth's Last Judgment and destruction,
And its fiery reconstruction,
May be drawn from other channels;
For we read in Hebrew annals
That there shall be altogether
Fifteen Judgment days; but whether   10
Following or interpolated,
Jerome saith, is nowhere stated.

DAY I

On the first day, loud upcrashing,
Shall the shoreless ocean, gnashing
With a dismal anaclysmal
Outrush from its deeps abysmal,
Lifted high by dread supernal,
Storm the mountain heights eternal!
Forty cubits of sheer edges,
Wall-like, o'er the summit-ridges   20
Stretching upright forth—a mirror
For the unutterable terror
Of the huddled howling nations,
Smit with sudden desolations,
Rushing hither, thither, drunken,
Half their pleasant realms sea-sunken!

DAY II

On the second day, down-pouring,
Shall the watery walls drop roaring
From the ruinous precipices
To the nethermost abysses,   30
With a horrible waterquaking
In the world-wide cataracts, shaking
Earth's foundations as they thunder
To the cavernous darkness under.—

437

Surf-plumed steeds of God Almighty,
Rock and pyramid, forest, city,
Through the flood-rent valleys scourging,
Wild in headlong ebb down-surging,
Down, till eye of man scarce reaches
Where, within its shrunken beaches,   40
Hidden from a world's amazement,
Cowers the Deep in self-abasement.

DAY III

On the third day, o'er the seething
Of the leprous ocean writhing,
Whale and dragon, orc and kraken,
And leviathan, forsaken
His unfathomable eyrie,
To and fro shall plunge—the dreary
Dumb death-sickness of creation
Startling with their ululation.   50
Men shall hear the monsters bellow
Forth their burden, as they wallow;
But its drift?—Let none demand it!
God alone shall understand it!

DAY IV

On the fourth day, blazing redly,
With a reek pitch-black and deadly,
A consuming flame shall quiver
From all seas and every river!
Every brook and beck and torrent
Leaping in a fiery current;   60
All the moats and meres and fountains
Lit, like beacons on the mountains;
Furnace-roar of smolten surges
Scaring earth's extremest verges!

DAY V

On the fifth day, Judgment-stricken,
Every green herb, from the lichen
To the cedar of the forest,
Shall sweat blood in anguish sorest!
On the same, all fowls of heaven
Into one wide field, fear-driven,   70
Shall assemble, cowed and shrinking,
Neither eating aught, nor drinking;

Kind with kind, all ranked by feather,
Doves with doves aghast together,
Swan with swan in downfal regal,
Wren with wren, with eagle, eagle!
Ah! when fowl feel such foreboding,
What shall be the Sinner's goading?

DAY VI

On the sixth day, through all nations
Shall be quaking of foundations,   80
With a horrible hollow rumbling—
All that all men builded crumbling
As the heel of Judgment tramples
Cot and palace, castles, temples,
Hall and minster, thorp and city;—
All men too aghast for pity
In the crashing and the crushing
Of that stony stream's downrushing!—
And a flame of fiery warning
Forth from sundown until morning   90
With a lurid coruscation
Shall reveal night's desolation!

DAY VII

On the seventh day, self-shattered,
Rifting fourfold, scarred and scattered,
Pounded in the Judgment's mortars,
Every stone shall split in quarters!
Pebble, whinstone, granite sparry,
Rock and boulder—stones of quarry,
Shaped or shapeless, all asunder
Shivering, split athwart and under;   100
And the splinters, each on other,
Shall make war against his brother,
Each one grinding each to powder,
Grinding, gnashing, loud and louder,
Grinding, gnashing on till even,
With a dolorous plea to Heaven.
What the drift?—Let none demand it!
God alone shall understand it!

DAY VIII

On the eighth, in dire commotion,
Shall the dry land heave like Ocean,   110

439

Puffed in hills and sucked in hollows,
Yawning into steep-down swallows—
Swelling, mountainously lifted,
Skyward from the plains uprifted—
With a universal clamour,
Rattling, roaring through the tremor;
While, flung headlong, all men living
Grovel in a wild misgiving!—
What, O Sinner, shall avail your
Might in solid Earth's own failure!   120

DAY IX

On the ninth day all the mountains
Shall drop bodily, like spent fountains,
All the cloud-capped pride of pristine
Peak and pinnacle amethystine
Toppling, drifting to the level,
Flooding all the dales with gravel;
One consummate moment blasting
All that seems so everlasting—
All men to the caves for shelter
Scurrying through the world-wide welter!   130

DAY X

On the tenth day, hither, thither,
Herding from their holes together,
With a glaring of white faces,
Through the desolate wildernesses
Men shall o'er that mountain ruin
Run as from a Death's pursuing,—
Each one with suspicious scowling,
Shrinking from his fellow's howling—
For all human speech confounded
Shall not sound as once it sounded.   140
None shall understand his brother—
Mother child, nor child his mother!

DAY XI

On the eleventh day, at dawning,
Every sepulchre wide yawning
At the approach of Earth's Assessor,
Shall upyield its white possessor;—
All the skeletons, close-serried,
O'er the graves where each lay buried,

Mute upstanding, white and bony,
With a dreadful ceremony   150
Staring from the morn till gloaming
Eastward for the Judge's coming;
Staring on, with sockets eyeless,
Each one motionless and cryless,
Save the dry, dead-leaf-like chattering,
Through that white-branched forest pattering.
What its drift?—Let none demand it!
God alone shall understand it!

DAY XII

On the twelfth, the Planets seven
And all stars shall drop from Heaven!   160
On the same day, scared and trembling,
All four-footed things assembling,
Each after his kind in order—
All the lions in one border,
Sheep with sheep—not needing shepherd—
Stag with stag—with leopard, leopard—
Shall be herded cowed and shrinking,
Neither eating aught, nor drinking,
But to Godward bellowing, shrieking,
Howling, barking, roaring, squeaking;—   170
What the drift?—Let none demand it!
God alone shall understand it!

DAY XIII

On the thirteenth awful morning
Shall go forth the latest warning,
With a close to all things mortal,
For the Judge is at the portal!
In an agony superhuman,
Every living man and woman,
Child and dotard—every breather—
Shall lie down and die together,   180
That all flesh in death's subjection
May abide the Resurrection!

DAY XIV

On the fourteenth, morn to even,
Fire shall feed on Earth and Heaven,
Through the skies and all they cover,
Under earth, and on, and over;

All things ghostly, human, bestial,
In the crucible celestial
Tested by the dread purgation
Of that final conflagration;   190
Till the intolerable whiteness
Dawn, of God's exceeding brightness
Through the furnace-flame's erasure
Of yon mortal veil of azure!

DAY XV

Last, the fifteenth day shall render
Earth a more than earthly splendour,
Once again shall Word be given:
'Let there be new Earth, new Heaven!'
And this fleeting world—this charnel,
Purified, shall wax eternal!—   200
Then all souls shall Michael gather
At the footstool of the Father,
Summoning from Earth's four corners,
All erst human saints; and scorners,
And without revenge or pity
Weigh them in the scales almighty!—

Sinner! Dost thou dread that trial?
Mark yon shadow on the dial!

Ast illi semper modò 'cras, cras,' umbra docebit.

EXPLICIT

(1865)

JAMES THOMSON ('B.V.')
1834–1882

353   from *Art*

III

SINGING is sweet; but be sure of this,
Lips only sing when they cannot kiss.

Did he ever suspire a tender lay
While her presence took his breath away?

Had his fingers been able to toy with her hair
Would they then have written the verses fair?

Had she let his arm steal round her waist
Would the lovely portrait yet be traced?

Since he could not embrace it flushed and warm
He has carved in stone the perfect form.   10

Who gives the fine report of the feast?
He who got none and enjoyed it least.

Were the wine really slipping down his throat
Would his song of the wine advance a note?

Will you puff out the music that sways the whirl,
Or dance and make love with a pretty girl?

Who shall the great battle-story write?
Not the hero down in the thick of the fight.

Statues and pictures and verse may be grand,
But they are not the Life for which they stand.   20

(Wr. 1865; pub. 1867)

354   ONCE in a saintly passion
          I cried with desperate grief,
        O Lord, my heart is black with guile,
          Of sinners I am chief.
        Then stooped my guardian angel
          And whispered from behind,
        'Vanity, my little man,
          You're nothing of the kind.'

(Wr. 1865; pub. 1884)

355   *Mr MacCall at Cleveland Hall*
           (April 15, 1866)

        MR MACCALL at Cleveland Hall,
        Sunday evening—date to fix—
        Fifteenth April, sixty-six,
        Speech reported and redacted
        By a fellow much distracted.

I

Who lectures? No mere scorner;
   Clear-brained, his heart is warm.

She sits at the nearest corner
   Of I will not say what form.

II

The Conflict of Opinions   10
   In the Present Day, saith Chair.

What muff in the British dominions
   Could dispute that she is fair?

III

Mammon-worship is horrid,
   Plutocracy is base.

Dark hair from a fine small forehead;
   I catch but the still side face.

IV

We wallow in mere dimension,
   The Big to us is Great.

If she stood at her utmost tension   20
   She *might* pass four feet eight.

V

We lay on colour in splashes,
   With a mop, or a broom for brush.

How dark are her long eyelashes!
   How pure is her cheek's slight flush!

VI

But we have no perception
   For form—the divinest—now.

Each curve there is perfection,
   In nostril, chin, and brow.

VII

Our women are good kind creatures,
    But they cannot dress at all.

Does her bonnet grace her features?—
    Clear blue with a black lace fall.

VIII

Low Church—very low—in the gutter;
    High Church—as ven'son high.

O'er the flower of her face gleams the flutter
    Of a smile like a butterfly.

IX

Herder, Wieland, Lessing;
    Bossuet, Montalembert.

Fine names, but the name worth guessing
    Is the name of the sweet girl there.

X

The individual; true man;
    Individuality.

A man's but one half; some woman
    The other half must be.

XI

Persistent valour the sternest,
    With love's most gentle grace.

How grand is the eye fixed earnest
    In the half-seen up-turned face!

XII

'How did you like the lecture?
    Was it not beautiful?'

I should think *she was!* 'I conjecture
    That your brains have been gathering wool!'

P.S.

The Chairman was a rare man;
   At every telling point
He smiled at his post like a jolly host
   Carving rich cuts from the joint;
Which the name he bore was Richard Moore
   Whom Heaven with grace anoint!

     That conflict of opinion   60
        It had its counterpart
     In conflict for dominion
        Between my head and heart.

           (Wr. 1866; pub. 1892)

356   *In the Room*

   'Ceste insigne fable et tragicque comedie'—RABELAIS.

I

THE sun was down, and twilight grey
   Filled half the air; but in the room,
Whose curtain had been drawn all day,
   The twilight was a dusky gloom:
Which seemed at first as still as death,
   And void; but was indeed all rife
With subtle thrills, the pulse and breath
   Of multitudinous lower life.

II

In their abrupt and headlong way
   Bewildered flies for light had dashed   10
Against the curtain all the day,
   And now slept wintrily abashed;
And nimble mice slept, wearied out
   With such a double night's uproar;
But solid beetles crawled about
   The chilly hearth and naked floor.

III

And so throughout the twilight hour
   That vaguely murmurous hush and rest
There brooded; and beneath its power
   Life throbbing held its throbs supprest: 20

446

Until the thin-voiced mirror sighed,
   I am all blurred with dust and damp,
So long ago the clear day died,
   So long has gleamed nor fire nor lamp.

IV

Whereon the curtain murmured back,
   Some change is on us, good or ill;
Behind me and before is black
   As when those human things lie still:
But I have seen the darkness grow
   As grows the daylight every morn;   30
Have felt out there long shine and glow,
   In here long chilly dusk forlorn.

V

The cupboard grumbled with a groan,
   Each new day worse starvation brings:
Since *he* came here I have not known
   Or sweets or cates or wholesome things:
But now! a pinch of meal, a crust,
   Throughout the week is all I get.
I am so empty; it is just
   As when they said we were to let.   40

VI

What is become, then, of our Man?
   The petulant old glass exclaimed;
If all this time he slumber can,
   He really ought to be ashamed.
I wish we had our Girl again,
   So gay and busy, bright and fair:
The girls are better than these men,
   Who only for their dull selves care.

VII

It is so many hours ago—
   The lamp and fire were both alight—   50
I saw him pacing to and fro,
   Perturbing restlessly the night.
His face was pale to give one fear,
   His eyes when lifted looked too bright;
He muttered; what, I could not hear:
   Bad words though; something was not right.

VIII

The table said, He wrote so long
  That I grew weary of his weight;
The pen kept up a cricket song,
  It ran and ran at such a rate: 60
And in the longer pauses he
  With both his folded arms downpressed
And stared as one who does not see,
  Or sank his head upon his breast.

IX

The fire-grate said, I am as cold
  As if I never had a blaze;
The few dead cinders here I hold,
  I held unburned for days and days.
Last night he made them flare; but still
  What good did all his writing do?   70
Among my ashes curl and thrill
  Thin ghosts of all those papers too.

X

The table answered, Not quite all;
  He saved and folded up one sheet,
And sealed it fast, and let it fall;
  And here it lies now white and neat.
Whereon the letter's whisper came,
  My writing is closed up too well;
Outside there's not a single name,
  And who should read me I can't tell.   80

XI

The mirror sneered with scornful spite,
  (That ancient crack which spoiled her looks
Had marred her temper), Write and write!
  And read those stupid, worn-out books!
That's all he does, read, write, and read,
  And smoke that nasty pipe which stinks:
He never takes the slightest heed
  How any of us feels or thinks.

XII

But Lucy fifty times a day
  Would come and smile here in my face,   90
Adjust a tress that curled astray,
  Or tie a ribbon with more grace:

448

She looked so young and fresh and fair,
  She blushed with such a charming bloom,
It did one good to see her there,
  And brightened all things in the room.

XIII

She did not sit hours stark and dumb
  As pale as moonshine by the lamp;
To lie in bed when day was come,
  And leave us curtained chill and damp.   100
She slept away the dreary dark,
  And rose to greet the pleasant morn;
And sang as gaily as a lark
  While busy as the flies sun-born.

XIV

And how she loved us every one;
  And dusted this and mended that,
With trills and laughs and freaks of fun,
  And tender scoldings in her chat!
And then her bird, that sang as shrill
  As she sang sweet; her darling flowers   110
That grew there in the window-sill,
  Where she would sit at work for hours.

XV

It was not much she ever wrote;
  Her fingers had good work to do;
Say, once a week a pretty note;
  And very long it took her too.
And little more she read, I wis;
  Just now and then a pictured sheet,
Besides those letters she would kiss
  And croon for hours, they were so sweet.   120

XVI

She had her friends too, blithe young girls,
  Who whispered, babbled, laughed, caressed,
And romped and danced with dancing curls,
  And gave our life a joyous zest.
But with this dullard, glum and sour,
  Not one of all his fellow-men
Has ever passed a social hour;
  We might be in some wild beast's den.

XVII

This long tirade aroused the bed,
    Who spoke in deep and ponderous bass,   130
Befitting that calm life he led,
    As if firm-rooted in his place:
In broad majestic bulk alone,
    As in thrice venerable age,
He stood at once the royal throne,
    The monarch, the experienced sage:

XVIII

I know what is and what has been;
    Not anything to me comes strange,
Who in so many years have seen
    And lived through every kind of change.   140
I know when men are good or bad,
    When well or ill, he slowly said;
When sad or glad, when sane or mad,
    And when they sleep alive or dead.

XIX

At this last word of solemn lore
    A tremor circled through the gloom,
As if a crash upon the floor
    Had jarred and shaken all the room:
For nearly all the listening things
    Were old and worn, and knew what curse   150
Of violent change death often brings,
    From good to bad, from bad to worse;

XX

They get to know each other well,
    To feel at home and settled down;
Death bursts among them like a shell,
    And strews them over all the town.
The bed went on, This man who lies
    Upon me now is stark and cold;
He will not any more arise,
    And do the things he did of old.   160

XXI

But we shall have short peace or rest;
    For soon up here will come a rout,
And nail him in a queer long chest,
    And carry him like luggage out.

They will be muffled all in black,
    And whisper much, and sigh and weep:
But he will never more come back,
    And some one else in me must sleep.

XXII

Thereon a little phial shrilled,
    Here empty on the chair I lie: 170
I heard one say, as I was filled,
    With half of this a man would die.
The man there drank me with slow breath,
    And murmured, Thus ends barren strife:
O sweeter, thou cold wine of death,
    Than ever sweet warm wine of life.

XXIII

One of my cousins long ago,
    A little thing, the mirror said,
Was carried to a couch to show,
    Whether a man was really dead.   180
Two great improvements marked the case:
    He did not blur her with his breath,
His many-wrinkled, twitching face
    Was smooth old ivory: verdict, Death.—

XXIV

It lay, the lowest thing there, lulled
    Sweet-sleep-like in corruption's truce;
The form whose purpose was annulled,
    While all the other shapes meant use.
It lay, the *he* become now *it*,
    Unconscious of the deep disgrace,   190
Unanxious how its parts might flit
    Through what new forms in time and space.

XXV

It lay and preached, as dumb things do,
    More powerfully than tongues can prate;
Though life be torture through and through,
    Man is but weak to plain of fate:
The drear path crawls on drearier still
    To wounded feet and hopeless breast?
Well, he can lie down when he will,
    And straight all ends in endless rest.   200

XXVI

And while the black night nothing saw,
    And till the cold morn came at last,
That old bed held the room in awe
    With tales of its experience vast.
It thrilled the gloom; it told such tales
    Of human sorrows and delights,
Of fever moans and infant wails,
    Of births and deaths and bridal nights.

(Wr. 1867–8; pub. 1872)

357　　　　*In a Christian Churchyard*

THIS field of stones, he said,
May well call forth a sigh;
Beneath them lie the dead,
On them the living lie.

(Wr. 1870; pub. 1871)

from *The City of Dreadful Night* (358–359)

358　　　　　　　IV

HE stood alone within the spacious square
    Declaiming from the central grassy mound,
With head uncovered and with streaming hair,
    As if large multitudes were gathered round:
A stalwart shape, the gestures full of might,
The glances burning with unnatural light:—

As I came through the desert thus it was,
As I came through the desert: All was black,
In heaven no single star, on earth no track;
A brooding hush without a stir or note,   10
The air so thick it clotted in my throat;
And thus for hours; then some enormous things
Swooped past with savage cries and clanking wings:
            But I strode on austere;
            No hope could have no fear.

As I came through the desert thus it was,
As I came through the desert: Eyes of fire
Glared at me throbbing with a starved desire;

The hoarse and heavy and carnivorous breath
Was hot upon me from deep jaws of death;   20
Sharp claws, swift talons, fleshless fingers cold
Plucked at me from the bushes, tried to hold:
      But I strode on austere;
      No hope could have no fear.

As I came through the desert thus it was,
As I came through the desert: Lo you, there,
That hillock burning with a brazen glare;
Those myriad dusky flames with points a-glow
Which writhed and hissed and darted to and fro;
A Sabbath of the Serpents, heaped pell-mell   30
For Devil's roll-call and some *fête* of Hell:
      Yet I strode on austere;
      No hope could have no fear.

As I came through the desert thus it was,
As I came through the desert: Meteors ran
And crossed their javelins on the black sky-span;
The zenith opened to a gulf of flame,
The dreadful thunderbolts jarred earth's fixed frame;
The ground all heaved in waves of fire that surged
And weltered round me sole there unsubmerged: 40
      Yet I strode on austere;
      No hope could have no fear.

As I came through the desert thus it was,
As I came through the desert: Air once more,
And I was close upon a wild sea-shore;
Enormous cliffs arose on either hand,
The deep tide thundered up a league-broad strand;
White foambelts seethed there, wan spray swept and flew;
The sky broke, moon and stars and clouds and blue:
      And I strode on austere;   50
      No hope could have no fear.

As I came through the desert thus it was,
As I came through the desert: On the left
The sun arose and crowned a broad crag-cleft;
There stopped and burned out black, except a rim,
A bleeding eyeless socket, red and dim;
Whereon the moon fell suddenly south-west,
And stood above the right-hand cliffs at rest:
      Still I strode on austere;
      No hope could have no fear.   60

As I came through the desert thus it was,
As I came through the desert: From the right
A shape came slowly with a ruddy light;
A woman with a red lamp in her hand,
Bareheaded and barefooted on that strand;
O desolation moving with such grace!
O anguish with such beauty in thy face!
        I fell as on my bier,
        Hope travailed with such fear.

As I came through the desert thus it was,
As I came through the desert: I was twain,
Two selves distinct that cannot join again;
One stood apart and knew but could not stir,
And watched the other stark in swoon and her;
And she came on, and never turned aside,
Between such sun and moon and roaring tide:
        And as she came more near
        My soul grew mad with fear. 70

As I came through the desert thus it was,
As I came through the desert: Hell is mild 80
And piteous matched with that accursèd wild;
A large black sign was on her breast that bowed,
A broad black band ran down her snow-white shroud;
That lamp she held was her own burning heart,
Whose blood-drops trickled step by step apart:
        The mystery was clear;
        Mad rage had swallowed fear.

As I came through the desert thus it was,
As I came through the desert: By the sea
She knelt and bent above that senseless me; 90
Those lamp-drops fell upon my white brow there,
She tried to cleanse them with her tears and hair;
She murmured words of pity, love, and woe,
She heeded not the level rushing flow:
        And mad with rage and fear,
        I stood stonebound so near.

As I came through the desert thus it was,
As I came through the desert: When the tide
Swept up to her there kneeling by my side,
She clasped that corpse-like me, and they were borne 100
Away, and this vile me was left forlorn;

I know the whole sea cannot quench that heart,
Or cleanse that brow, or wash those two apart:
    They love; their doom is drear,
    Yet they nor hope nor fear;
    But I, what do I here?

359   XVIII

I WANDERED in a suburb of the north,
  And reached a spot whence three close lanes led down,
Beneath thick trees and hedgerows winding forth
  Like deep brook channels, deep and dark and lown:
The air above was wan with misty light,
The dull grey south showed one vague blur of white.

I took the left-hand lane and slowly trod
  Its earthen footpath, brushing as I went
The humid leafage; and my feet were shod
  With heavy languor, and my frame downbent,   10
With infinite sleepless weariness outworn,
So many nights I thus had paced forlorn.

After a hundred steps I grew aware
  Of something crawling in the lane below;
It seemed a wounded creature prostrate there
  That sobbed with pangs in making progress slow,
The hind limbs stretched to push, the fore limbs then
To drag; for it would die in its own den.

But coming level with it I discerned
  That it had been a man; for at my tread   20
It stopped in its sore travail and half-turned,
  Leaning upon its right, and raised its head,
And with the left hand twitched back as in ire
Long grey unreverend locks befouled with mire.

A haggard filthy face with bloodshot eyes,
  An infamy for manhood to behold.
He gasped all trembling, What, you want my prize?
  You leave, to rob me, wine and lust and gold
And all that men go mad upon, since you
Have traced my sacred secret of the clue?   30

You think that I am weak and must submit;
   Yet I but scratch you with this poisoned blade,
And you are dead as if I clove with it
   That false fierce greedy heart. Betrayed! betrayed!
I fling this phial if you seek to pass,
And you are forthwith shrivelled up like grass.

And then with sudden change, Take thought! take thought!
   Have pity on me! it is mine alone.
If you could find, it would avail you naught;
   Seek elsewhere on the pathway of your own: 40
For who of mortal or immortal race
The lifetrack of another can retrace?

Did you but know my agony and toil!
   Two lanes diverge up yonder from this lane;
My thin blood marks the long length of their soil;
   Such clue I left, who sought my clue in vain:
My hands and knees are worn both flesh and bone;
I cannot move but with continual moan.

But I am in the very way at last
   To find the long-lost broken golden thread   50
Which reunites my present with my past,
   If you but go your own way. And I said,
I will retire as soon as you have told
Whereunto leadeth this lost thread of gold.

And so you know it not! he hissed with scorn;
   I feared you, imbecile! It leads me back
From this accursed night without a morn,
   And through the deserts which have else no track,
And through vast wastes of horror-haunted time,
To Eden innocence in Eden's clime: 60

And I become a nursling soft and pure,
   An infant cradled on its mother's knee,
Without a past, love-cherished and secure;
   Which if it saw this loathsome present Me,
Would plunge its face into the pillowing breast,
And scream abhorrence hard to lull to rest.

He turned to grope; and I retiring brushed
   Thin shreds of gossamer from off my face,
And mused, His life would grow, the germ uncrushed;
   He should to antenatal night retrace,   70
And hide his elements in that large womb
Beyond the reach of man-evolving Doom.

And even thus, what weary way were planned,
   To seek oblivion through the far-off gate
Of birth, when that of death is close at hand!
   For this is law, if law there be in Fate:
What never has been, yet may have its when;
The thing which has been, never is again.

(Wr. from 1870; pub. 1874)

C. S. CALVERLEY

1831–1884

Peace: A Study

360

HE stood, a worn-out City clerk—
   Who'd toiled, and seen no holiday,
For forty years from dawn to dark—
   Alone beside Caermarthen Bay.

He felt the salt spray on his lips;
   Heard children's voices on the sands;
Up the sun's path he saw the ships
   Sail on and on to other lands;

And laughed aloud. Each sight and sound
   To him was joy too deep for tears;   10
He sat him on the beach, and bound
   A blue bandana round his ears:

And thought how, posted near his door,
   His own green door on Camden Hill,
Two bands at least, most likely more,
   Were mingling at their own sweet will

Verdi with Vance. And at the thought
He laughed again, and softly drew
That Morning Herald that he'd bought
    Forth from his breast, and read it through.   20

                 (1866)

361   *Changed*

    I KNOW not why my soul is racked:
      Why I ne'er smile as was my wont:
    I only know that, as a fact,
        I don't.
    I used to roam o'er glen and glade
      Buoyant and blithe as other folk:
    And not unfrequently I made
        A joke.

    A minstrel's fire within me burned.
      I'd sing, as one whose heart must break,   10
    Lay upon lay: I nearly learned
        To shake.
    All day I sang; of love, of fame,
      Of fights our fathers fought of yore,
    Until the thing almost became
        A bore.

    I cannot sing the old songs now!
      It is not that I deem them low;
    'Tis that I can't remember how
        They go.   20
    I could not range the hills till high
      Above me stood the summer moon:
    And as to dancing, I could fly
        As soon.

    The sports, to which with boyish glee
      I sprang erewhile, attract no more;
    Although I am but sixty-three
        Or four.
    Nay, worse than that, I've seemed of late
      To shrink from happy boyhood—boys   30
    Have grown so noisy, and I hate
        A noise.

They fright me, when the beech is green,
    By swarming up its stem for eggs:
They drive their horrid hoops between
      My legs:—
It's idle to repine, I know;
    I'll tell you what I'll do instead:
I'll drink my arrowroot, and go
      To bed.   40

(1872)

362   *Contentment*

After the Manner of Horace

FRIEND, there be they on whom mishap
    Or never or so rarely comes,
That, when they think thereof, they snap
      Derisive thumbs:

And there be they who lightly lose
    Their all, yet feel no aching void;
Should aught annoy them, they refuse
      To be annoyed:

And fain would I be e'en as these!
    Life is with such all beer and skittles;   10
They are not difficult to please
      About their victuals:

The trout, the grouse, the early pea,
    By such, if there, are freely taken;
If not, they munch with equal glee
      Their bit of bacon:

And when they wax a little gay
    And chaff the public after luncheon,
If they're confronted with a stray
      Policeman's truncheon,   20

They gaze thereat with outstretched necks,
    And laughter which no threats can smother,
And tell the horror-stricken X
      That he's another.

459

In snowtime if they cross a spot
  Where unsuspected boys have slid,
They fall not down—though they would not
    Mind if they did:

When the spring rosebud which they wear
  Breaks short and tumbles from its stem,   30
No thought of being angry e'er
    Dawns upon them;

Though 'twas Jemima's hand that placed,
  (As well you ween) at evening's hour,
In the loved button-hole that chaste
    And cherished flower.

And when they travel, if they find
  That they have left their pocket-compass
Or Murray or thick boots behind,
    They raise no rumpus,   40

But plod serenely on without:
  Knowing it's better to endure
The evil which beyond all doubt
    You cannot cure.

When for that early train they're late,
  They do not make their woes the text
Of sermons in the Times, but wait
    On for the next;

And jump inside, and only grin
  Should it appear that that dry wag,   50
The guard, omitted to put in
    Their carpet-bag.

(1872)

363   *'Forever'*

FOREVER; 'tis a single word!
  Our rude forefathers deemed it two:
Can you imagine so absurd
    A view?

Forever! What abysms of woe
    The word reveals, what frenzy, what
Despair! For ever (printed so)
        Did not.

It looks, ah me! how trite and tame!
    It fails to sadden or appal
Or solace—it is not the same
        At all.

O thou to whom it first occurred
    To solder the disjoined, and dower
Thy native language with a word
        Of power:

We bless thee! Whether far or near
    Thy dwelling, whether dark or fair
Thy kingly brow, is neither here
        Nor there.

But in men's hearts shall be thy throne,
    While the great pulse of England beats.
Thou coiner of a word unknown
        To Keats!

And nevermore must printer do
    As men did long ago; but run
'For' into 'ever,' bidding two
        Be one.

Forever! passion-fraught, it throws
    O'er the dim page a gloom, a glamour:
It's sweet, it's strange; and I suppose
        It's grammar.

Forever! 'Tis a single word!
    And yet our fathers deemed it two:
Nor am I confident they erred;
        Are you?

                                            (1872)

461

THOMAS HARDY

1840–1928

364

Her Dilemma

(*In ——— church*)

THE two were silent in a sunless church,
Whose mildewed walls, uneven paving-stones,
And wasted carvings passed antique research;
And nothing broke the clock's dull monotones.

Leaning against a wormy poppy-head,
So wan and worn that he could scarcely stand,
—For he was soon to die,—he softly said,
'Tell me you love me!'—holding long her hand.

She would have given a world to breathe 'yes' truly,
So much his life seemed hanging on her mind,   10
And hence she lied, her heart persuaded throughly
'Twas worth her soul to be a moment kind.

But the sad need thereof, his nearing death,
So mocked humanity that she shamed to prize
A world conditioned thus, or care for breath
Where Nature such dilemmas could devise.

(Wr. 1866; pub. 1898)

365

Neutral Tones

WE stood by a pond that winter day,
And the sun was white, as though chidden of God,
And a few leaves lay on the starving sod;
    —They had fallen from an ash, and were gray.

Your eyes on me were as eyes that rove
Over tedious riddles of years ago;
And some words played between us to and fro
    On which lost the more by our love.

The smile on your mouth was the deadest thing
Alive enough to have strength to die;   10
And a grin of bitterness swept thereby
    Like an ominous bird a-wing . . .

Since then, keen lessons that love deceives,
    And wrings with wrong, have shaped to me
Your face, and the God-curst sun, and a tree,
    And a pond edged with grayish leaves.

(Wr. 1867; pub. 1898)

366   *Thoughts of Phena*

At News of Her Death

NOT a line of her writing have I,
    Not a thread of her hair,
No mark of her late time as dame in her dwelling, whereby
    I may picture her there;
    And in vain do I urge my unsight
    To conceive my lost prize
At her close, whom I knew when her dreams were upbrimming
    with light,
    And with laughter her eyes.

What scenes spread around her last days,
    Sad, shining, or dim?   10
Did her gifts and compassions enray and enarch her sweet ways
    With an aureate nimb?
    Or did life-light decline from her years,
    And mischances control
Her full day-star; unease, or regret, or forebodings, or fears
    Disennoble her soul?

Thus I do but the phantom retain
    Of the maiden of yore
As my relic; yet haply the best of her—fined in my brain
    It may be the more   20
    That no line of her writing have I,
    Nor a thread of her hair,
No mark of her late time as dame in her dwelling, whereby
    I may picture her there.

(Wr. 1890; pub. 1898)

Friends Beyond

WILLIAM DEWY, Tranter Reuben, Farmer Ledlow late at
 plough,
  Robert's kin, and John's, and Ned's,
And the Squire, and Lady Susan, lie in Mellstock churchyard
 now!

'Gone,' I call them, gone for good, that group of local hearts and
 heads;
  Yet at mothy curfew-tide,
And at midnight when the noon-heat breathes it back from walls
 and leads,

They've a way of whispering to me—fellow-wight who yet abide—
  In the muted, measured note
Of a ripple under archways, or a lone cave's stillicide:

'We have triumphed: this achievement turns the bane to antidote, 10
  Unsuccesses to success,
Many thought-worn eves and morrows to a morrow free of
 thought.

'No more need we corn and clothing, feel of old terrestrial stress;
  Chill detraction stirs no sigh;
Fear of death has even bygone us: death gave all that we possess.'

W. D.—'Ye mid burn the old bass-viol that I set such value by.'
Squire.—'You may hold the manse in fee,
  You may wed my spouse, may let my children's memory of me
 die.'

Lady S.—'You may have my rich brocades, my laces; take each
 household key;
  Ransack coffer, desk, bureau;   20
Quiz the few poor treasures hid there, con the letters kept by me.'

Far.—'Ye mid zell my favourite heifer, ye mid let the charlock grow,
  Foul the grinterns, give up thrift.'
Far. Wife.—'If ye break my best blue china, children, I shan't care or
 ho.'

All.—'We've no wish to hear the tidings, how the people's fortunes
 shift;
  What your daily doings are;
Who are wedded, born, divided; if your lives beat slow or swift.

'Curious not the least are we if our intents you make or mar,
    If you quire to our old tune,
If the City stage still passes, if the weirs still roar afar.'   30

—Thus, with very gods' composure, freed those crosses late and
    soon
    Which, in life, the Trine allow
(Why, none witteth), and ignoring all that haps beneath the moon,

William Dewy, Tranter Reuben, Farmer Ledlow late at plough,
    Robert's kin, and John's, and Ned's,
And the Squire, and Lady Susan, murmur mildly to me now.

(1898)

368   *At an Inn*

WHEN we as strangers sought
    Their catering care,
Veiled smiles bespoke their thought
    Of what we were.
They warmed as they opined
    Us more than friends—
That we had all resigned
    For love's dear ends.

And that swift sympathy
    With living love   10
Which quicks the world—maybe
    The spheres above,
Made them our ministers,
    Moved them to say,
'Ah, God, that bliss like theirs
    Would flush our day!'

And we were left alone
    As Love's own pair;
Yet never the love-light shone
    Between us there!   20
But that which chilled the breath
    Of afternoon,
And palsied unto death
    The pane-fly's tune.

The kiss their zeal foretold,
　　And now deemed come,
Came not: within his hold
　　Love lingered numb.
Why cast he on our port
　　A bloom not ours?　　　　　　　　　　　30
Why shaped us for his sport
　　In after-hours?

As we seemed we were not
　　That day afar,
And now we seem not what
　　We aching are.
O severing sea and land,
　　O laws of men,
Ere death, once let us stand
　　As we stood then!　　　　　　　　　　　40

　　　　　　　(1898)

369　　　　　　　　*'I Look into My Glass'*

I LOOK into my glass,
And view my wasting skin,
And say, 'Would God it came to pass
My heart had shrunk as thin!'

For then, I, undistrest
By hearts grown cold to me,
Could lonely wait my endless rest
With equanimity.

But Time, to make me grieve,
Part steals, lets part abide;　　　　　　　　　10
And shakes this fragile frame at eve
With throbbings of noontide.

　　　　　　　(1898)

THOMAS HARDY

370   *Drummer Hodge*

I

THEY throw in Drummer Hodge, to rest
    Uncoffined—just as found:
His landmark is a kopje-crest
    That breaks the veldt around;
And foreign constellations west
    Each night above his mound.

II

Young Hodge the Drummer never knew—
    Fresh from his Wessex home—
The meaning of the broad Karoo,
    The Bush, the dusty loam,   10
And why uprose to nightly view
    Strange stars amid the gloam.

III

Yet portion of that unknown plain
    Will Hodge for ever be;
His homely Northern breast and brain
    Grow to some Southern tree,
And strange-eyed constellations reign
    His stars eternally.

(Wr. and pub. 1899)

371   *A Wife in London*

(*December, 1899*)

I

SHE sits in the tawny vapour
    That the Thames-side lanes have uprolled,
    Behind whose webby fold on fold
Like a waning taper
    The street-lamp glimmers cold.

A messenger's knock cracks smartly,
    Flashed news is in her hand
    Of meaning it dazes to understand
Though shaped so shortly:
    He—has fallen—in the far South Land. . . .   10

467

II

'Tis the morrow; the fog hangs thicker,
    The postman nears and goes:
    A letter is brought whose lines disclose
By the firelight flicker
    His hand, whom the worm now knows:

Fresh—firm—penned in highest feather—
    Page-full of his hoped return,
    And of home-planned jaunts by brake and burn
In the summer weather,
    And of new love that they would learn.   20

                      (1901)

372   *An August Midnight*

I

A SHADED lamp and a waving blind,
And the beat of a clock from a distant floor:
On this scene enter—winged, horned, and spined—
A longlegs, a moth, and a dumbledore;
While 'mid my page there idly stands
A sleepy fly, that rubs its hands . . .

II

Thus meet we five, in this still place,
At this point of time, at this point in space.
—My guests besmear my new-penned line,
Or bang at the lamp and fall supine.   10
'God's humblest, they!' I muse. Yet why?
They know Earth-secrets that know not I.

                (Wr. 1899; pub. 1901)

373   *The Darkling Thrush*

I LEANT upon a coppice gate
    When Frost was spectre-gray,
And Winter's dregs made desolate
    The weakening eye of day.
The tangled bine-stems scored the sky
    Like strings of broken lyres,
And all mankind that haunted nigh
    Had sought their household fires.

The land's sharp features seemed to be
    The Century's corpse outleant,   10
His crypt the cloudy canopy,
    The wind his death-lament.
The ancient pulse of germ and birth
    Was shrunken hard and dry,
And every spirit upon earth
    Seemed fervourless as I.

At once a voice arose among
    The bleak twigs overhead
In a full-hearted evensong
    Of joy illimited;   20
An aged thrush, frail, gaunt, and small,
    In blast-beruffled plume,
Had chosen thus to fling his soul
    Upon the growing gloom.

So little cause for carolings
    Of such ecstatic sound
Was written on terrestial things
    Afar or nigh around,
That I could think there trembled through
    His happy good-night air   30
Some blessed Hope, whereof he knew
    And I was unaware.

          (Wr. and pub. 1900)

374   *Wives in the Sere*

I

NEVER a careworn wife but shows,
    If a joy suffuse her,
Something beautiful to those
    Patient to peruse her,
Some one charm the world unknows
    Precious to a muser,
Haply what, ere years were foes,
    Moved her mate to choose her.

II

But, be it a hint of rose
    That an instant hues her,
Or some early light or pose   10
    Wherewith thought renews her—

Seen by him at full, ere woes
    Practised to abuse her—
Sparely comes it, swiftly goes,
    Time again subdues her.

(1901)

375   *The Subalterns*

I

'POOR wanderer,' said the leaden sky,
    'I fain would lighten thee,
But there are laws in force on high
    Which say it must not be.'

II

—'I would not freeze thee, shorn one,' cried
    The North, 'knew I but how
To warm my breath, to slack my stride;
    But I am ruled as thou.'

III

—'To-morrow I attack thee, wight,'
    Said Sickness. 'Yet I swear   10
I bear thy little ark no spite,
    But am bid enter there.'

IV

—'Come hither, Son,' I heard Death say;
    'I did not will a grave
Should end thy pilgrimage to-day,
    But I, too, am a slave!'

V

We smiled upon each other then,
    And life to me had less
Of that fell look it wore ere when
    They owned their passiveness.   20

(1901)

376   *Long Plighted*

        Is it worth while, dear, now,
To call for bells, and sally forth arrayed
For marriage-rites—discussed, decried, delayed
        So many years?

        Is it worth while, dear, now,
To stir desire for old fond purposings,
By feints that Time still serves for dallyings,
        Though quittance nears?

        Is it worth while, dear, when
The day being so far spent, so low the sun,   10
The undone thing will soon be as the done,
        And smiles as tears?

        Is it worth while, dear, when
Our cheeks are worn, our early brown is gray;
When, meet or part we, none says yea or nay,
        Or heeds, or cares?

        Is it worth while, dear, since
We still can climb old Yell'ham's wooded mounds
Together, as each season steals its rounds
        And disappears?   20

        Is it worth while, dear, since
As mates in Mellstock churchyard we can lie,
Till the last crash of all things low and high
        Shall end the spheres?

                            (1901)

377   *A Commonplace Day*

        THE day is turning ghost,
And scuttles from the kalendar in fits and furtively,
        To join the anonymous host
Of those that throng oblivion; ceding his place, maybe,
        To one of like degree.

        I part the fire-gnawed logs,
Rake forth the embers, spoil the busy flames, and lay the ends
        Upon the shining dogs;
Further and further from the nooks the twilight's stride extends,
        And beamless black impends.   10

Nothing of tiniest worth
Have I wrought, pondered, planned; no one thing asking blame or
    praise,
        Since the pale corpse-like birth
Of this diurnal unit, bearing blanks in all its rays—
        Dullest of dull-hued Days!

        Wanly upon the panes
The rain slides as have slid since morn my colourless thoughts; and yet
        Here, while Day's presence wanes,
And over him the sepulchre-lid is slowly lowered and set,
        He wakens my regret.   20

        Regret—though nothing dear
That I wot of, was toward in the wide world at his prime,
        Or bloomed elsewhere than here,
To die with his decease, and leave a memory sweet, sublime,
        Or mark him out in Time. . . .

        —Yet, maybe, in some soul,
In some spot undiscerned on sea or land, some impulse rose,
        Or some intent upstole
Of that enkindling ardency from whose maturer glows
        The world's amendment flows;   30

        But which, benumbed at birth
By momentary chance or wile, has missed its hope to be
        Embodied on the earth;
And undervoicings of this loss to man's futurity
        May wake regret in me.

                                                        (1901)

378   *To Lizbie Browne*

                            I

                DEAR Lizbie Browne,
                Where are you now?
                In sun, in rain?—
                Or is your brow
                Past joy, past pain,
                Dear Lizbie Browne?

II

Sweet Lizbie Browne,
How you could smile,
How you could sing!—
How archly wile   10
In glance-giving,
Sweet Lizbie Browne!

III

And, Lizbie Browne,
Who else had hair
Bay-red as yours,
Or flesh so fair
Bred out of doors,
Sweet Lizbie Browne?

IV

When, Lizbie Browne,
You had just begun   20
To be endeared
By stealth to one,
You disappeared,
My Lizbie Browne!

V

Ay, Lizbie Browne,
So swift your life,
And mine so slow,
You were a wife
Ere I could show
Love, Lizbie Browne.   30

VI

Still, Lizbie Browne,
You won, they said,
The best of men
When you were wed. . . .
Where went you then,
O Lizbie Browne?

VII

Dear Lizbie Browne,
I should have thought,
'Girls ripen fast,'
And coaxed and caught   40
You ere you passed,
Dear Lizbie Browne!

VIII

But, Lizbie Browne,
I let you slip;
Shaped not a sign;
Touched never your lip
With lip of mine,
Lost Lizbie Browne!

IX

So, Lizbie Browne,
When on a day   50
Men speak of me
As not, you'll say,
'And who was he?'—
Yes, Lizbie Browne!

(1901)

379   *A Broken Appointment*

YOU did not come,
And marching Time drew on, and wore me numb.—
Yet less for loss of your dear presence there
Than that I thus found lacking in your make
That high compassion which can overbear
Reluctance for pure lovingkindness' sake
Grieved I, when, as the hope-hour stroked its sum,
        You did not come.

You love not me,
And love alone can lend you loyalty;   10
—I know and knew it. But, unto the store
Of human deeds divine in all but name,
Was it not worth a little hour or more
To add yet this: Once you, a woman, came
To soothe a time-torn man; even though it be
        You love not me?

(1901)

474

380 ## *The Self-Unseeing*

HERE is the ancient floor,
Footworn and hollowed and thin,
Here was the former door
Where the dead feet walked in.

She sat here in her chair,
Smiling into the fire;
He who played stood there,
Bowing it higher and higher.

Childlike, I danced in a dream;
Blessings emblazoned that day;　　　　　　　　　　10
Everything glowed with a gleam;
Yet we were looking away!

(1901)

DORA GREENWELL
1821–1882

381 ### *A Scherzo*
(A Shy Person's Wishes)

WITH the wasp at the innermost heart of a peach,
On a sunny wall out of tip-toe reach,
With the trout in the darkest summer pool,
With the fern-seed clinging behind its cool
Smooth frond, in the chink of an aged tree,
In the woodbine's horn with the drunken bee,
With the mouse in its nest in a furrow old,
With the chrysalis wrapt in its gauzy fold;
With things that are hidden, and safe, and bold,
With things that are timid, and shy, and free,　　　　10
Wishing to be;
With the nut in its shell, with the seed in its pod,
With the corn as it sprouts in the kindly clod,
Far down where the secret of beauty shows
In the bulb of the tulip, before it blows;
With things that are rooted, and firm, and deep,
Quiet to lie, and dreamless to sleep;

With things that are chainless, and tameless, and proud,
With the fire in the jagged thunder-cloud,
With the wind in its sleep, with the wind in its waking,   20
With the drops that go to the rainbow's making,
Wishing to be with the light leaves shaking,
Or stones on some desolate highway breaking;
Far up on the hills, where no foot surprises
The dew as it falls, or the dust as it rises;
To be couched with the beast in its torrid lair,
Or drifting on ice with the polar bear,
With the weaver at work at his quiet loom;
Anywhere, anywhere, out of this room!

(1867)

DIGBY MACKWORTH DOLBEN

1848–1867

382   *A Song*

THE world is young today:
  Forget the gods are old,
  Forget the years of gold
When all the months were May.

A little flower of Love
  Is ours, without a root,
  Without the end of fruit,
Yet—take the scent thereof.

There may be hope above,
  There may be rest beneath;   10
  We see them not, but Death
Is palpable—and Love.

(Wr. 1867; pub. 1880)

W. H. MALLOCK

1849–1923

383   *A Marriage Prospect*

(*From an Unfinished Drama*)

WHY should I heed their railings? What's a prude?
  A devil's scarecrow in the fields of good.
  Let them rail on. I think a wedding-day
  Looks best, as mountains do, some miles away,
Or squalid fishing-smacks far out to sea,
  Seen lily-sailed in sunshine and blue haze,
  Where the delicious lights are all men chase,
And no man ever reaches. And so I'm free
  Another six weeks—move in a rich half-light,
  A tenderest compromise of dark and bright,   10
A magic season, in short, when eyes that shine
And lips that whisper with soft words, combine
  The spice of wrong, the conscience-ease of right,
And deepest sighs come most luxuriously.
  Then too this twilight-time leads not to night
But sunrise—that at least will gladden me,
  The sunrise of my day of married life,
  Ere bride and bridegroom fade to man and wife:
And I meanwhile, a short time more, am free—
  Or half free; wherefore let me love my fill   20
Of half-loves, ere I consecrate my days,
  In sober, sombre truth, for good and ill,
To the one worship of a withering face.

                                        (Wr. 1868; pub. 1880)

384   *Christmas Thoughts, by a Modern Thinker*

(*After Mr Matthew Arnold*)

THE windows of the church are bright;
  'Tis Christmas Eve; a low wind breathes;
And girls with happy eyes to-night
  Are hanging up the Christmas wreaths;

And village voices by-and-by
  Will reach my windows through the trees,
With wild, sweet music: 'Praise on high
  To God: on earth, good-will and peace.'

Oh, happy girls, that hang the wreaths!
  Oh, village fiddlers, happy ye!   10
Christmas to you still truly breathes
  Good-will and peace; but not to me.

Yes, gladness is your simple rôle,
  Ye foolish girls, ye labouring poor;
But joy would ill beseem my soul—
  To sigh, my part is, and endure.

For once as Rousseau stood, I stand
  Apart, made picturesque by grief—
One of a small world-weary band,
  The orphans of a dead belief.   20

Through graveyards lone we love to stray,
  And sadly the sad tombs explore,
And contradict the texts which say
  That we shall rise once more.

Our faith is dead, of course; and grief
  Fills its room up; and Christmas pie
And turkey cannot bring relief
  To such as Obermann and I.

Ah, Obermann, and might I pass
  This English Christmas-tide with thee,   30
Far by those inland waves whose glass
  Brightens and breaks by Meillerie;

Or else amongst the sternest dells
  Alp shags with pine, we'd mix our sighs,
Mourn at the sound of Christmas bells,
  Sniff at the smell of Christmas pies.

But thou art dead; and long, dank grass
  And wet mould cool thy tired, hot brain;
Thou art lain down, and now, alas!
  Of course you won't get up again.   40

Yet, Obermann, 'tis better so;
    For if, sad slumberer, after all
You were to re-arise, you know
    'Twould make us feel so very small.

Best bear our grief this manlier way,
    And make our grief be balm to grief;
For if in faith sweet comfort lay,
    There lurks sweet pride in unbelief.

Wherefore, remembering this, once more
    Unto my childhood's church I'll go,   50
And bow my head at that low door
    I passed through standing, long ago.

I'll sit in the accustomed place,
    And make, while all the unlearnèd stare,
A mournful, atheistic face
    At their vain noise of unheard prayer.

Then, while they hymn the heavenly birth
    And angel voices from the skies,
My thoughts shall go where Weimar's earth
    For ever darkens Goethe's eyes;   60

Till sweet girls' glances from their books
    Shall steal towards me, and they sigh:
'How intellectual he looks,
    And yet how wistful! And his eye

Has that vain look of baffled prayer!'
    And then when church is o'er I'll run,
Comb misery into all my hair,
    And go and get my portrait done.

(1893)

GEORGE ELIOT
(MARIAN, formerly MARY ANN, EVANS)
1819–1880

from *Brother and Sister* (385–387)

385

VI

OUR brown canal was endless to my thought;
And on its banks I sat in dreamy peace,
Unknowing how the good I loved was wrought,
Untroubled by the fear that it would cease.

Slowly the barges floated into view
Rounding a grassy hill to me sublime
With some Unknown beyond it, whither flew
The parting cuckoo toward a fresh spring time.

The wide-arched bridge, the scented elder-flowers,
The wondrous watery rings that died too soon,   10
The echoes of the quarry, the still hours
With white robe sweeping-on the shadeless noon,

    Were but my growing self, are part of me,
    My present Past, my root of piety.

386

VII

THOSE long days measured by my little feet
Had chronicles which yield me many a text;
Where irony still finds an image meet
Of full-grown judgments in this world perplext.

One day my brother left me in high charge,
To mind the rod, while he went seeking bait,
And bade me, when I saw a nearing barge,
Snatch out the line, lest he should come too late.

Proud of the task, I watched with all my might
For one whole minute, till my eyes grew wide,   10
Till sky and earth took on a strange new light
And seemed a dream-world floating on some tide—

A fair pavilioned boat for me alone
Bearing me onward through the vast unknown.

VIII

BUT sudden came the barge's pitch-black prow,
Nearer and angrier came my brother's cry,
And all my soul was quivering fear, when lo!
Upon the imperilled line, suspended high,

A silver perch! My guilt that won the prey,
Now turned to merit, had a guerdon rich
Of hugs and praises, and made merry play,
Until my triumph reached its highest pitch

When all at home were told the wondrous feat,
And how the little sister had fished well.
In secret, though my fortune tasted sweet,
I wondered why this happiness befell.

'The little lass had luck,' the gardener said:
And so I learned, luck was with glory wed.

(Wr. 1869; pub. 1874)

GEORGE AUGUSTUS SIMCOX
1841–1905

Love's Votary

OTHERS have pleasantness and praise,
    And wealth; and hand and glove
They walk with worship all their days,
    But I have only Love.

And therefore if Love be a fire,
    Then he shall burn me up;
If Love be water out of mire,
    Then I will be the cup.

If Love come worn with wayfaring,
  My breast shall be his bed;   10
If he come faint and hungering,
  My heart shall be his bread.

If Love delight in vassalage,
  Then I will be his thrall,
Till, when I end my pilgrimage,
  Love give me all for all.

(1869)

T. E. BROWN

1830–1897

389   *The Well*

I AM a spring—
Why square me with a kerb?
Ah, why this measuring
Of marble limit? Why this accurate vault
Lest day assault,
Or any breath disturb?
And why this regulated flow
Of what 'tis good to feel, and what to know?
You have no right
To take me thus, and bind me to your use,   10
Screening me from the flight
Of all great wings that are beneath the heaven,
So that to me it is not given
To hold the image of the awful Zeus,
Nor any cloud or star
Emprints me from afar.
O cruel force,
That gives me not a chance
To fill my natural course;
With mathematic rod   20
Economising God;
Calling me to pre-ordered circumstance
Nor suffering me to dance
Over the pleasant gravel,
With music solacing my travel—

With music, and the baby buds that toss
In light, with roots and sippets of the moss!
A fount, a tank:
Yet through some sorry grate
A driblet faulters, till around the flank   30
Of burly cliffs it creeps; then, silver-shooting,
Threads all the patient fluting
Of quartz, and violet-dappled slate:
A puny thing, on whose attenuate ripples
No satyr stoops to see
His broken effigy,
No naiad leans the languor of her nipples.
One faith remains—
That through what ducts soe'er,
What metamorphic strains,   40
What chymic filt'rings, I shall pass
To where, O God, Thou lov'st to mass
Thy rains upon the crags, and dim the sphere.
So, when night's heart with keenest silence thrills,
Take me, and weep me on the desolate hills!

(Wr. 1870; pub. 1900)

390   HIGH overhead
                My little daughter
            Was going to bed:—
                Below
                In twenty fathoms of black water
                A cod went sulking slow—
            Perceived the light
            That sparkled on the height,
                Then swam
            Up to the filmy level,   10
                Brought's eye to bear
                With dull fixed stare,
                    Then—'Damn!'
            He said—and 'Devil!—
        I thought'—but what he thought who knows?
        One plunge, and off he goes
                East? North?
                Fares forth
        To Lundy? Cardiff? But of that keen probe
        That for an instant pierced the lobe   20

                Of his sad brain,
Tickling the phosphor-grit,
        How long will he retain
One bit?
        And then above
My little daughter kneels, and says her prayers.
        Quite right!
            My little love—
        Good night!
            Sweet pet!   30
        Put out the light!
            And so
            I go
        Downstairs—
And yet—and yet—
            That cod!
            O God!
            O God!

                        (Wr. 1877; pub. 1908)

391   *The Bristol Channel*

                        I

THE sulky old gray brute!
But when the sunset strokes him,
Or twilight shadows coax him,
He gets so silver-milky,
He turns so soft and silky,
He'd make a water-spaniel for King Knut.

                        II

This sea was Lazarus, all day
At Dives' gate he lay,
And lapped the crumbs.
Night comes;   10
The beggar dies—
Forthwith the Channel, coast to coast,
Is Abraham's bosom; and the beggar lies
A lovely ghost.

                        (Wr. 1878; pub. 1893)

392 *I Bended unto Me*

I BENDED unto me a bough of May,
That I might see and smell:
It bore it in a sort of way,
It bore it very well.
But, when I let it backward sway,
Then it were hard to tell
With what a toss, with what a swing,
The dainty thing
Resumed its proper level,
And sent me to the devil.   10
I know it did—you doubt it?
I turned, and saw them whispering about it.

(Wr. 1878; pub. 1900)

393 from *Roman Women*

XIII

O ENGLISHWOMAN on the Pincian,
I love you not, nor ever can—
Astounding woman on the Pincian!

I know your mechanism well-adjusted,
I see your mind and body have been trusted
To all the proper people:
I see you straight as is a steeple;
I see you are not old;
I see you are a rich man's daughter;
I see you know the use of gold,   10
But also know the use of soap-and-water;
And yet I love you not, nor ever can—
Distinguished woman on the Pincian!

You have no doubt of your preëminence,
Nor do I make pretence
To challenge it for my poor little slattern,
Whose costume dates from Saturn—
My wall-flower with the long, love-draggled fringes:
But then the controversy hinges
On higher forms; and you must bear   20
Comparisons more noble. Stare, yes, stare—
I love you not, nor ever can,
You peerless woman on the Pincian.

485

No, you'll not see her on the Pincian,
My Roman woman, wife of Roman man!
Elsewhere you may—
And she is bright as is the day;
And she is sweet, that honest workman's wife
Fulfilled with bounteous life:
Her body balanced like a spring   30
In equipoise of perfect natural grace;
Her soul unquestioning
Of ought but genial cares; her face,
Her frock, her attitude, her pace
The confluence of absolute harmonies—
And you, my Lady Margaret,
Pray what have you to set
'Gainst splendours such as these?
No, I don't love you, and I never can,
Pretentious woman on the Pincian!   40

But morals—beautiful serenity
Of social life, the sugar and the tea,
The flannels and the soup, the coals,
The patent recipés for saving souls,
And other things: the chill dead sneer
Conventional, the abject fear
Of form-transgressing freedom—I admit
That you have these; but love you not a whit
The more, nor ever can,
Alarming female on the Pincian!   50

Come out, O woman, from this blindness!
Rome, too, has women full of loving-kindness,
Has noble women, perfect in all good
That makes the glory of great womanhood—
But they are Women! I have seen them bent
On gracious errand; seen how goodness lent
The grave, ineffable charm
That guards from possibility of harm
A creature so divinely made,
So softly swayed   60
With native gesture free—
The melting-point of passionate purity.
Yes—soup and flannels too,
And tickets for them—just like you—
Tracts, books, and all the innumerable channels
Through which your bounty acts—
Well—not the tracts,

But certainly the flannels—
Her I must love, but you I never can,
Unlovely woman on the Pincian.   70

And yet—
Remarkable woman on the Pincian!—
We owe a sort of debt
To you, as having gone with us of old
To those bleak islands, cold
And desolate and grim,
Upon the Ocean's rim,
And shared their horrors with us—not that then
Our poor bewildered ken
Could catch the further issues, knowing only   80
That we were very lonely!
Ah well, you did us service in your station;
And how the progress of our civilisation
Has made you quite so terrible
It boots not ask; for still
You gave us stalwart scions,
Suckled the young sea-lions,
And smiled infrequent, glacial smiles
Upon the sulky isles—
For this and all His mercies—stay at home!   90
Here are the passion-flowers!
Here are the sunny hours!
O Pincian woman, do not come to Rome!

(Wr. from 1879; pub. 1895)

394   *A Sermon at Clevedon*

                        Good Friday

Go on! Go on!
Don't wait for me!
Isaac was Abraham's son—
Yes, certainly—
And as they clomb Moriah—
I know! I know!
A type of the Messiah—
Just so! just so!
Perfectly right; and then the ram
Caught in the—*listening?* Why of course I am!   10
*Wherefore, my brethren, that was counted—*yes—
To Abraham for righteousness—

487

Exactly, so I said—
At least—but go a-head!
Now mark
The conduct of the Patriarch—
'Behold the wood!'
Isaac exclaimed—By Jove, an Oxford hood!
'But where'—
What long straight hair!   20
'Where is the lamb?'
You mean—the ram:
No, no! I beg your pardon!
There's the Churchwarden,
In the Clerk's pew—
Stick tipped with blue—
Now Justification—
'By Faith?' I fancy; Aye, the old equation;
Go it, Justice! Go it, Mercy!
Go it, Douglas! Go it, Percy!   30
I back the winner,
And have a vague conception of the sinner—
Limbs nude,
Horatian attitude,
Nursing his foot in Sublapsarian mood—
More power
To you my friend! you're good for half-an-hour.
Dry bones! dry bones!
But in my ear the long-drawn west wind moans,
Sweet voices seem to murmur from the wave;   40
And I can sit, and look upon the stones
That cover Hallam's grave.

(1900)

395   *Dartmoor: Sunset at Chagford*

Is it ironical, a fool enigma,
This sunset show?
The purple stigma,
Black mountain cut upon a saffron glow—
Is it a mammoth joke,
A riddle put for me to guess,
Which having duly honoured, I may smoke,
And go to bed,
And snore,
Having a soothing consciousness   10

488

Of something red?
Or is it more?
Ah, is it, is it more?

A dole, perhaps?
The scraps
Tossed from the table of the revelling gods?—
What odds!
I taste them—Lazarus
Was nourished thus!
But, all the same, it surely is a cheat—   20
Is this the stuff they eat?
A cheat! a cheat!
Then let the garbage be—
Some pig-wash! let it vanish down the sink
Of night! 'tis not for me.
I will not drink
Their draff,
While, throned on high, they quaff
The fragrant sconce—
Has Heaven no cloaca for the nonce?   30

Say 'tis an anodyne—
It never shall be mine.
I want no opiates—
The best of all their cates
Were gross to balk the meanest sense;
I want to be co-equal with their fates;
I will not be put off with temporal pretence:
I want to be awake, and know, not stand
And stare at waving of a conjuror's hand.

But is it speech   40
Wherewith they strive to reach
Our poor inadequate souls?
The round earth rolls;
I cannot hear it hum—
The stars are dumb—
The voices of the world are in my ear
A sensuous murmur. Nothing speaks
But man, my fellow—him I hear,
And understand; but beasts and birds
And winds and waves are destitute of words.   50
What is the alphabet
The gods have set?

What babbling! what delusion!
And in these sunset tints
What gay confusion!
Man prints
His meaning, has a letter
Determinate. I know that it is better
Than all this cumbrous hieroglyph—
The *For*, the *If*   60
Are growth of man's analysis:
The gods in bliss
Scrabble a baby-jargon on the skies
For us to analyse!
Cumbrous? nay, idiotic—
A party-coloured symbolism,
The fragments of a shivered prism:
Man gives the swift demotic.

'Tis good to see
The economy   70
Of poor upstriving man!
Since time began,
He has been sifting
The elements; while God, on chaos drifting,
Sows broadcast all His stuff.
Lavish enough,
No doubt; but why this waste?
See! of these very sunset dyes
The virgin chaste
Takes one, and in a harlot's eyes   80
Another rots. They go by billion billions:
Each blade of grass
Ignores them as they pass;
The spiders in their foul pavilions,
Behold this vulgar gear,
And sneer;
Dull frogs
In bogs
Catch rosy gleams through rushes,
And know that night is near;   90
Wrong-headed thrushes
Blow bugles to it;
And a wrong-headed poet
Will strut, and strain the cogs
Of the machine, he blushes
To call his Muse, and maunder;
And, marvellous to relate!

These pseudo-messengers of state
Will wander
Where there is no intelligence to meet them,   100
Nor even a sensorium to greet them.
The very finest of them
Go where there's nought to love them
Or notice them: to cairns, to rocks
Where ravens nurse their young,
To mica-splints from granite-boulders wrung
By channels of the marsh, to stocks
Of old dead willows in a pool as dead.
Can anything be said
To these? The leech   110
Looks from its muddy lair,
And sees a silly something in the air—
Call you this *speech*?
O God, if it be speech,
Speak plainer,
If Thou would'st teach
That I shall be a gainer!
The age of picture-alphabets is gone:
We are not now so weak;
We are too old to con   120
The horn-book of our youth. Time lags—
O, rip this obsolete blazon into rags!
And speak! O, speak!

But, if I be a spectacle
In Thy great theatre, then do Thy will:
Arrange Thy instruments with circumspection;
Summon Thine angels to the vivisection!
But quick! O, quick!
For I am sick,
And very sad.   130
Thy pupils will be glad.
'See,' Thou exclaim'st, 'this ray!
How permanent upon the retina!
How odd that purple hue!
The pineal gland is blue.
I stick this probe
In the posterior lobe—
Behold the cerebellum
A smoky yellow, like old vellum!
Students will please observe   140
The structure of the optic nerve.

See! nothing could be finer—
That film of pink
Around the hippocampus minor.
Behold!
I touch it, and it turns bright gold.
Again!—as black as ink.
Another lancet—thanks!
That's Manx—
Yes, the delicate pale sea-green   150
Passing into ultra-marine—
A little blurred—in fact
This brain seems packed
With sunsets. Bring
That battery here; now put your
Negative pole beneath the suture—
That's just the thing.
Now then the other way—
I say! I say!
More chloroform!   160
(A little more will do no harm)
Now this is the most instructive of all
The phenomena, what in fact we may call
The most obvious justification
Of vivisection in general.
Observe (once! twice!)
That's very nice)—
Observe, I say, the incipient relation
Of a quasi-moral activity
To this physical agitation!   170
Of course, you see. . . .'
Yes, yes, O God,
I feel the prod
Of that dissecting knife.
Instructive, say the pupil angels, *very*:
And some take notes, and some take sandwiches and sherry;
And some are prying
Into the very substance of my brain—
I feel their fingers!
(My life! my life!)   180
Yes, yes! it lingers!
The sun, the sun—
Go on! go on!
Blue, yellow, red!
But please remember that I am not dead,
Nor even dying.

(1900)

GEORGE MacDONALD
1824–1905

396   *Winter Song*

THEY were parted then at last?
    Was it duty, or force, or fate?
Or did a worldly blast
    Blow-to the meeting-gate?

An old, short story is this!
    A glance, a trembling, a sigh,
A gaze in the eyes, a kiss—
    Why will it not go by!

                            (1871)

397   *Professor Noctutus*

NOBODY knows the world but me.
The rest go to bed; I sit up and see.
I'm a better observer than any of you all,
For I never look out till the twilight fall,
And never then without green glasses,
And that is how my wisdom passes.

I never think, for that is not fit:
I observe. I have seen the white moon sit
On her nest, the sea, like a fluffy owl,
Hatching the boats and the long-legged fowl!   10
When the oysters gape—you may make a note—
She drops a pearl into every throat.

I can see the wind: can you do that?
I see the dreams he has in his hat,
I see him shaking them out as he goes,
I see them rush in at man's snoring nose.
Ten thousand things you could not think,
I can write down plain with pen and ink!

You know that I know; therefore pull off your hat,
Whether round and tall, or square and flat: 20
You cannot do better than trust in me;
You may shut your eyes in fact—*I* see!
Lifelong I will lead you, and then, like the owl,
I will bury you nicely with my spade and showl.

(1871)

398   *The Shortest and Sweetest of Songs*

Come
Home.

(1893)

399   *No End of No-Story*

THERE is a river
whose waters run asleep
run run ever
singing in the shallows
dumb in the hollows
sleeping so deep
and all the swallows
that dip their feathers
in the hollows
or in the shallows   10
are the merriest swallows
and the nests they make
with the clay they cake
with the water they shake
from their wings that rake
the water out of the shallows
or out of the hollows
will hold together
in any weather
and the swallows   20
are the merriest fellows
and have the merriest children
and are built very narrow
like the head of an arrow
to cut the air
and go just where

494

the nicest water is flowing
and the nicest dust is blowing
and each so narrow
like the head of an arrow   30
is a wonderful barrow
to carry the mud he makes
for his children's sakes
from the wet water flowing
and the dry dust blowing
to build his nest
for her he loves best
and the wind cakes it
the sun bakes it
into a nest   40
for the rest
of her he loves best
and all their merry children
each little fellow
with a beak as yellow
as the buttercups growing
beside the flowing
of the singing river
always and ever
growing and blowing   50
as fast as the sheep
awake or asleep
crop them and crop
and cannot stop
their yellowness blowing
nor yet the growing
of the obstinate daisies
the little white praises
they grow and they blow
they spread out their crown   60
and they praise the sun
and when he goes down
their praising is done
they fold up their crown
and sleep every one
till over the plain
he is shining amain
and they're at it again
praising and praising
such low songs raising   70
that no one can hear them
but the sun so near them

and the sheep that bite them
but do not fright them
are the quietest sheep
awake or asleep
with the merriest bleat
and the little lambs
are the merriest lambs
forgetting to eat   80
for the frolic in their feet
and the lambs and their dams
are the whitest sheep
with the woolliest wool
for the swallow to pull
when he makes his nest
for her he loves best
and they shine like snow
in the grasses that grow
by the singing river   90
that sings for ever
and the sheep and the lambs
are merry for ever
because the river
sings and they drink it
and the lambs and their dams
would any one think it
are bright and white
because of their diet
which gladdens them quiet   100
for what they bite
is buttercups yellow
and daisies white
and grass as green
as the river can make it
with wind as mellow
to kiss it and shake it
as never was known
but here in the hollows
beside the river   110
where all the swallows
are the merriest fellows
and the nests they make
with the clay they cake
in the sunshine bake
till they are like bone
and as dry in the wind
as a marble stone

dried in the wind
the sweetest wind   120
that blows by the river
flowing for ever
and who shall find
whence comes the wind
that blows on the hollows
and over the shallows
where dip the swallows
and comes and goes
and the sweet life blows
into the river   130
that sings as it flows
and the sweet life blows
into the sheep
awake or asleep
with the woolliest wool
and the trailingest tails
and never fails
gentle and cool
to wave the wool
and to toss the grass   140
as the lambs and the sheep
over it pass
and tug and bite
with their teeth so white
and then with the sweep
of their trailing tails
smooth it again
and it grows amain
and amain it grows
and the wind that blows   150
tosses the swallows
over the hollows
and over the shallows
and blows the sweet life
and the joy so rife
into the swallows
that skim the shallows
and have the yellowest children
and the wind that blows
is the life of the river   160
that flows for ever
and washes the grasses
still as it passes
and feeds the daisies

the little white praises
and buttercups sunny
with butter and honey
that whiten the sheep
awake or asleep
that nibble and bite 170
and grow whiter than white
and merry and quiet
on such good diet
watered by the river
and tossed for ever
by the wind that tosses
the wool and the grasses
and the swallow that crosses
with all the swallows
over the shallows 180
dipping their wings
to gather the water
and bake the cake
for the wind to make
as hard as a bone
and as dry as a stone
and who shall find
whence comes the wind
that blows from behind
and ripples the river 190
that flows for ever
and still as it passes
waves the grasses
and cools the daisies
the white sun-praises
that feed the sheep
awake or asleep
and give them their wool
for the swallows to pull
a little away 200
to mix with the clay
that cakes to a nest
for those they love best
and all the yellow children
soon to go trying
their wings at the flying
over the hollows
and over the shallows
with all the swallows
that do not know 210

whence the wind doth blow
that comes from behind
a blowing wind

(1893)

FREDERICK LOCKER-LAMPSON
(formerly LOCKER)
1821–1895

400   *A Terrible Infant*

I RECOLLECT a nurse call'd Ann
   Who carried me about the grass,
And one fine day a fine young man
   Came up, and kiss'd the pretty lass.
She did not make the least objection!
   Thinks I, '*Aha!*
When I can talk I'll tell Mamma.'
—And that's my earliest recollection.

(1872)

EDWARD DOWDEN
1843–1913

401   *Burdens*

ARE sorrows hard to bear,—the ruin
   Of flowers, the rotting of red fruit,
A love's decease, a life's undoing,
   And summer slain, and song-birds mute,
And skies of snow and bitter air?
These things, you deem, are hard to bear.

But ah the burden, the delight
   Of dreadful joys! Noon opening wide,
Golden and great; the gulfs of night,
   Fair deaths, and rent veils cast aside,   10
Strong soul to strong soul rendered up,
And silence filling like a cup.

(Wr. 1872; pub. 1876)

ROBERT LOUIS STEVENSON

1850–1894

402
    IN Autumn when the woods are red
    And skies are grey and clear,
    The sportsmen seek the wild fowls' bed
    Or follow down the deer;
    And Cupid hunts by haugh and head,
    By riverside and mere,
    I walk, not seeing where I tread
    And keep my heart with fear,
    Sir, have an eye, on where you tread,
    And keep your heart with fear,   10
    For something lingers here;
    A touch of April not yet dead,
    In Autumn when the woods are red
    And skies are grey and clear.

(Wr. 1873–9?; pub. 1921)

403
    I SAW red evening through the rain,
    Lower above the steaming plain;
    I heard the hour strike small and still,
    From the black belfry on the hill.

    Thought is driven out of doors to-night
    By bitter memory of delight;
    The sharp constraint of finger tips,
    Or the shuddering touch of lips.

    I heard the hour strike small and still,
    From the black belfry on the hill.   10
    Behind me I could still look down
    On the outspread monstrous town.

    The sharp constraint of finger tips
    Or the shuddering touch of lips,
    And all old memories of delight
    Crowd upon my soul to-night.

    Behind me I could still look down
    On the outspread feverish town;
    But before me still and grey
    And lonely was the forward way.   20

(Wr. 1875; pub. 1921)

404 *Browning*

BROWNING makes the verses:
    Your servant the critique.
Browning wouldn't sing at all:
    I fancy I could speak.
Although the book was clever
    (To give the Deil his due)
I wasn't pleased with Browning
    Nor he with my review.

(Wr. 1875?; pub. 1915)

405 LAST night we had a thunderstorm in style.
The wild lightning streaked the airs,
As though my God fell down a pair of stairs.
The thunder boomed and bounded all the while;
All cried and sat by water-side and stile—
To mop our brow had been our chief of cares.
I lay in bed with a Voltairean smile,
The terror of good, simple guilty pairs,
And made this rondeau in ironic style,
Last night we had a thunderstorm in style.   10
Our God the Father fell down-stairs,
The stark blue lightning went its flight, the while,
The very rain you might have heard a mile—
The strenuous faithful buckled to their prayers.

(Wr. 1875-9?; pub. 1921)

406 *Requiem*

UNDER the wide and starry sky,
Dig the grave and let me lie.
Glad did I live and gladly die,
    And I laid me down with a will.

This be the verse you grave for me:
Here he lies where he longed to be;
Home is the sailor, home from sea,
    And the hunter home from the hill.

(Wr. 1880-4; pub. 1887)

407

Pirate Ditty

From Treasure Island

FIFTEEN men on the Dead Man's Chest—
  Yo-ho-ho, and a bottle of rum!
Drink and the devil had done for the rest—
  Yo-ho-ho, and a bottle of rum!

(Wr. and pub. 1881)

408

A Mile an' a Bittock

A MILE an' a bittock, a mile or twa,
Abüne the burn, ayont the law,
Davie an' Donal' an' Cherlie an' a',
  An' the müne was shinin' clearly!

Ane went hame wi' the ither, an' then
The ither went hame wi' the ither twa men,
An' baith wad return him the service again,
  An' the müne was shinin' clearly!

The clocks were chappin' in house an' ha',
Eleeven, twal an' ane an' twa;   10
An' the guidman's face was turnt to the wa',
  An' the müne was shinin' clearly!

A wind got up frae affa the sea,
It blew the stars as clear's could be,
It blew in the een of a' o' the three,
  An' the müne was shinin' clearly!

Noo, Davie was first to get sleep in his head,
'The best o' frien's maun twine,' he said;
'I'm weariet, an' here I'm awa' to my bed.'
  An' the müne was shinin' clearly!   20

Twa o' them walkin' an' crackin' their lane,
The mornin' licht cam gray an' plain,
An' the birds they yammert on stick an' stane,
  An' the müne was shinin' clearly!

O years ayont, O years awa',
My lads, ye'll mind whate'er befa'—
My lads, ye'll mind on the bield o' the law,
    When the müne was shinin' clearly.

(Wr. 1884; pub. 1887)

409   *Fragment*

THOU strainest through the mountain fern,
A most exiguously thin
    Burn.
For all thy foam, for all thy din,
Thee shall the pallid lake inurn,
With well-a-day for Mr Swin-
    Burne!
Take then this quarto in thy fin
And, O thou stoker huge and stern,
The whole affair, outside and in,   10
    Burn!
But save the true poetic kin,
The works of Mr Robert Burn!
And William Wordsworth upon Tin-
    Tern!

(Wr. 1884?; pub. 1916)

410   SO live, so love, so use that fragile hour,
         That when the dark hand of the shining power
         Shall one from other, wife or husband, take,
         The poor survivor may not weep and wake.

(Wr. c.1885; pub. 1916)

411   *To Mrs Will H. Low*

EVEN in the bluest noonday of July,
There could not run the smallest breath of wind
But all the quarter sounded like a wood;
And in the chequered silence and above
The hum of city cabs that sought the Bois,
Suburban ashes shivered into song.
A patter and a chatter and a chirp

And a long dying hiss—it was as though
Starched old brocaded dames through all the house
Had trailed a strident skirt, or the whole sky   10
Even in a wink had over-brimmed in rain.
Hark, in these shady parlours, how it talks
Of the near Autumn, how the smitten ash
Trembles and augurs floods! O not too long
In these inconstant latitudes delay,
O not too late from the unbeloved north
Trim your escape! For soon shall this low roof
Resound indeed with rain, soon shall your eyes
Search the foul garden, search the darkened rooms,
Nor find one jewel but the blazing log.   20

(Wr. 1886; pub. 1887)

412   *MY house*, I say. But hark to the sunny doves
           That make my roof the arena of their loves,
           That gyre about the gable all day long
           And fill the chimneys with their murmurous song:
           Our house, they say; and *mine*, the cat declares
           And spreads his golden fleece upon the chairs;
           And *mine* the dog, and rises stiff with wrath
           If any alien foot profane the path.
           So too the buck that trimmed my terraces,
           Our whilome gardener, called the garden his;   10
           Who now, deposed, surveys my plain abode
           And his late kingdom, only from the road.

(1887)

413   IT'S an owercome sooth for age an' youth
               And it brooks wi' nae denial,
           That the dearest friends are the auldest friends
               And the young are just on trial.

           There's a rival bauld wi' young an' auld
               And it's him that has bereft me;
           For the sürest friends are the auldest friends
               And the maist o' mines hae left me.

There are kind hearts still, for friends to fill
  And fools to take and break them;   10
But the nearest friends are the auldest friends
  And the grave's the place to seek them.

(1887)

414

FAIR Isle at Sea—thy lovely name
Soft in my ear like music came.
That sea I loved, and once or twice
I touched at isles of Paradise.

(Wr. 1888?; pub. 1916)

415

As with heaped bees at hiving time
The boughs are clotted, as (ere prime)
Heaven swarms with stars, or the city street
Pullulates with faring feet;
So swarmed my senses once; that now
Repose behind my tranquil brow,
Unsealed, asleep, quiescent, clear;
Now only the vast shapes I hear
Hear—and my hearing slowly fills—
Rivers and winds among the twisting hills,   10
And hearken—and my face is lit—
Life facing; death pursuing it.

(Wr. 1891–4?; pub. 1921)

416

THE morning drum-call on my eager ear
Thrills unforgotten yet; the morning dew
Lies yet undried along my field of noon.

But now I pause at whiles in what I do,
And count the bell, and tremble lest I hear
(My work untrimmed) the sunset gun too soon.

(1895)

417 I HAVE trod the upward and the downward slope;
I have endured and done in days before;
I have longed for all, and bid farewell to hope;
And I have lived and loved, and closed the door.

(1895)

WILLIAM ERNEST HENLEY
1849–1903

418 *Waiting*

A SQUARE, squat room (a cellar on promotion),
    Drab to the soul, drab to the very daylight;
    Plasters astray in unnatural-looking tinware;
    Scissors and lint and apothecary's jars.

Here, on a bench a skeleton would writhe from,
    Angry and sore, I wait to be admitted:
    Wait till my heart is lead upon my stomach,
    While at their ease two dressers do their chores.

One has a probe—it feels to me a crowbar.
    A small boy sniffs and shudders after bluestone.   10
    A poor old tramp explains his poor old ulcers.
    Life is (I think) a blunder and a shame.

(Wr. from 1873; pub. 1888)

419 *To W. R.*

MADAM LIFE'S a piece in bloom
    Death goes dogging everywhere:
She's the tenant of the room,
    He's the ruffian on the stair.

You shall see her as a friend,
    You shall bilk him once and twice;
But he'll trap you in the end,
    And he'll stick you for her price.

With his kneebones at your chest,
  And his knuckles in your throat,   10
You would reason—plead—protest!
  Clutching at her petticoat;

But she's heard it all before,
  Well she knows you've had your fun,
Gingerly she gains the door,
  And your little job is done.

(Wr. 1877; pub. 1898)

SYDNEY DOBELL

1824–1874

420   *Perhaps*

TEN heads and twenty hearts! so that this me,
Having more room and verge, and striking less
The cage that galls us into consciousness,
Might drown the rings and ripples of to be
In the smooth deep of being: plenary
Round hours; great days, as if two days should press
Together, and their wine-press'd night accresce
The next night to so dead a parody
Of death as cures such living: of these ordain
My years; of those large years grant me not seven,   10
Nor seventy, no, nor only seventy sevens!
And then, perhaps, I might stand well in even
This rain of things; down-rain, up-rain, side-rain;
This rain from Earth and Ocean, air and heaven,
And from the Heaven within the Heaven of Heavens.

(1875)

E. KEARY

fl. 1857–1882

421   *Old Age*

SUCH a wizened creature,
    Sitting alone;
    Every kind of ugliness thrown
Into each feature.

'I wasn't always so,'
    Said the wizened
    One; 'sweet motions unimprisoned
Were mine long ago.'

And again, 'I shall be—
    At least something   10
    Out of this outside me, shall wing
Itself fair and free.'

                                    (1874)

PHILIP BOURKE MARSTON

1850–1887

422   *After*

I

A LITTLE time for laughter,
    A little time to sing,
    A little time to kiss and cling,
And no more kissing after.

II

A little while for scheming
    Love's unperfected schemes;
    A little time for golden dreams,
Then no more any dreaming.

III

A little while 'twas given
  To me to have thy love;
  Now, like a ghost, alone I move
About a ruined heaven.

10

IV

A little time for speaking,
  Things sweet to say and hear;
  A time to seek, and find thee near,
Then no more any seeking.

V

A little time for saying
  Words the heart breaks to say;
  A short, sharp time wherein to pray,
Then no more need for praying;

20

VI

But long, long years to weep in,
  And comprehend the whole
  Great grief that desolates the soul,
And eternity to sleep in.

(1875)

LOUISA S. GUGGENBERGER
(formerly BEVINGTON)

1845–1895

423

Afternoon

PURPLE headland over yonder,
  Fleecy, sun-extinguished moon,
I am here alone, and ponder
  On the theme of Afternoon.

Past has made a groove for Present,
  And what fits it *is*: no more.
Waves before the wind are weighty;
  Strongest sea-beats shape the shore.

509

Just what is is just what can be,
   And the Possible is free;   10
'Tis by being, not by effort,
   That the firm cliff juts to sea.

With an uncontentious calmness
   Drifts the Fact before the 'Law';
So we name the ordered sequence
   We, remembering, foresaw.

And a law is mere procession
   Of the forcible and fit;
Calm of uncontested Being,
   And our thought that comes of it.   20

In the mellow shining daylight
   Lies the Afternoon at ease,
Little willing ripples answer
   To a drift of casual breeze.

Purple headland to the westward!
   Ebbing tide, and fleecy moon!
In the 'line of least resistance',
   Flows the life of Afternoon.

(1876)

424   *Twilight*

GREY the sky, and growing dimmer,
   And the twilight lulls the sea;
Half in vagueness, half in glimmer,
   Nature shrouds her mystery.

What have all the hours been spent for?
   Why the on and on of things?
Why eternity's procession
   Of the days and evenings?

Hours of sunshine, hours of gloaming,
   Wing their unexplaining flight,   10
With a measured punctuation
   Of unconsciousness, at night.

Just at sunset was translucence,
   When the west was all aflame;
So I asked the sea a question,
   And an answer nearly came.

Is there nothing but Occurrence?
   Though each detail seem an Act,
Is that whole we deem so pregnant
   But unemphasizèd Fact?   20

Or, when dusk is in the hollows
   Of the hill-side and the wave,
Are things just so much in earnest
   That they cannot but be grave?

Nay, the lesson of the Twilight
   Is as simple as 'tis deep;
Acquiescence, acquiescence,
   And the coming on of sleep.

         (1876)

425   *'Egoisme à Deux'*

WHEN the great universe hung nebulous
   Betwixt the unprevented and the need,
Was it foreseen that you and I should be?—
      Was it decreed?

While time leaned onward through eternities,
   Unrippled by a breath and undistraught,
Lay there at leisure Will that we should breathe?—
      Waited a Thought?

When the warm swirl of chaos-elements
   Fashioned the chance that woke to sentient strife,   10
Did there a Longing seek, and hasten on
      Our mutual life?

That flux of many accidents but now
   That brought you near and linked your hand in mine,—
That fused our souls in love's most final faith,—
      Was it divine?

         (1882)

426

Love and Language

LOVE that is alone with love
　　Makes solitudes of throngs;
Then why not songs of silences,—
　　Sweet silences of songs?

Parts need words: the perfect whole
　　Is silent as the dead;
When I offered you my soul
　　Heard you what I *said*?

(1882)

427

Am I to Lose You?

'AM I to lose you now?' The words were light;
　　You spoke them, hardly seeking a reply,
　　That day I bid you quietly 'Good-bye,'
And sought to hide my soul away from sight.
The question echoed, dear, through many a night,—
　　My question, not your own—most wistfully;
　　'Am I to lose him?'—asked my heart of me;
'Am I to lose him now, and lose him quite?'

And only you can tell me. Do you care
　　That sometimes we in quietness should stand　　　　10
　　As fellow-solitudes, hand firm in hand,
And thought with thought and hope with hope compare?
What is your answer? Mine must ever be,
　　'I greatly need your friendship: leave it me.'

(1882)

WILLIAM RENTON

fl. 1875–1905

428

The Foal

THE mouse-brown foal that fain had fed
From off the green his mother crops
So quietly in her own place,
Craning in vain and bending, stops,

Intent upon his match with space,
And rises beaten by half a head.
And last he sets himself to slide
His spidery-slender limbs aside,
If so be now to reach the mead.—
He must stride   10
Ere he can feed.

(1876)

429   *The Shadow of Himself*

AT evening the horse comes down unled
 With pace that is but his second best,
And with harness only about his head:
 He is half undrest,
And on his way to bed.
But he takes his share of the space and the light,
 His brown skin glisters warm and good,
And his shadow stretches as full a height
 As a horse's should;
For on the wall   10
 As he slouches down
Stalks a phantom, tall as he is tall
 And black as he is brown;
With the very gait and the very speed
 Of his Highness shown,
And I fear me a greed
 That matches his own;
For if his head should stoop to treat
With the wayside grasses—in a heat
 There stoops his friend's,   20
And their muzzles meet
 On the very tuft for which he contends.

(1876)

430   *Crescent Moon*

THE moon had risen an hour or more.
It was the younger moon, but shorn
Of those first pointing cusps she wore,
And bluff with blunted horn;
But poised upright
And golden bright,

Save where there hung a middle haze,
Soft as the golden air that lies
Upon the sunset's closing eyes
And plays   10
Between his glory-golden lids—
And none forbids.
And none forbade, as it did seem,
That this lorn haze should doat and dream
On such an eve of June
And cling about the middle moon,
That scarce was dimmer for such offending.
But none might stay its soft ascending,
Till each in turn the veilèd old
Was clear as dew,   20
And all the new
Was dusky gold;
And last, a wraith,
Exhaling like the breath
We breathed upon a golden jar,
Showed on the tip and went afar—
Upon the disc a moving spot
That would be, was, and now was not.

                                   (1876)

431   *After Nightfall*

AMPLE the air above the western peaks;
Within the peaks a silence uncompelled.
It is the hour of abnegation's self,
In clear obeisance of the mountain thrones,
And cloudless self-surrender of the skies:
The very retrospect of skiey calm,
And selfless self-approval of the hills.

                                   (1876)

432   *Moon and Candle-light*

BENEATH our eaves the moonbeams play,
  Where trumps of white convolvulus
Lean out askance, and have their say
  Half to the moon and half to us.

The foam-white tassel nestles still,
  Where the taperlight has laid,
In its corner by the sill,
  A black tassel for a shade.
It has laid the shadowy clasp
  Of the high-barred baby-chair   10
On the milkwhite casement hasp.
  The moon clasps and holds it there
With a darker, of her own
  Milkwhite standing casement bar:
Dusky hands, thus all alone,
  Clasped in each as lovers' are.
Through the sea of mellow space,
  Where the moon and candle-light,
Taking tender heart of grace,
  Mingle hands of holy white,   20
The moon looks between the bars
  On the bar-flecked baby-seat,
Thinks—*She!*—to wile away the scars.
  The taper smiles on her defeat.
Smiles, too, a steady shadow down
  Between the fore and hinder stays
Of the moon's dais: with a frown
  The table greets the carpet grays.
The moon turns to hide her smile . .
  Creep up the light two spokes of dust, 30
Like light-streaks in a dusty aisle,
  Beneath the chair—midway, are thrust
On the table shade in black.
  The taper shrugs and hums a tune,
Two black crutches stumble back
  On the wainscot to the moon.
. . . So the shadows make a raft
  Of the chamber gear to-night:
Play cross-purpose fore and aft
  By the moon and candle-light.   40

                              (1876)

433   *The Fork of the Road*

An utter moorland, high, and wide, and flat;
A beaten roadway, branching out in grave distaste;
And weather-beaten and defaced,
Pricking its ears along the solitary waste—
A signpost; pointing this way, pointing that.

                              (1876)

R. E. EGERTON WARBURTON
1804–1891

434   *Past and Present*

ON four-horse coach, whose luggage pierced the sky,
  Perch'd on back seat, like clerk on office-stool,
  While wintry winds my dangling heels kept cool,
  In Whitney white envelop'd and blue tie,
Unpillow'd slumber from my half-closed eye
  Scared by the shrill tin horn; when welcome Yule
  Brought holiday season, it was thus from school
  I homeward came some forty years gone by.
Thus two long days and one long night I rode,
  Stage after stage, till the last change of team   10
  Stopp'd, splash'd and panting, at my sire's abode.
How nowaday from school comes home my son?
  Through duct and tunnel by a puff of steam,
  Shot like a pellet from his own pop-gun.

(1877)

ALICE MEYNELL
1847–1922

435   *After a Parting*

FAREWELL has long been said; I have forgone thee;
  I never name thee even.
But how shall I learn virtues and yet shun thee?
  For thou art so near Heaven
That Heavenward meditations pause upon thee.

Thou dost beset the path to every shrine;
  My trembling thoughts discern
Thy goodness in the good for which I pine;
  And, if I turn from but one sin, I turn
Unto a smile of thine.   10

How shall I thrust thee apart
    Since all my growth tends to thee night and day—
To thee faith, hope, and art?
    Swift are the currents setting all one way;
They draw my life, my life, out of my heart.

(Wr. 1877; pub. 1890)

436   *Cradle-Song at Twilight*

THE child not yet is lulled to rest.
    Too young a nurse, the slender Night
So laxly holds him to her breast
    That throbs with flight.

He plays with her, and will not sleep.
    For other playfellows she sighs;
An unmaternal fondness keep
    Her alien eyes.

(1895)

437   *The Shepherdess*

SHE walks—the lady of my delight—
    A shepherdess of sheep.
Her flocks are thoughts. She keeps them white;
    She guards them from the steep;
She feeds them on the fragrant height,
    And folds them in for sleep.

She roams maternal hills and bright,
    Dark valleys safe and deep.
Into that tender breast at night
    The chastest stars may peep.   10
She walks—the lady of my delight—
    A shepherdess of sheep.

She holds her little thoughts in sight,
    Though gay they run and leap.
She is so circumspect and right;
    She has her soul to keep.
She walks—the lady of my delight—
    A shepherdess of sheep.

(1895)

438   *'I Am the Way'*

THOU art the Way.
Hadst Thou been nothing but the goal,
   I cannot say
If Thou hadst ever met my soul.

   I cannot see—
I, child of process—if there lies
   An end for me,
Full of repose, full of replies.

   I'll not reproach
The road that winds, my feet that err.   10
   Access, Approach
Art Thou, Time, Way, and Wayfarer.

       (1896)

439   *The Lady Poverty*

THE Lady Poverty was fair:
But she has lost her looks of late,
With change of times and change of air.
Ah slattern! she neglects her hair,
Her gown, her shoes; she keeps no state
As once when her pure feet were bare.

Or—almost worse, if worse can be—
She scolds in parlours, dusts and trims,
Watches and counts. O is this she
Whom Francis met, whose step was free,   10
Who with Obedience carolled hymns,
In Umbria walked with Chastity?

Where is her ladyhood? Not here,
Not among modern kinds of men;
But in the stony fields, where clear
Through the thin trees the skies appear,
In delicate spare soil and fen,
And slender landscape and austere.

       (1896)

HENRY BELLYSE BAILDON
1849–1907

440   *A Moth*

A CLUMSY clot of shadow in the fold
  Of the white blind,—a moth asleep or dead,
And hooked therein with still, tenacious hold,
  And dusky vans outspread.

Laid on my hand a wonder of dull dyes,
  A sombre miracle of mingled grain,
Grey etched on grey, faint as faint memories,
  Dim stain invading stain.

Each wing-edge scalloped clear as any shell's,
  With rippled repetitions ebbing in   10
Rhyme within rhyme, as when cathedral bells
  Remit their joyous din.

Complete is it of broken laceries,
  A pencilled maze of blending greys,
Mosaic of symmetric traceries,
  Assorted in sweet ways.

Black velvet grainings upon pearly ash,
  An elf-wrought broidery of hues they stole
From the black moss-blot, and the lichen-splash,
  From birch or beechen bole.   20

Strange-headed thing, in ruminative rest
  Stirring its flexile antlers dreamily,
With great ghoul-eyes and sable-feathered breast,
  In sleep's security.

'There rest thee, and sleep off thy drowsy fit,
  Till night shall triumph in the dusky glades,
And mass her conquering glooms, then rise and flit
  A shadow through the shades!'

                                      (1877)

GEORGE R. SIMS

1847–1922

A Garden Song

I SCORN the doubts and cares that hurt
　　The world and all its mockeries,
My only care is now to squirt
　　The ferns among my rockeries.

In early youth and later life
　　I've seen an up and seen a down,
And now I have a loving wife
　　To help me peg verbena down.

Of joys that come to womankind
　　The loom of fate doth weave her few,　　　　10
But here are summer joys entwined
　　And bound with golden feverfew,

I've learnt the lessons one and all
　　With which the world its sermon stocks,
Now, heedless of a rise or fall,
　　I've Brompton and I've German stocks.

In peace and quiet pass our days,
　　With nought to vex our craniums,
Our middle beds are all ablaze
　　With red and white geraniums.　　　　20

And like a boy I laugh when she,
　　In Varden hat and Varden hose,
Comes slyly up the lawn at me
　　To squirt me with the garden hose.

Let him who'd have the peace he needs
　　Give all his worldly mumming up,
Then dig a garden, plant the seeds,
　　And watch the product coming up.

(1879)

442

Undertones

By a lunatic laureate

THERE'S a feeling that comes with the daze of joy
    And goes with the knights of grief—
That stands on the top of a baby buoy,
    And floats with an anchor chief.
It rides on the back of a noted Bill,
    And fights where your collars fray;
It whispers in accents loud and shrill—
    To-morrow succeeds to-day.

We con the lessons of life betimes
    In the leaves of an open glade;   10
The frost on the window writes its rimes,
    We live and we learn be trayed.
The coals we heat and the apes we were
    Are gone where the Russians sleigh.
The moral is blown on the well-known air—
    To-morrow succeeds to-day.

In the bustle and jam of the daily strife,
    What matters if men preserve
The bosom of hope from the butcher's knife,
    And its train from the pointsman curve?   20
Remember the fate of the ready maid
    Who went where the preachers prey;
Take matter for thought from a new decayed—
    To-morrow succeeds to-day.

(1880)

JEAN INGELOW

1820–1897

443

The Long White Seam

As I came round the harbour buoy,
    The lights began to gleam,
No wave the land-locked water stirred,
    The crags were white as cream;

And I marked my love by candle-light
  Sewing her long white seam.
    It's aye sewing ashore, my dear,
      Watch and steer at sea,
    It's reef and furl, and haul the line,
      Set sail and think of thee.   10

I climbed to reach her cottage door;
  O sweetly my love sings!
Like a shaft of light her voice breaks forth,
  My soul to meet it springs
As the shining water leaped of old,
  When stirred by angel wings.
    Aye longing to list anew,
      Awake and in my dream,
    But never a song she sang like this,
      Sewing her long white seam.   20

Fair fall the lights, the harbour lights,
  That brought me in to thee,
And peace drop down on that low roof
  For the sight that I did see,
And the voice, my dear, that rang so clear
  All for the love of me.
    For O, for O, with brows bent low
      By the candle's flickering gleam,
    Her wedding gown it was she wrought,
      Sewing the long white seam.   30

                              (1880)

JOHN ADDINGTON SYMONDS
1840–1893

The Camera Obscura

INSIDE the skull the wakeful brain,
Attuned at birth to joy and pain,
Dwells for a lifetime; even as one
Who in a closed tower sees the sun
Cast faint-hued shadows, dim or clear,
Upon the darkened disc: now near,

Now far, they flit; while he, within,
Surveys the world he may not win:
Whate'er he sees, he notes; for nought
Escapes the net of living thought;   10
And what he notes, he tells again
To last and build the brains of men.
Shades are we; and of shades we weave
A trifling pleasant make-believe;
Then pass into the shadowy night,
Where formless shades blindfold the light.

(1880)

ROBERT BRIDGES

1844–1930

445   *London Snow*

WHEN men were all asleep the snow came flying,
In large white flakes falling on the city brown,
Stealthily and perpetually settling and loosely lying,
   Hushing the latest traffic of the drowsy town;
Deadening, muffling, stifling its murmurs failing;
Lazily and incessantly floating down and down:
   Silently sifting and veiling road, roof and railing;
Hiding difference, making unevenness even,
Into angles and crevices softly drifting and sailing.
   All night it fell, and when full inches seven   10
It lay in the depth of its uncompacted lightness,
The clouds blew off from a high and frosty heaven;
   And all woke earlier for the unaccustomed brightness
Of the winter dawning, the strange unheavenly glare:
The eye marvelled—marvelled at the dazzling whiteness;
   The ear hearkened to the stillness of the solemn air;
No sound of wheel rumbling nor of foot falling,
And the busy morning cries came thin and spare.
   Then boys I heard, as they went to school, calling,
They gathered up the crystal manna to freeze   20
Their tongues with tasting, their hands with snowballing;
   Or rioted in a drift, plunging up to the knees;
Or peering up from under the white-mossed wonder,
'O look at the trees!' they cried, 'O look at the trees!'
   With lessened load a few carts creak and blunder,

Following along the white deserted way,
A country company long dispersed asunder:
  When now already the sun, in pale display
Standing by Paul's high dome, spread forth below
His sparkling beams, and awoke the stir of the day.   30
  For now doors open, and war is waged with the snow;
And trains of sombre men, past tale of number,
Tread long brown paths, as toward their toil they go:
  But even for them awhile no cares encumber
Their minds diverted; the daily word is unspoken,
The daily thoughts of labour and sorrow slumber
At the sight of the beauty that greets them, for the charm they have
    broken.

                              (1880)

446   *On a Dead Child*

PERFECT little body, without fault or stain on thee,
  With promise of strength and manhood full and fair!
    Though cold and stark and bare,
The bloom and the charm of life doth awhile remain on thee.

Thy mother's treasure wert thou;—alas! no longer
  To visit her heart with wondrous joy; to be
    Thy father's pride;—ah, he
Must gather his faith together, and his strength make stronger.

To me, as I move thee now in the last duty,
  Dost thou with a turn or gesture anon respond;   10
    Startling my fancy fond
With a chance attitude of the head, a freak of beauty.

Thy hand clasps, as 'twas wont, my finger, and holds it:
  But the grasp is the clasp of Death, heartbreaking and stiff;
    Yet feels to my hand as if
'Twas still thy will, thy pleasure and trust that enfolds it.

So I lay thee there, thy sunken eyelids closing,—
  Go lie thou there in thy coffin, thy last little bed!—
    Propping thy wise, sad head,
Thy firm, pale hands across thy chest disposing.   20

So quiet! doth the change content thee?—Death, whither hath he taken
    thee?
  To a world, do I think, that rights the disaster of this?
        The vision of which I miss,
Who weep for the body, and wish but to warm thee and awaken thee?

Ah! little at best can all our hopes avail us
  To lift this sorrow, or cheer us, when in the dark,
      Unwilling, alone we embark,
And the things we have seen and have known and have heard of, fail us.

                            (1880)

447   THE evening darkens over.
                After a day so bright
                The windcapt waves discover
                That wild will be the night.
                There's sound of distant thunder.

                The latest sea-birds hover
                Along the cliff's sheer height;
                As in the memory wander
                Last flutterings of delight,
                White wings lost on the white.   10

                There's not a ship in sight;
                And as the sun goes under
                Thick clouds conspire to cover
                The moon that should rise yonder.
                Thou art alone, fond lover.

                        (1890)

JOSEPH SKIPSEY

1832–1903

448   *'Get Up!'*

'GET up!' the caller calls, 'Get up!'
    And in the dead of night,
To win the bairns their bite and sup,
    I rise a weary wight.

My flannel dudden donn'd, thrice o'er
    My birds are kiss'd, and then
I with a whistle shut the door,
    I may not ope again.

                                    (1881)

449   *Not as Wont*

'WE'LL meet no more as wont!' she said;
    And moons went by of keen regret,
Before once more beneath the shade
    We met, where we so oft had met.

Till then in Life's grim strife I'd kept
    A heart unquelled, an eye unwet;
But now like any child I wept—
    We'd met, but not as wont we'd met.

                                    (1892)

WILLIAM WATSON

1858–1935

450   *An Epitaph*

HIS friends he loved. His direst earthly foes—
    Cats—I believe he did but feign to hate.
My hand will miss the insinuated nose,
    Mine eyes the tail that wagg'd contempt at Fate.

                        (Wr. 1881; pub. 1884)

WILLIAM FREDERICK STEVENSON

fl. 1883

451

Life and Impellance

THERE went most passionately to Life, Impellance,
And thrilled it with the high perception of divines;
And through a blight of gloom its request fought for
Heaven, its hospice, light, investure ante-natal,
And hope, impact of fathom, lucid suavity.

(1883)

452

A Planet of Descendance

A PLANET of descendance rent,
   A scatter of an effluence;
Before the princes of content,
   Angels of deliverance.

See, methought, the silent hills,
   And the valleys, and the sea;
There is propent death of skills,
   And invalid's puissancy.

(1883)

EUGENE LEE-HAMILTON

1845–1907

453

Sunken Gold

IN dim green depths rot ingot-laden ships;
   And gold doubloons, that from the drowned hand fell,
   Lie nestled in the ocean-flower's bell
With love's old gifts, once kissed by long-drowned lips.

And round some wrought gold cup the sea-grass whips,
   And hides lost pearls, near pearls still in their shell,
   Where sea-weed forests fill each ocean dell
And seek dim twilight with their restless tips.

So lie the wasted gifts, the long-lost hopes,
   Beneath the now hushed surface of myself,   10
In lonelier depths than where the diver gropes;

They lie deep, deep; but I at times behold
   In doubtful glimpses, on some reefy shelf,
The gleam of irrecoverable gold.

                      (1884)

454   *Idle Charon*

THE shores of Styx are lone for evermore,
   And not one shadowy form upon the steep
   Looms through the dusk, as far as eyes can sweep,
To call the ferry over as of yore;

But tintless rushes, all about the shore,
   Have hemmed the old boat in, where, locked in sleep,
   Hoar-bearded Charon lies; while pale weeds creep
With tightening grasp all round the unused oar.

For in the world of Life strange rumours run
   That now the Soul departs not with the breath,   10
But that the Body and the Soul are one;

And in the loved one's mouth, now, after death,
   The widow puts no obol, nor the son,
To pay the ferry in the world beneath.

                      (1884)

455   *Noon's Dream-Song*

THE day is long; the worn Noon dreams.
He shifts in vain, to ease his pain,
And through what seems, he hears a song:

A forest song, whose high note seems
To tell of pain, endured in vain,
And fills his dreams with things lost long.

A dead love seems to thrill that song;
Hope nursed in vain, years passed in pain,
Leaves fallen long, a tide that dreams.

Then, as he dreams, the shades grow long;   10
And, in his pain, he moans in vain,
While fades the song of what but seems.

(1899)

456   *Among the Firs*

AND what a charm is in the rich hot scent
   Of old fir forests heated by the sun,
   Where drops of resin down the rough bark run,
And needle litter breathes its wonderment.

The old fir forests heated by the sun,
   Their thought shall linger like the lingering scent,
   Their beauty haunt us, and a wonderment
Of moss, of fern, of cones, of rills that run.

The needle litter breathes a wonderment;
   The crimson crans are sparkling in the sun;   10
   From tree to tree the scampering squirrels run;
The hum of insects blends with heat and scent.

The drops of resin down the rough bark run;
   And riper, ever riper, grows the scent;
   But eve has come, to end the wonderment,
And slowly up the tree trunk climbs the sun.

(1899)

AMY LEVY
1861–1889

457   *Epitaph*

(*On a commonplace person who died in bed*)

THIS is the end of him, here he lies:
The dust in his throat, the worm in his eyes,
The mould in his mouth, the turf on his breast;
This is the end of him, this is best.
He will never lie on his couch awake,
Wide-eyed, tearless, till dim daybreak.

Never again will he smile and smile
When his heart is breaking all the while.
He will never stretch out his hands in vain
Groping and groping—never again.   10
Never ask for bread, get a stone instead,
Never pretend that the stone is bread.
Never sway and sway 'twixt the false and true,
Weighing and noting the long hours through.
Never ache and ache with the chok'd-up sighs;
This is the end of him, here he lies.

(1884)

458   *On the Threshold*

O GOD, my dream! I dreamed that you were dead;
Your mother hung above the couch and wept
Whereon you lay all white, and garlanded
With blooms of waxen whiteness. I had crept
Up to your chamber-door, which stood ajar,
And in the doorway watched you from afar,
Nor dared advance to kiss your lips and brow.
I had no part nor lot in you, as now;
Death had not broken between us the old bar;
Nor torn from out my heart the old, cold sense   10
Of your misprision and my impotence.

(1889)

A. MARY F. ROBINSON
(MME. DARMESTETER, MME. DUCLAUX)
1857–1944

459   *Aubade Triste*

THE last pale rank of poplar-trees
    Begins to glimmer into light,
    With stems and branches faintly white
Against a heaven one dimly sees
    Beyond the failing night.

A point of grey that grows to green
    Fleck'd o'er with rainy yellow bars,—
    A sudden whitening of the stars,
A pallor where the moon has been,
    A peace the morning mars;   10

When, lo! a shiver of the breeze
    And all the ruffled birds awake,
    The rustling aspens stir and shake;
For, pale, beyond the pallid trees,
    The dawn begins to break.

And now the air turns cool and wan,
    A drizzling rain begins to fall,
    The sky clouds over with a pall—
The night, that was for me, is gone;
    The day has come for all.   20

                                        (1886)

460   *Pallor*

THE great white lilies in the grass
    Are pallid as the smile of death;
For they remember still—alas!—
    The graves they sprang from underneath.

The angels up in heaven are pale—
    For all have died, when all is said;
Nor shall the lutes of Eden avail
    To let them dream they are not dead.

                                        (1886)

461   *Neurasthenia*

I WATCH the happier people of the house
    Come in and out, and talk, and go their ways;
I sit and gaze at them; I cannot rouse
    My heavy mind to share their busy days.

I watch them glide, like skaters on a stream,
    Across the brilliant surface of the world.
But I am underneath: they do not dream
    How deep below the eddying flood is whirl'd.

They cannot come to me, nor I to them;
   But, if a mightier arm could reach and save,   10
Should I forget the tide I had to stem?
   Should I, like these, ignore the abysmal wave?

Yes! in the radiant air how could I know
How black it is, how fast it is, below?

                (1888)

462   *An Orchard at Avignon*

THE hills are white, but not with snow:
   They are as pale in summer time,
For herb or grass may never grow
   Upon their slopes of lime.

Within the circle of the hills
   A ring, all flowering in a round,
An orchard-ring of almond fills
   The plot of stony ground.

More fair than happier trees, I think,
   Grown in well-watered pasture land   10
These parched and stunted branches, pink
   Above the stones and sand.

O white, austere, ideal place,
   Where very few will care to come,
Where spring hath lost the waving grace
   She wears for us at home!

Fain would I sit and watch for hours
   The holy whiteness of thy hills,
Their wreath of pale auroral flowers,
   Their peace the silence fills.   20

A place of secret peace thou art,
   Such peace as in an hour of pain
One moment fills the amazèd heart,
   And never comes again.

                (1888)

E. NESBIT
1858–1924

463   *Song*

Oh, baby, baby, baby dear,
We lie alone together here;
The snowy gown and cap and sheet
With lavender are fresh and sweet;
Through half-closed blinds the roses peer
To see and love you, baby dear.

We are so tired, we like to lie
Just doing nothing, you and I,
Within the darkened quiet room.
The sun sends dusk rays through the gloom,   10
Which is no gloom since you are here,
My little life, my baby dear.

Soft sleepy mouth so vaguely pressed
Against your new-made mother's breast.
Soft little hands in mine I fold,
Soft little feet I kiss and hold,
Round soft smooth head and tiny ear,
All mine, my own, my baby dear.

And he we love is far away!
But he will come some happy day,   20
You need but me, and I can rest
At peace with you beside me pressed.
There are no questions, longings vain,
No murmuring, nor doubt, nor pain,
Only content and we are here,
          My baby dear.

                                        (1886)

464   *Among His Books*

A silent room—gray with a dusty blight
          Of loneliness;
A room with not enough of life or light
          Its form to dress.

533

Books enough though! The groaning sofa bears
    A goodly store—
Books on the window-seat, and on the chairs,
    And on the floor.

Books of all sorts of soul, all sorts of age,
    All sorts of face—   10
Black-letter, vellum, and the flimsy page
    Of commonplace.

All bindings, from the cloth whose hue distracts
    One's weary nerves,
To yellow parchment, binding rare old tracts
    It serves—deserves.

Books on the shelves, and in the cupboard books,
    Worthless and rare—
Books on the mantelpiece—where'er one looks
    Books everywhere!   20

Books! books! the only things in life I find
    Not wholly vain.
Books in my hands—books in my heart enshrined—
    Books in my brain.

My friends are they: for children and for wife
    They serve me too;
For these alone, of all dear things in life,
    Have I found true.

They do not flatter, change, deny, deceive—
    Ah no—not they!   30
The same editions which one night you leave
    You find next day.

You don't find railway novels where you left
    Your Elzevirs!
Your Aldines don't betray you—leave bereft
    Your lonely years!

And yet this common book of Common Prayer
    My heart prefers,
Because the names upon the fly-leaf there
    Are mine and hers.   40

It's a dead flower that makes it open so—
    Forget-me-not—
The Marriage Service . . . well, my dear, you know
    Who first forgot.

Those were the days when in the choir we two
    Sat—used to sing—
When I believed in God, in love, in you—
    In everything.

Through quiet lanes to church we used to come,
    Happy and good,   50
Clasp hands through sermon, and go slowly home
    Down through the wood.

Kisses? A certain yellow rose no doubt
    That porch still shows,
Whenever I hear kisses talked about
    I smell that rose!

No—I don't blame you—since you only proved
    My choice unwise,
And taught me books should trusted be and loved,
    Not lips and eyes!   60

And so I keep your book—your flower—to show
    How much I care
For the dear memory of what, you know,
    You never were.

                (1888)

465   *The Gray Folk*

THE house, with blind unhappy face,
    Stands lonely in the last year's corn,
    And in the grayness of the morn
The gray folk come about the place.

By many pathways, gliding gray
    They come past meadow, wood, and wold,
    Come by the farm and by the fold
From the green fields of yesterday.

Past lock and chain and bolt and bar
   They press, to stand about my bed,   10
   And like the faces of the dead
I know their hidden faces are.

They will not leave me in the day
   And when night falls they will not go,
   Because I silenced, long ago,
The only voice that they obey.

(1895)

466   *Love's Guerdons*

DEAREST, if I almost cease to weep for you,
   Do not doubt I love you just the same;
'Tis because my life has grown to keep for you
   All the hours that sorrow does not claim.

All the hours when I may steal away to you,
   Where you lie alone through the long day,
Lean my face against your turf and say to you
   All that there is no one else to say.

Do they let you listen—do you lean to me?
   Know now what in life you never knew,   10
When I whisper all that you have been to me,
   All that I might never be to you?

Dear, lie still. No tears but mine are shed for you,
   No one else leaves kisses day by day,
No one's heart but mine has beat and bled for you,
   No one else's flowers push mine away.

No one else remembers—do not call to her,
   Not alone she treads the churchyard grass;
You are nothing now who once were all to her,
   Do not call her—let the strangers pass!   20

(1895)

467   *The Claim*

OH! I admit I'm dull and poor,
   And plain and gloomy, as you tell me;
And dozens flock around your door
   Who in all points but one excel me.

You smile on them, on me you frown,
   They worship for the wage you pay;
I lay life, love, and honour down
   For you to walk on every day.

I am the only one who sees
   That though such gifts can never move you,   10
A meagre price are gifts like these
   For life's high privilege—to love you.

I am the one among your train
   Who sees that loving you is worth
A thousand times the certain gain
   Of all the heaped-up joys of earth.

And you, who know as well as I,
   What your glass tells you every morning—
A kindred soul you should descry,
   Dilute with sympathy your scorning.   20

At least you should approve the intense
   Love that gives all for you to waste;
Your other lovers have more sense,
   Admit that I have better taste.

                    (1895)

468   *Villeggiatura*

MY window, framed in pear-tree bloom,
   White-curtained shone, and softly lighted:
So, by the pear-tree, to my room
   Your ghost last night climbed uninvited.

Your solid self, long leagues away,
   Deep in dull books, had hardly missed me;
And yet you found this Romeo's way,
   And through the blossom climbed and kissed me.

I watched the still and dewy lawn,
   The pear-tree boughs hung white above you;   10
I listened to you till the dawn,
   And half forgot I did not love you.

Oh, dear! what pretty things you said,
   What pearls of song you threaded for me!
I did not—till your ghost had fled—
   Remember how you always bore me!

                    (1895)

RUDYARD KIPLING
1865–1936

469   *The Story of Uriah*

'Now there were two men in one city; the one rich, and the other poor'

JACK BARRETT went to Quetta
  Because they told him to.
He left his wife at Simla
  On three-fourths his monthly screw.
Jack Barrett died at Quetta
  Ere the next month's pay he drew.

Jack Barrett went to Quetta.
  He didn't understand
The reason of his transfer
  From the pleasant mountain-land.   10
The season was September,
  And it killed him out of hand.

Jack Barrett went to Quetta
  And there gave up the ghost,
Attempting two men's duty
  In that very healthy post;
And Mrs Barrett mourned for him
  Five lively months at most.

Jack Barrett's bones at Quetta
  Enjoy profound repose;   20
But I shouldn't be astonished
  If *now* his spirit knows
The reason of his transfer
  From the Himalayan snows.

And, when the Last Great Bugle Call
  Adown the Hurnai throbs,
And the last grim joke is entered
  In the big black Book of Jobs,
And Quetta graveyards give again
  Their victims to the air,   30
I shouldn't like to be the man
  Who sent Jack Barrett there.

(1886)

470 *Danny Deever*

'WHAT are the bugles blowin' for?' said Files-on-Parade.
'To turn you out, to turn you out,' the Colour-Sergeant said.
'What makes you look so white, so white?' said Files-on-Parade.
'I'm dreadin' what I've got to watch,' the Colour-Sergeant said.
 For they're hangin' Danny Deever, you can hear the Dead March
  play,
  The regiment's in 'ollow square—they're hangin' him to-day;
  They've taken of his buttons off an' cut his stripes away,
  An' they're hangin' Danny Deever in the mornin'.

'What makes the rear-rank breathe so 'ard?' said Files-on-Parade.
'It's bitter cold, it's bitter cold,' the Colour-Sergeant said.   10
'What makes that front-rank man fall down?' said Files-on-Parade.
'A touch o' sun, a touch o' sun,' the Colour-Sergeant said.
  They are hangin' Danny Deever, they are marchin' of 'im round,
  They 'ave 'alted Danny Deever by 'is coffin on the ground;
  An' 'e'll swing in 'arf a minute for a sneakin' shootin' hound—
  O they're hangin' Danny Deever in the mornin'!

''Is cot was right-'and cot to mine,' said Files-on-Parade.
''E's sleepin' out an' far to-night,' the Colour-Sergeant said.
'I've drunk 'is beer a score o' times,' said Files-on-Parade.
''E's drinkin' bitter beer alone,' the Colour-Sergeant said.   20
  They are hangin' Danny Deever, you must mark 'im to 'is place,
  For 'e shot a comrade sleepin'—you must look 'im in the face;
  Nine 'undred of 'is county an' the Regiment's disgrace,
  While they're hangin' Danny Deever in the mornin'.

'What's that so black agin the sun?' said Files-on-Parade.
'It's Danny fightin' 'ard for life,' the Colour-Sergeant said.
'What's that that whimpers over'ead?' said Files-on-Parade.
'It's Danny's soul that's passin' now,' the Colour-Sergeant said.
 For they're done with Danny Deever, you can 'ear the quickstep
  play,
  The regiment's in column, an' they're marchin' us away;   30
  Ho! the young recruits are shakin', an' they'll want their beer to-day,
  After hangin' Danny Deever in the mornin'!

           (1890)

471   *Gentlemen-Rankers*

To the legion of the lost ones, to the cohort of the damned,
   To my brethren in their sorrow overseas,
Sings a gentleman of England cleanly bred, machinely crammed,
   And a trooper of the Empress, if you please.
Yes, a trooper of the forces who has run his own six horses,
   And faith he went the pace and went it blind,
And the world was more than kin while he held the ready tin,
   But to-day the Sergeant's something less than kind.
       We're poor little lambs who've lost our way,
         Baa! Baa! Baa!
       We're little black sheep who've gone astray,   10
         Baa—aa—aa!
       Gentlemen-rankers out on the spree,
       Damned from here to Eternity,
       God ha' mercy on such as we,
         Baa! Yah! Bah!

Oh, it's sweet to sweat through stables, sweet to empty kitchen slops,
   And it's sweet to hear the tales the troopers tell,
To dance with blowzy housemaids at the regimental hops
   And thrash the cad who says you waltz too well.   20
Yes, it makes you cock-a-hoop to be 'Rider' to your troop,
   And branded with a blasted worsted spur,
When you envy, O how keenly, one poor Tommy living cleanly
   Who blacks your boots and sometimes calls you 'Sir'.

If the home we never write to, and the oaths we never keep,
   And all we know most distant and most dear,
Across the snoring barrack-room return to break our sleep,
   Can you blame us if we soak ourselves in beer?
When the drunken comrade mutters and the great guard-lantern
      gutters
   And the horror of our fall is written plain,   30
Every secret, self-revealing on the aching whitewashed ceiling,
   Do you wonder that we drug ourselves from pain?

We have done with Hope and Honour, we are lost to Love and Truth,
   We are dropping down the ladder rung by rung,
And the measure of our torment is the measure of our youth.
   God help us, for we knew the worst too young!

Our shame is clean repentance for the crime that brought the sentence,
　　Our pride it is to know no spur of pride,
And the Curse of Reuben holds us till an alien turf enfolds us
　　And we die, and none can tell Them where we died.　　　　　40
　　　　　We're poor little lambs who've lost our way,
　　　　　　　Baa! Baa! Baa!
　　　　　We're little black sheep who've gone astray,
　　　　　　　Baa—aa—aa!
　　　　　Gentlemen-rankers out on the spree,
　　　　　Damned from here to Eternity,
　　　　　God ha' mercy on such as we,
　　　　　　　Baa! Yah! Bah!

　　　　　　　　　　　　　　　　　　　　　　　　(1892)

472　　　　　　　*In the Neolithic Age*

IN the Neolithic Age savage warfare did I wage
　　For food and fame and woolly horses' pelt.
I was singer to my clan in that dim, red Dawn of Man,
　　And I sang of all we fought and feared and felt.

Yea, I sang as now I sing, when the Prehistoric spring
　　Made the piled Biscayan ice-pack split and shove;
And the troll and gnome and dwerg, and the Gods of Cliff and Berg
　　Were about me and beneath me and above.

But a rival of Solutré, told the tribe my style was *outré—*
　　'Neath a tomahawk, of diorite, he fell.　　　　　　　　10
And I left my views on Art, barbed and tanged, below the heart
　　Of a mammothistic etcher at Grenelle.

Then I stripped them, scalp from skull, and my hunting-dogs fed full,
　　And their teeth I threaded neatly on a thong;
And I wiped my mouth and said, 'It is well that they are dead,
　　'For I know my work is right and theirs was wrong'.

But my Totem saw the shame; from his ridgepole-shrine he came,
　　And he told me in a vision of the night:—
'There are nine and sixty ways of constructing tribal lays,
　　'And every single one of them is right!'　　　　　　　　20

　　　　　.　　.　　.　　.　　.　　.　　.

Then the silence closed upon me till They put new clothing on me
　　Of whiter, weaker flesh and bone more frail;
And I stepped beneath Time's finger, once again a tribal singer,
　　And a minor poet certified by Traill!

Still they skirmish to and fro, men my messmates on the snow,
  When we headed off the aurochs turn for turn;
When the rich Allobrogenses never kept amanuenses,
  And our only plots were piled in lakes at Berne.

Still a cultured Christian age sees us scuffle, squeak, and rage,
  Still we pinch and slap and jabber, scratch and dirk;   30
Still we let our business slide—as we dropped the half-dressed hide—
  To show a fellow-savage how to work.

Still the world is wondrous large,—seven seas from marge to marge—
  And it holds a vast of various kinds of man;
And the wildest dreams of Kew are the facts of Khatmandhu,
  And the crimes of Clapham chaste in Martaban.

Here's my wisdom for your use, as I learned it when the moose
  And the reindeer roared where Paris roars to-night:—
'*There are nine and sixty ways of constructing tribal lays,*
  '*And—every—single—one—of—them—is—right!*'   40

                               (1892)

473   *The Vampire*

A FOOL there was and he made his prayer
(Even as you and I!)
To a rag and a bone and a hank of hair
(We called her the woman who did not care)
But the fool he called her his lady fair—
(Even as you and I!)

Oh, the years we waste and the tears we waste
And the work of our head and hand
Belong to the woman who did not know
(And now we know that she never could know)   10
And did not understand!

A fool there was and his goods he spent
(Even as you and I!)
Honour and faith and a sure intent
(And it wasn't the least what the lady meant)
But a fool must follow his natural bent
(Even as you and I!)

Oh, the toil we lost and the spoil we lost
And the excellent things we planned
Belong to the woman who didn't know why   20
(And now we know that she never knew why)
And did not understand!

The fool was stripped to his foolish hide
(Even as you and I!)
Which she might have seen when she threw him aside—
(But it isn't on record the lady tried)
So some of him lived but the most of him died—
(Even as you and I!)

And it isn't the shame and it isn't the blame
That stings like a white hot brand—   30
It's coming to know that she never knew why
(Seeing, at last, she could never know why)
And never could understand!

(1897)

474   *Recessional*

1897

GOD of our fathers, known of old,
    Lord of our far-flung battle-line,
Beneath whose awful Hand we hold
    Dominion over palm and pine—
Lord God of Hosts, be with us yet,
Lest we forget—lest we forget!

The tumult and the shouting dies;
    The Captains and the Kings depart:
Still stands Thine ancient sacrifice,
    An humble and a contrite heart.   10
Lord God of Hosts, be with us yet,
Lest we forget—lest we forget!

Far-called, our navies melt away;
    On dune and headland sinks the fire:
Lo, all our pomp of yesterday
    Is one with Nineveh and Tyre!
Judge of the Nations, spare us yet,
Lest we forget—lest we forget!

If, drunk with sight of power, we loose
   Wild tongues that have not Thee in awe,   20
Such boastings as the Gentiles use,
   Or lesser breeds without the Law—
Lord God of Hosts, be with us yet,
Lest we forget—lest we forget!

For heathen heart that puts her trust
   In reeking tube and iron shard,
All valiant dust that builds on dust,
   And guarding, calls not Thee to guard,
For frantic boast and foolish word—
Thy mercy on Thy People, Lord!   30

(Wr. and pub. 1897)

WILLIAM CANTON

1845–1926

475   *Day-Dreams*

BROAD August burns in milky skies,
   The world is blanched with hazy heat;
The vast green pasture, even, lies
   Too hot and bright for eyes and feet.

Amid the grassy levels rears
   The sycamore against the sun
The dark boughs of a hundred years,
   The emerald foliage of one.

Lulled in a dream of shade and sheen,
   Within the clement twilight thrown   10
By that great cloud of floating green,
   A horse is standing, still as stone.

He stirs nor head nor hoof, although
   The grass is fresh beneath the branch;
His tail alone swings to and fro
   In graceful curves from haunch to haunch.

He stands quite lost, indifferent
   To rack or pasture, trace or rein;
He feels the vaguely sweet content
   Of perfect sloth in limb and brain.   20

(1887)

OSCAR WILDE

1854–1900

476   *Les Ballons*

AGAINST these turbid turquoise skies
   The light and luminous balloons
   Dip and drift like satin moons,
Drift like silken butterflies;

Reel with every windy gust,
   Rise and reel like dancing girls,
   Float like strange transparent pearls,
Fall and float like silver dust.

Now to the low leaves they cling,
   Each with coy fantastic pose,   10
   Each a petal of a rose
Straining at a gossamer string.

Then to the tall trees they climb,
   Like thin globes of amethyst,
   Wandering opals keeping tryst
With the rubies of the lime.

(1887)

477   *Symphony in Yellow*

AN omnibus across the bridge
   Crawls like a yellow butterfly,
   And, here and there, a passer-by
Shows like a little restless midge.

Big barges full of yellow hay
   Are moved against the shadowy wharf,
   And, like a yellow silken scarf,
The thick fog hangs along the quay.

The yellow leaves begin to fade
  And flutter from the Temple elms,
  And at my feet the pale green Thames 10
Lies like a rod of rippled jade.

(1889)

from *The Ballad of Reading Gaol* (478–479)

478

I

HE did not wear his scarlet coat,
  For blood and wine are red,
And blood and wine were on his hands
  When they found him with the dead,
The poor dead woman whom he loved,
  And murdered in her bed.

He walked amongst the Trial Men
  In a suit of shabby gray;
A cricket cap was on his head,
  And his step seemed light and gay; 10
But I never saw a man who looked
  So wistfully at the day.

I never saw a man who looked
  With such a wistful eye
Upon that little tent of blue
  Which prisoners call the sky,
And at every drifting cloud that went
  With sails of silver by.

I walked, with other souls in pain,
  Within another ring,
And was wondering if the man had done 20
  A great or little thing,
When a voice behind me whispered low,
  'That fellow's got to swing.'

Dear Christ! the very prison walls
  Suddenly seemed to reel,
And the sky above my head became
  Like a casque of scorching steel;
And, though I was a soul in pain,
  My pain I could not feel. 30

I only knew what hunted thought
   Quickened his step, and why
He looked upon the garish day
   With such a wistful eye;
The man had killed the thing he loved,
   And so he had to die.

     .   .   .   .   .

Yet each man kills the thing he loves,
   By each let this be heard,
Some do it with a bitter look,
   Some with a flattering word,   40
The coward does it with a kiss,
   The brave man with a sword!

Some kill their love when they are young,
   And some when they are old;
Some strangle with the hands of Lust,
   Some with the hands of Gold:
The kindest use a knife, because
   The dead so soon grow cold.

Some love too little, some too long,
   Some sell, and others buy;   50
Some do the deed with many tears,
   And some without a sigh:
For each man kills the thing he loves,
   Yet each man does not die.

He does not die a death of shame
   On a day of dark disgrace,
Nor have a noose about his neck,
   Nor a cloth upon his face,
Nor drop feet foremost through the floor
   Into an empty space.   60

     .   .   .   .   .

He does not sit with silent men
   Who watch him night and day;
Who watch him when he tries to weep,
   And when he tries to pray;
Who watch him lest himself should rob
   The prison of its prey.

He does not wake at dawn to see
  Dread figures throng his room,
The shivering Chaplain robed in white,
  The Sheriff stern with gloom,   70
And the Governor all in shiny black,
  With the yellow face of Doom.

He does not rise in piteous haste
  To put on convict-clothes,
While some coarse-mouthed Doctor gloats, and notes
  Each new and nerve-twitched pose,
Fingering a watch whose little ticks
  Are like horrible hammer-blows.

He does not know that sickening thirst
  That sands one's throat, before   80
The hangman with his gardener's gloves
  Slips through the padded door,
And binds one with three leathern thongs,
  That the throat may thirst no more.

He does not bend his head to hear
  The Burial Office read,
Nor, while the terror of his soul
  Tells him he is not dead,
Cross his own coffin, as he moves
  Into the hideous shed.   90

He does not stare upon the air
  Through a little roof of glass:
He does not pray with lips of clay
  For his agony to pass;
Nor feel upon his shuddering cheek
  The kiss of Caiaphas.

479   III

In Debtors' Yard the stones are hard,
  And the dripping wall is high,
So it was there he took the air
  Beneath the leaden sky,
And by each side a Warder walked,
  For fear the man might die.

Or else he sat with those who watched
   His anguish night and day;
Who watched him when he rose to weep,
   And when he crouched to pray;   10
Who watched him lest himself should rob
   Their scaffold of its prey.

The Governor was strong upon
   The Regulations Act:
The Doctor said that Death was but
   A scientific fact:
And twice a day the Chaplain called,
   And left a little tract.

And twice a day he smoked his pipe,
   And drank his quart of beer: 20
His soul was resolute, and held
   No hiding-place for fear;
He often said that he was glad
   The hangman's hands were near.

But why he said so strange a thing
   No Warder dared to ask:
For he to whom a watcher's doom
   Is given as his task,
Must set a lock upon his lips,
   And make his face a mask.   30

Or else he might be moved, and try
   To comfort or console:
And what should Human Pity do
   Pent up in Murderers' Hole?
What word of grace in such a place
   Could help a brother's soul?

.   .   .   .   .

With slouch and swing around the ring
   We trod the Fools' Parade!
We did not care: we knew we were
   The Devil's Own Brigade: 40
And shaven head and feet of lead
   Make a merry masquerade.

We tore the tarry rope to shreds
  With blunt and bleeding nails;
We rubbed the doors, and scrubbed the floors,
  And cleaned the shining rails:
And, rank by rank, we soaped the plank,
  And clattered with the pails.

We sewed the sacks, we broke the stones,
  We turned the dusty drill: 50
We banged the tins, and bawled the hymns,
  And sweated on the mill:
But in the heart of every man
  Terror was lying still.

So still it lay that every day
  Crawled like a weed-clogged wave:
And we forgot the bitter lot
  That waits for fool and knave,
Till once, as we tramped in from work,
  We passed an open grave.   60

With yawning mouth the yellow hole
  Gaped for a living thing;
The very mud cried out for blood
  To the thirsty asphalte ring:
And we knew that ere one dawn grew fair
  Some prisoner had to swing.

Right in we went, with soul intent
  On Death and Dread and Doom:
The hangman, with his little bag,
  Went shuffling through the gloom: 70
And each man trembled as he crept
  Into his numbered tomb.

            .   .   .   .   .   .

That night the empty corridors
  Were full of forms of Fear,
And up and down the iron town
  Stole feet we could not hear,
And through the bars that hide the stars
  White faces seemed to peer.

He lay as one who lies and dreams
  In a pleasant meadow-land,   80
The watchers watched him as he slept,
  And could not understand
How one could sleep so sweet a sleep
  With a hangman close at hand.

But there is no sleep when men must weep
  Who never yet have wept:
So we—the fool, the fraud, the knave—
  That endless vigil kept,
And through each brain on hands of pain
  Another's terror crept.   90

Alas! it is a fearful thing
  To feel another's guilt!
For, right within, the sword of Sin
  Pierced to its poisoned hilt,
And as molten lead were the tears we shed
  For the blood we had not spilt.

The Warders with their shoes of felt
  Crept by each padlocked door,
And peeped and saw, with eyes of awe,
  Grey figures on the floor,   100
And wondered why men knelt to pray
  Who never prayed before.

All through the night we knelt and prayed,
  Mad mourners of a corse!
The troubled plumes of midnight were
  The plumes upon a hearse:
And bitter wine upon a sponge
  Was the savour of Remorse.

          .   .   .   .   .   .

The grey cock crew, the red cock crew,
  But never came the day: 110
And crooked shapes of Terror crouched,
  In the corners where we lay:
And each evil sprite that walks by night
  Before us seemed to play.

They glided past, they glided fast,
  Like travellers through a mist:
They mocked the moon in a rigadoon
  Of delicate turn and twist,
And with formal pace and loathsome grace
  The phantoms kept their tryst.   120

With mop and mow, we saw them go,
  Slim shadows hand in hand:
About, about, in ghostly rout
  They trod a saraband:
And the damned grotesques made arabesques,
  Like the wind upon the sand!

With the pirouettes of marionettes,
  They tripped on pointed tread:
But with flutes of Fear they filled the ear,
  As their grisly masque they led,   130
And loud they sang, and long they sang,
  For they sang to wake the dead.

'Oho!' they cried, 'The world is wide,
  But fettered limbs go lame!
And once, or twice, to throw the dice
  Is a gentlemanly game,
But he does not win who plays with Sin
  In the secret House of Shame.'

No things of air these antics were,
  That frolicked with such glee: 140
To men whose lives were held in gyves,
  And whose feet might not go free,
Ah! wounds of Christ! they were living things,
  Most terrible to see.

Around, around, they waltzed and wound;
  Some wheeled in smirking pairs;
With the mincing step of a demirep
  Some sidled up the stairs:
And with subtle sneer, and fawning leer,
  Each helped us at our prayers.   150

The morning wind began to moan,
　　But still the night went on:
Through its giant loom the web of gloom
　　Crept till each thread was spun:
And, as we prayed, we grew afraid
　　Of the Justice of the Sun.

The moaning wind went wandering round
　　The weeping prison-wall:
Till like a wheel of turning steel
　　We felt the minutes crawl:　　　　　　160
O moaning wind! what had we done
　　To have such a seneschal?

At last I saw the shadowed bars,
　　Like a lattice wrought in lead,
Move right across the whitewashed wall
　　That faced my three-plank bed,
And I knew that somewhere in the world
　　God's dreadful dawn was red.

At six o'clock we cleaned our cells,
　　At seven all was still,　　　　　　　170
But the sough and swing of a mighty wing
　　The prison seemed to fill,
For the Lord of Death with icy breath
　　Had entered in to kill.

He did not pass in purple pomp,
　　Nor ride a moon-white steed.
Three yards of cord and a sliding board
　　Are all the gallows' need:
So with rope of shame the Herald came
　　To do the secret deed.　　　　　　　180

We were as men who through a fen
　　Of filthy darkness grope:
We did not dare to breathe a prayer,
　　Or to give our anguish scope:
Something was dead in each of us,
　　And what was dead was Hope.

For Man's grim Justice goes its way,
    And will not swerve aside:
It slays the weak, it slays the strong,
    It has a deadly stride: 190
With iron heel it slays the strong,
    The monstrous parricide!

We waited for the stroke of eight:
    Each tongue was thick with thirst:
For the stroke of eight is the stroke of Fate
    That makes a man accursed,
And Fate will use a running noose
    For the best man and the worst.

We had no other thing to do,
    Save to wait for the sign to come: 200
So, like things of stone in a valley lone,
    Quiet we sat and dumb:
But each man's heart beat thick and quick,
    Like a madman on a drum!

With sudden shock the prison-clock
    Smote on the shivering air,
And from all the gaol rose up a wail
    Of impotent despair,
Like the sound that frightened marshes hear
    From some leper in his lair.   210

And as one sees most fearful things
    In the crystal of a dream,
We saw the greasy hempen rope
    Hooked to the blackened beam,
And heard the prayer the hangman's snare
    Strangled into a scream.

And all the woe that moved him so
    That he gave that bitter cry,
And the wild regrets, and the bloody sweats,
    None knew so well as I: 220
For he who lives more lives than one
    More deaths than one must die.

                    (Wr. 1897–8; pub. 1898)

ANDREW LANG

1844–1912

480

The Last Chance

WITHIN the streams, Pausanias saith,
  That down Cocytus valley flow,
Girdling the grey domain of Death,
  The spectral fishes come and go;
The ghosts of trout flit to and fro.
  Persephone, fulfil my wish,
And grant that in the shades below
  My ghost may land the ghosts of fish.

(1888)

LIONEL JOHNSON

1867–1902

481

Victory

To George Moore

DOWN the white steps, into the night, she came;
Wearing white roses, lit by the full moon:
And white upon the shadowy lawn she stood,
Waiting and watching for the dawn's first flame,
Over the dark and visionary wood.
Down the white steps, into the night, she came;
Wearing white roses, lit by the full moon.

Night died away: and over the deep wood
Widened a rosy cloud, a chilly flame:
The shadowy lawn grew cold, and clear, and white.   10
Then down she drew against her eyes her hood,
To hide away the inexorable light.
Night died away: and over the deep wood
Widened a rosy cloud, a chilly flame.

Then back she turned, and up the white steps came,
And looked into a room of burning lights.
Still slept her loveless husband his brute sleep,
Beside the comfortless and ashen flame:

Her lover waited, where the wood was deep.
She turned not back: but from the white steps came,   20
And went into the room of burning lights.

(Wr. 1888; pub. 1897)

482   *Lambeth Lyric*

SOME seven score Bishops late at Lambeth sat,
Gray-whiskered and respectable debaters:
Each had on head a well-strung curly hat;
          And each wore gaiters.

And when these prelates at their talk had been
Long time, they made yet longer proclamation,
Saying: 'These creeds are childish! both Nicene,
          And Athanasian.

True, they were written by the Holy Ghost;
So, to re-write them were perhaps a pity.   10
Refer we their revision to a most
          Select Committee!

In ten years' time we wise Pan Anglicans
Once more around this Anglo Catholic table
Will meet, to prove God's word more weak than man's,
          His truth, less stable.'

So saying homeward the good Fathers go;
Up Mississippi some and some up Niger.
For thine old mantle they have clearly no
          More use, Elijah!   20

Instead, an apostolic apron girds
Their loins, which ministerial fingers tie on:
And Babylon's songs they sing, new tune and words,
          All over Zion.

The Creeds, the Scriptures, all the Faith of old,
They hack and hew to please each bumptious German,
Windy and vague as mists and clouds that fold
          Tabour and Hermon.

Happy Establishment in this thine hour!
Behold thy bishops to their sees retreating!   30
'Have at the Faith!' each cries: 'good bye till our
          Next merry meeting!'

(Wr. 1888; pub. 1953)

483

A Stranger

To Will Rothenstein

HER face was like sad things: was like the lights
Of a great city, seen from far off fields,
Or seen from sea: sad things, as are the fires
Lit in a land of furnaces by night:
Sad things, as are the reaches of a stream
Flowing beneath a golden moon alone.
And her clear voice, full of remembrances,
Came like faint music down the distant air.
As though she had a spirit of dead joy
About her, looked the sorrow of her ways: 10
If light there be, the dark hills are to climb
First: and if calm, far over the long sea.
Fallen from all the world apart she seemed,
Into a silence and a memory.
What had the thin hands done, that now they strained
Together in such passion? And those eyes,
What saw they long ago, that now they dreamed
Along the busy streets, blind but to dreams?
Her white lips mocked the world, and all therein:
She had known more than this; she wanted not   20
This, who had known the past so great a thing.
Moving about our ways, herself she moved
In things done, years remembered, places gone.
Lonely, amid the living crowds, as dead,
She walked with wonderful and sad regard:
With us, her passing image: but herself
Far over the dark hills and the long sea.

(Wr. 1889; pub. 1897)

484

The Roman Stage

To Hugh Orange

A MAN of marble holds the throne,
With looks composed and resolute:
Till death, a prince whom princes own,
Draws near to touch the marble mute.

The play is over: good my friends!
Murmur the pale lips: *your applause!*
With what a grace the actor ends:
How loyal to dramatic laws!

A brooding beauty on his brow;
Irony brooding over sin: 10
The next imperial actor now
Bids the satyric piece begin.

(Wr. 1891; pub. 1895)

485   *The Dark Angel*

DARK Angel, with thine aching lust
To rid the world of penitence:
Malicious Angel, who still dost
My soul such subtile violence!

Because of thee, no thought, no thing,
Abides for me undesecrate:
Dark Angel, ever on the wing,
Who never reachest me too late!

When music sounds, then changest thou
Its silvery to a sultry fire: 10
Nor will thine envious heart allow
Delight untortured by desire.

Through thee, the gracious Muses turn
To Furies, O mine Enemy!
And all the things of beauty burn
With flames of evil ecstasy.

Because of thee, the land of dreams
Becomes a gathering place of fears:
Until tormented slumber seems
One vehemence of useless tears.   20

When sunlight glows upon the flowers,
Or ripples down the dancing sea:
Thou, with thy troop of passionate powers,
Beleaguerest, bewilderest, me.

Within the breath of autumn woods,
Within the winter silences:
Thy venomous spirit stirs and broods,
O Master of impieties!

The ardour of red flame is thine,
And thine the steely soul of ice: 30
Thou poisonest the fair design
Of nature, with unfair device.

Apples of ashes, golden bright;
Waters of bitterness, how sweet!
O banquet of a foul delight,
Prepared by thee, dark Paraclete!

Thou art the whisper in the gloom,
The hinting tone, the haunting laugh:
Thou art the adorner of my tomb,
The minstrel of mine epitaph.   40

I fight thee, in the Holy Name!
Yet, what thou dost, is what God saith:
Tempter! should I escape thy flame,
Thou wilt have helped my soul from Death:

The second Death, that never dies,
That cannot die, when time is dead:
Live Death, wherein the lost soul cries,
Eternally uncomforted.

Dark Angel, with thine aching lust!
Of two defeats, of two despairs: 50
Less dread, a change to drifting dust,
Than thine eternity of cares.

Do what thou wilt, thou shalt not so,
Dark Angel! triumph over me:
Lonely, unto the Lone I go;
Divine, to the Divinity.

(Wr. 1893; pub. 1894)

GERALD MASSEY

1828–1907

486   As proper mode of quenching legal lust,
          A Roué takes unto Himself a Wife:
        'Tis Cheaper when the bones begin to rust,
        And there's no other Woman you can trust;
        But, mind you, in return, Law says you must
          Provide her with the physical means of life:
        And then the blindest beast may wallow and roll;
        The twain are One flesh, never mind the Soul:
        You may not cruelly beat her, but are free
        To violate the life in sanctuary;   10
        In virgin soil renew old seeds of Crime
        To blast eternity as well as time:
            She must show black and blue, or no divorce
            Is granted by the Law of Physical Force.

                                                    (1889)

487   *The Diakka*

        You are the Merry men, dwarfs of soul,
        Who can get your hand through the tiniest hole,
        And make your bells jingle outside of the show;
        Prove there's life beyond, and on that we go!
        'Tis trying to find that we ARE more near
        To you than to those we have held more dear,
        But I think they are backing you all the while;
        And down on our efforts benignly may smile
        To see how we strive and are ever unable
        To meet and shake hands with the leg of a table.   10
            So holloa, boys, ring the bells, let them see how
            You can wake up the world with YOUR row-de-dow.

        Folk say you are Devils: then act as such!
        Give them a touch of the devil's clutch.
        In times like ours 'tis a comfort to know
        For certain there *may* be a devil or so!
        We need them to prove how the lusts of old
        For women or wine, for gore or gold,
        Are not to be quenched with their burning breath
        By the waters of Winter that drown us in death,   20

But still live on, all a-crave to be fed
In the earth-life lived by the homeless dead.
    Holloa, boys, ring the bells, let us see how
    You can wake up the world with YOUR row-de-dow.

Many a fathom deep under the ground
Souls like toads in the rock lie bound,
Awaiting the resurrection sound
Of the Crack of doom, for them to be found!
Nothing short of an earthquake-kick
Will send them heavenward, make them quick.   30
Spirits far off, invisible, mute,
Can no more reach to the buried root,
Than we upon earth to the moon can shoot,
Or open oysters by playing a flute!
    Holloa, boys, ring the bells, show them how
    You can wake up the world with YOUR row-de-dow.

(1889)

488 *Womankind*

DEAR things! we would not have you learn too much—
    Your Ignorance is so charming! We've a notion
That greater knowledge might not lend you such
    Sure aid to blind obedience and devotion.

(1889)

COSMO MONKHOUSE
1840–1901

489 *Any Soul to Any Body*

SO we must part, my body, you and I
    Who've spent so many pleasant years together.
'Tis sorry work to lose your company
    Who clove to me so close, whate'er the weather,
From winter unto winter, wet or dry;
    But you have reached the limit of your tether,
And I must journey on my way alone,
And leave you quietly beneath a stone.

They say that you are altogether bad
   (Forgive me, 'tis not my experience),   10
And think me very wicked to be sad
   At leaving you, a clod, a prison, whence
To get quite free I should be very glad.
   Perhaps I may be so, some few days hence,
But now, methinks, 'twere graceless not to spend
A tear or two on my departing friend.

Now our long partnership is near completed,
   And I look back upon its history;
I greatly fear I have not always treated
   You with the honesty you showed to me.   20
And I must own that you have oft defeated
   Unworthy schemes by your sincerity,
And by a blush or stammering tongue have tried
To make me think again before I lied.

'Tis true you're not so handsome as you were,
   But that's not your fault and is partly mine.
You might have lasted longer with more care,
   And still looked something like your first design;
And even now, with all your wear and tear,
   'Tis pitiful to think I must resign   30
You to the friendless grave, the patient prey
Of all the hungry legions of Decay.

But you must stay, dear body, and I go.
   And I was once so very proud of you:
You made my mother's eyes to overflow
   When first she saw you, wonderful and new.
And now, with all your faults, 'twere hard to find
   A slave more willing or a friend more true.
Ay—even they who say the worst about you
Can scarcely tell what I shall do without you.   40

(1890)

ARTHUR SYMONS
1865–1945

490 *Pastel: Masks and Faces*

THE light of our cigarettes
Went and came in the gloom:
It was dark in the little room.

Dark, and then, in the dark,
Sudden, a flash, a glow,
And a hand and a ring I know.

And then, through the dark, a flush
Ruddy and vague, the grace
(A rose!) of her lyric face.

(Wr. 1890; pub. 1892)

491 *The Absinthe-Drinker*

GENTLY I wave the visible world away.
Far off, I hear a roar, afar yet near,
Far off and strange, a voice is in my ear,
And is the voice my own? the words I say
Fall strangely, like a dream, across the day;
And the dim sunshine is a dream. How clear,
New as the world to lovers' eyes, appear
The men and women passing on their way!

The world is very fair. The hours are all
Linked in a dance of mere forgetfulness.
I am at peace with God and man. O glide,   10
Sands of the hour-glass that I count not, fall
Serenely: scarce I feel your soft caress,
Rocked on this dreamy and indifferent tide.

(Wr. 1890; pub. 1892)

492 *Rain on the Down*

NIGHT, and the down by the sea,
And the veil of rain on the down;
And she came through the mist and the rain to me
From the safe warm lights of the town.

563

The rain shone in her hair,
And her face gleamed in the rain;
And only the night and the rain were there
As she came to me out of the rain.

(Wr. 1890; pub. 1892)

493   *During Music*

THE music had the heat of blood,
A passion that no words can reach;
We sat together, and understood
Our own heart's speech.

We had no need of word or sign,
The music spoke for us, and said
All that her eyes could read in mine
Or mine in hers had read.

(Wr. 1890; pub. 1892)

494   *At the Cavour*

WINE, the red coals, the flaring gas,
Bring out a brighter tone in cheeks
That learn at home before the glass
The flush that eloquently speaks.

The blue-grey smoke of cigarettes
Curls from the lessening ends that glow;
The men are thinking of the bets,
The women of the debts, they owe.

Then their eyes meet, and in their eyes
The accustomed smile comes up to call,   10
A look half miserably wise,
Half heedlessly ironical.

(Wr. 1890; pub. 1892)

495

At Dieppe

To Walter Sickert

THE grey-green stretch of sandy grass,
Indefinitely desolate;
A sea of lead, a sky of slate;
Already autumn in the air, alas!

One stark monotony of stone,
The long hotel, acutely white,
Against the after-sunset light
Withers grey-green, and takes the grass's tone.

Listless and endless it outlies,
And means, to you and me, no more   10
Than any pebble on the shore,
Or this indifferent moment as it dies.

(Wr. 1893; pub. 1895)

496

Paris

MY Paris is a land where twilight days
Merge into violent nights of black and gold;
Where, it may be, the flower of dawn is cold:
Ah, but the gold nights, and the scented ways!

Eyelids of women, little curls of hair,
A little nose curved softly, like a shell,
A red mouth like a wound, a mocking veil:
Phantoms, before the dawn, how phantom-fair!

And every woman with beseeching eyes,
Or with enticing eyes, or amorous,   10
Offers herself, a rose, and craves of us
A rose's place among our memories.

(Wr. 1894; pub. 1895)

497

The Barrel-Organ

ENIGMATICAL, tremulous,
Voice of the troubled wires,
What remembering desires
Wail to me, wandering thus

Up through the night with a cry,
Inarticulate, insane.
Out of the night of the street and the rain
Into the rain and the night of the sky?

Inarticulate voice of my heart,
Rusty, a worn-out thing,   10
Harsh with a broken string,
Mended, and pulled apart,
All the old tunes played through,
Fretted by hands that have played,
Tremulous voice that cries to me out of the shade,
The voice of my heart is crying in you.

(Wr. 1895; pub. 1897)

W. B. YEATS
1865–1939

498   *A Cradle Song*

'*Coth yani me von gilli beg,*
'*N heur ve thu more a creena.*'

THE angels are bending
  Above your white bed,
They weary of tending
  The souls of the dead.

God smiles in high heaven
  To see you so good,
The old planets seven
  Grow gay with his mood.

I kiss you and kiss you,
  With arms round my own,   10
Ah, how shall I miss you,
  When, dear, you have grown.

(1890)

The Pity of Love

A PITY beyond all telling,
  Is hid in the heart of love;
The folk who are buying and selling,
  The stars of God where they move,
The mouse-grey waters on flowing,
  The clouds on their journey above,
And the cold wet winds ever blowing,
  All threaten the head that I love.

(1892)

The Sorrow of Love

THE quarrel of the sparrows in the eaves,
  The full round moon and the star-laden sky,
And the loud song of the ever-singing leaves
  Had hid away earth's old and weary cry.

And then you came with those red mournful lips,
  And with you came the whole of the world's tears,
And all the sorrows of her labouring ships,
  And all burden of her myriad years.

And now the sparrows warring in the eaves,
  The crumbling moon, the white stars in the sky,   10
And the loud chanting of the unquiet leaves,
  Are shaken with earth's old and weary cry.

(Wr. 1891; pub. 1892)

When You Are Old

WHEN you are old and grey and full of sleep,
And nodding by the fire, take down this book,
And slowly read, and dream of the soft look
Your eyes had once, and of their shadows deep;

How many loved your moments of glad grace,
And loved your beauty with love false or true,
But one man loved the pilgrim soul in you,
And loved the sorrows of your changing face;

And bending down beside the glowing bars,
Murmur, a little sadly, how Love fled   10
And paced upon the mountains overhead
And hid his face amid a crowd of stars.

(Wr. 1891; pub. 1892)

502   *Who Goes with Fergus?*

WHO will go drive with Fergus now,
And pierce the deep wood's woven shade,
And dance upon the level shore?
Young man, lift up your russet brow,
And lift your tender eyelids, maid,
And brood on hopes and fear no more.

And no more turn aside and brood
Upon love's bitter mystery;
For Fergus rules the brazen cars,
And rules the shadows of the wood,   10
And the white breast of the dim sea
And all dishevelled wandering stars.

(1892)

503   *He Thinks of Those who have Spoken Evil of His*
                          Beloved

HALF close your eyelids, loosen your hair,
And dream about the great and their pride;
They have spoken against you everywhere,
But weigh this song with the great and their pride;
I made it out of a mouthful of air,
Their children's children shall say they have lied.

(1898)

504   *He Wishes for the Cloths of Heaven*

HAD I the heavens' embroidered cloths,
Enwrought with golden and silver light,
The blue and the dim and the dark cloths
Of night and light and the half-light,

I would spread the cloths under your feet:
But I, being poor, have only my dreams;
I have spread my dreams under your feet;
Tread softly because you tread on my dreams.

(1899)

WILLIAM CORY
(formerly JOHNSON)
1823–1892

505

Hersilia

I SEE her stand with arms a-kimbo,
A blue and blonde *sub aureo nimbo*;
She scans her literary limbo,
The reliques of her teens;
Things like the chips of broken stilts,
Or tatters of embroidered quilts,
Or nosegays tossed away by jilts,
Notes, ballads, tales, and scenes.

Soon will she gambol like a lamb,
Fenced, but not tethered, near the Cam.   10
Maybe she'll swim where Byron swam,
And chat beneath the limes,
Where Arthur, Alfred, Fitz, and Brooks
Lit thought by one another's looks,
Embraced their jests and kicked their books,
In England's happier times;

Ere magic poets felt the gout,
Ere Darwin whelmed the Church in doubt,
Ere Apologia had found out
The round world must be right;   20
When Gladstone, bluest of the blue,
Read all Augustine's folios through;
When France was tame, and no one knew
We and the Czar would fight.

'Sixty years since' (said dear old Scott;
We're bound, you know, to quote Sir Wat)
This isle had not a sweeter spot

Than Neville's Court by Granta;
No Newnham then, no kirtled scribes,
No Clelia to harangue the tribes,   30
No race for girls, no apple bribes
To tempt an Atalanta.

We males talked fast, we meant to be
World-betterers all at twenty-three,
But somehow failed to level thee,
Oh, battered fort of Edom!
Into the breach our daughters press,
Brave patriots in unwarlike dress,
Adepts at thought-in-idleness,
Sweet devotees of freedom.   40

And now it is your turn, fair soul,
To see the fervent car-wheels roll,
Your rivals clashing past the goal,
Some sly Milanion leading.
Ah! with them may your Genius bring
Some Celia, some Miss Mannering;
For youthful friendship is a thing
More precious than succeeding.

(1891)

JAMES LOGIE ROBERTSON
1846–1922

506   *The Discovery of America*
(*Seen from the Ochils through the perspective of four centuries*)

ALL the mill-horses of Europe
    Were plodding round and round;
All the mills were droning
    The same old sound.

The drivers were dozing, the millers
    Were deaf—as millers will be;
When, startling them all, without warning
    Came a great shout from the sea!

It startled them all. The horses,
    Lazily plodding round,   10
Started and stopp'd; and the mills dropp'd
    Like a mantle their sound.

The millers look'd over their shoulders,
    The drivers open'd their eyes:
A silence, deeper than deafness,
    Had fallen out of the skies.

'Halloa there!'—this time distinctly
    It rose from the barren sea;
And Europe, turning in wonder,
    Whisper'd, 'What can it be?'   20

'Come down, come down to the shore here!'
    And Europe was soon on the sand;—
It was the great Columbus
    Dragging his prize to land.

                (1891)

507 *A Schule Laddie's Lament on the Lateness o' the Season*

THE east wind's whistlin' cauld an' shrill,
The snaw lies on the Lomont Hill;
It's simmer i' the almanack,
But when 'ill simmer days be back?

There's no' a bud on tree or buss;
The craws are at a sair nonplus,—
Hoo can they big? hoo can they pair?
Wi' them sae cauld, and winds sae bare.

My faither canna saw his seed,—
The hauf o' th' laund's to ploo, indeed;   10
The lambs are deein', an' the yowes
Are trauchled wanderin' owre the knowes.

There's no' a swallow back as yet,
The robin doesna seek to flit;
There's no' a buckie, nor a bud,
On ony brae, in ony wud.

507   trauchled] fatigued by walking   buckie] shell

It's no' a time for barefit feet
When it may be on-ding o' sleet.
The season's broken a' oor rules,—
It's no' the time o' year o' bools;   20

It's no' the time o' year o' peeries.
I think the year's gane tapsalteeries!
The farmers may be bad, nae doot—
It pits hiz laddies sair aboot.

(1891)

DOLLIE RADFORD
1858–?

508   *Soliloquy of a Maiden Aunt*

THE ladies bow, and partners set,
And turn around and pirouette
          And trip the Lancers.

But no one seeks my ample chair,
Or asks me with persuasive air
          To join the dancers.

They greet me, as I sit alone
Upon my solitary throne,
          And pass politely.

Yet mine could keep the measured beat,   10
As surely as the youngest feet,
          And tread as lightly.

No other maiden had my skill
In our old homestead on the hill—
          That merry May-time

When Allan closed the flagging ball,
And danced with me before them all,
          Until the day-time.

507   on-ding] driving or beating on

572

Again I laugh, and step alone,
And curtsey low as on my own   20
   His strong hand closes.

But Allan now seeks staid delight,
His son there, brought my niece to-night
   These early roses.

Time orders well, we have our Spring,
Our songs, and may-flower gathering,
   Our love and laughter.

And children chatter all the while,
And leap the brook and climb the stile
   And follow after.   30

And yet—the step of Allan's son,
Is not as light as was the one
   That went before it.

And that old lace, I think, falls down
Less softly on Priscilla's gown
   Than when I wore it.

        (1891)

J. K. STEPHEN

1859–1892

509   *England and America*

I. ON A RHINE STEAMER

REPUBLIC of the West,
 Enlightened, free, sublime,
Unquestionably best
 Production of our time.

The telephone is thine,
 And thine the Pullman Car,
The caucus, the divine
 Intense electric star.

To thee we likewise owe
  The venerable names
Of Edgar Allan Poe,
  And Mr Henry James.

In short it's due to thee,
  Thou kind of Western star,
That we have come to be
  Precisely what we are.

But every now and then,
  It cannot be denied,
You breed a kind of men
  Who are not dignified,

Or courteous or refined,
  Benevolent or wise,
Or gifted with a mind
  Beyond the common size,

Or notable for tact,
  Agreeable to me,
Or anything, in fact,
  That people ought to be.

2. ON A PARISIAN BOULEVARD

Britannia rules the waves,
  As I have heard her say;
She frees whatever slaves
  She meets upon her way.

A teeming mother she
  Of Parliaments and Laws;
Majestic, mighty, free:
  Devoid of common flaws.

For her did Shakspere write
  His admirable plays:
For her did Nelson fight
  And Wolseley win his bays.

Her sturdy common sense
  Is based on solid grounds:
By saving numerous pence
  She spends effective pounds.

The Saxon and the Celt
    She equitably rules;
Her iron rod is felt
    By countless knaves and fools.   20

In fact, mankind at large,
    Black, yellow, white and red,
Is given to her in charge,
    And owns her as a head.

But every here and there—
    Deny it if you can—
She breeds a vacant stare
    Unworthy of a man:

A look of dull surprise;
    A nerveless idle hand: 30
An eye which never tries
    To threaten or command:

In short, a kind of man,
    If man indeed he be,
As worthy of our ban
    As any that we see:

Unspeakably obtuse,
    Abominably vain,
Of very little use,
    And execrably plain.   40

                        (1891)

510   *In the Backs*

As I was strolling lonely in the Backs,
I met a woman whom I did not like.
I did not like the way the woman walked:
Loose-hipped, big-boned, disjointed, angular.
If her anatomy comprised a waist,
I did not notice it: she had a face
With eyes and lips adjusted thereunto,
But round her mouth no pleasing shadows stirred,
Nor did her eyes invite a second glance.
Her dress was absolutely colourless,   10
Devoid of taste or shape or character;
Her boots were rather old, and rather large,

                        575

And rather shabby, not precisely matched.
Her hair was very far from beautiful
And not abundant: she had such a hat
As neither merits nor expects remark.
She was not clever, I am very sure,
Nor witty nor amusing; well-informed
She may have been, and kind, perhaps, of heart;
But gossip was writ plain upon her face.   20
And so she stalked her dull unthinking way;
Or, if she thought of anything, it was
That such a one had got a second class,
Or Mrs So-and-So a second child.
I do not want to see that girl again:
I do not like her: and I should not mind
If she were done away with, killed, or ploughed.
She did not seem to serve a useful end:
And certainly she was not beautiful.

(1891)

511   *A Remonstrance*

LOVE is what lacks then: but what does it mean to you?
    Where did you hear of it, feel it, or see?
What has the truth, or the good of it been to you?
    How love some other, yet nohow love me?

If there were any conspicuous fault in me,
    Any defect it were torture to bear,
Low-lying levels, too deep to exalt, in me,
    Dread possibilities in me to fear:

If I were ugly or old or untractable,
    Mean in my methods or low in my views: 10
If I were dull or unpleasant: in fact able
    Neither to please, nor elate, nor amuse:—

That makes you angry, impatient; we'll take it, then,
    I am a man that to know 's to esteem:
That's the admission you make to me: make it then:
    Well why not love me? what's love but a dream?

Only of course in the sense you bestow on it:
    I have a meaning for love, that is plain:
Further than passion, and longing, and so on, it
    Means to me liking and liking again: 20

Liking, and liking, and liking—that's plain enough;—
　　Something depending on qualities then?
Yes: for they give you both pleasure and pain enough,
　　Qualities common in women and men.

Still not a doubt that, the love being brought about,
　　Liking made love, there is more that will come:
All the good qualities ever yet thought about:—
　　Yes, they fall short of that excellent sum.

Like a man: like him: and let there be more of it,
　　That which he is he'll be liked for: at last　　　30
Love in a minute will flash—I am sure of it—
　　Whether the wedding be future or past.

You who consider it quite immaterial
　　Whether the person is worthy or not:
You who are looking for something ethereal,
　　Something celestial, transcending our lot:

You to whom every excellent quality
　　Means but a cypher: who hope to behold
Love at a burst in his mighty totality
　　Change all the grey of the world into gold:　　　40

You dream a priceless love: I feel a penny one:
　　My reason plods, while your fancy can range:—
Therefore, I ask, since you'll never love any one,
　　Why should you not marry me for a change?

　　　　　　　　　　　　　　　　　(1891)

512　　　　　*After the Golden Wedding*

　　　　　　(*Three Soliloquies*)

I. THE HUSBAND'S

　SHE'S not a faultless woman; no!
　　She's not an angel in disguise:
　She has her rivals here below:
　　She's not an unexampled prize:

　She does not always see the point
　　Of little jests her husband makes:
　And, when the world is out of joint,
　　She makes a hundred small mistakes:

577

She's not a miracle of tact:
   Her temper's not the best I know: 10
She's got her little faults in fact,
   Although I never tell her so.

But this, my wife, is why I hold you
   As good a wife as ever stepped,
And why I meant it when I told you
   How cordially our feast I kept:

You've lived with me these fifty years,
   And all the time you loved me dearly:
I may have given you cause for tears:
   I may have acted rather queerly.   20

I ceased to love you long ago:
   I loved another for a season:
As time went on I came to know
   Your worth, my wife: and saw the reason

Why such a wife as you have been
   Is more than worth the world beside;
You loved me all the time, my Queen;
   You couldn't help it if you tried.

You loved me as I once loved you,
   As each loved each beside the altar: 30
And whatsoever I might do,
   Your loyal heart could never falter.

And, if you sometimes fail me, sweetest,
   And don't appreciate me, dear,
No matter: such defects are meetest
   For poor humanity, I fear.

And all's forgiven, all's forgot,
   On this our golden wedding day;
For, see! she loves me: does she not?
   So let the world e'en go its way.   40

I'm old and nearly useless now,
   Each day a greater weakling proves me:
There's compensation anyhow:
   I still possess a wife that loves me.

2. THE WIFE'S

Dear worthy husband! good old man!
  Fit hero of a golden marriage:
I'll show towards you, if I can,
  An absolutely wifely carriage.

The months or years which your career
  May still comprise before you perish,
Shall serve to prove that I, my dear,
  Can honour, and obey, and cherish.

Till death us part, as soon he must,
  (And you, my dear, should show the way)   10
I hope you'll always find me just
  The same as on our wedding day.

I never loved you, dearest: never!
  Let that be clearly understood:
I thought you good, and rather clever,
  And found you really rather good.

And, what was more, I loved another,
  But couldn't get him: well, but, then
You're just as bad, my erring brother,
  You most impeccable of men:—   20

Except for this: my love was married
  Some weeks before I married you:
While you, my amorous dawdler, tarried
  Till we'd been wed a year or two.

You loved me at our wedding: I
  Loved some one else: and after that
I never cast a loving eye
  On others: you—well, tit for tat!

But after all I made you cheerful:
  Your whims I've humoured: saw the point   30
Of all your jokes: grew duly tearful,
  When you were sad, yet chose the joint

You liked the best of all for dinner,
  And soothed you in your hours of woe:
Although a miserable sinner,
  I *am* a good wife, as wives go.

I bore with you and took your side,
   And kept my temper all the time:
I never flirted; never cried,
   Nor ranked it as a heinous crime,   40

When you preferred another lady,
   Or used improper words to me,
Or told a story more than shady,
   Or snored and snorted after tea,

Or otherwise gave proofs of being
   A dull and rather vain old man:
I still succeeded in agreeing
   With all you said, (the safest plan),

Yet always strove my point to carry,
   And make you do as I desired: 50
I'm *glad* my people made me marry!
   They hit on just what I required.

Had love been wanted—well, I couldn't
   Have given what I'd not to give;
Or had a genius asked me! wouldn't
   The man have suffered? now, we live

Among our estimable neighbours
   A decent and decorous life:
I've earned by my protracted labours
   The title of a model wife.   60

But when beneath the turf you're sleeping,
   And I am sitting here in black,
Engaged, as they'll suppose, in weeping,
   I shall not wish to have you back.

3. THE VICAR'S

A good old couple! kind and wise!
   And oh! what love for one another!
They've won, those two, life's highest prize,
   Oh! let us copy them, my brother.

(1891)

KATHARINE TYNAN
1861–1931

513   *The Witch*

MARGARET GRADY—I fear she will burn—
Charmed the butter off my churn;
'Tis I would know it the wide world over,
Yellow as saffron, scented with clover.

At Omagh market the witch displayed it:
Ill she had gathered, ill she had made it.
Hid in my cloak's hood, one glance I threw it,
Passed on smiling; my troth! I knew it!

Sheila, the kindest cow in the parish,
Mild and silken, and good to cherish,   10
Shame her own gold butter should leave her
To enrich the milk of a low-bred heifer!

I said not Yea or Nay to the mocker,
But called the fairy-man over from Augher;
Like a russet he is that's withered,
Bent in two with his wisdom gathered.

He touched the butter, he peered and pondered,
And crooned strange rhymes while I watched and wondered:
Then he drew me out through the gloaming
O'er the fields where the mist was coming.   20

He bewitched me so that I know not
Where they may grow, where they may grow not;
Those witch-hazels he plucked and plaited,
Crooning on while the twigs he mated.

There's the wreath on the churn-dash yonder.
All the neighbours view it with wonder;
And 'spite of Father Tom I avow it
The yield is doubled since that came to it.

I bless the fairy-man though he be evil;
Yet fairy-spells come not from the Devil;   30
And Margaret Grady—I fear she will burn—
I do forgive her, with hate and scorn.

(1891)

ERNEST DOWSON
1867–1900

Ah, dans ces mornes séjours
Les jamais sont les toujours.
PAUL VERLAINE

YOU would have understood me, had you waited,
   I could have loved you, dear! as well as he:
Had we not been impatient, dear! and fated
     Always to disagree.

What is the use of speech? Silence were fitter:
   Lest we should still be wishing things unsaid.
Though all the words we ever spake were bitter,
     Shall I reproach you dead?

Nay, let this earth, your portion, likewise cover
   All the old anger, setting us apart: 10
Always, in all, in truth was I your lover;
     Always, I held your heart.

I have met other women who were tender,
   As you were cold, dear! with a grace as rare.
Think you, I turned to them, or made surrender,
     I who had found you fair?

Had we been patient, dear! ah, had you waited,
   I had fought death for you, better than he:
But from the very first, dear! we were fated
     Always to disagree.   20

Late, late, I come to you, now death discloses
   Love that in life was not to be our part:
On your low lying mound between the roses,
     Sadly I cast my heart.

I would not waken you: nay! this is fitter;
   Death and the darkness give you unto me;
Here we who loved so, were so cold and bitter,
     Hardly can disagree.

(Wr. 1891; pub. 1894)

515 ## *Terre Promise*

For Herbert P. Horne

EVEN now the fragrant darkness of her hair
Had brushed my cheek; and once, in passing by,
Her hand upon my hand lay tranquilly:
What things unspoken trembled in the air!

Always I know, how little severs me
From mine heart's country, that is yet so far;
And must I lean and long across a bar,
That half a word would shatter utterly?

Ah might it be, that just by touch of hand,
Or speaking silence, shall the barrier fall;   10
And she shall pass, with no vain words at all,
But droop into mine arms, and understand!

(Wr. 1893; pub. 1896)

516 ## *Spleen*

For Arthur Symons

I WAS not sorrowful, I could not weep,
And all my memories were put to sleep.

I watched the river grow more white and strange,
All day till evening I watched it change.

All day till evening I watched the rain
Beat wearily upon the window pane.

I was not sorrowful, but only tired
Of everything that ever I desired.

Her lips, her eyes, all day became to me
The shadow of a shadow utterly.   10

All day mine hunger for her heart became
Oblivion, until the evening came,

And left me sorrowful, inclined to weep,
With all my memories that could not sleep.

(1896)

517   *Vitae summa brevis spem nos vetat incohare longam.*

THEY are not long, the weeping and the laughter,
        Love and desire and hate:
I think they have no portion in us after
        We pass the gate.

They are not long, the days of wine and roses:
        Out of a misty dream
Our path emerges for a while, then closes
        Within a dream.

                              (Wr. and pub. 1896)

JOHN GRAY
1866–1934

518   *Les Demoiselles de Sauve*

        To S.A.S. Alice, Princesse de Monaco

BEAUTIFUL ladies through the orchard pass;
Bend under crutched-up branches, forked and low;
Trailing their samet palls o'er dew-drenched grass.

Pale blossoms, looking on proud Jacqueline,
Blush to the colour of her finger tips,
And rosy knuckles, laced with yellow lace.

High-crested Berthe discerns, with slant, clinched eyes,
Amid the leaves pink faces of the skies;
She locks her plaintive hands Sainte-Margot-wise.

Ysabeau follows last, with languorous pace;   10
Presses, voluptuous, to her bursting lips,
With backward stoop, a bunch of eglantine.

Courtly ladies through the orchard pass;
Bow low, as in lords' halls; and springtime grass
Tangles a snare to catch the tapering toe.

                              (1892)

519   *Wings in the Dark*

FORTH into the warm darkness faring wide—
More silent momently the silent quay—
Towards where the ranks of boats rock to the tide,
Muffling their plaintive gurgling jealously.

With gentle nodding of her gracious snout,
One greets her master till he step aboard;
She flaps her wings impatient to get out;
She runs to plunder, straining every cord.

Full-winged and stealthy like a bird of prey,
All tense the muscles of her seemly flanks;   10
She, the coy creature that the idle day
Sees idly riding in the idle ranks.

Backward and forth, over the chosen ground,
Like a young horse, she drags the heavy trawl
Content; or speeds her rapturous course unbound,
And passing fishers through the darkness call,

Deep greeting, in the jargon of the sea.
Haul upon haul, flounders and soles and dabs,
And phosphorescent animalculæ,
Sand, sea drift, weeds, thousands of worthless crabs.   20

Darkling upon the mud the fishes grope,
Cautious to stir, staring with jewel eyes;
Dogs of the sea, the savage congers mope,
Winding their sulky march meander-wise.

Suddenly all is light and life and flight,
Upon the sandy bottom, agate strewn.
The fishers mumble, waiting till the night
Urge on the clouds, and cover up the moon.

(1893)

The Barber

I

I DREAMED I was a barber; and there went
Beneath my hand, oh! manes extravagant.
Beneath my trembling fingers, many a mask
Of many a pleasant girl. It was my task
To gild their hair, carefully, strand by strand;
To paint their eyebrows with a timid hand;
To draw a bodkin, from a vase of kohl,
Through the closed lashes, pencils from a bowl
Of sepia to paint them underneath;
To blow upon their eyes with a soft breath.   10
They lay them back and watched the leaping bands.

II

The dream grew vague. I moulded with my hands
The mobile breasts, the valley; and the waist
I touched; and pigments reverently placed
Upon their thighs in sapient spots and stains,
Beryls and crysolites and diaphanes,
And gems whose hot harsh names are never said.
I was a masseur; and my fingers bled
With wonder as I touched their awful limbs.

III

Suddenly, in the marble trough, there seems   20
O, last of my pale mistresses, Sweetness!
A twy-lipped scarlet pansie. My caress
Tinges thy steelgray eyes to violet.
Adown thy body skips the pit-a-pat
Of treatment once heard in a hospital
For plagues that fascinate, but half appal.

IV

So, at the sound, the blood of me stood cold.
The chaste hair ripened into sullen gold.
The throat, the shoulders, swelled and were uncouth.
The breasts rose up and offered each a mouth.   30
And on the belly pallid blushes crept,
That maddened me, until I laughed and wept.

(1893)

521

Mishka

To Henri Teixeira de Mattos

MISHKA is poet among the beasts.
When roots are rotten, and rivers weep,
The bear is at play in the land of sleep.
Though his head be heavy between his fists.
The bear is poet among the beasts.

THE DREAM:
Wide and large are the monster's eyes,
Nought saying, save one word alone:
Mishka! Mishka, as turned to stone,
Hears no word else, nor in anywise
Can see aught save the monster's eyes.   10

Honey is under the monster's lips;
And Mishka follows into her lair,
Dragged in the net of her yellow hair,
Knowing all things when honey drips
On his tongue like rain, the song of the hips

Of the honey-child, and of each twin mound.
Mishka! there screamed a far bird-note,
Deep in the sky, when round his throat
The triple coil of her hair she wound.
And stroked his limbs with a humming sound.   20

Mishka is white like a hunter's son;
For he knows no more of the ancient south
When the honey-child's lips are on his mouth,
When all her kisses are joined in one,
And his body is bathed in grass and sun.

The shadows lie mauven beneath the trees,
And purple stains, where the finches pass,
Leap in the stalks of the deep, rank grass.
Flutter of wing, and the buzz of bees,
Deepen the silence, and sweeten ease.   30

The honey-child is an olive tree,
The voice of birds and the voice of flowers,
Each of them all and all the hours,
The honey-child is a wingèd bee,
Her touch is a perfume, a melody.

(1893)

587

522

The Vines

To André Chevrillon

'HAVE you seen the listening snake?'
Bramble clutches for his bride,
Lately she was by his side,
Woodbine, with her gummy hands.

In the ground the mottled snake
Listens for the dawn of day;
Listens, listening death away,
Till the day burst winter's bands.

Painted ivy is asleep,
Stretched upon the bank, all torn,   10
Sinewy though she be; love-lorn
Convolvuluses cease to creep.

Bramble clutches for his bride,
Woodbine, with her gummy hands,
All his horny claws expands;
She has withered in his grasp.

'Till the day dawn, till the tide
Of the winter's afternoon.'
'Who tells dawning?'—'Listen, soon.'
Half-born tendrils, grasping, gasp.   20

(1893)

523

Poem

To Arthur Edmonds

GERANIUM, houseleek, laid in oblong beds
On the trim grass. The daisies' leprous stain
Is fresh. Each night the daisies burst again,
Though every day the gardener crops their heads.

A wistful child, in foul unwholesome shreds,
Recalls some legend of a daisy chain
That makes a pretty necklace. She would fain
Make one, and wear it, if she had some threads.

Sun, leprous flowers, foul child. The asphalt burns,
The garrulous sparrows perch on metal Burns.   10
Sing! Sing! they say, and flutter with their wings.
He does not sing, he only wonders why
He is sitting there. The sparrows sing. And I
Yield to the strait allure of simple things.

(1893)

524   *Spleen*

THE roses every one were red,
And all the ivy leaves were black.

Sweet, do not even stir your head,
Or all of my despairs come back.

The sky is too blue, too delicate:
Too soft the air, too green the sea.

I fear—how long had I to wait!—
That you will tear yourself from me.

The shining box-leaves weary me,
The varnished holly's glistening,   10

The stretch of infinite country;
So, saving you, does everything.

(1893)

525   *Battledore*

THE sheltered garden sleeps among the tall
Black poplars which grow round it, next the wall.
The wall is very high, green grown on red.
All is within, white convent, chapel, all.

Slight supper past, the evening office said,
Gardening tools locked up, the poultry fed,
Little is done but lazy chaplets told,
Weeds plucked, and garden calvaries visited.

Some pace and stitch; some read in little, old,
Worn, heavily bound missals, which they hold   10
With both red hands, where lawns are foiled with flowers,
Lily and Ladybell and Marygold.

This is the least unhushed of evening hours,
When blessed peace best wears its dearest dowers;
Quietly grouped are nuns and novices;
Two tiny ladies play with battledores.

Drunk with the blows, unsteady with the whizz
Of whirling flight, the shuttlecock seems, is
Alive and fluttering at each new shock.
Sisters are drawing close by twos and threes.   20

Asthmatic mother, as the shuttlecock
Flies straight at her, allows herself to knock
It onward with her leaf fan, muttering,
Half as excuse: 'Tis nearly nine o'clock.

What better warrant for a foolish thing:
With swift inventiveness the sisters bring
Whatever light thing strikes; old copybooks
Fulfil the purpose well. Such fluttering

Within the convent walls the sober rooks
Who live among the poplar branches—Sooks!—   30
Had seldom seen. Now all the place prevails
With cries and laughter to its furthest nooks.

The novices and nuns catch up their tails,
Better to bustle, darting till their veils
Float back and tangle in the merry fuss,
Till sombre weeds swell out like lusty sails. . . .

Peace, croaks the mother, Peace, the angelus!

(1896)

526   THEY say, in other days,
           When Jove in Heaven, and Pluto ruled in Hell,
           Man, walking in a haze,
           Exceeding good, or did exceeding ill.

           So, when he came to Dis,
           And man must face his three infernal judges,
           Having greatly done amiss,
           The devils grin, and fellow fellow nudges.

They say that many a prince
Came with such load of crime upon his back,   10
That Tartarus would rinse
His jaws, that Hell would shudder and be black.

First Æacus would hear the tale
Against the sinner of his sin,
And for a pain condemn the pale
Ghost to the lower court, wherein

Dread Minos gave a like award,
And sent him Rhadamanthusward.

There was no pain for man that Hell could reach
Like this pain. Yet the devils would beseech   20

Their master, and entreat the Dreadful One
To judge as strangely as the thing was done.

Then Pluto judged; that is to say, his face was bare;
Whereof I may not tell if it were harsh or fair;

But this I may: a man might howl a space
Of many years who once had seen his face.

(1896)

527   *Tobias and the Angel*

TOBIAS, journeying to Ecbatane,
Takes with him Azarias as he fares,
Which is an angel, serving unawares,
To guide and bring him to his house again.

Raphael walks mid-picture, sandal-shod;
Three fingers in three fingers leads the boy;
Holding sweet speech, the distance to employ;
The little curly dog sniffs out his road.

Tobias, jerkined, belted, simply cloaked,
With naked shanks, except for limp-legged boots   10
Against rough stones or harsh and prickly roots,
Bareheaded, querulous and wonderlooked.

591

Glorious archangel, Medicine of God,
Kind courier, peacock-plumed thy pinions be,
Sign of thine ancient immortality,
Folded for fare on mortal stone and sod.

Thy glory floats and glints twixt hair and wing;
Thou wearest man's attention on thy face;
Though somewhat else Tobias doth half trace
Therein, whiles thou art wise of trafficking.   20

Tobias bears his fish, and neatly slung,
Lest its scales soil, or it should leave a reek;
Raphael the gall, old Tobit's eyes being sick,
By sparrows' hospitality quick stung.

Hard to each hand, Tobias doth not see
Great Michael, armed and exquisite, alert,
The prince, the Warrior, lest any hurt;
Lest Asmodeus lurk to thwart, walks he.

And gentle Gabriel, the ambassador;
His arm a lily-stalk, with triple bloom,   30
And three locked lilies (tidings yet to come).
One with an angel maketh one of four.

Much sky and little earth complete arrear,
Tree-fledged and island-strawn, the Tigris, bland,
Creeps lower. (Pilgrims trudge on mountain land.)
Flower and thorn and stone are frequent near.

Hasting to speed thy marriage, thou and he,
Tobias, hardly yet at man's first scope,
Sprung of staunch kindliness and godly hope,
Brought up and nourished in captivity.   40

Forth from the river, come to take thy bath,
Leaped fleshly passion, eager to devour;
'Seize him,' the angel said; and in that hour
Slit out his gall, his lust, his bilious wrath.

To medicine the gall at bidding turned
Of him who leadeth thee; the heart laid by;
The liver too, to purpose presently,
To fright the demon, being spoiled & burned.

Mark how Tobias, setting out for gain,
Under the angel guidance halts halfway   50
For greater gain; the guide resumes the way,
Wise and alone, to spare his ward the pain.

He sees in Azarias one of his tribe,
A man discreet and just, but hired for wages
To bring him into Media, to Rages;
Back to the city of Sennacherib.

Of Raphael's work, and how he handled it,
With fish's gall how he gave Tobit sight,
Purgation of the demon-haunted night,
Is written in the book which Tobit writ.   60

All things being done, and done exceeding well,
The guide replied to him, when said Tobias:
'Give we the half of gain to Azarias:'
'Call me not so, my name is Raphael.'

There liveth no Tobias graced with power
To take angelic counsel, to uproot
Swarth lust, meek purity to substitute,
But meets the angel in the proper hour.

(1896)

528

*Magnae deus potentiae
qui fertili natos aqua
partim relinquis gurgiti
partim levas in aera.*

The Flying Fish

I

MYSELF am Hang the buccaneer,
whom children love and brave men fear,
master of courage, come what come,
master of craft, and called Sea-scum;

student of wisdom and waterways,
course of moons and the birth of days;
to him in whose heart all things be
I bring my story of the sea.

The same am I as that sleek Hang
whose pattens along the stone quay clang   10
in sailing time, whose pile is high
on the beach when merchants come to buy.

Am he who cumbers his lowly hulk
with refuse bundles of feeble bulk;
turns sailor's eyes to the weather skies;
bows low to the Master of Merchandise;

who hoists his sails with the broken slats;
whose lean crew are scarcely food for his rats;
am he who creeps from tower-top ken
and utmost vision of all men: 20

ah then, am he who changeth line,
and which man knoweth that course of mine?
Am he, sir Sage, who sails to the sea
where an island and other wonders be.

After six days we sight the coast,
and my palace top, should a sailor boast;
sails rattle down; and then we ride,
mean junk and proud, by my palace side.

For there lives a junk in that ancient sea
where the gardens of Hang and his palace be,   30
o my fair junk! which once aboard
the pirate owns no living lord.

Its walls are painted water-green
like the green sea's self, both shade and sheen,
lest any mark it. The pirate's trade
is to hover swiftly and make afraid.

Its sails are fashioned of lithe bamboo,
all painted blue as the sky is blue,
so it be not seen till the prey be nigh.
Hang loves not that the same should fly.   40

In midst of the first a painted sun
gleams gold like the celestial yon;
in midst of the second a tender moon,
that a lover might kiss his flute and swoon;

or maid touch lute at sight of the third,
pictured with all the crystal herd;
so the silly ships are mazed at sight
of night by day and day by night.

For wind and water a goodlier junk
than any that ever sailed or sunk;   50
which junk was theirs; none fiercer than
my fathers since the fall of man.

So cotton rags lays Hang aside:
lays bare the sailor's gristly hide;   ·
and wraps his body in vests of silk;
ilk is as beautiful as ilk.

Then Hang puts on his ancient mail,
silver and black, and scale on scale
like dragons', which his grandsire bore
before him, and his grandsire before.   60

He binds his legs with buskins grim,
tawny and gold for the pride of him;
his feet are bare like his who quelled
the dragon, his feet are feet of eld.

His head is brave with a lacquered casque,
the donning which is a heavy task;
its flaps are feathered like Yuen Yin;
'tis strapped with straps of tiger-skin.

The passions of his fathers whelm
the heart of Hang when he wears their helm.   70
Then Hang grows wrinkled betwixt his eyes;
he frowns like a devil, devil-wise;

his eyeballs start; his mask is red
like his who at last shall judge the dead;
his nostrils gape; his mouth is the mouth
of the fish that swims in the torrid south;

his beard the pirate Hang lets flow;
he lays his hand on his father's bow,
wherewith a cunning man of strength
might shoot an arrow the vessel's length.   80

I have another of sun-red lac,
of a great man's height, so the string be slack;
the charge departs with a fiery clang;
'tis drawn with the foot, the foot of Hang.

Such house and harness become me, when
I wait upon laden merchantmen;
'Twixt tears and the sea, 'twixt brine and brine,
they shudder at sight of me and mine.

II

Of the birds that fly in the farthest sea
six are stranger than others be:
under its tumble, among the fish,
six are a marvel passing wish.

First is a hawk, exceeding great;
he dwelleth alone; he hath no mate;
his neck is wound with a yellow ring;
on his breast is the crest of a former king.

The second bird is exceeding pale,
from little head to scanty tail;   10
she is striped with black on either wing,
which is rose-lined, like a princely thing.

Though small the bulk of the brilliant third,
of all blue birds 'tis the bluest bird;
they fly in bands; and, seen by day,
by the side of them the sky is grey.

I mind the fifth, I forget the fourth,
unless that it comes from the east by north.
The fifth is an orange white-billed duck;
he diveth for fish, like the god of Luck;   20

he hath never a foot on which to stand;
for water yields and he loves not land.
This is the end of many words
save one, concerning marvellous birds.

The great-faced dolphin is first of fish;
he is devil-eyed and devilish;
of all the fishes is he most brave,
he walks the sea like an angry wave.

The second the fishes call their lord;
himself a bow, his face is a sword;   30
his sword is armed with a hundred teeth,
fifty above and fifty beneath.

The third hath a scarlet suit of mail;
the fourth is naught but a feeble tail;
the fifth is a whip with a hundred strands,
and every arm hath a hundred hands.

The last strange fish is the last strange bird;
Of him no sage hath ever heard;
he roams the sea in a gleaming horde
in fear of the dolphin and him of the sword.   40

He leaps from the sea with a silken swish;
he beats the air does the flying fish.
His eyes are round with excess of fright,
bright as the drops of his pinions' flight.

In sea and sky he hath no peace;
for the five strange fish are his enemies;
and the five strange fowls keep watch for him;
they know him well by his crystal gleam.

Oftwhiles, sir Sage, on my junk's white deck
have I seen this fish-bird come to wreck,   50
oftwhiles (fair deck) 'twixt bow and poop
have I seen this piteous sky-fish stoop.

Scaled bird, how his snout and gills dilate,
all quivering and roseate:
he pants in crystal and mother-of-pearl
while his body shrinks and his pinions furl.

His beauty passes like bubbles blown;
the white bright bird is a fish of stone;
the bird so fair, for its putrid sake,
is flung to the dogs in the junk's white wake.   60

III

Have thought, son Pirate, some such must be
as the beast thou namest in yonder sea;
else, bring me a symbol from nature's gear
of aspiration born of fear.

Hast been, my son, to the doctor's booth
some day when Hang had a qualm to soothe?
Hast noted the visible various sign
Of each flask's virtue, son of mine?

Rude picture of insect seldom found,
of plant that thrives in marshy ground,   10
goblin of east wind, fog or draught,
sign of the phial's potent craft?

'Tis even thus where the drug is sense,
where wisdom is more than frankincense,
wit's grain than a pound of pounded bones,
where knowledge is redder than ruby stones.

Hast thou marked how poppies are sign of sin?
how bravery's mantle is tiger-skin?
how earth is heavy and dumb with care?
how song is the speech of all the air?   20

A tree is the sign most whole and sure
of aspiration plain and pure;
of the variation one must wend
in search of the sign to the sea's wild end.

Thy fish is the fairest of all that be
in the throbbing depths of yonder sea.
He says in his iridescent heart:
I am gorgeous-eyed and a fish apart;

my back hath the secret of every shell,
the Hang of fishes knoweth well;   30
scales of my breast are softer still,
the ugly fishes devise my ill.

He prays the Maker of water-things
not for a sword, but cricket's wings,
not to be one of the sons of air,
to be rid of the water is all his prayer;

all his hope is a fear-whipped whim;
all directions are one to him.
There are seekers of wisdom no less absurd,
son Hang, than thy fish that would be a bird.   40

(1896)

529 *On the South Coast of Cornwall*

THERE lives a land beside the western sea
The sea-salt makes not barren, for its hills
Laugh even in winter time; the bubbly rills
Dance down their grades, and fill with melody
The fishers' hearts; for these, where'er they be,
Sing out salt choruses; the land-breeze fills
Their sweetened lungs with wine which it distils
From emerald fat field and gorse gold lea.
Like a thrown net leans out the ample bay.
The fishers' huddled cabins crowd and wedge,   10
Greedy, against the rugged treacherous edge
Of their great liquid mine renewed alway.
The fishers have no thought but of the strong
Sea, whence their food, their crisp hair, and their song.

(1897)

MICHAEL FIELD
(KATHARINE BRADLEY, 1846–1914, and
EDITH COOPER, 1862–1913)

530 *Cyclamens*

THEY are terribly white:
There is snow on the ground,
  And a moon on the snow at night;
  The sky is cut by the winter light;
Yet I, who have all these things in ken,
Am struck to the heart by the chiselled white
  Of this handful of cyclamen.

(1893)

531 *Noon*

FULL summer and at noon; from a waste bed
Convolvulus, musk-mallow, poppies spread
The triumph of the sunshine overhead.

Blue on refulgent ash-trees lies the heat;
It tingles on the hedge-rows; the young wheat
Sleeps, warm in golden verdure, at my feet.

The pale, sweet grasses of the hayfield blink;
The heath-moors, as the bees of honey drink,
Suck the deep bosom of the day. To think

Of all that beauty by the light defined   10
None shares my vision! Sharply on my mind
Presses the sorrow: fern and flower are blind.

(1893)

JOHN DAVIDSON

1857–1909

532   *Thirty Bob a Week*

I COULDN'T touch a stop and turn a screw,
    And set the blooming world a-work for me,
Like such as cut their teeth—I hope, like you—
    On the handle of a skeleton gold key;
I cut mine on a leek, which I eat it every week:
    I'm a clerk at thirty bob as you can see.

But I don't allow it's luck and all a toss;
    There's no such thing as being starred and crossed;
It's just the power of some to be a boss,
    And the bally power of others to be bossed: 10
I face the music, sir; you bet I ain't a cur;
    Strike me lucky if I don't believe I'm lost!

For like a mole I journey in the dark,
    A-travelling along the underground
From my Pillar'd Halls and broad Suburbean Park,
    To come the daily dull official round;
And home again at night with my pipe all alight,
    A-scheming how to count ten bob a pound.

And it's often very cold and very wet,
  And my missis stitches towels for a hunks;   20
And the Pillar'd Halls is half of it to let—
  Three rooms about the size of travelling trunks.
And we cough, my wife and I, to dislocate a sigh,
  When the noisy little kids are in their bunks.

But you never hear her do a growl or whine,
  For she's made of flint and roses, very odd;
And I've got to cut my meaning rather fine,
  Or I'd blubber, for I'm made of greens and sod:
So p'r'aps we are in Hell for all that I can tell,
  And lost and damn'd and served up hot to God.   30

I ain't blaspheming, Mr Silver-tongue;
  I'm saying things a bit beyond your art:
Of all the rummy starts you ever sprung,
  Thirty bob a week's the rummiest start!
With your science and your books and your the'ries about spooks,
  Did you ever hear of looking in your heart?

I didn't mean your pocket, Mr, no:
  I mean that having children and a wife,
With thirty bob on which to come and go,
  Isn't dancing to the tabor and the fife: 40
When it doesn't make you drink, by Heaven! it makes you think,
  And notice curious items about life.

I step into my heart and there I meet
  A god-almighty devil singing small,
Who would like to shout and whistle in the street,
  And squelch the passers flat against the wall;
If the whole world was a cake he had the power to take,
  He would take it, ask for more, and eat them all.

And I meet a sort of simpleton beside,
  The kind that life is always giving beans;   50
With thirty bob a week to keep a bride
  He fell in love and married in his teens:
At thirty bob he stuck; but he knows it isn't luck:
  He knows the seas are deeper than tureens.

601

And the god-almighty devil and the fool
   That meet me in the High Street on the strike,
When I walk about my heart a-gathering wool,
   Are my good and evil angels if you like.
And both of them together in every kind of weather
   Ride me like a double-seated bike.   60

That's rough a bit and needs its meaning curled.
   But I have a high old hot un in my mind—
A most engrugious notion of the world,
   That leaves your lightning 'rithmetic behind:
I give it at a glance when I say 'There ain't no chance,
   Nor nothing of the lucky-lottery kind.'

And it's this way that I make it out to be:
   No fathers, mothers, countries, climates—none;
No Adam was responsible for me,
   Nor society, nor systems, nary one: 70
A little sleeping seed, I woke—I did, indeed—
   A million years before the blooming sun.

I woke because I thought the time had come;
   Beyond my will there was no other cause;
And everywhere I found myself at home,
   Because I chose to be the thing I was;
And in whatever shape of mollusc or of ape
   I always went according to the laws.

I was the love that chose my mother out;
   I joined two lives and from the union burst;   80
My weakness and my strength without a doubt
   Are mine alone for ever from the first:
It's just the very same with a difference in the name
   As 'Thy will be done.' You say it if you durst!

They say it daily up and down the land
   As easy as you take a drink, it's true;
But the difficultest go to understand,
   And the difficultest job a man can do,
Is to come it brave and meek with thirty bob a week,
   And feel that that's the proper thing for you.   90

It's a naked child against a hungry wolf;
　It's playing bowls upon a splitting wreck;
It's walking on a string across a gulf
　With millstones fore-and-aft about your neck;
But the thing is daily done by many and many a one;
　And we fall, face forward, fighting, on the deck.

(1894)

533　　　　　　　*A Northern Suburb*

NATURE selects the longest way,
　And winds about in tortuous grooves;
A thousand years the oaks decay;
　The wrinkled glacier hardly moves.

But here the whetted fangs of change
　Daily devour the old demesne—
The busy farm, the quiet grange,
　The wayside inn, the village green.

In gaudy yellow brick and red,
　With rooting pipes, like creepers rank,　　　　　10
The shoddy terraces o'erspread
　Meadow, and garth, and daisied bank.

With shelves for rooms the houses crowd,
　Like draughty cupboards in a row—
Ice-chests when wintry winds are loud,
　Ovens when summer breezes blow.

Roused by the fee'd policeman's knock,
　And sad that day should come again,
Under the stars the workmen flock
　In haste to reach the workmen's train.　　　　　20

For here dwell those who must fulfil
　Dull tasks in uncongenial spheres,
Who toil through dread of coming ill,
　And not with hope of happier years—

The lowly folk who scarcely dare
　Conceive themselves perhaps misplaced,
Whose prize for unremitting care
　Is only not to be disgraced.

(1896)

MARY E. COLERIDGE
1861–1907

534   *An Insincere Wish Addressed to a Beggar*

WE are not near enough to love,
   I can but pity all your woe;
For wealth has lifted me above,
   And falsehood set you down below.

If you were true, we still might be
   Brothers in something more than name;
And were I poor, your love to me
   Would make our differing bonds the same.

But golden gates between us stretch,
   Truth opens her forbidding eyes;   10
You can't forget that I am rich,
   Nor I that you are telling lies.

Love never comes but at love's call,
   And pity asks for him in vain;
Because I cannot give you all,
   You give me nothing back again.

And you are right with all your wrong,
   For less than all is nothing too;
May Heaven beggar me ere long,
   And Truth reveal herself to you!   20

(Wr. 1895; pub. 1908)

535   *The Nurse's Lament*

THE flower is withered on the stem,
The fruit hath fallen from the bough.
None knows nor thinks of them.
There's no child in the house now.

The bird that sang sings not here.
Where is the bonny lark?
When shall I behold my dear?
The fire is out, the house dark.

(Wr. before 1896; pub. 1954)

604

536   *The Three Musicians*

ALONG the path that skirts the wood,
    The three musicians wend their way,
Pleased with their thoughts, each other's mood,
    Franz Himmel's latest roundelay,
The morning's work, a new-found theme, their breakfast and the
       summer day.

One's a soprano, lightly frocked
    In cool, white muslin that just shows
Her brown silk stockings gaily clocked,
    Plump arms and elbows tipped with rose,
And frills of petticoats and things, and outlines as the warm wind blows.   10

Beside her a slim, gracious boy
    Hastens to mend her tresses' fall,
And dies her favour to enjoy,
    And dies for *réclame* and recall
At Paris and St Petersburg, Vienna and St James's Hall.

The third's a Polish Pianist
    With big engagements everywhere,
A light heart and an iron wrist,
    And shocks and shoals of yellow hair, ·
And fingers that can trill on sixths and fill beginners with despair.   20

The three musicians stroll along
    And pluck the ears of ripened corn,
Break into odds and ends of song,
    And mock the woods with Siegfried's horn,
And fill the air with Gluck, and fill the tweeded tourist's soul with
       scorn.

The Polish genius lags behind,
    And, with some poppies in his hand,
Picks out the strings and wood and wind
    Of an imaginary band,
Enchanted that for once his men obey his beat and understand.   30

The charming cantatrice reclines
      And rests a moment where she sees
Her château's roof that hotly shines
      Amid the dusky summer trees,
And fans herself, half shuts her eyes, and smoothes the frock about her
      knees.

The gracious boy is at her feet,
      And weighs his courage with his chance;
His fears soon melt in noonday heat.
      The tourist gives a furious glance,
Red as his guide-book grows, moves on, and offers up a prayer for
      France.   40

                                                (Wr. 1895; pub. 1896)

537   *The Ballad of a Barber*

                  HERE is the tale of Carrousel,
                  The barber of Meridian Street.
                  He cut, and coiffed, and shaved so well,
                  That all the world was at his feet.

                  The King, the Queen, and all the Court,
                  To no one else would trust their hair,
                  And reigning belles of every sort
                  Owed their successes to his care.

                  With carriage and with cabriolet
                  Daily Meridian Street was blocked,   10
                  Like bees about a bright bouquet
                  The beaux about his doorway flocked.

                  Such was his art he could with ease
                  Curl wit into the dullest face;
                  Or to a goddess of old Greece
                  Add a new wonder and a grace.

                  All powders, paints, and subtle dyes,
                  And costliest scents that men distil,
                  And rare pomades, forgot their price
                  And marvelled at his splendid skill.   20

The curling irons in his hand
Almost grew quick enough to speak,
The razor was a magic wand
That understood the softest cheek.

Yet with no pride his heart was moved;
He was so modest in his ways!
His dainty task was all he loved,
And now and then a little praise.

An equal care he would bestow
On problems simple or complex;   30
And nobody had seen him show
A preference for either sex.

How came it then one sunny day,
Coiffing the daughter of the King,
He lengthened out the least delay
And loitered in his hairdressing?

The Princess was a pretty child,
Thirteen years old, or thereabout.
She was as joyous and as wild
As spring flowers when the sun is out.   40

Her gold hair fell down to her feet
And hung about her pretty eyes;
She was as lyrical and sweet
As one of Schubert's melodies.

Three times the barber curled a lock,
And thrice he straightened it again;
And twice the irons scorched her frock,
And twice he stumbled in her train.

His fingers lost their cunning quite,
His ivory combs obeyed no more;   50
Something or other dimmed his sight,
And moved mysteriously the floor.

He leant upon the toilet table,
His fingers fumbled in his breast;
He felt as foolish as a fable,
And feeble as a pointless jest.

He snatched a bottle of Cologne,
And broke the neck between his hands;
He felt as if he was alone,
And mighty as a king's commands.   60

The Princess gave a little scream,
Carrousel's cut was sharp and deep;
He left her softly as a dream
That leaves a sleeper to his sleep.

He left the room on pointed feet;
Smiling that things had gone so well.
They hanged him in Meridian Street.
You pray in vain for Carrousel.

(Wr. 1895; pub. 1896)

A. E. HOUSMAN
1859–1936

from *A Shropshire Lad* (538–544)

538

I

1887

FROM Clee to heaven the beacon burns,
    The shires have seen it plain,
From north and south the sign returns
    And beacons burn again.

Look left, look right, the hills are bright,
    The dales are light between,
Because 'tis fifty years to-night
    That God has saved the Queen.

Now, when the flame they watch not towers
    About the soil they trod,   10
Lads, we'll remember friends of ours
    Who shared the work with God.

To skies that knit their heartstrings right,
  To fields that bred them brave,
The saviours come not home to-night:
  Themselves they could not save.

It dawns in Asia, tombstones show
  And Shropshire names are read;
And the Nile spills his overflow
  Beside the Severn's dead. 20

We pledge in peace by farm and town
  The Queen they served in war,
And fire the beacons up and down
  The land they perished for.

'God save the Queen' we living sing,
  From height to height 'tis heard;
And with the rest your voices ring,
  Lads of the Fifty-third.

Oh, God will save her, fear you not:
  Be you the men you've been,
Get you the sons your fathers got, 30
  And God will save the Queen.

539

XII

WHEN I watch the living meet,
  And the moving pageant file
Warm and breathing through the street
  Where I lodge a little while,

If the heats of hate and lust
  In the house of flesh are strong,
Let me mind the house of dust
  Where my sojourn shall be long.

In the nation that is not
  Nothing stands that stood before;
There revenges are forgot, 10
  And the hater hates no more;

Lovers lying two and two
  Ask not whom they sleep beside,
And the bridegroom all night through
  Never turns him to the bride.

540   XVI

IT nods and curtseys and recovers
    When the wind blows above,
The nettle on the graves of lovers
    That hanged themselves for love.

The nettle nods, the wind blows over,
    The man, he does not move,
The lover of the grave, the lover
    That hanged himself for love.

541   XXX

OTHERS, I am not the first,
Have willed more mischief than they durst:
If in the breathless night I too
Shiver now, 'tis nothing new.

More than I, if truth were told,
Have stood and sweated hot and cold,
And through their reins in ice and fire
Fear contended with desire.

Agued once like me were they,
But I like them shall win my way   10
Lastly to the bed of mould
Where there's neither heat nor cold.

But from my grave across my brow
Plays no wind of healing now,
And fire and ice within me fight
Beneath the suffocating night.

542   XL

INTO my heart an air that kills
    From yon far country blows:
What are those blue remembered hills,
    What spires, what farms are those?

That is the land of lost content,
    I see it shining plain,
The happy highways where I went
    And cannot come again.

543   XLVIII

Be still, my soul, be still; the arms you bear are brittle,
    Earth and high heaven are fixt of old and founded strong.
Think rather,—call to thought, if now you grieve a little,
    The days when we had rest, O soul, for they were long.

Men loved unkindness then, but lightless in the quarry
    I slept and saw not; tears fell down, I did not mourn;
Sweat ran and blood sprang out and I was never sorry:
    Then it was well with me, in days ere I was born.

Now, and I muse for why and never find the reason,
    I pace the earth, and drink the air, and feel the sun.   10
Be still, be still, my soul; it is but for a season:
    Let us endure an hour and see injustice done.

Ay, look: high heaven and earth ail from the prime foundation;
    All thoughts to rive the heart are here, and all are vain:
Horror and scorn and hate and fear and indignation—
    Oh why did I awake? when shall I sleep again?

544   LX

Now hollow fires burn out to black,
    And lights are guttering low:
Square your shoulders, lift your pack,
    And leave your friends and go.

Oh never fear, man, nought's to dread,
    Look not left nor right:
In all the endless road you tread
    There's nothing but the night.

                        (Wr. 1895–6; pub. 1896)

545   Because I liked you better
                              Than suits a man to say,
                          It irked you, and I promised
                              To throw the thought away.

                          To put the world between us
                              We parted, stiff and dry;
                          'Good-bye', said you, 'forget me.'
                              'I will, no fear', said I.

If here, where clover whitens
  The dead man's knoll, you pass,   10
And no tall flower to meet you
  Starts in the trefoiled grass,

Halt by the headstone naming
  The heart no longer stirred,
And say the lad that loved you
  Was one that kept his word.

(Wr. from 1893; pub. 1936)

546   HER strong enchantments failing,
  Her towers of fear in wreck,
Her limbecks dried of poisons
  And the knife at her neck,

The Queen of air and darkness
  Begins to shrill and cry,
'O young man, O my slayer,
  To-morrow you shall die.'

O Queen of air and darkness,
  I think 'tis truth you say,   10
And I shall die to-morrow;
  But you will die to-day.

(Wr. 1895; pub. 1922)

547   YONDER see the morning blink:
  The sun is up, and up must I,
To wash and dress and eat and drink
And look at things and talk and think
  And work, and God knows why.

Oh often have I washed and dressed
  And what's to show for all my pain?
Let me lie abed and rest:
Ten thousand times I've done my best
  And all's to do again.   10

(Wr. 1895; pub. 1922)

548

OH who is that young sinner with the handcuffs on his wrists?
And what has he been after that they groan and shake their fists?
And wherefore is he wearing such a conscience-stricken air?
Oh they're taking him to prison for the colour of his hair.

'Tis a shame to human nature, such a head of hair as his;
In the good old time 'twas hanging for the colour that it is;
Though hanging isn't bad enough and flaying would be fair
For the nameless and abominable colour of his hair.

Oh a deal of pains he's taken and a pretty price he's paid
To hide his poll or dye it of a mentionable shade;
But they've pulled the beggar's hat off for the world to see and stare,   10
And they're haling him to justice for the colour of his hair.

Now 'tis oakum for his fingers and the treadmill for his feet
And the quarry-gang on Portland in the cold and in the heat,
And between his spells of labour in the time he has to spare
He can curse the God that made him for the colour of his hair.

(Wr. from 1895; pub. 1937)

549   HERE dead lie we because we did not choose
         To live and shame the land from which we sprung.
      Life, to be sure, is nothing much to lose,
         But young men think it is, and we were young.

(Wr. 1895–1900?; pub. 1936)

550   WHEN the bells justle in the tower
         The hollow night amid,
      Then on my tongue the taste is sour
         Of all I ever did.

(Wr. 1895–1900?; pub. 1930)

551   THE laws of God, the laws of man,
      He may keep that will and can;
      Not I: let God and man decree
      Laws for themselves and not for me;

And if my ways are not as theirs
Let them mind their own affairs.
Their deeds I judge and much condemn,
Yet when did I make laws for them?
Please yourselves, say I, and they
Need only look the other way.   10
But no, they will not; they must still
Wrest their neighbour to their will,
And make me dance as they desire
With jail and gallows and hell-fire.
And how am I to face the odds
Of man's bedevilment and God's?
I, a stranger and afraid
In a world I never made.
They will be master, right or wrong;
Though both are foolish, both are strong.   20
And since, my soul, we cannot fly
To Saturn nor to Mercury,
Keep we must, if keep we can,
These foreign laws of God and man.

(Wr. *c.*1900; pub. 1922)

552

WHEN the eye of day is shut,
    And the stars deny their beams,
And about the forest hut
    Blows the roaring wood of dreams,

From deep clay, from desert rock,
    From the sunk sands of the main,
Come not at my door to knock,
    Hearts that loved me not again.

Sleep, be still, turn to your rest
    In the lands where you are laid;   10
In far lodgings east and west
    Lie down on the beds you made.

In gross marl, in blowing dust,
    In the drowned ooze of the sea,
Where you would not, lie you must,
    Lie you must, and not with me.

(Wr. 1900; pub. 1922)

553   SOME can gaze and not be sick,
       But I could never learn the trick.
       There's this to say for blood and breath,
       They give a man a taste for death.

                          (Wr. 1900–1?; pub. 1937)

554   THE sigh that heaves the grasses
            Whence thou wilt never rise
       Is of the air that passes
            And knows not if it sighs.

       The diamond tears adorning
            Thy low mound on the lea,
       Those are the tears of morning,
            That weeps, but not for thee.

                        (Wr. soon after 1900; pub. 1922)

VICTOR PLARR

1863–1929

555   *Shadows*

       A SONG of shadows: never glory was
            But it had some soft shadow that would lie
       On wall, on quiet water, on smooth grass,
            Or in the vistas of the phantasy:

       The shadow of the house upon the lawn,
            Upon the house the shadow of the tree,
       And through the moon-steeped hours unto the dawn
            The shadow of thy beauty over me.

                                      (1896)

556   *Of Change of Opinions*

       As you advance in years you long
            For what you scorned when but a boy:
       Then 'twas the town, now the birds' song
            Is your obsession and your joy.

And, as you lie and die, maybe
  You will look back, unreconciled
To that dark hour, and clearly see
  Yourself a little wistful child.

Into the jaws of death you'll bring
  No virile triumph, wrought with pain;
But only to the monster fling
  The daydream and the daisy-chain,

The lispéd word, the gentle touch,
  The wonder, and the mystic thought,
For old gray Death upon his crutch
  To rake into his Bag of Nought.

(1899)

HILAIRE BELLOC

1870–1953

557   *The Justice of the Peace*

DISTINGUISH carefully between these two,
  This thing is yours, that other thing is mine.
You have a shirt, a brimless hat, a shoe
  And half a coat. I am the Lord benign
Of fifty hundred acres of fat land
To which I have a right. You understand?

I have a right because I have, because,
  Because I have—because I have a right.
Now be quite calm and good, obey the laws,
  Remember your low station, do not fight
Against the good, because, you know, it pricks
Whenever the uncleanly demos kicks.

I do not envy you your hat, your shoe.
  Why should you envy me my small estate?
It's fearfully illogical in you
  To fight with economic force and fate.
Moreover, I have got the upper hand,
And mean to keep it. Do you understand?

(1896)

FRANCIS THOMPSON
1859–1907

558   *The End of It*

SHE did not love to love, but hated him
For making her to love; and so her whim
  From passion taught misprision to begin.
  And all this sin
Was because love to cast out had no skill
Self, which was regent still.
Her own self-will made void her own self's will.

(1897)

FREDERICK TENNYSON
1807–1898

559   *Old Age*

AS when into the garden paths by night
One bears a lamp, and with its sickly glare
Scatters the burnished flowers a-dreaming there,
Palely they show like spectres in his sight,
Lovely no more, disfurnished of delight,
Some folded up and drooping o'er the way,
Their odours spent, their colour changed to gray,
Some that stood queen-like in the morning light
Fallen discrowned: so the low-burning loves
That tremble in the hearts of aged men   10
Cast their own light upon the world that moves
Around them, and receive it back again.
Old joys seem dead, old faces without joys;
Laughter is dead. There is no mirth in boys.

(1913)

DORA SIGERSON SHORTER
1866–1918

560   *The Wind on the Hills*

Go not to the hills of Erinn
When the night winds are about,
Put up your bar and shutter,
And so keep the danger out.

For the good-folk whirl within it,
And they pull you by the hand,
And they push you on the shoulder,
Till you move to their command.

And lo! you have forgotten
What you have known of tears,   10
And you will not remember
That the world goes full of years;

A year there is a lifetime,
And a second but a day,
And an older world will meet you
Each morn you come away.

Your wife grows old with weeping,
And your children one by one
Grow grey with nights of watching,
Before your dance is done.   20

And it will chance some morning
You will come home no more;
Your wife sees but a withered leaf
In the wind about the door.

And your children will inherit
The unrest of the wind,
They shall seek some face elusive,
And some land they never find.

When the wind is loud, they sighing
Go with hearts unsatisfied,   30
For some joy beyond remembrance,
For some memory denied.

And all your children's children,
They cannot sleep or rest,
When the wind is out in Erinn
And the sun is in the West.

(1899)

SOURCES AND NOTES

For further details of poems in copyright, see also p. 627.

1–9. Thomas Lovell Beddoes. **1–5.** *Poems* (1851). **6.** *Works*, ed. H. W. Donner (1935). **7–9.** *Death's Jest-Book* (1850). Texts, except 6, *Plays and Poems*, ed. H. W. Donner (1950).

10–41. Alfred Tennyson. **10–12, 14–15.** *Poems* (1842). **13.** *Poems* (1851). **16–17.** *The Princess* (1847). **18–29.** *In Memoriam* (1850). **30–1, 33–6.** *Maud* (1855). **32.** *The Examiner* (9 Dec. 1854). **37.** *Idylls of the King* (1859). **38.** *Cornhill* (Feb. 1860). **39.** *The Holy Grail* (1869, title page '1870'); the glosses are Tennyson's. **40.** *Tiresias* (1885). **41.** *Demeter* (1889). Texts, *Works* (1907–8).

42–58. Emily Jane Brontë. **42–3, 45–9, 54–6.** Privately printed, New York (1902). **44, 50–3.** *Complete Poems*, ed. C. Shorter (1910). **57–8.** *Poems* by Currer, Ellis and Acton Bell (1846). Texts, except 57–8, *Complete Poems*, ed. C. W. Hatfield (1941).

59. Emily Jane Brontë and Charlotte Brontë. *Wuthering Heights and Agnes Grey* (1850), emending 'love's' to 'loves'. Charlotte Brontë excerpted the first three stanzas from a long poem, from which Emily Brontë had excerpted and published 'The Prisoner' (58); Charlotte Brontë supplied the last two stanzas; *Complete Poems of Emily Jane Brontë*, ed. C. W. Hatfield (1941).

60–1. Leigh Hunt. **60.** *Monthly Chronicle* (Nov. 1838). **61.** *Correspondence*, ii (1862). Texts, *Poetical Works*, ed. H. S. Milford (1923).

62–8. Walter Savage Landor. **62.** R. R. Madden, *Countess of Blessington* (1855). **63.** *Works* (1846). **64.** *The Examiner* (3 Feb. 1849). **65.** *Last Fruit* (1853). **66–7.** *Dry Sticks* (1858). **68.** *Heroic Idyls* (1863). Texts, *Poems*, ed. S. Wheeler (1937).

69. Winthrop Mackworth Praed. *Poetical Works* (1864); text, *Selected Poems*, ed. K. Allott (1953).

70–2. Thomas Hood. *New Monthly* (Sept.–Nov. 1840); text, *Poetical Works*, ed. W. Jerrold (1906).

73–95. William Barnes. **73.** *Dorset County Chronicle* (4 June 1840). **74.** *DCC* (15 July 1841). **75.** *DCC* (19 Aug. 1841). **76.** *DCC* (20 Nov. 1856). **77.** *DCC* (10 Sept. 1857). **78.** *DCC* (1 April 1858). **79–80.** *Poems of Rural Life in the Dorset Dialect* (1879), but placed there within Barnes's Second Collection (1859). **81.** *DCC* (18 June 1859). **82.** *DCC* (22 Aug. 1861). **83.** *DCC* (31 Oct. 1861). **84.** *DCC* (19 Dec. 1861). **85.** *DCC* (24 July 1862). **86.** *Macmillan's* (May 1864). **87–9, 91–5.** *Poems*, ed. B. Jones (1962). **90.** *DCC* (20 Feb. 1873). Texts, *Poems*, ed. B. Jones (1962), correcting 73, line 45, to 'wer'. The glosses are from Barnes's glossary.

96–7. James Clarence Mangan. **96.** *Dublin University Magazine* (June 1840); the gloss is Mangan's. **97.** *The Nation* (18 April 1846). Texts, *Poems*, ed. D. J. O'Donoghue (1910).

98. Anonymous. *The Curiosities of Street Literature* (1871); text, *The Common Muse*, ed. V. de S. Pinto and A. E. Rodway (1957).

99. William Miller. *Whistle-Binkie* (1841).

100. Charles Dickens. *The Examiner* (7 Aug. 1841).

101–2. William Wordsworth. **101.** *Poems* (1842). **102.** *Poems* (1849–50). Texts, *Poetical Works*, ed. E. de Selincourt and H. Darbishire (1954).

103–7. Elizabeth Barrett Browning. **103.** *Graham's Magazine* (Dec. 1842). **104.** *Sonnets from the Portuguese* (1850). **105.** *Aurora Leigh* (1857). **106–7.** *Last Poems* (1862). Texts, *Poems*, ed. C. Porter and H. A. Clarke (1900).

108–26. Robert Browning. **108–9.** *Dramatic Lyrics* (1842). **110.** *Hood's Magazine* (March 1845). **111–12.** *Dramatic Romances and Lyrics* (1845). **113–19.** *Men and Women* (1855). **120–2.** *Dramatis Personae* (1864). **123.** Laura Troubridge, *Memories and Reflections* (1925); *Poems*, ed. J. Pettigrew and T. J. Collins (1981). **124.** *Jocoseria* (1883). **125–6.** *Asolando* (1889). Texts, except **123**, *Poetical Works* (1888–9), but supplying some end-of-line punctuation.

127–9. Ebenezer Jones. *Studies of Sensation and Event* (1843); texts, 1879 ed.

130–55. John Clare. **130, 132, 137, 147, 152.** *Poems of John Clare's Madness*, ed. G. Grigson (1949). **131, 134, 144, 146, 154.** *Later Poems*, ed. E. Robinson and D. Powell (1984). **133.** *Madrigals and Chronicles*, ed. E. Blunden (1924). **135, 141.** J. L. Cherry, *Life and Remains* (1873). **136.** *Bedford Times* (1 Jan. 1848). **138.** *Bedford Times* (18 Dec. 1847). **139.** *Bedford Times* (29 Jan. 1848). **140, 145, 148, 155.** *Later Poems*, ed. E. Robinson and G. Summerfield (1964). **142–3.** *Poems*, ed. J. W. Tibble (1935). **149–51, 153.** *Poems from Manuscript*, ed. E. Blunden and A. Porter (1920). Texts, *Later Poems*, ed. E. Robinson and D. Powell (1984). The glosses are from Robinson and Powell's glossary.

156–7. John Ruskin. **156.** *Book of Beauty* (1845). **157.** *Poems* (1903). Texts, *Poems*, ed. E. T. Cook and A. Wedderburn (1903).

158. Thomas Babington Macaulay. *Miscellaneous Writings* (1860).

159–67. Lewis Carroll. **159.** *Collected Verse* (1932). **160.** *Comic Times* (8 Sept. 1855); then *Alice's Adventures in Wonderland* (1865). **161–2.** *Alice's Adventures in Wonderland* (1865). **163–5.** *Through the Looking-Glass* (1872). **166.** *The Hunting of the Snark* (1876). **167.** i–vii, *Sylvie and Bruno* (1889); viii, *Sylvie and Bruno Concluded* (1893). Texts, *Complete Works* (1939).

168–71. Charlotte Brontë. **168.** *Brontë Society Transactions* (1924). **169.** *Brontë Poems*, ed. A. C. Benson (1915), with the title 'Eventide' and without the last line. **170.** *Poems*, ed. T. J. Wise and J. A. Symington (1934), with the title 'Lost in the Hills'. **171.** *Poems*, ed. T. Winnifrith (1984). Texts, kindly supplied by Juliet R. V. Barker; variants are not recorded here, but it should be noted that in **168** 'void' is the alternative written above 'still' (uncancelled), and that in **170** 'life's light's' is not credited by Dr Barker but the MS is too faint for a guess different from 1934.

172. Charlotte Brontë, perhaps Emily Jane Brontë. *Wuthering Heights and Agnes Grey* (1850). For discussion of the authorship, see *Complete Poems of Emily Jane Brontë*, ed. C. W. Hatfield (1941).

173–6. Edward Lear. **173.** i–iii, *A Book of Nonsense* (1846); iv, *More Nonsense* (1872). **174–5.** *Laughable Lyrics* (1877). **176.** *Nonsense Songs* (1894). Text for **173**, *Complete Nonsense* (1947).

177–8. Charles Kingsley. **177.** *The Saint's Tragedy* (1848). **178.** *Poems* (1884). Texts, *Poems* (1889).

179–87. Arthur Hugh Clough. **179.** *Ambarvalia* (1849). **180.** *The Crayon* (Aug.

1855). **181**. *Putnam's Magazine* (July 1853). **182**. *Atlantic Monthly* (Feb.–May 1858). **183**. *Poems* (1862). **184–5**. *Letters and Remains* (1865). **186–7**. *Poems and Prose Remains* (1869). Texts, *Poems*, ed. F. L. Mulhauser (1974), but with corrections in **182** from 1869: I, line 224 ('than'), I, line 277 ('hast'), II, line 276 ('Time'), III, line 220 ('gaze').

188–96. Dante Gabriel Rossetti. **188**. *The Germ* (1850). **189**. *Collected Works* (1886). **190, 192–5**. *Poems* (1870). **191**. *Poems: An Offering to Lancashire*, ed. I. Craig (1863). **196**. *Works* (1911). Texts, *Works*, ed. W. M. Rossetti (1911).

197–220. Christina G. Rossetti. **197, 199, 201, 204, 206–7, 210**. *Goblin Market* (1862). **198**. *The Germ* (Feb. 1850). **200**. *The Century* (May 1884). **202**. *Macmillan's* (March 1863). **203, 211**. *New Poems* (1896). **205**. *Macmillan's* (April 1861). **208**. *A Round of Days* (1866). **209, 218–20**. *Time Flies* (1885). **212–14**. *The Prince's Progress* (1866). **215**. *The Argosy* (Jan. 1874). **216**. *Scribner's* (Jan. 1872). **217**. *A Pageant* (1881). Texts, *Complete Poems*, ed. R. W. Crump (i, 1979; ii, 1986), except **203, 211, 220**, which (pending Crump's vol. iii) are from *Poetical Works*, ed. W. M. Rossetti (1904).

221–3. Ebenezer Elliott. *More Verse and Prose by the Cornlaw Rhymer* (1850).

224–31. Matthew Arnold. **224–5**. *Empedocles on Etna* (1852). **226, 228–9**. *New Poems* (1867). **227**. *Poems* (1853). **230**. *Cornhill* (Nov. 1869), within an article on St Paul. **231**. *Fortnightly Review* (Jan. 1881). Texts, *Poetical Works*, ed. C. B. Tinker and H. F. Lowry (1950).

232–41. William Allingham. **232–4**. *Poems* (1850). **235**. *Songs, Ballads and Stories* (1877). **236–7**. *Evil May-Day* (1882). **238**. *Blackberries* (1884). **239**. *Flower Pieces* (1888). **240**. *Life and Phantasy* (1889). **241**. *Thought and Word* (1890). Texts, except **240**, *Poems* (1912).

242–8. Coventry Patmore. **242**. *The Betrothal* (1854). **243–4**. *The Espousals* (1856). **245**. *Pall Mall Gazette* (6 July 1876). **246**. *Pall Mall Gazette* (30 Nov. 1876). **247**. *The Unknown Eros* (1877). **248**. *The Week* (5 Jan. 1878). Texts, *Poems*, ed. F. Page (1949).

249. Ernest Jones. *Notes to the People* (1852).

250. William Makepeace Thackeray. *Southern Literary Messenger* (Nov. 1853); text, *Ballads* (1908).

251–8. James Henry. **251–6**. *A Half Year's Poems* (1854). **257–8**. *Poematia* (1866). Henry's accent-marks have been removed.

259–62. William Bell Scott. **259**. *Poems* (1854); text, *Poems* (1875). **260**. *Poems* (1854). **261**. *Poems* (1875). **262**. *A Poet's Harvest Home* (1882).

263–4. Mortimer Collins. **263**. *Idyls and Rhymes* (1855). **264**. *Athenaeum* (2 Sept. 1876); text, *Selections* (1886).

265. Shirley Brooks. *Punch* (24 May 1856).

266. Edward FitzGerald. *Rubáiyát of Omar Khayyám* (1859).

267–8. Elizabeth Siddal. **267**. *Burlington Magazine* (May 1903). **268**. W. M. Rossetti, *Ruskin: Rossetti: Pre-Raphaelitism* (1899). Texts, *Poems and Drawings*, ed. R. Lewis and M. S. Lasner (1978); the titles were apparently supplied by W. M. Rossetti.

269–73. William Morris. **269**. *The Defence of Guenevere* (1858). **270**. *The Legend of the Briar Rose* (1890). **271–3**. *Poems by the Way* (1891). Texts, *Collected Works*, ed.

M. Morris, i (1910), ix (1911), but correcting from 1858 the punctuation of **269**, line 11.

274–5. Thomas Ashe. **274**. *Poems* (1871). **275**. *Songs Now and Then* (1876). Texts, *Poems* (1886).

276. T. L. Peacock. *Gryll Grange*; Fraser's (April–Dec. 1860); volume, 1861; text, 1861.

277. Adelaide Anne Procter. *Legends and Lyrics* (1866).

278–80. Richard Watson Dixon. *Christ's Company* (1861).

281–99. George Meredith. **281–97**. *Modern Love* (1862). **298–9**. *Poems and Lyrics of the Joy of Earth* (1883). Texts, *Poems*, ed. P. B. Bartlett (1978).

300. J. Stanyan Bigg. *Shifting Scenes* (1862).

301–9. Algernon Charles Swinburne. **301**. *The Spectator* (17 May 1862). **302**. *The Spectator* (24 May 1862). **303–7**. *Poems and Ballads* (1866). **308**. *Notes on Poems and Reviews* (1866). **309**. *Athenaeum* (22 July 1876). Texts, *Poems* (1905), but dropping Swinburne's paragraph-note, French, to **306**.

310–16. John Leicester Warren, Lord de Tabley. **310–11**. *Praeterita* (1863) by William Lancaster. **312**. *Rehearsals* (1870). **313–14**. *Searching the Net* (1873, **314** re-writing a poem of 1863). **315–16**. *Poems Dramatic and Lyrical* (1893). Texts, *Collected Poems* (1903).

317. Robert Stephen Hawker. *All the Year Round* (10 Sept. 1864); text, *Poetical Works* (1879).

318–27. Charles Turner. **318**. *Sonnets* (1864). **319–21**. *Small Tableaux* (1868). **322**. *Sonnets, Lyrics and Translations* (1873). **323–7**. *Collected Sonnets* (1880). Texts, *Collected Sonnets* (1880).

328–47. Gerard M. Hopkins. **328**. *Note-Books*, ed. H. House (1937). **329, 333, 343, 347**. *The Poets and the Poetry of the Century*, ed. A. H. Miles (1893). **330**. First stanza in *The Spirit of Man*, ed. R. Bridges (1916); complete, *Poems*, ed. R. Bridges (1918). **331, 335–8, 341–2, 344–6**. *Poems*, ed. R. Bridges (1918). **332**. *Lyra Sacra*, ed. H. C. Beeching (1895). **334**. *The Spirit of Man*, ed. R. Bridges (1916). **339**. *A Book of Christmas Verse*, ed. H. C. Beeching (1895). **340**. *Stonyhurst Magazine* (March 1883). Texts, *Poems*, ed. W. H. Gardner and N. H. MacKenzie (1967), but adopting in **332**, line 12, 'eastwards', and in **337**, line 7, 'its self', from *Gerard Manley Hopkins*, ed. C. Phillips (1986).

348. John Henry Newman. *The Month* (April–May 1865); text, *Verses on Various Occasions* (1868).

349–51. Arthur Munby. *Verses, New and Old* (1865).

352. Sebastian Evans. *Brother Fabian's Manuscript* (1865).

353–9. James Thomson. **353**. *National Reformer* (17 Feb. 1867). **354**. *A Voice from the Nile* (1884). **355**. *Poems, Essays and Fragments*, ed. J. M. Robertson (1892). **356**. *National Reformer* (19 May 1872). **357**. *National Reformer* (7 May 1871). **358–9**. *National Reformer* (22 March–17 May 1874). Texts, *Poetical Works* (1895).

360–3. C. S. Calverley. **360**. *Once a Week* (24 Nov. 1866). **361–3**. *Fly Leaves* (1872). Texts, *English Poems*, ed. H. D. Spear (1974).

364–80. Thomas Hardy. **364–9**. *Wessex Poems* (1898). **370**. *Literature* (25 Nov.

1899). **371–2, 375–80.** *Poems of the Past and the Present* (1901, title-page '1902'). **373.** *The Graphic* (29 Dec. 1900). **374.** *The Tatler* (31 July 1901). Texts, *Complete Poetical Works*, ed. S. Hynes, i (1982).

381. Dora Greenwell. *Poems* (1867).

382. Digby Mackworth Dolben. *Lyra Viginti Chordarum*, printed by J. A. Symonds (1880?); text, *Poems*, ed. R. Bridges (1911).

383–4. W. H. Mallock. **383.** *Poems* (1880). **384.** *Verses* (1893).

385–7. George Eliot. *The Legend of Jubal* (1874); text, *Works* (1878–80, Cabinet Ed.).

388. George Augustus Simcox. *Poems and Romances* (1869).

389–95. T. E. Brown. **389, 392, 394–5.** *Collected Poems* (1900). **390.** *Poems* (1908). **391.** *Old John* (1893). **393.** *New Review* (Aug. 1895). Texts, *Poems* (1908).

396–9. George MacDonald. **396–7.** *Works of Fancy and Imagination*, iii (1871). **398–9.** *Poetical Works* (1893). Texts, *Poetical Works* (1893).

400. Frederick Locker-Lampson. *London Lyrics* (1872); text, 1876 ed.

401. Edward Dowden. *Poems* (1876).

402–17. Robert Louis Stevenson. **402–3, 405, 415.** *Poems* (1921). **404.** *Poetical Fragments* (1915). **406, 408, 411–13.** *Underwoods* (1887). **407.** *Treasure Island* (serialized 1881, volume 1883). **409–10, 414.** *Poems* (1916). **416–17.** *Songs of Travel* (1895). Texts, *Collected Poems*, ed. J. Adam Smith (1950).

418–19. William Ernest Henley. **418.** *A Book of Verses* (1888); entirely re-writing the hospital sequence first published in *Cornhill* (July 1875). **419.** *Poems* (1898).

420. Sydney Dobell. *Poetical Works* (1875).

421. E. [Eliza] Keary. *Little Seal-Skin* (1874).

422. Philip Bourke Marston. *All in All* (1875).

423–7. Louisa S. Guggenberger. **423–4.** *Key-Notes* (1876) by Arbor Leigh; texts, 1879 ed. **425–7.** *Poems, Lyrics, and Sonnets* (1882).

428–33. William Renton. *Oils and Watercolours* (1876).

434. R. E. Egerton Warburton. *Poems, Epigrams and Sonnets* (1877).

435–9. Alice Meynell. **435.** *Scots Observer* (31 May 1890). **436.** *Saturday Review* (6 July 1895). **437.** *Pall Mall Gazette* (3 Dec. 1895). **438–9.** Privately printed (1896). Texts, *Poems*, ed. F. Page (1940).

440. Henry Bellyse Baildon. *Morning Clouds* (1877).

441–2. George R. Sims. **441.** *The Dagonet Ballads* (1879). **442.** *Ballads of Babylon* (1880).

443. Jean Ingelow. *Poems* (1880).

444. John Addington Symonds. *New and Old* (1880).

445–7. Robert Bridges. **445–6.** *Poems, Third Series* (1880). **447.** *Shorter Poems* (1890). Texts, *Poetical Works* (1936), but supplying a full-stop in **447**, line 1.

448–9. Joseph Skipsey. **448.** *A Book of Lyrics* (1881). **449.** *Songs and Lyrics* (1892).

450. William Watson. *Epigrams* (1884); text, *Collected Poems* (1898).

451–2. William Frederick Stevenson. *Qualte and Peedra* (1883).

453–6. Eugene Lee-Hamilton. **453–4.** *Apollo and Marsyas* (1884). **455–6.** *Forest Notes* (1899). Texts, *Dramatic Sonnets, Poems, and Ballads* (1903).

457–8. Amy Levy. **457.** *A Minor Poet* (1884). **458.** *A London Plane-Tree* (1889).

459–62. A. Mary F. Robinson. **459–60.** *An Italian Garden* (1886). **461–2.** *Songs, Ballads, and a Garden Play* (1888). Texts, *Collected Poems* (1902).

463–8. E. [Edith] Nesbit. **463.** *Lays and Legends* (1886). **464.** *Leaves of Life* (1888). **465–8.** *A Pomander of Verse* (1895).

469–74. Rudyard Kipling. **469.** *Civil and Military Gazette* (3 March 1886). **470.** *Scots Observer* (22 Feb. 1890). **471.** *Barrack-Room Ballads* (1892). **472.** *The Idler* (Dec. 1892). **473.** *The Vampire* (wrappers, 1897). **474.** *The Times* (17 July 1897). Texts, *Verse* (1940).

475. William Canton. *A Lost Epic* (1887).

476–9. Oscar Wilde. **476.** *Lady's Pictorial, Christmas Number* (1887). **477.** *Centennial Magazine* (5 Feb. 1889). **478–9.** *The Ballad of Reading Gaol* (1898). Texts, *Poems* (1908).

480. Andrew Lang. *Grass of Parnassus* (1888).

481–5. Lionel Johnson. **481, 483.** *Ireland* (1897). **482.** *Poems* (1953). **484.** *Poems* (1895). **485.** *Second Book of the Rhymers' Club* (1894). Texts, *Poems*, ed. I. Fletcher (1953).

486–8. Gerald Massey. *My Lyrical Life* (1889).

489. Cosmo Monkhouse. *Corn and Poppies* (1890).

490–7. Arthur Symons. **490–4.** *Silhouettes* (1892). **495–6.** *London Nights* (1895). **497.** *Amoris Victima* (1897). Texts, *Collected Works* (1924).

498–504. W. B. Yeats. **498.** *Scots Observer* (19 April 1890). **499–502.** *The Countess Kathleen* (1892). **503.** *The Dome* (May 1898). **504.** *The Wind Among the Reeds* (1899). Texts, *Collected Poems* (1950), except for **498–500** (1892).

505. William Cory. *Ionica* (1891).

506–7. James Logie Robertson. *Ochil Idylls* (1891) by Hugh Haliburton; the glosses are from the glossary.

508. Dollie Radford. *A Light Load* (1891).

509–12. J. K. Stephen. **509–10.** *Lapsus Calami* (1891). **511–12.** *Quo Musa Tendis?* (1891). Texts, *Lapsus Calami* (1896).

513. Katharine Tynan. *Ballads and Lyrics* (1891).

514–17. Ernest Dowson. **514.** *Second Book of the Rhymers' Club* (1894). **515–17.** *Verses* (1896). Texts, *Poetical Works*, ed. D. Flower (1967).

518–29. John Gray. **518.** *The Dial* (1892); text, *Silverpoints* (1893). **519.** *Silverpoints* (1893); text, *A Sailor's Garland*, ed. J. Masefield (1906). **520–4.** *Silverpoints* (1893). **525.** *The Dial* (1896). **526–7.** *Spiritual Songs* (1896). **528.** *The Dial* (1896); text, *The Long Road* (1926). **529.** *The Pageant* (1897). Gray's poems, never collected, are being authoritatively edited by I. Fletcher.

530–1. Michael Field. *Underneath the Bough* (1893).

532–3. John Davidson. **532.** *Yellow Book* (July 1894). **533.** *The Speaker* (9 May 1896). Texts, *Poems*, ed. A. Turnbull (1973).

534–5. Mary E. Coleridge. **534.** *Poems* (1908). **535.** *Collected Poems* (1954). Texts, *Collected Poems*, ed. T. Whistler (1954).

536–7. Aubrey Beardsley. **536.** *The Savoy* (Jan. 1896). **537.** *The Savoy* (July 1896).

538–54. A. E. Housman. **538–44.** *A Shropshire Lad* (1896). **545, 549.** *More Poems* (1936). **546–7, 551–2, 554.** *Last Poems* (1922). **548, 553.** Laurence Housman, *A.E.H.* (1937). **550.** Printed by J. Carter and J. Sparrow as a Christmas card (1930); then 1937. Texts, *Collected Poems* (1939).

555–6. Victor Plarr. **555.** *In the Dorian Mood* (1896). **556.** *The Garland of New Poetry* (1899). Texts, *Collected Poems*, ed. I. Fletcher (1974).

557. Hilaire Belloc. *Verses and Sonnets* (1896).

558. Francis Thompson. *New Poems* (1897); text, *Poems*, ed. T. J. Connolly (1932).

559. Frederick Tennyson. *Shorter Poems*, ed. C. Tennyson (1913).

560. Dora Sigerson Shorter. *Ballads and Poems* (1899); text, *Collected Poems* (1907).

*

The editor and publisher are grateful for permission to include the following copyright material in this anthology:

Hilaire Belloc: 'The Justice of the Peace' from *Complete Verse*. Reprinted by permission of Gerald Duckworth & Co. Ltd.

John Clare: 'Love's Pains', 'A Vision', 'The thunder mutters', 'Hesperus', 'The Shepherd Boy', 'There is a charm', 'I went my Sunday' and 'The Yellowhammer' from *John Clare: A Selection*, edited by Eric Robinson and David Powell; 'I've Had Many', 'Black absence', 'The Old Year', 'The Winters Spring', 'Evening', 'The passing', 'Soft falls', 'To Miss B', 'Hymn to the Creator', 'First Love', 'Love's memories', 'The mist rauk' and 'An Anecdote of Love' from *The Later Poems of John Clare 1837–1864*, edited by Eric Robinson, David Powell and Margaret Grainger; 'I Am', 'An Invite to Eternity', 'I am', 'I hid my love' and 'I wish I was' from *Selected Poems and Prose of John Clare*, edited by Eric Robinson and Geoffrey Summerfield. Copyright Eric Robinson. Reproduced by permission of Curtis Brown Ltd.

Gerard Manley Hopkins: 'It was a hard thing to undo this knot' from *The Poems of Gerard Manley Hopkins*, 4th ed., 1967, edited by W. H. Gardner and N. H. MacKenzie. Reprinted by permission of Oxford University Press.

Agnes Mary F. Robinson: 'Aubade Triste', 'Pallor', 'Neurasthenia' and 'An Orchard at Avignon' from *Collected Poems* (T. Fisher Unwin, 1902). Reprinted by permission of A. & C. Black (Publishers) Ltd.

Arthur Symons: 'Pastel: Masks and Faces', 'The Absinthe-Drinker', 'Rain on the Down', 'During Music', 'At the Cavour', 'At Dieppe', 'Paris' and 'The Barrel-Organ'. Reprinted by permission of the Literary Estate of Arthur Symons.

W. B. Yeats: 'A Cradle Song', 'The Pity of Love', 'The Sorrow of Love', 'When You Are Old', 'Who Goes with Fergus?', 'He Thinks of Those who have Spoken Evil of His Beloved' and 'He Wishes for the Cloths of Heaven' from *The Collected Poems of W. B. Yeats* (New York: Macmillan, 1956). Reprinted by permission of A. P. Watt Ltd., and Macmillan Publishing Co., Inc.

INDEX OF TITLES AND FIRST LINES

The references are to the poem numbers

INDEX OF TITLES AND FIRST LINES

INDEX OF TITLES AND FIRST LINES

INDEX OF AUTHORS

The references are to the poem numbers